NEIGHBORS
&
STRANGERS

BOOKS BY WILLIAM R. POLK

Backdrop to Tragedy: The Struggle for Palestine (with David Stamler and Edmund Asfour)

The Opening of South Lebanon: A Study of the Impact of the West on the Middle East

The United States and the Arab World

Passing Brave (with William Mares)

The Elusive Peace: The Middle East in the Twentieth Century

The Arab World

Tales for Eliza

The Arab World Today

Blind Man's Buff (a novel)

No Apples for Eden (a novel)

EDITED BY WILLIAM R. POLK

The Developmental Revolution

Beginnings of Modernization in the Middle East; The Golden Ode

WILLIAM R. POLK

NEIGHBORS & STRANGERS

THE FUNDAMENTALS OF FOREIGN AFFAIRS

The University of Chicago Press
Chicago & London

WILLIAM R. POLK is a former professor of history
at the University of Chicago and past president of
the Adlai Stevenson Institute of International
Affairs. He was a member of the Policy Planning
Council in the Department of State during the
Kennedy and Johnson administrations.

The University of Chicago Press, Chicago 60637
The University of Chicago Press, Ltd., London
© 1997 by The University of Chicago
All rights reserved. Published 1997
Printed in the United States of America
06 05 04 03 02 01 00 99 98 97   1 2 3 4 5

ISBN: 0-226-67329-4 (cloth)

Library of Congress Cataloging-in-Publication Data

Polk, William Roe, 1929–
    Neighbors and strangers : the fundamentals of
foreign affairs / William R. Polk.
        p.   cm.
    Includes bibliographical references and index.
    ISBN 0-226-67329-4 (cloth : alk. paper)
    1. International relations.   I. Title.
  JX1391.P66   1997
  327—dc21   97-2353
                                          CIP

For George Polk,

a son who grew, year by year,

with the book, each year less a

stranger; each year more a

neighbor, until at last

almost a brother too.

CONTENTS

Acknowledgments / ix

Introduction / 1

PART I THE BOTTOM LINE

1 Staying Alive in a Dangerous World / 13

2 Out of the Mists of the Past / 24

3 *Our* Possessions / 36

PART II DEFENSE

4 Keeping *Them* Out / 47

5 Rome, Walled China, and Medieval Europe / 58

6 Modern Walls / 66

PART III ARMIES AND WARFARE

7 The First Armies / 75

8 Assyria and Rome / 84

9 Soldiers, Mercenaries, and Guerrillas / 92

10 The Colonial Auxiliary / 101

11 Weapons / 108

12 Modern Armies / 116

PART IV NONGOVERNMENTAL RELATIONS

13 Trade / 129

14 The Trader / 139

15 European Trade and Finance / 152

16 The Amateurs / 165

PART V INTELLIGENCE AND ESPIONAGE

17 Getting to Know *Them* / 175

18 Spies and Spymasters / 182

19 Tools of the Trade / 195

20 Espionage and Counterintelligence / 203

PART VI DIPLOMACY

21 Peaceful Relations between States / 217

22 Worldviews and Strategy / 224

23 The Conduct of Relations / 233

24 The Medieval School of Statecraft / 243

25 Diplomats and Their Masters / 252

26 Intervention and International Law / 268

PART VII GETTING RID OF THE ALIEN

27 Parting Company / 281

28 Ethnic Cleansing / 293

29 Coming Together / 311

Notes / *321*

Index / *351*

ACKNOWLEDGMENTS

In writing this book, I have profited from the suggestions and criticisms of a number of colleagues. While it is not possible to name them all, I single out William McNeill, Speros Vryonis, L. P. Harvey, John Campbell, McGeorge Bundy, Walt W. Rostow, Richard Barnet, and Murray Kempton.

INTRODUCTION

Getting along with foreigners, as the media constantly remind us, is the most dangerous problem of our age. We can hardly pass a day without witnessing on television or reading in the press evidence of failures to find ways to coexist with those whose skin color, customs, or religions are not ours. Even in intervals of peace, we prudently prepare for conflicts to come.

As we observe contemporary foreigners, armed with awesome weapons, able quickly to fall upon us, and driven by ancient hatreds, we long for some golden age when, however noxious they may have been, they were at least farther away. Alas, all the evidence indicates that those tranquil times exist only in our imaginations. During the whole of the human experience, the stranger has always been a neighbor.

Fear of the foreigner arises not just from a reading of his pronouncements or an analysis of his politics. It is not just conceptual or intellectual; it is visceral and inbred. All our senses tell us that with him we lack bonds of kinship, shared memories of childhood, intimacies of ritual and religion, and a comforting similarity. No matter how maddening the brother or the cousin, we see something of ourselves in him. But the foreigner looks different, speaks incomprehensibly, and even smells odd. His clothes are outlandish, his habits often violate our norms, and his religion challenges or insults the true faith we cherish; his very existence parodies our lives or calls into question the systems under which we live; or worse, in the ways he is most like us, as we often suspect, he may actually be at his most dangerous. The taste we share may be for the same garden or the same gold.

Such fears are a mixture of rational and irrational impulses so pervasive and deep-seated as to transcend individual experience or even historical memory. And they are directed not just toward identified enemies but toward all aliens. Indeed, ancient, medieval, and modern societies have commonly used their words for "foreigner" and "enemy" almost interchangeably. In their contacts with "the barbarians at the gates," peoples throughout history have evinced stark terror. This deep fear remains, and sometimes with good reason, a major ingredient in modern foreign affairs.

Yet, the alien cannot be eliminated. Even the grandest empires never managed to remove or kill off all their alien neighbors. As Edward Gibbon reflected in *The Decline and Fall of the Roman Empire*, "All conquest must be ineffectual unless it could be universal, since the increasing circle must be involved in a larger sphere of hostility." Each expansion of "our" safe area brings us into contact with more of "them." Foreigners are always just over the next hill, and each push of our frontiers outward brings more of them into our midst. Just as there is no "final solution," so is there no real possibility of isolation.

There is a compensation, however: the tension arising from having to live near those who are different has been one of the most stimulating and productive of human experiences. It forced our ancestors—as it forces us today—to learn, invent, and grow. Without that challenge our civilization is scarcely conceivable.

In order to meet that challenge, our ancestors invented a medley of responses ranging from isolationism to colonialism, trade to imperialism, diplomacy to espionage, liberation to enslavement, and missionary activity to extermination. These responses form the subject of this book: the origin and elaboration of the complex means of adjustments among peoples who lived too near to be ignored but who, in ways contemporaries thought to be critical or vital, remained strangers.

As I will discuss in chapter 1, this problem is not an abstract one: it mirrors the daily battles, adjustments, and exchanges that are fought *within* our bodies, which host a variety of strangers as well. Some of them are pernicious, even potentially lethal; others help us digest our food and perform a variety of other necessary tasks. We can no more eliminate them than we can the aliens who live around us. As we invent stronger and more sophisticated medical interventions, our bodily guests mutate or otherwise learn to protect themselves. Sometimes, as on the larger stage of international affairs, our efforts at defense are not only ineffectual but self-defeating, as when our medicines kill or disable our bodily allies. A careful examination of how the components of our bodily systems work shows that our bodies have developed responses that could be said to resemble those that make up international affairs—arriving at accommodations through a kind of diplomacy, exchanging goods and services, walling off areas against intruders, mounting sophisticated intelligence collection programs, and fighting all-out wars. Although I do not wish to push the analogy too far, I find no essential discontinuity between what happens within our bodies and what happens among societies.

These responses fall within a limited range and follow identifiable patterns; so, as I will show in the following chapters, what we do today in foreign affairs is far less "modern" than we realize.

In analyzing the history of foreign affairs, my object is twofold. First, I wish to reveal the patterns as they developed and as they have recurred. Thus, while I trace the means invented by our forebears to deal with foreigners, I will show that such strategies apply to our times as well. Second, I aim to illuminate the complexity and interdependence of the "tools" of foreign affairs by juxtaposing the fundamental categories of actions— defense, warfare and armies, espionage, diplomacy, trade and aid, nongovernmental action, ethnic cleansing, and incorporation. All too often, in concentrating on one facet observers lose sight of the whole. In the real world, foreign affairs is not just diplomacy or trade or intelligence or military relations but all of them together.

◆ ◆ ◆

Why do this? I find that we have forgotten much or most of the inherited experience of dealing with neighbors and strangers. As George Santayana memorably wrote, "Those who cannot remember the past are condemned to repeat it." And in forgetting, we have narrowed the scope of and ossified our concepts with occasionally painful, costly, or even deadly results.

Of course, if my inquiry were "just academic," it would be of concern only to scholars, but it is not. Not only do foreign affairs affect us all powerfully and in ways of which we are often unaware, but our ways of reacting and understanding them are dynamic. They are powerfully influenced by interactions among scholars and practitioners. Indeed, there is no clear division between the two groups. Scholars have rarely remained in their cloisters; today even fewer do. Many enter public service, whereas others seek to be thought "relevant" by advising policy makers. Conversely, government officials periodically go back into academic institutions for advanced training and are constantly influenced by the writings of university professors; so there is a regular interchange out of which emerges a shared worldview that shapes national budgets and sets military and civil doctrine.

My own experiences illustrate these points. Looking back, I find that I have learned about foreign affairs in four stages: first academically, as a student and then as a university professor; next as a policy planner in the United States government; then as the president of an international affairs research institute; and finally as an adviser to various international agencies, foundations, and businesses. Personal experience in all four fields of activity has enabled me to see how complex are our relationships with other societies. Let me briefly explain.

In universities I read and taught the more or less traditional views of diplomatic history and international relations. Foreign affairs were what happened between, say, Germany and France when they were not at war. This concept was embodied in treaties, dispatches, and pronouncements written by diplomats and ministers or heads of state. The records, housed in the great state archives in London, Paris, Berlin, and Vienna, showed what these officials found it useful to do together and what they forced one another to do separately.

This view of foreign affairs is based mainly on the experience of the nineteenth century; it was (and is) of considerable influence on foreign affairs establishments around the world. The great European statesmen— Metternich, Talleyrand, Castlereagh, Palmerston—were the exemplars; their agents were ambassadors stationed at the courts of London, Paris, Berlin, Vienna, and a few petty states. Their methods grew out of the etiquette and mores of the European aristocracy. Students and practitioners learned about them through the research of scholars who spent much of their lives in the great archives reading the diplomatic dispatches from which they distilled guides for their contemporaries. These guides aimed to impart a view of the past so that statesmen could understand the present and make it like the past. Sir Charles Webster has left us a classic example of this circular process. In order to show British diplomats at the 1919 Paris Peace Conference how to conduct themselves, he wrote the *Peace Conference Handbook,* in which he described how their predecessors had acted at the 1814–15 Congress of Vienna. In essence the message of such works, of which their were many, was that the craft of foreign affairs was coterminous with diplomacy, and diplomacy was what European gentlemen did together when they were not fighting.

My government service shocked me out of this comfortable view. From the first day, it was evident that diplomacy was only one part of relations with foreigners; within a short time, it was also evident that few diplomats, living or dead, had comprehended the complex range of transnational contacts.

That was the first lesson. The second was that what I had studied and taught was reality seen through a glass darkly: it was based on the records diplomats and statesmen had written and so, obviously, was limited to what they knew or thought to be significant. But because we have developed a fuller vision of the period that produced our foreign affairs concepts, we can see how incomplete or faulty was their understanding of the forces at work in their own times. Economics, religion, political agitation, social unrest, and many other forces were simply beyond the ken, often beyond the interest, of the gentlemen who wrote the documents.

Are comparable oversights possible today? I believe I can answer both as an American and as a student of other societies and states. As a member of the Policy Planning Council of the U.S. Department of State from 1961 to 1965, I had the opportunity not only to participate in "the decision-making process" but also to read the most confidential papers of my American contemporaries and predecessors. I came to see that our archives did not, indeed, could not, contain the whole or perhaps even the essential story. In my direct experience, the records of many of the major episodes of the 1960s, including the Cuban missile crisis, the various Arab-Israeli wars, and the Vietnam War, were confused, incomplete, or misleading. The reason, in large part, I believe, is that our approach— that of Americans, Europeans, and those who studied in their schools— to foreign affairs arose from and was codified on the basis of the limited experience of a few countries in Europe during about three centuries. In that period, because of the nature of governments, foreign affairs could be treated both as separate from politics and as an extension of the aristo-cratic social order. Being locked into that definition, we were frequently baffled when what we faced in our world did not fit.

The "mainline" concept of the foreign affairs establishments of the United States, the Soviet Union, and other countries received a major challenge in the 1950s and 1960s. The challenge was brought about by the introduction of the "strategist" alongside the diplomat. Actually, like many figures and roles I shall discuss below, the strategist was not a mod-ern invention: he existed in ancient India, China, and other societies, and he periodically appeared and disappeared as opportunity, need, or danger demanded. Often he wrote memoranda of advice, what we term "mirrors for princes," such as Niccolò Machiavelli's *The Prince* or Sun Tzu's *The Art of War*. In recent times, he has received his inspiration from such mathe-maticians as John von Neumann and is now called a "politico-military ex-pert." Emphasizing programming, planning, and gaming, he has pro-claimed the advent of a new "science" of international affairs. Relations among nations, like the economy in Adam Smith's perception, he has asserted, are guided by a sort of "hidden hand": governments are "good" (that is, predictable) when they understand and act in accordance with their own interest, "bad" (that is, unpredictable) when they do not. In his view, diplomacy had virtually no role, since this brave new world is a world of self-evident logic.

In this rarefied atmosphere, strategy was thought to be both the medium and the message, both the means of communication and the essence of foreign affairs. The foreigner was seen as making his decisions based on criteria and in ways different from the way we make ours. The world in which he lives is not the world we see about us. His world, and the one we enter when we deal with him, is closer to the war game—as Carl von Clausewitz told us—than to the political process at work in even the most dictatorial societies. It is chess, not negotiation. This view was as limiting in its own way as the old diplomacy.

That, I think, is why outsiders did not comprehend the *politics* of Vietnam, the Arab-Israeli wars, and more recently the terrible conflicts in Africa, India, Sri Lanka, the Balkans, and Central Asia. Even the domestic imperatives of America's closest European allies have often baffled the strategists: How could the Europeans miss or avoid the self-evident answers to such "strategic" issues as the role of NATO? Our strategists saw the issues clearly; how could their politicians see them differently? To try to find out, government officials played and replayed war games. But this approach only deepened their confusion and annoyance. What they could not comprehend was that the European governments were, of course, governed by *their* domestic criteria: neither they *nor any other government* normally acted on the strategic criteria they ascribed to international affairs.

By the time I left government service in 1965, I had concluded that both of these views of foreign affairs, and our lack of a historical appreciation of how we got where we are, had skewed the American vision, locking us into a narrow view that did not accord with the real world.

A lecturing visit to the Institute of World Economy and International Relations of the Soviet Academy of Sciences showed me that Americans were not alone. However much the Russians sought to fit the challenges they encountered into their ideology, they shared with us a "strategic worldview." In Moscow as elsewhere, scholars regarded that view as a datum to which they reacted intellectually and within the confines of which they trained teachers and bureaucrats and advised their government and party. Lecturing in Germany, France, England, Canada, and the United States, I met with dozens of scholars and officials and found that they shared a similar approach.

But it has become increasingly clear in recent years that much of the activity that takes place among nations is not carried on by the agents of governments. It is truly, to use the Russian word, *mezhdunarodnii,* "among peoples." This also is not a new concept although probably most of us think it is. The first of what today we call "nongovernmental organizations" (NGOs) appears to have been set up about four thousand years ago. Today there are scores of thousands including everything from giant multinational corporations (of which a number are larger, at least financially, than many nations) to such organizations as The Red Cross, Médecins sans Frontières, Human Rights Watch, Amnesty International, and Greenpeace. These organizations and two other kinds—specialized agencies of the United Nations and official multinational organizations of many shapes—arguably are as important on many issues today as governments.

. . .

With the prejudice of a historian, I have emphasized the long but mainly forgotten development of such concepts and ventures. As I read myself into the record, it became clear that time after time we and our predecessors have reinvented the wheel, doing things and coming up with concepts that in some cases go back beyond history. But most twentieth-century studies implicitly assume that "it all began" in the past century or so. Take diplomacy again. True, a few scholars have tried to widen our perception of its history. Garrett Mattingly showed us that the men of the Renaissance devoted considerable energies to diplomacy (and quite a bit also to espionage), and Harold Nicholson lightly considered the "interurban" experience of ancient Greece. But that was as far as it went: the more remote and harder-to-read records of China or India or the vast and complex— international—world of Islam were the preserve of Orientalists whose studies were hardly noticed by "mainline" historians and those political scientists who were concerned with foreign affairs, while the ancient world of the Egyptians, the Babylonians, the Phoenicians, the Hittites, and the Assyrians was never considered.

When we look outside of diplomacy into "peripheral" fields, we see them largely dismissed as also irrelevant. Maynard Keynes's analysis of the Versailles treaty marked out the road that led to the catastrophe of World War II, but his work was considered *just* economics. The vast proliferation of international business organizations was exotic to most academic and governmental experts. The growth of an increasingly homogenized world culture, a product of the cinema, television, and a consumer-oriented economy, was little appreciated. And the great shared issues of poverty, race, population, and the environment were at best tolerated sidelines in foreign offices and schools of international relations.

Fortuitously, my appointment in 1967 as president of the Adlai Stevenson Institute of International Affairs offered me an opportunity to pull back and look afresh at such issues. On them, I found stimulus in work being done by archaeologists, anthropologists, and historians of other civilizations and in such new fields as sociobiology and ethology. Was it possible that beneath the language of Metternich, Bismarck, and Dulles lay concepts of which we, and certainly they, were unaware but which influenced our ideas and actions? Once one has reflected on territoriality, dominance, display, boundary maintenance, and other animal attitudes toward *their* aliens, concepts not common in academies of foreign affairs, the moves in the war game, or in diplomatic concourse, look somewhat different.

In trying to fathom how our "deeper" attitudes are formed and retained, issues that are rarely comprehended by the participants, I turned to neurophysiology and psychiatry. Psychiatrists have from time to time addressed the issues of our "deep fears" and the balance of our civilized and animal natures, as did Jung in the concept of the "collective unconscious," M. E. P. Seligman in "Phobias and Preparedness," and Freud in "Why War?" and "Civilization and Its Discontents."

Having gone back more than two centuries and having spread my inquiry beyond Europe, I began to see much repetition of patterns, ideas, and roles. Did these things evolve naturally, or were they "programmed"? In order to find out, I decided to try to start all over again by going back to the hypothetical beginnings of our species, using studies of contemporary primitive peoples and of animal behavior before turning to the more customary fields of foreign affairs. It has been a massive undertaking, and what I present here is only the summary of a few points selected to throw into relief the range of ways in which others have reacted to their neighbors. Although in practice the ways in which we approach foreigners are not so clearly or logically differentiated, I have organized my materials in several broad categories for purposes of description and analysis.

In part 1, I begin with the human body. This enables me to show how personal and yet indistinct are boundaries between "us and them," that "foreign affairs" actually begin in our bodies. In the ways in which we manage our most intimate biological relationships, we find the beginnings of a continuity that ultimately takes us, without significant changes of pattern, to the social level. With "primitive" societies we can see, in a different if not always a clearer perspective, responses and ideas that we can recognize in "sophisticated" societies. So, using observations of contemporary or near-contemporary primitive tribes supplemented by studies of animal behavior, we can guess how some of our basic concepts may have evolved. But at the point of transition to settled human society, a new concept—property—arises and begins to alter profoundly our response to aliens.

Part 2 discusses how societies organized to keep "them" out, with emphasis on static defense, wall-building, and the elaboration of cultural barriers. It would be convenient if, as we like to believe today, there were a sharp distinction between "defense" and "offense," but the historical record makes clear that this is not always so.

Part 3 traces the evolution and growth of armies and warfare from primitive conditions to our most advanced. I do not attempt to cover all armies, and certainly not all wars, and with few exceptions spend little time on weapons systems per se, except as they have significant impact on societies.

Part 4 deals with how people swapped what they had for what they wanted: the growth of trade and aid. Discussion of the merchant leads to a more general treatment of the role of the nonprofessional in foreign affairs.

Part 5 describes how nations learned the secrets of their neighbors and tried to keep others from learning theirs and how some used espionage to "destabilize" or vanquish their enemies.

Part 6 explores how groups negotiated with their neighbors, the rise and development of concepts, techniques and mores of diplomacy, the selection and training (if any) of diplomats, the occasional breakdown of diplomacy in military intervention, and the attempts to create restraints on governments through international law.

Part 7 discusses how first clans and then societies occasionally split apart or were moved or ejected from their homelands in attempts at "ethnic cleansing" and the formation of new societies.

Within each part, although not seeking to be comprehensive, I have illustrated my theme with examples drawn from the earliest recorded times down to the present time and from various parts of the world. Obviously, other examples could have been brought forward, and I make no claim that the ones I have chosen are the best, but they serve my comparative and analytic purpose. In choosing them I have tried not to act promiscuously—that is, by ascribing uniformity to what is only an apparently similar "role" in different societies or by neglecting the analogy of apparently diverse activities that accomplish related purposes. Where I judged it useful or necessary, I have given enough detail so that the reader is made aware of these matters. Where space does not allow full coverage, or where what I write is obscure or controversial, I point the reader to where he can find more.

• • •

One incidental benefit of ranging widely across cultures and over millennia is a revised view of the general role of foreign affairs in actually forming and shaping societies. As I learned more about the earliest villages and progressed through the city-states of the ancient world to the great empires and finally to our own times, I have come to a view that is almost the mirror image of the popular modern conception of foreign affairs as something separate from domestic affairs: measures taken to create a defense against the invasion of strangers, particularly the building of walls and mobilization of armies, were crucial ingredients among the complex mix that created civilizations. Today the challenge of the neighbor still fires the furnaces of national development. I confess that I take little pleasure in this finding, since often it has led to war and catastrophe. But like it or not, I will argue that the evolution of individual societies depended crucially on both the example and the threat of the foreigner.

My purpose, then, is to broaden the concept of foreign affairs by showing how its major components—trade, defense, warfare, diplomacy, espionage, exclusion, and conversion—have evolved and how they interact. If I succeed, I will not only have entertained or stimulated, although these are certainly part of my purpose; I will have made more flexible our view of a great and unending task—getting along with our neighbors.

PART I THE BOTTOM LINE

. . . .

1 STAYING ALIVE IN A DANGEROUS WORLD

Our beautiful little planet floats near enough to the sun to receive the energy on which we live while neither coming close enough to burn nor wandering far enough to freeze; tilting slightly as it circles the sun, it provides us with a change of climates within a moderate range; and, blessed with abundant water and oxygen, it sustains us and all those on whom we depend for life. The species are myriad, ranging from the microscopic to the gargantuan. And all of us separate species and billions of individuals face similar problems of feeding ourselves, procreating, adapting to change, and preserving our lives. Consequently, despite the enormous range of our sizes, shapes, habitats, and habits, our accommodation to the basic imperatives of life fall within a finite range and evince a continuity between the microscopic and the macroscopic. Thus, although we are more accustomed to think of relations with others on the social rather than the biological level, we can usefully begin by examining the adaptations, organizations, and mores that we have made on and in our individual bodies.

How "individual," in fact, are our bodies? When he faced the question of whether apparent reality actually exists, the seventeenth-century French philosopher René Descartes wrote, "Je pense, donc je suis." It was, he asserted, the fact that he thought that proved his existence. Were he alive today and a biologist, he would have had to amend his statement to read something like "Je suis, donc je suis une société."

The "I" that Descartes believed he could firmly assert existed turns out to be not a singularity but a multitude. Although common sense tells us that each of us is what we see and feel—an individual, discrete, homogeneous body—a microscope proves that, in fact, "I" had better be written "we." In this chapter I will show how the dilemmas of coping with the foreigner are, for each of us, the constant and fundamental challenge and that "foreign relations" begin not "over there" but in and on the skin of each of us. I will discuss briefly how complex our body's systems are, how they are attacked by pathogens, how the growth of a world community affects our health and, finally, what the body does about the challenge of staying alive. First, our bodily systems.

. . .

Political philosophers have often evoked the metaphor of the body to characterize the state: being "organic," some have asserted, it is born, matures, and ultimately dies. As a metaphor at least, this notion proved a powerful stimulus to thought about the "body politic," but it seems to me that the metaphor is more suggestive when put another way: whether or not we can say that states or societies are organic and go through a life cycle, it is certainly true that what happens on the "microscale" of our bodies provides a model for much of what happens on the "macroscale" *among* societies. Each of our bodies is not a single thing but rather is a composite of "us" and "them," self and non-self; so it is both possible and provocative to think of the body as a complex system of relationships among neighbors and strangers or as a sort of arena of foreign affairs writ small.

When we look in a mirror, we see what we conventionally think of as ourselves, a complete, unattached being that we can weigh, move, and employ and that by responses of pleasure and pain make us aware of all of its dimensions. Commanded by a brain, it certainly seems a single unit. Yet, as Descartes admitted, reality is not necessarily the same as appearance. In sickness, as I will discuss below, we are aware that the body can be invaded by external agents. But even in health, there is much in us that is not, strictly speaking, us. Bacteria are the prime example: in their countless billions, they live everywhere. They inhabit our intestines, where they help us process our food. Without them *we* would starve, sicken and die. And, as *they* die off, they are expelled with our feces. In fact, about half of the bulk of our feces is composed of their dead bodies. But they are constantly renewed: with an almost unbelievable zest for life, they multiply more than a million times in less than a day. And they are extraordinarily adaptable. It has recently been discovered that one variety, *Helicobacter pylori,* manages to live in the acid chamber of our stomach and duodenum where, it was thought, nothing could survive. Others have been discovered that can thrive in bleach or on that very bulwark of our defense, a bar of soap.

Moreover, as I shall discuss below, even if we consider the components of our blood system as "us," it is clear that they are not, strictly speaking, under "our" control but move and act according to imperatives of which at least our conscious brains are unaware. Whatever "us" is, it is constantly being redefined by relations with "non-us," rebuilt by borrowings from internal neighbors and external strangers so that the frontier between "us" and "them" is fungible, elastic, blurred.

And there are many visible or nearly visible creatures that live on our skins or within our bodies that cannot be considered "us." Since, until recently everywhere/and still in many places, clothing and bedding were rarely changed, they provided ideal habitats for all sorts of bodily pests. Our ancestors were literally plagued by lice. To lure them away, people often put a piece of fur on the bed or floor thinking that the lice would prefer the fur to a naked human form. Picking lice off one's mate or lover was, apparently, a major social occupation. Fortunately for their peace of mind, no one then knew how dangerous such parasites were, but medieval and Renaissance literature is full of references to them. The great English poet John Donne tried to put a romantic interpretation on their visitations. Like most of our ancestors, he lived closer to our bodies' guests than we now think fashionable. Fleas particularly caught his imagination, as they must have demanded his constant attention; so in "The Flea" we find him writing to his beloved that

> It suck'd me first, and now sucks thee,
>> And in this flea, our two bloods mingled bee . . .
> Where wee almost, yea more than maryed are.
>> This flea is you and I, and this
>> Our mariage bed, and mariage temple is.

Having distanced ourselves, at least somewhat and usually, from fleas and lice, and believing in bodily cleanliness, we do not share Donne's romanticism. But, more than we realize, we share our bodies with their kind. They are just one variety among many potential or actual visitors, but, until the seventeenth century, they were among the smallest that anyone could see. Then the Dutch microscopist Antonie van Leeuwenhoek put together a crude microscope that enabled his contemporaries to see that even fleas are themselves infested by still smaller creatures—tiny mites—as our bedclothes, carpets, and skins still are. Some of these give us allergies and we try, without success, to rid our bodies and our houses of them. It is well that we do not succeed because even those we think of as most disgusting are often beneficial in that they feed on the flakes of dead skin we constantly shed.

More disturbing are other creatures. Today, Americans and others are particularly sensitive to the invasions of their bodies by ticks because some species carry a microscopic organism that causes disease among humans. One form, known as "Rocky Mountain spotted fever," has been recognized for years, and, more recently, Lyme disease and human granulocytic ehrlichiosis (HGE) have become endemic in large areas of North America and are being spread abroad. So it would seem reasonable to think of getting rid of the carriers. But it is a virtually impossible task as long as we live on this fecund earth. Anyone walking across a field in the summer knows that ticks are everywhere.

They are not alone. An assault force of worms, scabies and other kinds of lice, fleas, and mites stands ready to move against our bodies when conditions favor them. When seen under microscopes, some appear formidable creatures, like tiny tanks, armor-plated against attack and equipped with tools that resemble bulldozers to dig into our hides. In former times, our ancestors accepted their attentions with resignation; today, the more affluent of us have managed to drive at least some of them away, but others remain our permanent guests. One that we have to tolerate would terrify us if we could see it for what it is—a miniature crocodile. Like its large cousin, the follicle mite slithers down into a swamp where it feeds, breeds, and eventually dies. The swamp in question is us—the follicle mite lives in the warm, wet holes, or follicles, from which the hairs on our bodies grow.

I have described ubiquitous bacteria as being too small to have been seen by Leeuwenhoek's microscope; even smaller are viruses, which cannot be seen by anything less powerful than an electron microscope. These organisms share a common characteristic: in order to reproduce, they must enter one of the cells of another creature. Then, after multiplying, they explode the host cell and migrate to others. Viruses come in many shapes and have many manifestations; some forms have a remarkable capacity to move from one body to another. Particularly dangerous, because of their mobility, are the so-called aerosol forms. The common cold is the one we know best: we catch it often because it is sent through the air by someone coughing or sneezing. Our bodies are also hosts to various forms of "mushrooms," or fungi. Since they spread most easily by air, it is natural that they live primarily in our lungs. Rarely dangerous in themselves, fungus infestations can complicate other diseases (such as diabetes) or stressful situations (such as pregnancy). Sadly if romantically, we can contract, as Snow White did, an infection of fungus called *Sporotrichosis* from the thorn of a rose.

To quote John Donne again, but taking him in the biological sense rather than in the moral or political sense he meant, we perfectly exemplify his often-quoted line that "no man is an island, entire of itself." Each of us takes a position in the hierarchy of life, not only as the predator of some and the prey of others but also a composite of highly complex, interacting forms, part host, part guest, part helper, part foe.

What do these neighbors and strangers do to or for us? I have already mentioned that we cannot live without at least some of them, since, among other things, they process our food into forms we can utilize. Others we could well do without. These we term *pathogens,* and I have mentioned some already. Most do not normally harm us; some, however, become pernicious when they are unable to feed themselves in their accustomed ways or when they invade territories where they do not belong. Like all forms of life, they seize opportunities to grow and spread, and we inadvertently provide such opportunities when we are weakened by hunger, exhaustion, or pollution. Inevitably, we provide openings as we age.

Ironically, we also create scope for them when we intervene with medicines that upset the checks and balances of our systems that constitute what we think of as health. As Laurie Garrett has written, "Since World War II, public health strategy has focused on the eradication of microbes. Using powerful weaponry developed during the postwar period—antibiotics, antimalarials, and vaccines—political and scientific leaders in the United States and around the world pursued a military-style campaign to obliterate viral, bacterial, and parasitic enemies."[1]

Despite great optimism and much reported progress, the campaign has failed, for reasons I will shortly discuss. But it is probably well that it has since, in our quest for ever more powerful medicines, we sometimes attack our benign neighbors more effectively than the dangerous strangers. Chemotherapy is an outstanding example: in the course of killing some cancer cells, it destroys our bodily allies. Another example is our use of broadband antibiotics: in the attempt to create a "safe" environment we often kill benign bacteria, disrupting the balance of forces that had protected us. Moreover, this often happens in the most sterile of environments, the hospital. Outside our bodies, and on a larger scale, we now know that DDT and other pesticides similarly upset the balance of forces in the environment, with pernicious results.

As I will discuss below, we can see that similar policies—attacking the nearby, the obvious, and the relatively benign and thus opening a way for the truly dangerous—have been repeatedly played out among societies on the macroscopic level of foreign affairs. The Romans gave us a lesson on this kind of policy when they so weakened their near neighbors (the Gauls) that the wilder barbarians (the Goths and the Huns) could break through their defenses. As we shall see, this is a lesson that empire after empire failed to heed, at a fatal cost.

To reverse the image, we observe that such strategists as Machiavelli, Sun Tzu, and Vishnugupta might well have been discussing the politics of the virus world when they showed their princes how they could profit from hostilities among their neighbors. Fortunately for us—indeed, vital for us—our viral allies are engaged in unceasing warfare against our viral enemies. They cure our wounds, destroy our infections, heal our sicknesses. Compared to them, our "miracle" drugs are paltry contrivances. Without these allies, who are the front line of our defenses and whom we occasionally render impotent or destroy, sometimes by misguided attempts to keep ourselves healthy, we sicken and die.

It is only by triggering our bodily allies, not by inventing new medicines, that we have been able, for example, to contain smallpox. In the seventeenth century, the Ottoman Turks discovered that by injecting a small amount of serum from an infected person into another person, the latter would be prevented from contracting the disease. The wife of a British ambassador to Constantinople learned of this treatment in 1717 and, on her return to London, suggested that it be tried. There was strong reason since practically everyone in England then contracted smallpox and nearly half a million people died from it every year. The discovery was not greeted with enthusiasm, however: the English were not only skeptical (of its efficacy) and disdainful (since it was suggested by an "Oriental" people) but were outraged on religious grounds (since the source was non-Christian). When vaccination was tried, however, it was found to prevent the onset of disease. What it did, we now know, was to provoke the body's immune system into reacting against the invading virus; it did this by exposing the body to a small amount of the invader, which, being relatively weak, could be overwhelmed without serious damage to the body. Then the immune system, having been alerted to this particular invader, was ready and able to meet subsequent and more serious attacks successfully.

Vaccination is an example of how we assist our intracellular system. From this perspective we may consider our evolution as a long program of immunization: some diseases that ravaged the earth in earlier times killed off huge numbers of our ancestors' relatives. The survivors, our ancestors, had or developed immunities. As their heirs, we have profited from their legacy. But naturally, we, like the Ottoman Turks, want to improve our chances. In our efforts, we face four kinds of problems: the first, of which we are painfully aware as we observe cancer and AIDS, is our lack of knowledge; the second is that, in our attempts to control sickness, we often use antibiotics in a haphazard way so that when we most need them they are ineffective; third, we are increasingly often and rapidly traveling to areas where our bodies are not accustomed to local varieties of pathogens and where the local population is not immune to ours; and last, in our occasionally misguided attempts to improve our lives or to cater to our desires, we harm the environment in which we must live.

At the same time, we pride ourselves that we have wiped out most of the great invading "armies" of the past. Smallpox, cholera, diphtheria, leprosy, and other plagues that terrorized our ancestors are now mostly vague memories or occur only in far-off places among little-known peoples. We rest assured that the "magic bullets" of modern medicine together with public sanitation have effectively disposed of them.

But have they? No, sadly, they have not. Many strains of viruses and bacteria are capable of rapid mutation.[2] Thus, we should think of them as spectrums along which we have identified and attacked only a single, if the most common, band. As the virus mutates along the spectrum, almost like an army camouflaging itself, regrouping, or digging in, it appears in new configurations that may be immune to the only kind of defense we know how to mount. Then, in periods of severe weather, when our bodies are weakened, or in times of disruption such as war or famine, we quickly fall prey to new attacks. Flu (influenza) is an example. It is always a nuisance, but at the end of World War I, when many people were malnourished and living in stressful conditions, it killed about twenty million people.

An earlier pandemic, then known as "the pestilence," today known as the "Black Death," spread across Europe in the middle decades of the fourteenth century. Specialists are divided over what it really was, where it came from, and how it spread. But its effects were unambiguous: it wiped out a quarter of the population in just a few years, killing about twenty-five million people. That is, the pandemic matched the proportional scale of the loss of life that could be anticipated in a nuclear war.

The pestilence was one of the most catastrophic events in history, but it certainly was not unique. As Thucydides tells us, the plague of 430–429 B.C.E. demoralized the Athenians in their great war with Sparta "in attacks almost too grievous for human nature to endure."[3] And plague after plague has been reported from China to the New World. As I indicate in chapter 29, it is now believed that the effects of the diseases that Europeans brought to the New World and that ravaged the native populations dwarf even the horrible devastation of the Black Death. They virtually depopulated whole areas, killing upwards of one hundred million people. In our time, we have been lucky, so far, that the Ebola virus has not effectively spread from Africa since we have no immunity or effective medicines (or, apparently, biological allies) against it. But a disease nearly as bad— the deadly dengue virus—has broken out in southern Asia and Latin America, whence it is spreading to Europe and North America. It may become a major plague because it is linked with another invader, the Japanese "tiger" mosquito, which is the perfect host not only for dengue but also for yellow fever and encephalitis.

Fleas, rats, mosquitoes, bacteria, and viruses have limited ranges, but we do not; often we take them along with us in our travels. And, because each day more than one million of us cross international frontiers, we introduce them into new environments. Indeed, we inadvertently provide them with networks. This is true internationalism, but put into the world social context, it is one part of the trilogy that sets the scene for a pandemic. The second part of the trilogy is the concentration of populations. Within a few years there will be twenty-four cities with populations of more than ten million. Some already are well beyond that figure, and in them public sanitation is lacking or breaking down. The third part is poverty and attendant malnutrition. As human populations become packed together more densely, with vast numbers afflicted by mass poverty, and yet are thrown into frequent contact with others throughout the world, the chances of transnational epidemics grow. A recent (and so far relatively small-scale) example now affecting the poor in Africa and Asia is cerebrospinal meningitis, which for some years has been spreading among Muslim pilgrims to Mecca who then take it back to their countries of origin. We are fortunate that the Ebola virus, which has already been taken from West Africa by plane to Europe and America, has not yet managed to establish itself and spread effectively in these regions. But even with lesser diseases the world's healthcare systems could break down. It is predicted that AIDS, which is in principle far easier to contain, will have cost more than $500 billion by the year 2000.

Even short of a pandemic, the World Health Organization reported in 1996 that nearly fifty thousand people are dying each day from such "traditional" infectious diseases as cholera, malaria, and tuberculosis. Moreover, the report continued, in just the past twenty years some thirty new forms of infectious diseases have been detected and for them we have no effective prevention or efficacious treatment. Some of those making a comeback, such as the "w-strain" of tuberculosis, are mutations of "old" diseases that we thought we had conquered.

And, as though these threats were not dangerous enough, we have given the baleful side of nature a helping hand. As an adjunct to nuclear weapons, the major powers have developed, produced, stockpiled, and occasionally used materials for biological warfare. Like many aspects of foreign affairs, this is not the invention of our age. Induced disease has been a weapon of war, albeit a crude and generally ineffective one, for centuries. Mongol armies, perhaps more as a terror tactic than as an attempt at biological warfare, are said to have catapulted bodies of plague victims into the city of Kaffa, which they were besieging, in 1346; as I describe in chapter 29, the United States army was said to have passed out to Indians blankets that were thought to be infected with smallpox. Before and during World War II, both the Germans and the Japanese conducted horrifying experiments in biological warfare on civilians and on military prisoners. Subsequently, both the United States and the Soviet Union mounted biological warfare programs that produced massive quantities of lethal materials. Although fortunately never employed in combat, they have bequeathed us huge stockpiles and vast contaminated areas. So far attempts to stop the development and spread of such weapons have resulted only in the weak 1972 Biological Weapons Convention.

Our bodies were not, of course, designed to cope with all of the dangers, stresses, and opportunities of life as we know it in the twentieth century and war as we could experience it; they evolved over hundreds of thousands of years in conditions in which people rarely moved outside of their neighborhoods and rarely met strangers. When those conditions began to change in what was, biologically speaking, just yesterday, our ancestors began to pay the fearful price of epidemics against which they had no immunities. Yet, despite this radical change in the level of danger, the elaborate mechanisms and protocols our bodies did evolve over tens of thousands of generations remain today, despite the marvels of modern medicine, our first line of defense in a very dangerous world. Our bodies are thus where foreign relations come home to all of us, where we are forced to coexist—if we wish to exist at all—with a variety of neighbors and strangers. How we do it is the marvel of life. To that world of tolerance and diplomacy, of trade and embargo, of espionage and counterintelligence, of wall-building and warfare, I now turn.

. . .

The first element is not a mechanism so much as an attitude. Each of us is born as a society. As we emerge from our mothers' wombs, we already have identified the myriad creatures that live within us as part of our communities. And with them we are prepared to engage in the peaceful arts of trade and what might be considered biological "diplomacy." Bacteria that process our food are more or less what the Germans call *Gastarbeiter,* "guest workers." Our bodies need them even if, as on the social level, we occasionally find them annoying to the point that sometimes we (mistakenly) try to get rid of them.

Our bodies also tolerate a fair number of creatures that do not contribute to our well-being and of which some can be expected to harm us given the chance. All our bodies contain cancer cells. Even more prevalent in our systems is the highly dangerous and drug-resistant staphylococcus bacterium. But we have negotiated what amount to cease-fires with these creatures: provided they remain in certain identified areas our bodies' defensive forces do not attack them and they do not attack our bodies. We shall see later that comparable "safe areas" or sanctuaries were mankind's first attempt to limit the damage of constant hostilities.

Second are mechanisms. In order to cope with the complex, ever-changing adjustments to the environment and bodily transformations we undergo as we are born and grow, wax and wane in health and sickness, get fat or thin, rest or grow weary, and ingest the nourishment and air we need to live, sophisticated systems in our bodies are engaged in a constant vigil. Overseeing the vast number of cells with whom "we" cohabit our bodies, this counterespionage service is composed of white blood cells known as B lymphocytes, whose task it is to investigate visitors and infiltrators. Those they identify as harmful aliens are targeted. The lymphocytes then alert our immune systems to produce antibodies.

The forces they call into action are miraculous in their power and sensitivity: they command more than a hundred million kinds of responses to the varieties of alien intrusion. And, like a good counterintelligence service, the B cells keep historical records on the nature of the intrusion; this enables them to call for precisely the antibody required to deal with the intruder should it return at a later date. This is what happens when one is given a smallpox vaccination, as I mentioned above.

In the 1960s it was learned that the immune system works in other ways also.[4] Two types of what are called "T cells" were discovered. "Helper" (or CD4) T cells are engaged in counterespionage: on finding a suspicious creature, they put out chemical signals that cause other cells to produce what amount to "special forces" teams (known as CD8 T cells). These extremely sophisticated teams do not "fight" but apparently perform their tasks by activating the intruder's own self-destruct program.

As in human warfare, a prime target of an invading enemy is the intelligence force of the defender. For this reason, HIV, for example, targets the CD4, or helper, cells while trying to evade the main battle groups of the defender. It is here where the decisive conflict takes place. The scale of the military operations is staggering: every day, in a patient with HIV, about a billion viruses are produced, and the body, in response, produces about a billion defensive cells. The two "armies" fight literally to the death. But gradually, as the initially rare HIV mutants multiply, the invader begins to triumph.

And, as in human warfare, some of the enemy forces are likely to evade capture or destruction and regroup for a new assault. Cells that get away from the CD8 T teams travel the body's highway, the bloodstream, along with food and oxygen. But soon they are stopped for inspection at checkpoints known as lymph nodes. There they are again inspected and, if noxious, will be attacked by main battle groups, known as macrophages. Macrophages simply consume everything that has been identified as alien or sick.

With these powerful, well-positioned, and well-informed defenders, the body is normally capable of handling even the most dangerous of its guests. But here three problems can be identified. The first is that sometimes the intruder escapes apprehension. This appears to be the major problem with cancer. The second is that on the cellular level we are as apt to overreact as we are on the national level. On perceiving a threat, the body often throws itself into "general war" in which its weapons may pose a greater threat to our survival than the "disease" they are fighting. The high fever we experience with flu, for example, is a manifestation not of the disease but of the body's attempt to fight it. Even more dramatic, in viral or serum hepatitis—a disease that affects about three hundred million people today—the virus itself causes no damage to the liver; rather, it is the reaction or counterattack of the immune system that is often lethal. And so it follows that many of our medical interventions are really not attacks on disease but are attempts to moderate the violence of the immune system's reaction.

The third problem is that we cannot seal off our bodies from the outside any more than we can live in isolated societies. This is why, after millions of years of evolution, we still have chinks in our armor: we need foreigners. Indeed, we would never be born if we did not have mechanisms to allow them in. If our bodies could not accommodate alien intrusion, the female body would destroy sperm. Like cancer cells, which the body sometimes fails to recognize, the sperm arrives undercover, as it were, coated with a substance that makes it "invisible" to the female's defenses. The female's body cooperates in the deception by adding another coating to further disguise the alien. Finally, as the fetus begins to grow, the mother interposes a "wall," the tropoblast, in the placenta to keep out her own patrolling "security force" cells. At this point, the fetus begins to mount its own defense by producing chemicals that cause the mother temporarily to suppress her immune system.

Last, as in the human "dirty" wars of espionage, the body systems harbor "moles" who penetrate the defense establishment and turn it to their own use. More sophisticated and powerful than the Greeks in the Trojan Horse, they not only gain entry but also turn the defenders' forces against them. In tuberculosis, for example, if the attack is strong enough, some bacilli may manage to get inside the macrophages. Once inside, they multiply and when ready burst out, destroying the macrophage in which they have lodged and, even worse, cause the body's defending T cells to attack the macrophages, which they now identify with the invaders.

In summary, as I show in the following chapters, although the scale is different and the shape and identity of the actors are obviously not the same, there is a remarkable continuity from the biological to the social scale in our approach to the fundamental problem of living in a world of neighbors and strangers. That is the world where the concept of "foreign relations" comes home to all of us.

. . . .

2 OUT OF THE MISTS OF THE PAST

During the past fifty thousand generations human bodies have changed relatively little, but during the past five hundred we have gone through revolutionary cultural transformations. These have created patterns of culture and activities; even when the pattern per se has been radically altered, as it has for most of us, aspects remain that influence or shape our thoughts and acts. So, moving from the microscopic to the social scale, I will sketch what we can say about the most primitive of our foreign relations. I begin with the problems we encounter in trying to understand our remote ancestors.

The first problem is that researchers tend to find what they are looking for, and usually that is shaped or colored by what they believe about their own times. But slowly, with many false steps, we are beginning to piece together this unrecorded heritage. There still are many gaps, and even where we have information it is usually open to a wide range of interpretations. The parameters of these interpretations were set by the pioneering students of civil society, Hobbes, Locke, Montesquieu, and a few other philosophers who began to speculate on the "state of nature"—the way they thought early man lived.

I take up this point because the way these early thinkers approached the legacy of this dim and distant past has not only shaped many of our political institutions but also influenced both the questions asked by later sociologists, psychologists, and political scientists and the answers they have given about the present.

Hobbes and Locke differed over their political solutions, and each justified his position by recourse to what he argued was the original condition of mankind. Hobbes, reacting to the turmoil of revolution in his time, sought stability and security; these required strong government, which he believed always had been necessary. So he has influenced what we might call a "muscular" view of the past. But he did not think the concept was merely a polemical contrivance; for him, it was real. As he wrote, "There are many places, where they live so now . . . [including] the savage people in many places of *America*."[5]

Locke, who was to exercise a profound influence on the growth of political concepts and on American political institutions, saw the past through different eyes and used it for a different purpose. His concept of "the state of nature" was more benign. People were guided by social instincts and generally acted reasonably. Indeed, there was evidence that this was so. Like many of his contemporaries, Locke was fascinated by the sorts of tales we know from Richard Hakluyt's *Voyages* and particularly by the then current discoveries of primitive peoples whose ways of life, many thought, suggested the basic or "true conditions" of all mankind.[6] Grounded thus in the primitive condition of man, Locke found the root of all social relationships, including those with the alien neighbor.

Both the fascination with primitive societies and the ways the Enlightenment philosophers looked at them were still "in the air" when Charles Darwin came to write *The Origin of Species* in 1859. In that work he thought of evolution in largely individual terms: there were just too many babies, not all could survive, and, since it is evident that competition within a single species is generally more severe than that between species, he saw evolution as a "war of every man against every man" in which "the strongest survive and the weakest die."

But from his observations of animal life and reproduction Darwin had come to realize by 1871, when he published *The Descent of Man,* that his original emphasis on extreme individualism and hostility was logically untenable. In a world of such untempered mayhem as he had imagined, the survival of the species would be unlikely. Thus, Darwin came to think that "communities which included the greatest number of the most sympathetic members would flourish best and rear the greatest number of off-spring." But Darwin understood, as Freud would later emphasize, that co-operation and competition were not mutually exclusive. Indeed, cooperation often arises from competition: "When two tribes of primeval man, living in the same country, came into competition, if the one tribe included (other circumstances being equal) a greater number of coura-geous, sympathetic, and faithful members, who were always ready to warn each other of danger, to aid and defend each other, this tribe would with-out doubt succeed best and conquer the other."[7]

Love of one's fellow man, what Darwin calls the instinct of sympathy, would not, however, bring about peace in foreign relations. "It is no argu-ment against savage man being a social animal that the tribes inhabiting adjacent districts are almost always at war with each other," he wrote, "for the social instincts never extend to all the individuals of the same species. . . . Many instances could be given of the noble fidelity of savages toward each other, but not to strangers."[8]

More recently, Sigmund Freud and his followers have argued that each of us carries within his modern, adult, "civilized" self both primitive man and infantile man. If one accepts that proposition, for which there seems to be increasing physiological evidence,[9] then something like "the state of nature" again becomes significant. Humans carry over from the remote past instincts or propensities to actions and phobias that are inap-propriate in modern life. Unfortunately, in order to live with others, Freud said, people must suppress precisely those instincts that made for survival "in nature." Since this suppression is painful to the primitive man lurking within us, he will, if pressed too hard, attempt to break loose, as Mr. Hyde did from behind the civilized mask of Dr. Jekyll, to commit what to our civilized selves seem atrocities but what enabled primitive man to survive. Judged "by the wishes in our unconscious," he wrote despairingly, "we are, like primitive man, simply a gang of murderers. It is well that these wishes do not possess the potency which was attributed to them by primitive man; in the cross-fire of mutual maledictions mankind would long since have perished."[10]

We may find such positions extreme or unsupported by evidence, but even today—although working with much larger databases than the pioneers—paleoanthropologists, ethologists, and biologists are driven by motivations that arise from contemporary views and personal predilec-tions. One man's fact is often another man's politics. In its modern guise, the study of ancient mankind is only a century old, but it has evolved in great controversy as we have penetrated more deeply into the exotic world.

There were practical or pragmatic motivations for such penetration:

the West had conquered all of the Americas, most of Africa, and much of Asia. In order to administer these regions economically and effectively, the new European officials believed that they had not only to learn native languages but also to discover how native societies "ticked." At the same time, other Europeans, fired by missionary zeal, sought to "uplift" and convert the natives; to do their job, they too felt that they needed to understand, even if they deprecated or even sought to destroy, what existed. Relatively few studies resulted from "pure" curiosity about exotic peoples. But for whatever motive, the researchers have created a vast literature on scores of peoples in Africa, the Americas, Asia, and the Pacific islands.

However different these peoples are from one another, they are certainly very different from us, lacking many or most of the tools, technologies, and possessions of our societies; so logically, many believed, they should be more similar to the early human society from which both we and they evolved. There are significant problems, however, in using insights from modern primitive peoples to understand those of the remote past. The first is that few of the peoples we have been able to observe in the past century or so are truly "primitive" in the sense of early humans. Practically all of even the most primitive of contemporary peoples have themselves evolved, for example, keeping domesticated animals and practicing agriculture. These developments spread among our ancestors only during the past ten thousand years, so such people do not live as everyone did in the millions of years before the "Neolithic revolution." Second, in our act of studying them, they come to know about us. Even if only indirectly or only recently, we have entered their lives and have injected into them ideas, tools, goods, and "needs" that skew the picture we get. And third, something was decisively different between them and our ancestors: for reasons that we cannot know, the rate of transformation among them is obviously different than among our ancestors.

We cannot, therefore, exactly equate a modern primitive group with premodern mankind. We see the past through this lens at best darkly and with undefined distortions. Yet, undeniably our insights into ancient peoples would be poorer, even more flawed than they now are, without the stimuli we derive from studies of the lives of their closest modern counterparts.

Aware of this dilemma, students have staked out a new approach to the remote past. It is the view we can get from the study of animals. One of the pioneers in the attempt to use that means to draw a picture of the life of early men was Sir Arthur Keith,[11] who suggested that they must have lived together rather like a nomadic baboon troop. Only in such a group, he argued, were chances of individual survival good.

When Keith first set forth his analysis, little was known about any of our primate relatives. But it seemed logical that we were more likely to be similar to them than, say, to elephants or wolves. Consequently, over the last half-century many researchers have observed and analyzed the primates, seeking, in part, clues to how early men might have lived.

Clues is the right word since no more (indeed, probably less) than primitive tribes do primates present a satisfactory picture of early man. For one thing, primates differ from what we guess about early man in diet. This is significant since, living at a subsistence level, early men must have oriented their lives toward the acquisition of food. And we know that the few remaining hunter-gatherer societies derive about a third of their calories from fresh meat whereas chimpanzees, our nearest primate relatives, get only 1 percent to 5 percent from meat. Early in human evolution, change in diet must have had a considerable impact on all aspects of human society, including relations among groups.

With few facts and many suppositions in mind, a number of ethologists have turned to the study of those animals that, presumably, more closely resemble early mankind in diet—the carnivores. Among the carnivores are "social" animals such as wolves, lions, and hyenas, which live in packs, hunt together, and adapt to their environment as we suppose that early men must have done. But they also, of course, do not provide us a completely satisfying analogy to early mankind.

Nor does paleoanthropology shed much light on how early humans lived. We don't have many skeletons and from them we learn little more than an occasional insight into diet, the acquisition of fire and tools, and the migrations that gradually peopled the earth. So, while suggestive, in this as in the other fields facts are meager and analogies must be used with care. However, there are certain conclusions to which all the evidence—from bones, primates, carnivores, and primitive tribesmen—points. And some of these, moreover, appear a logical extension to the social scale of what we know from the biological scale. So a picture begins to emerge that appears reasonable.

◆ ◆ ◆

Now I will address a few points essential for my analysis of intergroup relations—societies as kindred groups, living and feeding in discrete territories, separated from yet occasionally interacting with similar groups on neighboring territories but terrified of and hostile to more alien groups with whom they would have been thrown as groups split apart and as some were forced to migrate. As we shall see, albeit occasionally in disguise or under other names, elements of these adaptations to environment are a significant part of our heritage and play important roles in our history and in current affairs. I begin with the size of the effective society.

It is difficult for us to imagine a society composed of only a few people. Yet, until "recently"—in terms of human evolution, just the past six or eight thousand years—social groups were very small. In some parts of the world, they remain so today. Kinship defined "us," and the fundamental social fact in the life of early men is that "us" must have meant the immediate family that we discovered in infancy. "Them" meant everyone else. To return to the analogy of our immune system, there is evidence that "at or near the time of birth, the newborn (or the almost-born, depending on the species) animal takes one last look around, and basically says: 'Okay, this is it; this is me. Anything other than this I see from now on is foreign.' "[12] Biology was the definition of society not only among people but also among animals; it was reasserted and accepted generation after generation for millions of years, and so it formed the norm on which other relationships were built as human ecology changed. As we shall see, the concept of kinship became the model of ruling establishments and, by extension, set the tone of the international "family" of rulers and their dependents.

Moreover, kinship is not only the relationship from which neighborly ties have generally devolved but also the ideal toward which all non-hostile relationships are expected to evolve under favorable conditions. So, as we should expect, it is normal that when all of those nearby are no longer kinsmen, but act as though they are, they are designated by kinship terms. "Brotherhood" encompasses those who act like brothers. It is the inherited and common memory of peaceful, cooperative, and intimate relationships with nearby persons. So connected are these concepts that many people use the same words for them all. *Kinship* is the word for "peace" among the Sudanese Nuer, whereas among the Fijians, "living in peace" is the phrase meaning to "live as relatives." And the expressions "to be acquainted," "to know one another" are synonyms of "to be related."[13] English speakers will not find such usage exotic because we treat our "kin" as "kindred" should be treated, "kindly," all from the same Old English word traced ultimately back to the common ancestor of the Indo-European word *gen,* "to give birth." Passing through Greek into Latin and medieval French, *gen* spawned many English words, including *gentle, generous, genial,* and *benign*—all the things we should think about our kin.

Ecology forced on both animals and men another category, between the immediate kindred and aliens: neighbors. The Greeks, as usual, had a word for them: *deme.* Biology explains such groups as being composed of members who are more likely to exhibit histocompatibility—to be able to accept organ transplants—than aliens and more likely to accept those from neighboring demes, nearby aliens, than from those that are more remote. Such affinities arise from the processes of subdivision and migration of groups and intermarriage. They have, as we shall see, complex manifestations. On one hand, demes find peaceful interaction possible or normal under certain circumstances, but, on the other, it appears that a high proportion of serious conflict occurs within them rather than among true aliens. Indeed, the crosscurrents of this relationship may be said to lie at the base of most aspects of early foreign contacts.

When later I describe the beginnings of interstate associations in the Tigris-Euphrates complex, Anatolia, Egypt, and China, I will show that in periods of peace, when rulers emphasized nonviolent contacts, they characterized their relationships to one another in kinship terms and that the earliest diplomatic correspondence is couched in precisely the same sentiments and observations as among tribal peoples. Rulers addressed one another as "brother" and so, by extension, equated diplomacy to relationships among kindred—as distinct from war, which, by implication, is what occurs among strangers. These were more articulate, more sophisticated manifestations of what appears to have been a common substratum. So consider what that basis was. Given their level of technology, kindred groups of early peoples were defined by fairly precise margins: they had to be large enough to accomplish the minimum chores of a seminomadic scavenging, hunting, and gathering economy and to defend themselves but small enough to keep in contact with one another and to keep themselves in proportion to the accessible supply of food.

These are the ecological conditions that prevail, although softened by cultural and technological improvements, in the deserts and steppes of Asia and Africa today and that set the limits of clans among groups as geographically and culturally diverse as the Bushmen, the Bedouin, and the Siberian Tunguz, among whom the common band is composed of the progeny of a single man over several generations. Studies of extant primitive peoples indicate a prevailing group size of twenty-five to fifty. It takes a major leap in imagination for us to conceive not only of a group so small but also of a "world" in which everyone was a grandfather, father, uncle, brother, cousin, son, nephew, or grandson (or their female equivalents). Kinship was not just an abstraction; it was the basis for all action and sentiment.

Where resources were scarce and the margin between life and death was thin, each group would naturally have been driven by its absolute need to defend the means it had to feed itself. The "fit" in Darwin's sense were those who defended it effectively. What they fed themselves on was, of course, a territory; so "territoriality," identification with a discrete piece of the earth, is deeply implanted in the human experience. This, along with kinship, can be observed at every level of experience, from the workings of our bodies through studies of animals and primitive societies up to and including our own attitudes and actions toward the world in which we live. Territoriality is the ancestor of nationalism, which is still today the most powerful political sentiment.

But "ownership" of a territory, to be effective, must be identifiable by neighbors. We do not know how early men defined their territories, but what we see in living animal societies and among primitive tribes suggests that they must have found means to warn intruders off. Many species of animals mark their territories in recognizable ways and defend them as groups against intruders. Hyenas, for example, urinate, defecate, and paw at known places along their frontiers. Their markings are unnoticed by other animals but are immediately recognized by other hyenas.[14] Usually they will not cross into alien territory, and, if they do, they are likely to be mauled or killed by the defending pack. I will describe in chapter 4 the ways in which later human societies have employed elaborate physical devices and formulated complex abstract concepts to define and protect their increasingly large and often scattered territories.

Given the low level of their technology, early men probably saw few people who were not kinsmen since each group would have required a large territory to feed itself and had no means of transport. This is certainly true of groups of primates, and it became even more true for early men as they became increasingly carnivorous, because carnivores require more space than vegetarians. The size of the territory would have varied depending on terrain and climate, but a reasonable average for a clan of fifty or so people would be about half the size of Long Island. Thus, as with primates and such groups as the Bedouin and the Bushmen, the shock and danger of encounters with aliens would have been lessened by their rarity. Moreover, since no one could have migrated very far in a generation or so, most neighbors would have been relatives who had lived together in recent memory, that is, members of the same deme.

We know of another "mechanism," charmingly called the "dear enemy" effect, that may also have mitigated the shock of encounters. Among birds, where the effect was identified, the playing of a recorded song of a bird from a remote area produces a paroxysm of rage, whereas the song of a neighbor evokes a more restrained reaction.[15] The inference is that neighborhood has a calming effect on strangeness. Among animals, scent seems to play a similar role. Perhaps odor, appearance, and speech similarly affected our ancestors.

We do not know under what circumstances the "dear enemies" over-came their antipathy and fear to form larger associations. The study of our nearest animal relatives, bonobos and chimpanzees, may provide clues. They also normally live in small groups but, on occasion, affiliate with others to form larger societies. We see similar accommodations among primitive peoples. The desert will not sustain large congregations, so the de facto or effective unit of Bedouin society—the clan—must be small. The Bedouin recognize, however, what we might term a de jure or conceptual society composed of several clans—the tribe—in which neigh-borhood and the memory of kinship allow conduct (for example, the end-ing of blood feuds without shame) not permitted with the true alien. Such affiliations are unstable, and relations within them are usually tense.

Perhaps the most studied among contemporary primitive peoples are the !Kung Bushmen of the Kalahari Desert. Their area is remote and harsh, so they must live in widely separated seminomadic groups. Intensely fearful of strangers, Bushmen hide or run away at the sight or sound of any alien.[16]

Obviously, each clan would like to live in isolation. Yet, like all hunter-gatherers, Bushmen are at the mercy of the climate and must fre-quently alter the shape of their territories. Were this not so, they would have had a simple foreign relations problem: just to maintain the estab-lished frontiers. But in years of severe drought they must have access to much larger areas than they need normally. This causes an ebb and flow of concentration and dispersion and even of incursion into the territories of neighbors and strangers.[17] The theoretical alternative to expansion or contraction of the territory is expansion or contraction of the number of inhabitants. Some hunter-gatherer groups practice infanticide in their attempts to stay within their accustomed territories, but even with this dra-conian measure they cannot adjust population size rapidly enough to adapt to changes in weather, availability of animals, and other random or unpredictable factors. Nor was infanticide a sufficient policy for the settled agricultural communities of the early Greeks, yet they and many other societies (including some still in existence today) have practiced it. Even if a group could manage perfectly to balance population and resources, there are social or biological imperatives for extragroup relationships. One is that clans need to gain access, peacefully or not, to other groups in order to secure mates. A second, which I discuss in chapter 28, is the expulsion of members. Thus, however feared it may be, contact with alien groups is a fundamental if sporadic condition of primitive life.

Contacts were probably infrequent since territory sizes, relative to capacity to move, were vast, but when chance or the sharing of such strate-

gic resources as water holes threw unrelated and unfamiliar groups together, they probably reacted as do packs of animals on the same plains
today: the weaker or already satiated group would loudly but rapidly decamp. Among baboon troops in such circumstances, fighting is rare, but
among carnivores, which occupy more territory and meet less frequently,
fighting on contact is more common. And among primitive human beings
it is even more frequent.

In addition to the protection of territory as a hunting and food-
gathering area, there is another reason for keeping the stranger out: fear.
As George B. Schaller mentions in *The Serengeti Lion,* some lions are "nomads" that, uninhibited by kinship ties or neighborhood restrictions, attack the prides and kill the cubs in the territories they invade. Nomads
are the outlaws of the lion kingdom. And, not surprisingly, we find that
in nearly all premodern societies, the inhabitants fear and hate those who,
like lion nomads, are rootless or alien. In folktales, the stranger is often
a demon in disguise; among nomads, a traveler without a local sponsor
is literally an outlaw; and even a few hundred years ago in Europe an
interloper might be executed on apprehension. Xenophobia was not invented by the Greeks: as we have seen, it is characteristic of our immune
systems and it is documented in studies of "virtually every group of animals
displaying higher forms of social organization."[18] I think, therefore, that
we must regard it as the norm from which other kinds of conduct vary
rather than the reverse.

Nothing so triggers our interest—and hostility—as the strange foot-
print on our turf. Among all the carnivores and among many of the primates, strangers are rarely, and only after initiation, accepted.[19] Even in
modern, complex, and sophisticated societies, as many of us are painfully
aware, true membership often remains rooted in kinship and its racial
extensions.

But if kinship was usually a necessary condition for membership, it
was occasionally not sufficient. Failure to maintain internal peace, even
where kinship was clear and where external dangers were present, and
failure to fit the changing capacities of their territory forced societies to
get rid of some kinsmen. Although over time and in various ecologies
there must have been considerable variation, something like the following
was probably typical: a single group of people grew to a larger size than
their territory would feed, and some division, say, between the descendants of each of two sons of the patriarch, was already evident. The cousins
would have been less motivated by what Darwin called "the instinct of
sympathy" than would the brothers. Push could have come to shove in
many ways—over the division of a kill, over women, over status—all of

which are common in animal and human societies. As a result of probably many conflicts, hostility grew until the weaker group fled.

It is difficult for us to imagine the terror embodied in that move. Living at a subsistence level, the emigres would have had no supplies to take with them to sustain them while they searched for a safe haven and food; being previously confined to their own territory, they would have known nothing about the surrounding areas, probably not even where they could find water. The chances are that anyone they met as they foraged would have regarded them as lion "nomads" and would have tried to kill them or drive them away. Knowing this, they probably would have reacted like other animals. So strong is the fear of the protectors of territory that, even in hot pursuit, hunting hyenas sometimes " 'stop dead in their tracks' when the quarry crosses into another clan's range."[20] Thus, however we may regard Hobbes's concept of the "state of nature" in general, his description—"continuall feare, and danger of violent death; and the life of man, solitary, poore, nasty, brutish, and short"—probably fit the little bands of refugees as they fled through the African night.

Yet, almost incredibly, from a few early sites our species spread over the whole planet into areas with environments far more difficult and less attractive than those of East Africa. To get to the remote areas in which they established themselves and where we are still discovering isolated groups today, they had to climb mountains, cross swamp and sea, desert and glacier, and endure the fury of the elements with virtually no equipment and no surplus supplies, encumbered with the aged and the very young. Not many could have survived, and nothing would have softened the survivors' reactions to those they encountered. Having no alternatives, they would have used the traditional weapons of the weak—cunning, ferocity, and terror. Starving as they undoubtedly were, they would have not only killed but probably also eaten the strangers.

This asserts behavior more violent than one might expect from studies of intraclan behavior among animals and humans precisely because, by the time little bands fled or were driven out of their clans and home territories, the mechanisms of kinship and territory had broken down. When kindred fight, usually the weaker member cowers and then takes his place down the social hierarchy, but when strangers invade a territory, there are no rules. I discuss the more modern manifestations of this outward thrust in chapter 28; here I will simply mention that, from at least two million years ago, groups began to migrate outward from their presumed place of origin along the Rift Valley until they covered the globe.

When we examine mankind's earliest records, we observe that despite their greater technological capacity, hunger impelled the Archaic

Greek and early Italian societies to force their "excess" population to migrate. Similar imperatives peopled the New World and continue to influence movements in our own epoch; today, entry of such migrants is a major political problem in Europe and America and often evokes a comparable "primal" hostility. Indeed, more generally, the fact that migrations continued intermittently for millions of years may have encouraged the hatred and fear that seems such an integral aspect of our view of the foreigner.

As we shall see, the apparent opposites of flight and attack, defense and offense, are often merely a matter of the position of the observer: groups running away from their oppressors have been some of the greatest aggressors of history. So probably it always was. Those of us alive today descend from the victors. Among them were the *Homo sapiens,* who about a hundred thousand years ago invaded territories that had been controlled by the so-called Neanderthals. Whether the Neanderthals suddenly died out or were "replaced" (slaughtered?) by invading *Homo sapiens,* the two species certainly coexisted for tens of thousands of years. We may never *know* what kind of relationship the two groups had, but we can infer some aspects of the probable "average" relationship from two facts and two analogies. The first fact is that *Homo sapiens* "replaced" the Neanderthals. There are none left anywhere in the world today, nor have there been, as far as is now known, for perhaps twenty thousand years. The second fact is that *Homo sapiens* moved into areas that had been the hunting preserves of the Neanderthals.

Everything we know about animal and primitive human behavior argues that protecting their territories would have been of fundamental, often vital, importance to the Neanderthals. Thus, I think we must presume, each small clan would have tried to repel the invaders. That is the first analogy; the second analogy with animals and primitive tribesmen suggests that the winners would have killed the males and children and raped the females. Experts disagree over how to interpret what evidence we have. One group argues that interbreeding of Neanderthals and migrants probably took place and would have given an advantage to the mutants (our ancestors) in coping with conditions in their new homeland.[21] The opposite position was most recently put forward by James Shreeve,[22] who maintains that the two species did not (possibly could not) interbreed and possibly did not even notice each other because they were physically so different as not to regard each other as competitors. I find this unlikely. While we do not have any Neanderthals to study, tests done on *Homo sapiens* and his nearest living primate relatives, the chimpanzee and the bonobo, show that we are as close as sibling species of other organisms, with at least 98 percent identity in nonrepeated DNA. The difference is so small, indeed, as to suggest that a hybrid might be viable. Neanderthals are closer to us than either of these primates, but whether or not they could have paired with *H. sapiens* to produce offspring, they certainly were competing for the same food supplies. In any event, there is evidence at many periods and places that, at least among *H. sapiens,* the invading males took over the females and disposed of the males. This brutal conflict, reinforced repeatedly over thousands of years, must have augmented the "deep fears" of the night, of fiends, and of monsters that our ancient ancestors often equated with the foreigner. As I will point out below, I believe this "deep fear" of the ultimate alien underlies the fear of the "barbarian" so evident in the Roman and Chinese Empires. It is a fear that still haunts many of us and underlies the tragedies of ethnic cleansing.

Until fairly recently there were almost no countervailing forces. It is difficult to imagine trade in the circumstances of ancient man.[23] Each group must have been autarkic. As seminomads without any form of animal assistance, they could not have afforded the luxury of possessions. And, living as they did on the edge of starvation, they could not have produced articles for barter. Perhaps some learned earlier than others how to acquire salt or shells from those nearer to the sea, but it was not until recently—say, the past thousand generations, or twenty thousand years—that we can begin to speak of trade. So early man had everything to lose and almost nothing to gain in encounters with strangers.

In short, his world was very small, his "nation" very compact. That probably would have been the end of the story had population and knowledge been static. But as people grew in number, those who adapted survived. And among the most significant of their adaptations were their methods of dealing with those who were too close to be ignored but too different to be treated as kindred, the neighbors who were also strangers.

. . . .

3 *OUR* POSSESSIONS

Living in an acquisitive, materialistic society, we find it hard to imagine conditions in which people were not comforted (and burdened) by possessions. Today, we all too often see photographs of refugees from war areas and "street people" pushing carts full of their meager goods while those of us who move from time to time are painfully and expensively aware that we accumulate almost immovable quantities of "things." Arab Bedouin call this process *qantara,* which means both to possess something bulky and to settle down. With possessions, it is hard to move.

In this chapter I consider possessions under five categories and try to show their influence on how we interact with foreigners. The categories are our most intimate possessions, *our bodies,* the *territories* on which early hunter-gatherers depended; immovable *facilities* that by their creation endowed territories with *goods* that could be stolen or seized by raiders; and, finally, our intangible possession, *pride.*

Our bodies. Our bodies are vital to us, but they are useful to others only under certain conditions. The least complicated of these conditions is hunger. Even though we may be revolted by the idea of cannibalism, this taboo was by no means universally shared until fairly recent times. Indeed, in times of famine and social chaos, instances of cannibalism have been recorded even in Europe in this century. Still practiced in some areas, it was widely reported in the ancient world, where it sometimes took on a religious or magical aspect. But cannibalism was also practical because it was easier to kill men, or at least women and children, than large, fast, and ferocious animals. And, with a diet made up primarily of fruits, grains, berries, grubs, and grasses[24] and often at the point of starvation, our ancestors must often have hungered for protein. It would have been surprising if they did not eat one another.

The bodies of women were particularly valuable, of course, because in small hunting bands, enough women of the right ages would not always have been available as mates. So, presumably, women were seized in raids among neighboring clans as they have been throughout history. For example, materials in graves of the fourth millennium B.C.E. in the Ukraine suggest that most females were local whereas the males, particularly those in richer graves, were foreign. In their settlement of the western Mediterranean in the eighth century B.C.E., the Greeks, whose population was at first were almost entirely male, "acquired" local women who certainly would have seemed to them entirely alien. Many other examples could be cited. The large-scale rape of Bosnian women by Serbs in 1994 and 1995 is thus not so unusual as we would wish.

The human body did not acquire other values for millions of years. Those values have come only as the development of agriculture and settled life put a premium on people as a new form of domesticated animal—slaves—who could plow, harvest, dig, and build. We begin to see this around five to six thousand years ago. In short, people then became an adjunct to other forms of property; so I will turn next to these.

Territories. In Paleolithic times, when everyone gleaned a living from a hunting and gathering territory, the territory itself was the only "real" property. It was a resource whose value depended mainly on its animal and plant population, but since everyone consumed everything he acquired, there was nothing that could be seized by an invader. If he drove away the inhabitants, the intruder could benefit from their territory only if he moved in and took their place. This was an attractive option only if he had been forced out of his own territory or if he found the new territory richer. That may have been only a slight advantage, but it might have spelled the difference between survival and extinction since to track down and kill wild animals was at best problematical. Early man survived in conditions beyond the skill and hardihood of most of us, and for him the specter of starvation was never far away. Those who think that life might have been easy *on average,* with frequent periods of idleness and a glut of food, forget that since primitive societies had no reserves, even a single accident, a brief bout of sickness, or a short run of bad hunting could be fatal.

Facilities and goods. Over thousands of years, early men must have probed at this weakness and gradually come to realize that if they made a kill that gave them more than they could consume, they could conserve some of the meat and useful bones for a future date. Given the conditions that often pertained during the long ice ages, it was easy to construct what amounted to deep freezes simply by digging pits. Examples of these have been discovered on the central Russian plain that date back about forty thousand years.[25] (Similar techniques are still used today by Eskimos.) For the first time, there was something in a territory that could be taken from it by invaders—a cache of food.

People eventually figured out that when they trapped or wounded more animals than they could consume they need not kill them. They could "store" wounded or immature animals. This option became particularly attractive as climatic changes and improved hunting techniques began to deplete animal populations. In some areas, only those who practiced storage would have survived. Larger pits, believed to have been used as pens for wild animals and to date from about seventeen thousand years ago, have been found in India, where similar pits, today called *keddahs,* are still in use.[26]

As finding and catching animals became harder and less sure, it must have seemed smart to keep some for longer periods. Some of the wounded would have been pregnant females, and their progeny may gradually have taught hunters to "manage" herds of still wild but smaller, less dangerous animals. Certainly by the end of the Neolithic period animals had come to be valued for the milk and wool they could give only while alive.[27] True domestication, however, was a complex process, involving changes in bodily structure, and it was many thousands of years before animals other than the dog were made a permanent part of man's household.

Probably about the same time that some pits were being used to hold captured animals, others began to be used to store wild grains. This became more common as people learned how to employ milling stones to break down the tough glume on wild grains to make them more digestible. Around 11,000 B.C.E. pits became more elaborate and, for the first time, were lined with clay to protect the stored grain. People were making a commitment to settle down.[28]

More efficient storage of what had been gathered and caught probably served to encourage the growth of numbers in those communities that took advantage of them. They would have increased not only absolutely but also relative to more backward neighbors. The strong and successful would have been less likely than the weak and less progressive to migrate into the unknown dangers; they were more able to defend themselves and had acquired a new motivation to stay put: the migrant could not take along his storage pit or his pen of animals.

With fewer wild animals to hunt and probably more people to feed, social groups needed larger territories. For the first time, clans must have frequently clashed. For the first time also, property in the form of stored grain and animals provided a tangible incentive for attack. Men had nearly reached the threshold of war.

Meanwhile, other men were not the only enemy: the elements made daily life often a misery and survival a constant battle. Paleolithic hunter-gatherers, probably crouching beside the bodies of the large animals they had killed for protection against winds and freezing rain, got the idea of peeling off the hide and propping it up with bones. A "house" of that kind dated to around 40,000 B.C.E., found in the Ukraine, was an early step toward settled life.[29] That shelter would not have lasted long, but as they became anchored by storage pits and assured of a supply of food, groups began, possibly first with reeds and ultimately with stone, to build semipermanent dwellings.

The next step was long in coming. Casually, probably at first even accidentally, people began to plant seed. The earliest such planting now known was along the flanks of the Taurus and Zagros mountains and along the edge of the Fertile Crescent. The northern Syrian site of Mureybet appears to have been the "first attested case of cultivation by man of wild cereals, carefully transported from their natural habitat in the hills [one hundred kilometers (sixty miles) away] into a foreign and man-made environment."[30] Even though the grain that was being harvested was still wild and not very productive, it was of great value; so the tasks of planting, weeding, protecting, and harvesting crops forced at least some of the inhabitants to stay put permanently. Agriculture made Mureybet perhaps the first village.

The decision to settle was of obvious importance; what has been less appreciated is that for the first time in human affairs, something of great value was accumulated and preserved long enough to make war profitable. Unlike the *territory* of the neighbor, which could be utilized only by an invading group that had lost or was willing to give up its own territory, a store of harvested grain could be consumed or carried back to the invaders' territory. The humble storage pit may thus mark a major divide in the development of foreign relations. It brought on communities a new kind of danger they had not previously experienced by making them targets for their neighbors. As we shall see, there is evidence that shortly after the pit's introduction communities felt impelled to build walls or to change their form of house construction to keep strangers out. Never again could men afford to live, as they always had, in the open. Yet, for all the danger, grain storage was of such great importance to the growing late Paleolithic populations that its use spread widely throughout the Near East, Asia, Africa, and Europe.

For thousands of years, settlements remained, at most, temporary villages: much of the population was probably absent for at least part of the year and the common form was not, indeed, what we would call a village. Rather, it was more like the African "compound" in which each person created a rudimentary shelter for himself near his fellows. We get a more accurate idea if we think of these early settlements as "base camps"— storehouses, retreats, and assembly points in which hunter-gatherers kept their increasingly larger collections of goods. These villages, small though they were, constituted a revolutionary change: once populations numbering in the scores collected, they started to change the pattern of their shelters, intensified their occupation, and marshaled their living space. Those who took these steps outclassed their less numerous and less advanced neighbors in compounds. The archaeological record suggests that those who lived in compounds could not effectively compete for living space and were driven away, absorbed, or forced to copy their larger neighbors. Thus villages were the dominant human association in many parts of the world for many centuries and even today are common in the world's marginal lands.

About ten thousand years ago, in a dry and barren area near the

Dead Sea, there was a four-hectare (ten-acre) plot that we can call the first true town. Jericho's two thousand inhabitants were too numerous to have been close kinsmen, yet they were living and working together. The site was not new, having been inhabited for a thousand years, but in earlier years the people must have had little to attract the envy or acquisitiveness of neighbors. By about 8350 B.C.E., however, the town had grown rich enough to have to consider its defense.

By about 6500 B.C.E., the Anatolian settlement of Çatal Hüyük had grown to three times the size of Jericho. The buildings of its six thousand inhabitants covered thirteen hectares (thirty-two acres). Excluding the alien was a major preoccupation of both Jericho and Çatal Hüyük. Indeed, they illustrate the two basic methods of defending a community. In Çatal Hüyük, the dwellings of the inhabitants, windowless and doorless, with the entrance on the roof, collectively formed a fortress. This arrangement was reinvented time after time, as I learned when I lived in such a dwelling in the Lebanese mountains in the 1950s. The arrangement was cheaper to construct than a wall and did not require a community organization since each family looked to its own defense, but it was not very effective. Thus, Jericho's common wall, although chronologically earlier, was more advanced; in fact, it was the world's first great public works project. To build it required not only the perception of foreign threat but, more important, a concept of community and a system of mobilization that lifted Jericho above all known contemporary societies; indeed, the act of building walls played a significant role in creating the city-state, the nation, and the empire.

Walls and the new irrigation works that began to be built would also force a revaluation of the human body. People were still slaughtered in their myriads, as they are still in our century, but increasingly, the more successful of the societies recognized that each new advance created more wealth but required more labor. Vast numbers were required to build the walls of the new cities, to dig and tend the irrigation works that fed them, and to work the quarries and mines that supplied them. Many were more or less free immigrants from neighboring villages, but demand rapidly exceeded that source of supply. Thus we are not surprised to find that the process of animal "domestication," seen as early as Çatal Hüyük, began to be extended to people. The relationship would be made clear in an early Assyrian statement and in a much later Roman edict. Both slaves and animals taken in battle were referred to by the Romans as "live booty"; the Assyrian term for submission was *eli erbi ritti pasalu* (walking on all fours), that is, becoming like a (domesticated) animal.[31] The source of these auxiliaries also becomes clear from the terms by which they were designated: the Sumerian word for "slave" is related to the word for "foreigner"; its Egyptian counterpart also meant "Asiatic."[32]

The growth of cities enormously magnified the need for labor. As trade became more important, cities competed for markets as nations do today and sought cheaper and more numerous labor forces. In one Syrian city, Mari, the main source of workers in the palace workshops was capture in war; elsewhere, workers—not unlike Turks in Germany, Hispanics in America, and Indians in England—were lured from abroad and given special status. By the end of the third millennium B.C.E., labor on a massive scale was being employed in every city: to build just one of the temple terraces of Uruk, for example, has been estimated to have required about 5.5 million man-hours, that is, a force of fifteen hundred men working ten hours a day for a year. But it was Rome that developed slavery to such an extent that one can almost describe it as a slave state. It has been estimated that the proportion of foreign slaves in the population rose from 15 percent in 225 B.C.E. to 35 percent in 31 B.C.E. The influx was constant and occasionally massive. Following the battle of Pydna in 168 B.C.E., for example, 150,000 Epirotes were enslaved, and even larger numbers came to slavery from the destruction of Corinth in 146 B.C.E. and from Caesar's conquest of Gaul.[33]

To slavery the Romans adapted quickly and happily. Most, or at least those whose voices we hear, became unquestioning beneficiaries of the new order. Romans found it natural and pleasurable to have crops planted, chores performed, lusts satisfied,[34] and minds stimulated by slaves. When opportunity offered or danger demanded, the slaves could be armed and even turned into private armies.

By the end of the second century B.C.E. about two million foreign slaves were living in what is now Italy. A population movement of that magnitude brought a qualitative change as well: particularly in the wars with the Greeks, the Romans began to acquire as slaves scores of thousands of educated, formerly wealthy men and women who were too valuable simply to be worked to death in remote mines or used as field hands. Many entered the houses of the rich and powerful as secretaries to the masters and as tutors to their children. Naturally, they taught what they knew and so gave a powerful impulse to the move toward Hellenization. Horace was certainly right in his often-quoted saying that "captive Greece overcame her barbarous conqueror and brought civilization to wild Latins."[35]

Since ancient times, slavery and indentured servitude have periodically been rediscovered and widely used, as with the Spanish and Portuguese enslavement of Africans and inhabitants of the New World in the fifteenth and sixteenth centuries, the importation of Africans into the New World in the seventeenth and eighteenth centuries, and the massive export of "indentured" South Asians to sugar and tea plantations in the nineteenth century.

Pride. Impressive as were these changes in the creation of wealth, in the growth of new facilities, and in the revaluation of human bodies, almost more seminal was the introduction, probably first by the people of Çatal Hüyük, of a new emotional element into the concept of possession. These early villagers began to bury their dead under their solidly built houses in ways that suggest an attempt to convey to the dead the means to continue the life of this world. By bringing the dead *into* their houses, they made the houses not only the domiciles of the living generation but also the residences of the family, living and dead, over long spans of time. The burial site thus perpetuates the connection of the community with its land.

The kindred as a transgenerational group merged emotionally with the land: more than ever before, people were committed to a long-term process in a settled place from which they could move only at great cost, with great effort, and with the loss of a past that now was physically present in the bones of ancestors. This joining of lineage to land further reinforced the sense of apartness from the alien, who was excluded from both. The seed of nationalism had been planted. It would take root and grow in the most diverse possible environments. The very pride of accomplishment, physically embodied in cities, would turn into a sort of love affair, a mystical union, first signified in Çatal Hüyük, of man and land. From that vague beginning, we have hardly ever looked back. We see it today in the faces of the people of Bosnia, where in 1996 refugees dug up the bodies of their dead and took them, sometimes in preference to their possessions, with them to their places of refuge.

◆ ◆ ◆

We have seen that from having a value of not more than his weight in meat, the human being, like the formerly wild animal, became himself a potential domesticated animal, a builder, farmer, digger, servant, bodyguard, soldier, concubine; that a territory from which a seminomadic band gleaned a subsistence diet became a farming area that, in supporting a compact and growing population, could become the pivot of a trading network; that this community could coalesce to construct facilities that were themselves of great value; that these facilities could become, among other things, storehouses for gathered wealth; and that the task of creating such facilities encouraged people to invest what amounted to their spirit in their land and so, in a rudimentary form, began to formulate what in later times we could call nationalism. Subsequent civilizations would elaborate these basic concepts, but by about six thousand years ago, the framework was already in place.

PART II DEFENSE

· · · · · · ·

4 KEEPING *THEM* OUT

Keeping enemies, both human and animal, out of "our" camp is a very old human activity. Remains have been found of what appears to have been a defensive wall—mammoth tusks stuck into the ground and surrounded by brush—at a site in central Europe that has been radiocarbon dated to 23,000 B.C.E.[1] Long before that time, and in many places, people doubtless made use of natural defenses, surrounded themselves (as tribesmen still do in Africa) with thorn bushes, and dug ditches or improved existing gullies. Remains of these activities would not today be identifiable, so we have no way of knowing about them. Around ten thousand years ago, however, as we have seen, not only did societies begin to accumulate goods that they wished to protect (and that they presumed that others wished to steal), but some societies also began to become populous enough to construct more elaborate defenses, as mentioned in chapter 3. It is at Jericho near the Dead Sea that we can identify the first significant venture in urban defense: the building of a wall.

About ten to twelve thousand years ago, a series of mutually reinforcing actions began to be taken by Jericho's inhabitants. Profiting from the relative advantages of good water, the presence of wild grains, and plentiful nearby animals, they no longer felt the need to move after their prey. Beginning to profit from new tools and new methods of preparing what they gleaned, they found it possible, with the same amount of work, to gather more than they consumed. In turn, being less mobile, they could accumulate and store the surplus. This surplus gave them, for the first time in the human experience, things both to exchange and to protect from others. Increased contact with foreigners enriched them but also, they apparently felt, endangered them by inciting their neighbors' covetousness. Whether or not their fear of foreigners was justified, they thought the danger clear and present enough to begin to invest their labor in defense on a far larger scale than anyone before had ever done.

Jericho's common wall was the world's first great public works project. By 7000 B.C.E. the four-hectare (ten-acre) site was surrounded by massive stone walls about 4 meters (13 feet) high and 3 meters (10 feet) thick and at least 700 meters (2,300 feet) long. To build it, a staggering 10,000 cubic meters of rock and earth—roughly 5 cubic meters for each of the 2,000 inhabitants—were moved by hand, without animal or mechanical aids. And the inhabitants periodically mobilized themselves to rebuild the walls as well. Between 3000 and 2300 B.C.E., they built or elaborated on twenty walls. The last, as the spiritual hymn puts it, came "a-tumblin' down" about 1500 B.C.E.

Jericho's are the best known, but walls were independently invented as the prime defensive element in settlements throughout the ancient world. Often, as in the roughly contemporary village of Shengavit in Central Asia, they were elaborately and massively constructed at enormous, indeed sometimes ruinous, cost to the inhabitants. So closely identified with the city did walls become in both Chinese ideographs and Egyptian hieroglyphics that the same word was used for both.

Three aspects of wall construction demand our attention at this point. First, walls embodied the new reality of foreign affairs: those who were becoming urban and were acquiring new forms of property realized that they had more to fear from neighbors and strangers than had their ancestors. They had not only their bodies to protect but also their investments in real estate and various forms of movable goods. As I outlined in the previous chapter, wealth had become a central factor in foreign relations.

Second, the coherent and discrete visual properties of the wall contributed to and indeed defined a new and more flexible sense of kinship. While keeping *them* out, walls delineate *us:* the two thousand inhabitants of Jericho were not, in the traditional sense, kin, but their residence together in a city gave them a new form of affinity based not on biology but on neighborhood. And to this expansive sense of *us* may be traced the origins of larger societies and, ultimately, nations and civilizations.

Third, and perhaps most important, the very task of building a wall helped—indeed, I believe, it may have been the key element—in the creation of two of the major characteristics of historical civilization: a sense of *capacity* that came from having worked together as communities on large projects and a sense of *pride* in accomplishment.

These new manifestations were by no means unique to the Middle

KEEPING *THEM* OUT / 49

East, but they had their first dramatic impact there. Nor does the historical record suggest that when the backbreaking tasks were largely carried out by foreign slave labor these results of massive public works projects were significantly diminished. Of course, we have no way of accessing the minds or emotions of the hundreds of thousands of humans who toiled on the projects I will describe; it was not they, however, but rather those who ordered, organized, and directed them whose emotions and beliefs predominate in forming the currents of history.

Ironically but understandably, the most "productive" aspect of wall-building was its cost. Jericho was about as small as a city could be and still have critical mass. It could not have put more than about two hundred men to work on the walls. That was probably the minimum that could have built or defended them. The proportional cost was nearly unbearable even if the inhabitants judged it to be absolutely vital. Over centuries, urban societies discovered that the only way to reduce the proportional cost was by growth, as we can see mathematically. Imagine a square two hundred meters on each side. That will give an interior space of forty thousand square meters to house those who must build, maintain, and defend eight hundred meters of wall, but adding 50 percent to the length of the walls will protect twice as much interior space. Size itself thus became a factor in safety and stability. Jericho was an early tributary in what became the great river of urbanization.

Appropriately, that river poured forth its bounty first in the great valleys of the Tigris-Euphrates, the Indus, the Nile, and (later) the Huang (Yellow) Rivers. Into all of them, previously nomadic or seminomadic peoples migrated and, enriched by agricultural innovations and trade, established first villages and then towns. One third-millennium document, described as a "geographical gazetteer" and found at the northern Syrian trading center of Ebla, lists 289 nearby urban trading partners.[2] As settlements proliferated and trade grew, warfare became persistent and pitiless. Those who fell behind quickly found that they could not meet the challenge of foreign affairs. The cost of defense, most evident in wall-building, forced them to merge, and it was from these mergers that the major urban centers evolved. We see this clearly in the growth of the early city of Uruk (the biblical Erech), one of the successful centers, which "leached" the settlements around it so that between 3000 and 2500 B.C.E. its 146 neighbors shrank to only 24.[3]

By 2500 B.C.E. Uruk required a city wall that stretched nearly ten kilometers (six miles), at least parts of which were apparently double, and much or all of which was at least seven meters (twenty-three feet) high.[4]

The cost was enormous. Since building such walls was beyond the capacities of the traditional small communities, they were forced to congregate in units of unprecedented size—true city-states—or die. Thus, the very cost of wall-building conferred on those who made the investment the benefits of the unfolding urban revolution.

Uruk was successful, but what about the villages that did not follow its lead? Obviously, some societies that did not organize themselves to build walls were unable to defend themselves against invaders. We might term this the *tactical* failure of these societies. The results of failure were often dramatic and must have been horrifying to contemporaries, but for us, at this safe distance, more interesting is that, lacking the experience of community activity on a grand scale, they also failed to achieve a *strategic* capacity. Here are two examples.

In Southeast Asia, Wilhelm Solheim has observed, "given the spread of plant and animal domestication, the advances in metallurgy and the development of trade, it is surprising that . . . [the period] after 8000 B.C. was unmarked by the kind of social evolution that accompanied the same events in the Middle East. We find neither the rise of cities nor the growth of centralized political power. Even as late as the second and first millenniums B.C. fortifications are unknown anywhere in Southeast Asia, which strongly suggests that organized warfare was also unknown."[5]

And in Europe, despite promising beginnings associated with the agricultural revolution, the "next step" was not taken. By roughly 5500 B.C.E., towns in southeastern Europe may have had populations of up to one thousand. That was too small to become a Jericho, but, given the degree of social organizational they had attained, European communities *could* have carried out modest public projects that probably would have set the process in motion. The towns stopped growing, however; so Neolithic Europeans built no major cities, dug no vast irrigation works, created no monumental art, formed no great political associations, and built no significant walls.

Why is this? Clearly, the Europeans were not lacking in skills—in some fields they were in advance of those in other areas—but the skills they demonstrated were not in mass organization; rather, they were in individual or small-scale invention. I mention four cases to make this point: *agriculture* was practiced in Europe by at least 6000 B.C.E. At about the same time, the Europeans mastered the *mining* and working of copper. Similarly, to take that favorite index of the archaeologist, at approximately the same time as in the Near East, roughly 6700–6500 B.C.E., they began to *manufacture* baked and burnished pottery. Indeed, in central Europe, ceramic technology had reached impressive sophistication even earlier. Even more striking, European experiments with what appears to have been *writing* began by approximately 5300–5200 B.C.E., or about two millennia *earlier* than the Sumerians'. Although these achievements testify to impressive cultural vitality, what is absent may be crucial: missing was a stimulus or an example. They were not invigorated by the perception of a foreign threat, nor were they stimulated by the example of foreign trading partners. Rather, in their security and isolation, Neolithic Europeans resembled the people of Southeast Asia, who, having made similar promising early progress, also failed to bring it to fruition in large-scale, agriculture-based urban civilization. Thus, although there probably was no single "trigger" that set urbanization in motion, I am impressed by what was so evident in those who succeeded and so obviously absent in those who did not.

To carry the argument one step further, we have at least one example to show that "success" in warfare did not necessarily provide the "trigger" to community development. When Indo-European nomads began to invade the Ukraine and eastern Europe after 4400 B.C.E., the residents were unable to resist,[6] and there, as later in India, the invaders not only wrecked much of what had been developed but also subjugated the native peoples. The invaders had organized at least sufficiently to conquer, but that kind of organization did not lead them to large-scale urban civilization. Thus, both "Old Europe" and its destroyers fade from the illuminated stage of history.

At roughly the same time as the Sumerians in Mesopotamia, Dravidian-speaking peoples in the Indus valley were experimenting with agriculture and animal domestication. Wheat and barley were grown by 7000 B.C.E.[7] As in the Near East, technological achievement, particularly in agriculture and animal husbandry, fostered a rise in population that in turn made possible the growth of fortified towns, which laid the basis for a sophisticated urban civilization.

We still know practically nothing about the early towns and little about the later cities of the Indus valley. One of the main sites, Harappa, whose name we affix to the civilization, was demolished in British colonial times to provide bricks to build the bed of a railway. The British were either uninterested in the Indian past or dismissive of Indian achievements. Writing in 1921 in *The Cambridge History of India,* A. Berriedale Keith scoffed at the idea that India had ever had great cities, explaining away the Sanskrit word *pur,* which at least later meant "city," by saying that it "may well have then meant no more than an earthwork strengthened by a palisade or possibly occasionally by stone. Stockades of this kind are often made by primitive peoples, and are so easily constructed that we can understand the repeated references in the Rigveda to the large numbers of such fortifications which were captured and destroyed by the Aryan hosts."[8] We now know that Keith was wrong, but just how wrong is only beginning to emerge. What little scholarly excavation has been done has shown that the Indus was dotted with significant cities that rivaled or surpassed Uruk.

At least two Indus cities had populations of forty to fifty thousand inhabitants. The city we call Harappa covered about 133 hectares (330 acres), while Mohenjo-daro and Ganweriwala, which probably were contemporary, were almost five times as large. What has been so far uncovered shows a remarkable degree of technical and organizational capacity: advanced systems of infrastructure—sewers, drains, a municipal water supply, and wide streets—which suggest centralized and well-organized city governments; fortifications and major public works projects, which in turn indicate capacity to mobilize; fear of foreign attack; and attempts to control floods. The facts that bricks were made to a standard size and that a unified system of weights existed imply broad cultural uniformity throughout the area, but it is unknown whether each city was a state, as in contemporary Mesopotamia, and later Greece and Etruscan Italy, or whether some form of overarching empire or federation existed.

Moreover, as more is learned about the extensive trade and cultural contacts among ancient peoples, ties between them begin to emerge, so that some scholars believe that the Indus, Nile, and Tigris-Euphrates valleys should be regarded as one great complex, with each part contributing to the whole.[9]

In India, this prosperous, advanced, and wide-ranging civilization was destroyed in the savage attacks of Indo-European-speaking Aryan tribesmen in the second millennium B.C.E. Its collapse is celebrated in the *Rig Veda*, composed some centuries later, in which the Aryan patron god Indra is described as the *puramdara*, or "city destroyer," who "rends forts as age consumes a garment."[10] Why the Indus civilization collapsed, or even exactly when it happened, is unknown. As I set out in chapter 28, I believe the causes were complex and occurred over generations. But it seems clear, at least, that the people who then lived along the Indus, despite their ancestors' construction of cities and fortifications, failed to cooperate in defense of one another, like the later Etruscans in Italy, and for this failure paid the supreme penalty when the barbarians were at their gates.

Meanwhile, beginning in the eighteenth century B.C.E., far away in

China, the Shang were developing a civilization comparable to those of the Indus peoples, the Sumerians, and the predynastic Egyptians. The basis of their wealth also was agriculture (millet, rice, and wheat), but substantial industries developed from silk production and from the mining and smelting of copper and tin. The building of walled towns was a major activity of the dynasty since its towns served as military outposts used to subdue the nearby inhabitants and to convert surrounding lands into tribute-paying districts.

Reflecting the very different ecological conditions of China, however, the Shang dynasty was both urban and seminomadic. It moved its seat of power at least eight times, but each time it made prodigious investments in its temporary capital. Like the earlier Sumerians and the contemporary Hittites, the dynasty was acutely aware of dangerous foreigners— Shang records list thirty-three *fang*, or alien/enemy states, in what is today China—and against them it built vast defenses. One Shang capital at Cheng-chou was surrounded by a pounded earthen wall seven kilometers (nearly five miles) long and more than nine meters (thirty feet) high. Thousands of man-years of labor provided by foreign slaves went into building it.[11]

As Herbert Franke has written, "The importance of walled towns to the power structure in traditional China can hardly be overrated."[12] Control of the countryside was the object, but in pursuit of that object, the Shang created a string of secondary effects. Doubtless, the undertaking of such massive projects played a role in China similar to that played by wall-building in the Near East—forcing urbanization, growth, and increased competence. The very organizational skills and technical expertise that they had to master raised the Shang above potential opponents. Fearing the stranger, capturing him, and learning how to exploit him were key ingredients in the rise of China. Caught up in the process, the Shang rode it, like a wave, past their rivals to become the first known Chinese urban civilization.

Is the connection between wall-building and the rise of civilization merely accidental? Is it fair to conclude that those who did not build walls failed to establish coherent civilizations? Surely such notions are disproved by Egypt, which seems to violate the "standard" model. Urban civilization does not appear to have evolved from an agricultural base there as in the Fertile Crescent and, when we can first "see" dynastic Egypt, it does not have walled cities. When we take a closer look, however, we find significant similarities. Begin at roughly the same time as proto-Sumerians were migrating into Mesopotamia; then around 4500 B.C.E. Egypt also received an intrusion of new peoples. Like the Sumerians, the Egyptian newcomers established themselves along the river in what appear to have been independent and mutually hostile villages and towns.[13] Predynastic Egypt lasted until approximately 3400 B.C.E., when a leader we know as Menes or Narmer created the first dynasty by conquering the delta and uniting upper and lower Egypt. It was then that Egypt, like the goddess Athena, seemed to come forth fully grown. But, of course, it did not happen that way; our perception arises only because that was the time when we begin to be able to "see." Just how it really happened we do not know. As one of the foremost scholars of this period has somberly warned us, "it seems best to state categorically that nothing is known in detail about the specific social or political institutions of Predynastic Egypt,"[14] but two inferences, significant for my purposes, can reasonably be drawn from later evidence. First, those who later created the pictorial hieroglyphic system found it logical or at least understandable to signify "town" by showing a wall. And second, even without this admittedly indirect evidence, we would have inferred that the predynastic Egyptians must have had considerable experience in large-scale building projects since, without a long period of experimentation, they would not have had the technical and organizational skills they exhibited early in dynastic times in the construction of the pyramids. To carry this argument a step further, I believe we can say that the pyramids became possible not only because the millennium of interurban hostility with its attendant wall-building had given the Egyptians the required skills but also because the unification of Egypt, with its attendant suppression of all local political, military, and commercial activity, enabled—possibly even forced—the government to divert its human resources and skills from military to monumental purposes.

We have seen that Jericho and other towns felt that building was vital for them, but why was a transformation that, to our eyes, conferred little or no contemporary economic or social benefit undertaken in Egypt? In a rather casual aside, the great English economist John Maynard Keynes might have touched on a more significant point than he realized when he suggested that the building of pyramids actually enriched the builders.[15] He does not pursue this line, but Carlo Cipolla points to what we may see to be a similar venture in medieval Europe: there, where comparably vast resources went into building cathedrals, the effort played a crucial role in bringing hoarded money back into circulation and so prevented stagnation of commerce.[16] Economics aside, there were dramatic intellectual and cultural results. Wisely, I believe, the eminent Egyptologist J. H. Breasted described the work on the pyramids and related structures as "a document in the history of the human mind. It clearly discloses man's sense of sovereign power in his triumph over material forces."[17]

Perhaps Narmer, having succeeded in unifying the country, needed to find another channel for the energies and organizational skills that had earlier been used on (and had developed from) activities the state would no longer tolerate. Wall-building might have been one; free-enterprise commerce certainly was another. Whatever his motivations, he and his successors threw Egypt's energies into the pyramid projects. And vast projects they were. The great pyramid of Khufu (or, as we learned to call him from the Greeks, Cheops) near Giza contains nearly 2.5 million stone blocks, each weighing from 2.5 to 15 tons.[18] Napoleon, with his usual panache, proclaimed that this one structure contained enough stone to build a wall ten feet high around France.

Almost as impressive as the walling of their early towns is what the Egyptians did culturally to defend themselves: in their religion, they created an impalpable or "virtual" wall—the result of the application of the skills and energies of the governing elite over many centuries—that in itself required almost as much investment as physical walls. Intangible though it was, it protected "Egyptianness" for thousands of years.

In order to understand the defensive aspects of this type of wall-building, we must put it into context. At least by the advent of the first dynasty, Egyptians believed their country to be the chief concern of the gods. Ruled by a pharaoh who was himself both a god and the earthly representative of the pantheon, it was also the home of a culture that brought into focus the human and the divine. Egypt was thus a unique land, personified as divine, blessed by the unique and miraculous bounty of the Nile.

It is within this system of belief that we must seek to understand the Egyptian practice of what we would term magic to thwart or ward off the alien. When the enemy alien (as in the period of the invasion of the so-called Hyksos) painfully challenged the Egyptian self-image, the invader was exorcised either by having his name left off the monumental wall inscriptions—thus becoming a "nonperson"—or by calling down the gods against him in the so-called execration texts. Ritual inscription of a name in such texts damned the bearer. When during the reign of the twelfth-dynasty pharaoh Sesostris III the Egyptians undertook an aggressive foreign policy, they employed with equal fervor conventional military force and magic. Pictures of troublesome foreign rulers, often represented as bound captives, and symbols of their peoples, often inscribed on pottery bowls, were smashed, as the figures they symbolized were to be smashed with the help of the gods.[19]

Lest this seem too bizarre (or "Oriental") to be taken seriously—either by them or by us—recall that medieval Europeans relied on comparable practices to ward off invaders. The city fathers (and the inhabitants) of Toulouse, Lyon, Paris, and Constantinople ceremonially paraded icons, relics, and other religious objects around their walls in the belief that this invocation of divine intervention would prevent Vikings, Huns, and others from breaking in. Who can doubt that this magical "line of defense" seemed to them no less real than a physical wall?[20]

And, lest it seem too medieval, consider what happened while the British were evacuating Dunkirk and German armies were pouring into France in May 1940. On May 19, French premier Paul Reynaud, "who publicly declared his faith in miracles, attended public prayers held at Notre Dame; on the twenty-sixth the relics of Saint Généviève, who had saved Paris before, were solemnly carried in procession; on the thirty-first, at the Basilica of the Sacre Coeur, France was reconsecrated to the Sacred Heart of Jesus. Old canticles abandoned by a disenchanted age were being dusted off for the emergency."[21]

The Egyptians also created a "virtual wall" in their hieroglyphic language, which demarcated them culturally from foreigners as sharply as any physical wall. And they were not unique in this. Indeed, their system was surpassed in complexity, cost, and consequence among the Chinese, who were themselves conscious of a great challenge by aliens.

In their conquest of the ancient Shang dynasty, the Chou (which had been one of the rival *fang*, or alien states) marched into eastern China at the head of a group of non-Chinese, "barbarian" tribes. The new dynasty rewarded these alien tribes for their military support by the grant of more than a thousand fiefs, which were the seeds of a new China, planted, as was to be done over and over again in Chinese history, by and for barbarian invaders.

Anchoring its supporters to the land with fiefs was a crucial but conventional part of the response of the Chou dynasty to its challenges. More innovative was the cultural response. Like dynastic Egypt, Chou China also created an inner defense system into which its intellectuals poured energies and skills comparable to those later to be devoted to building the many walls.

The heart of the highly articulated and remarkably unyielding Chinese culture is language. Comparable to English, Russian, and Arabic, Chinese is of vast proportions. And like Arabic, because it embodies sacrosanct texts, it takes on an almost mythic importance to its speakers. Like other complex languages, it was codified on the basis of a single dialect, but that dialect was then separated from the vernacular and protected from rapid change and alien intrusion. Venerated and relished by those who knew it, written Chinese constituted in its own special way as formidable a barrier to entry into China as the Great Wall.

During the Shang and the Chou periods, some forty thousand characters were created, so separate from—in some cases so unrelated to—the spoken language that a precise meaning could not be conveyed by hearing a passage read aloud but only by seeing the written text. Even more significant, so embodied in the classical literature did the written language become that only by mastering the literature as well as the written language could one fully understand a written text. In short, in the terms meaningful to the Chinese, as their historical experience evolved, the very act of mastering the medium transformed not the message, which remained inviolate, but both the messenger and the audience.

The Chinese linguistic-literary barrier was erected, like the Great Wall, over time and without prior design. Probably no other civilization has erected so impregnable, indestructible, yet intangible a barrier between itself and the alien.

But cultural barriers or "virtual" walls of the sort the ancient Egyptians and the Chinese elaborated are neither unique nor merely antiquarian. They have been, mutatis mutandis, echoed in our times by the Soviet Union's employment of Communism as a security barrier in Eastern Europe. Largely through the imposition of ideology, the peoples of the Soviet bloc were cut off from Westerners almost as effectively as the Egyptians and Chinese had been cut off from their neighbors. Like the Chinese, however, the Soviets realized that this barrier could not prevent physical intrusion (or extrusion); so in addition both undertook what was to become a vast program of wall-building. In China, each fief holder initially "built a city-fortress, a 'burgh' and settled as an island in the sea of natives. This is the origin of the typical Chinese quadrangular city, which is so similar to the Roman city."[22] And in this new kind of city were housed not military-agricultural colonists on the Shang pattern but members or associates of the ruling dynasty. The Chou city as a whole was not walled—only the headquarters of the administrator and his immediate entourage. The peasantry, obviously, was regarded as expendable or not worth protecting. But later, when the Chou was losing its grip on the countryside, the walled center, the ruler's redoubt, became—as in medieval Europe in times of comparable insecurity—the nucleus of the city.

The intimate relationship of the city and its wall, as I mentioned above when discussing the similar Egyptian conjunction, is encapsulated in the Chinese language's ideography: the two words for city, *ch'eng* and *shih*, arise from the characters for wall. *Ch'eng* is the word normally used to name a city, whereas a *shih* was originally a military colony or fort. *Shih*, when used as a verb, not surprisingly means "to repel barbarians."[23]

Thus the major early civilizations used walls—both physical and "virtual"—to pull themselves together as societies, protect what they were becoming from dangerous intruders, and acquire the capacities that raised them above the level of their contemporaries.

* * * * * * *

5 ROME, WALLED CHINA, AND MEDIEVAL EUROPE

In the ninth century B.C.E., the Chou dynasty began to lose control, and scores of its former provinces and districts split off into separate states. At first these states jostled against one another as though in ceremonial tournaments, but by the fifth century B.C.E. their conflict had changed character. In this period, the so-called warring states period, anarchy turned into perpetual warfare and warfare became unprecedented in the scale of its savagery. Belatedly realizing their mortal danger, the small states hurried to protect themselves as best they could with vast extensions of walls and fortifications. No longer designed merely to protect the administrative centers and the castles of the governors, they encircled whole cities and, toward the end of the period, extended along hundreds of miles of frontiers.

The surviving state, Qin, unified China in 222 B.C.E. and immediately turned its attention to the external threat: the nomads or "barbarians" along its northern frontier. Being of barbarian origin itself, the Qin knew well the peril it faced. Having inherited massive systems of fortifications built by the formerly independent northern states, the Qin emperor joined and extended the *Ai* (the Barrier) as the centerpiece of an elaborate system composed of military settlers' towns, garrisons, and devastated no-man's-lands.

Immediately after the Qin, the dynasty known as the Former Han built a massive centerpiece for its state. The capital at Chang-an was surrounded by 16 miles of walls 50 feet high and 40 feet wide at the top, backed by a terreplein (a level space for troops behind the parapet) more than 200 feet wide and raised about 20 feet above ground level; the whole was protected by a moat 150 feet wide and 15 feet deep. The earth-moving alone required scores of thousands of man-years of labor, and the wall-building required not only an enormous investment of labor but also the application of new technologies.

Although it would be difficult or perhaps impossible to prove the etiology of the massive projects of wall-building, in and of themselves, in the formation of Chinese technical and managerial skills, that conclusion seems to me inescapable. Each state and subsequently each dynasty faced the challenge of frontier defense by mobilizing tens or hundreds of thousands of craftsmen, designers, architects, engineers, surveyors, brick makers, bricklayers, stonemasons, drovers, carters, work-gang supervisors, and others who produced or fashioned, transported or laid millions of tons of earth, brick, and rock. Men had to be recruited, trained, supervised, fed, housed, and paid; animals bought or requisitioned; kilns built; and tools produced and delivered. There can be little doubt, I believe, that wall-building was one of the major causes of Chinese material civilization, the "school" of each successive dynasty. In the building of walls, China literally built itself. The process begun by the earlier dynasties would carry China to the pinnacle of world technology in the later Sung, Yuan, and Ming dynasties.

The discussion below of the Atlantic Wall, built by the Germans during World War II, will show that similar tasks could be accomplished only by what was then perhaps the largest, most efficient, and technologically most capable industrial and construction organization in the world, *Organisation Todt,* using modern construction equipment and impressed labor.

At roughly the same time as the warring states period in China and closely resembling the political organization of Sumerian Mesopotamia and Harappan India, a collection of city-states was being formed by the Etruscans in northern Italy. Roughly a thousand years later, during the Middle Ages, comparable city-states were to arise again on the same hills, by then called Tuscany. The Etruscans (or, as they called themselves, the Rasenna) were technologically advanced and, like the other peoples I have discussed, had learned the art of defensive architecture the hard and dangerous way—in response to the fear of invasion by rapacious foreigners. Their threat came from the seminomadic Gauls (a collection of Celtic Indo-European peoples) on their northern frontier. Walls they could build, but, like the Sumerians and (apparently) like the Dravidian Indians, the Etruscans never managed to join together to defend themselves. Each city-state looked to its narrow interests, so all were vulnerable to extortion by the Gauls; paying blackmail was the bedrock of their foreign policy. It was their weakness in disunity, according to legend, that gave Rome both its first serious challenge and its main chance.

At the end of the fifth century B.C.E., Rome was still a small and "primitive Iron age" city-state.[24] It had virtually no fortifications, presumably feeling safe behind the screen of the Etruscan cities (which were, in any event, richer targets for the Gauls), and its defense, such as it was, depended on a poorly organized, badly armed, and rather casual militia. These very weaknesses, however, may have given it, as they gave other small and unthreatening states, some status as a neutral arbitrator.

Although it is hard to disentangle myth from history—if the two are ever, indeed, far apart—Livy recounts that in or about 391 B.C.E. the Etruscan city of Clusium found itself besieged by Gallic raiders who were apparently demanding an excessive amount of protection money. Receiving no help from the other Etruscan cities, Clusium sought the intervention of Rome. Complimented but cautious, the Romans offered Clusium rather low-level (as we should say today) diplomatic assistance in scaling down the terms of the extortion. The Gauls apparently were annoyed; insults must have been exchanged; and the inexperienced Roman mediators got embroiled in a brawl. Furious, the Gauls followed them back to Rome determined to loot the city. What happened then seemed to the later Romans utterly shameful. Even the patriot historian Livy marveled. I think we may believe him because it must have embarrassed him to write that "at the first sound of the Gallic war-cry . . . [the Romans] hardly waited even to see the strange enemy . . . but fled before they had lost a single man."[25] That was to be Rome's darkest hour for nearly a thousand years.

Livy tells us that the little city-state had then virtually no fortifications; so, having defeated Roman troops outside the city, the Gauls walked in to loot and burn. When they withdrew, the Romans faced the task of rebuilding. Characteristically, they soberly analyzed what had happened and decided to implement reforms that would give their soldiers more mobility and better armor. And, fearing that the Gauls would return, they began a vast program of wall-building on the Etruscan model. Etruscan engineers also taught them how to organize and build public works in drainage and flood control. Apparently, this vast organizational effort had an effect on the Romans comparable with its effect on the Sumerians and others in the ancient world—it gave them a new sense of civic purpose, pride in accomplishment, and communal skills. It was surely a stronger, more determined Rome that twelve years later turned back to the task of conquering the peninsula—and then of conquering the known world.

I return now, after an interval of a thousand years, to China. There, wall-building had been actively pursued by dynasty after dynasty. In the many eras of unrest or revolution virtually every city was walled, but the most concentrated efforts in frontier defense were made by the Ming dynasty, which seized power from the faltering Yuan (Mongol) dynasty in 1368. Putting that date on the assumption of Ming rule suggests a clarity that history does not bear out: although the Mongol dynasty fell, Mongols continued to challenge the Ming for much of its 250-year reign. Time after time they mounted large-scale raids into China and in 1449 even captured and held hostage the Ming emperor. So it was apposite that the Ming would become China's greatest wall-builders. For them wall-building was truly, to use an often-misused expression, "a vital national purpose."

The marvel of the Ming dynasty was the most massive defensive construction of all time; the *ch'ang ch'eng* (Great Wall) is said to be the only human construction that is large enough to be visible from the moon. Approximately six thousand kilometers (nearly four thousand miles) long, anchored in the east on the extension of the Pacific Ocean, it marches close to Beijing and then snakes along the edge of the loess plateau, steppe, and desert lands of Mongolia, fording the upper reaches of the Huang (Yellow) River, and terminates in Central Asia near the vast Turpan Depression, where the desolate sands of the Taklimakan desert form what amounts to another ocean. Indeed, it cuts Asia in half—to its south are the "rice bowl" and land-bound peasantry of China and to its north are the nomadic peoples of Manchuria, Mongolia, and the Kazakh steppes. Unlike any other manmade creation, the Great Wall is more than a national divide: it is also a cultural and ecological bulkhead.

In every dimension, the wall can only be described as gigantic. Not all of it still stands, but enough does to enable us to infer what is now missing. Much of it was nine meters (thirty feet) high, and along the top was a roadway nearly as wide as the wall was high for the rapid movement of frontier guards. Periodic towers, as many as forty thousand of them, loomed twelve meters (forty feet). We get a sense of the scale of investment of labor from reports that it took a work force of forty thousand men about half a year to build one section of roughly six hundred miles.[26] But this was, apparently, a sort of record, and it may have been accomplished along prepared or relatively easy terrain. The whole project could not have taken less than a million man-years of labor. Arthur Waldron points out that the wall was really a fragmented and complex system rather than a single unit.[27]

In themselves, the components of the wall were daunting defensive installations, and since the wall often followed the ridge of mountains, many towers commanded virtually an aerial view of the surrounding countryside. Thus, they doubled as platforms for signaling by fire, smoke, and explosion so that early warning of concentrations of nomads could be transmitted to regional headquarters. In many areas the terrain was so rugged that with this elaborate and effective system of surveillance and communication government troops could be rushed to danger points before the would-be raiders could reach the wall.

China rarely used its wall as a springboard for attack, but the wall did give it that capacity. Able to rush troops along the roadway atop the battlements, it could assemble fighting forces, supply them, and prepare them more easily than could "barbarians" who were confined to the rugged ravines and hillocks over which it looked. Although the nomads had little capacity to pierce its screen, China could move its forces out at will. I mention this because, although walls should normally be considered as defensive, there are circumstances when they provide springboards for offensive operations, as is the case with the walls of Athens during the Peloponnesian War.

Neither Athens nor Sparta had learned how to conduct sophisticated siege operations, so Pericles's strategy was to withdraw behind Athens's twenty miles of walls, devastate its own countryside, and avoid battle with the formidable Spartan infantry.[28] From their safe redoubt, the Athenians carried the war to Sparta in their powerful fleet through commando raids. Their encounter was the battle of the elephant and the whale. As long as the Athenians stayed inside their city, the Spartans could not prevail; indeed, except for an outbreak of plague and a costly failed adventure, the Athenians might have won the war. Not surprisingly, a major aim of the Spartans in the peace they later imposed on the defeated Athenians was to destroy the walls that, to them, were springboards of offense.

Again I skip ahead many centuries, to Europe after the collapse of the Roman empire in the West. With Rome's heavy hand no longer maintaining law and order, anarchy prevailed. Large areas of previously densely settled land fell vacant as the inhabitants of the most dangerous areas abandoned their exposed dwellings and rushed to places where they could cower behind some sort of defense. At a time in which most people, and certainly all rural people, hovered at the brink of starvation, they didn't have much more than their bodies to protect. But over time, as they gathered together, worked and accumulated, and played host to itinerant traders, the little hamlets into which they had fled became towns. Some of these towns, and the old Roman administrative centers, gradually grew into cities, and, weighed in the scale of the age, the city was a prize beyond the dreams of avarice. It was a market where merchants displayed and traded the riches of distant lands and where churches hoarded away the

inherited treasures of past generations. Inside there was only minimal security but outside there was virtually none. Bandits were a scourge everywhere, and far worse were pillaging bands of Vikings, Magyars, and Normans.

The core of most of the new towns was the church, and it was on
the church that the blows of the raiders fell most heavily. Only in the
church was glittering wealth evident. So, in exposed areas such as inlets
from the sea where Vikings could appear suddenly, churches and abbeys
were abandoned. And the reach of the Vikings was long. Raiding parties
circled Europe, coming around the Atlantic coast into the Mediterranean
and down the Russian rivers into the Black Sea. Where they could find
shelter, people gathered to defend the church because defending it was
the only way to defend themselves. When they could, clergy and laymen
fought side by side against the invaders. And when they could not, they
invoked their holy relics to bring about divine intervention. But more important, they did two other things: they gave up a large part of what little
freedom they had to those who promised to defend them—initially bishops, barons, and kings—and they set about under the leadership of such
men to build walls.

Their aim was to achieve security, but in the quest for security they
began to acquire something the "pioneers" would never have dreamed of
trying to achieve: a new civic capacity. As Henri Pirenne wrote of the European medieval cities, construction of ramparts was

> the first public work undertaken by the towns and one which,
> down to the end of the Middle Ages, was their heaviest financial
> burden. Indeed, it may be truly said to have been the starting-
> point of their financial organisation, whence, for example, the
> name of *firmitas*, by which the communal tax was always known
> at Liège, and the appropriation in a number of cities *ad opus
> castri* (i.e., for the improvement of the fortifications) of a part
> of the fines imposed by the borough court. The fact that to-
> day municipal coats of arms are surrounded by a walled crown
> shows the importance accorded to the ramparts. There were
> no unfortified towns in the Middle Ages.[29]

Beginning with enhanced security and new organizational skills, some of
the towns underwent explosive growth. Pisa is a good example: in the
eleventh century, its walls encompassed only 30 hectares (74 acres), but
the town multiplied fivefold in a little over a century so that in 1162 it

required a new wall to encompass an additional 114 hectares (282 acres); a century later a new wall was built to take in another 185 hectares (456 acres).[30]

Fortification became an Italian specialty. At first walls were relatively simple constructions, with height the most important aspect. They were designed simply to keep out raiders who had little ability to breach them, but by the fifteenth century, as artillery was coming into use, the traditional thin, high, and flat walls proved vulnerable to shot. In the sixteenth century, the Italians responded to the "gunpowder revolution" by building much more imposing fortifications. These were far more expensive to build but also proved to be ruinously expensive to attack. The *trace italienne*, a much thicker, lower, and more intricate design of fortification virtually impervious to artillery, forced on the attacker long sieges and so raised the ante of warfare. In attempting to maintain his huge empire, Philip II of Spain was forced into such heavy expenditures for ammunition and sieges that he was forced to repudiate his debts and was unable to pay his soldiers on time. By the end of the century, at least 40 percent of government revenues had to be applied to the service of the debts he had incurred. This figure more or less equates to the crushing burden of debt common among developing countries today and played a major role in the decline of Spain to the status of a second-class power.

We also see the impact of the increased cost of warfare in the sixteenth-century conflict between the city-states of Florence and Siena. As the threat escalated, Siena was forced to spend so much on its walls that not enough remained to man them or to sustain the productive economy that had made them possible.

Thus, "walls" (taken broadly) have not only defensive value but offensive potential: they enabled Athens to neutralize Spartan power so that the Athenians could fully use their own; walls enabled the Italian possessions of Hapsburg Spain virtually to bankrupt it. But pushed to excess, the quest for security that walls represent can be ruinous. Forcing Siena to spend more than it could afford on defense, Florence brought about its collapse. Using similar tactics, Ronald Reagan forced the Soviet Union virtually to commit suicide.[31]

Finally, walls also reveal for us another insight: in addition to their importance in the rise of civic competence, their effect on the nature of warfare, and their role in state economics, they constituted a legacy for future times. Almost as important as their building was their dismantling. Walls that no longer were required for defense were often the quarries from which Renaissance and early modern cities were built. But the process of dismantling them could take on an even more impressive and formative role. I take Vienna as my example.

Until 1850, Vienna remained an almost medieval city. Whereas for hundreds of years, indeed from the high Middle Ages, most of the cities of Germany, France, and England had governed themselves, Vienna remained not only the seat but also the "manor" of the Hapsburg emperor. Popular discontent with the growing disparity between the paternalistic government of Vienna and political life of the cities of Western Europe was manifested in the revolution of 1848. Although the revolutionaries failed, their attempt sobered the Hapsburg ruling establishment into granting a statute proclaiming self-rule for Vienna in the spring of 1850. This new vision of the city set in motion a fever of land speculation that, in turn, created pressures to dismantle the vast belt of fortifications that for centuries had surrounded the *Hofburg* (the emperor's headquarters) and the inner city. The "new men" of Vienna wanted to get their hands on what they saw as the useless walls, moat, and broad glacis that penned them in the old city, not just to tear them down but to use them.

Their hopes frightened the army high command almost as much as the revolutionaries had. Generals are famous for fighting the last war, and Austrian generals were better known for this than most. To them, giving up the great battlements appeared a reckless proposal, and they stoutly opposed it. They pointed out that the Ottoman Turks had twice besieged the city in the distant past (1529 and 1683), scaring away the emperor and his court, and that, within living memory, the city had been twice (1805 and 1809) occupied by Napoleon's army. Even if the old fortifications were no proof against the weapons of their age, they argued, they had been of some value in the 1848 popular uprising (when the imperial court had yet again run away). But inglorious and painful as these freshly remembered events were, they would have been far more painful and perhaps totally disastrous, the conservatives pointed out, if the inner city had lain completely open. Faced with these arguments, the emperor moved cautiously but, at the end of 1857, proclaimed his intent to allow the expansion of the city.

A variety of developments make it clear that during the decade in which this policy was being discussed, the inhabitants of Vienna had educated themselves about the possibilities before them, and new figures came to the fore in city planning, architecture, and finance. So when the decision was taken to "open" this wide swath of land and the *Stadtplanung* (City Expansion Commission) was established to supervise the development, there was an explosion of activity. In taking control of their own environment, the Viennese gained a sudden accretion of confidence and the willingness to commit resources and ideas on a theretofore unimagined scale. Without exaggeration, we may say that the dismantling of the walls and the decision to build the *Ringstrasse* gave rise to modern Vienna.

. . . .

6 MODERN WALLS

World War I created a new version of a very old concept of fortification—the ditch. The western front, stretching from Switzerland to the English Channel, became a maze of interlocking barbed-wire entanglements, trenches with frequent sandbag, wooden-beam, and concrete pillboxes that separated the millions of soldiers of the Allies and the Central powers and was the graveyard of hundreds of thousands of them. As a result, often buried in the mud, warfare—which Europeans had come to see as a march of pomp and circumstance—turned into a dreary dirge of death in which "victories" were measured in yards of territory and the winning side was the one that had the most blood to let.

And as men were impaled on barbed wire, mown down by machine guns, or blown apart by high explosives, blood was spilled in unprecedented amounts. In the first five months of the war, Germany and France each suffered one million casualties—France lost 300,000 in two weeks in the August battles; it would lose an average of 1,000 men a day throughout the war. Over 2,500,000 were killed, gassed, or mutilated. British losses were smaller only because the British had committed fewer men, but in the single battle of Ypres, 54,105 men were killed or wounded. By the end of the war, both France and Britain had lost virtually a whole generation. France, which had suffered proportionally more than any other combatant, was economically and psychologically shattered. The wall as a system of frontier defense seemed to many to have reached beyond the grotesque to the absurd.

To many, but not all. The static defense into which the armies on the western front were locked from 1914 to 1918 was to influence the leaders of both France and Germany as they moved toward a renewal of their confrontation.

The French, even more than the various states that had recently formed Germany, had a tradition of fortification going back to medieval times but made famous by Louis XIV's great military planner, Marshal Sébastien de Vauban. Ironically, Vauban's main contribution to siege warfare was in the demolition of fortresses rather than in their construction, but that aspect of his heritage was largely forgotten when, in the aftermath of the stunning Prussian invasion of 1870–71, the French set about constructing a "wall" stretching from the channel to the Mediterranean. By 1885, some two hundred forts had been built.[32] Although redoubts had played an insignificant part in the war of 1870–71, French military planners found it logical to build on Vauban's tradition.

Thus, it was a combination of the horrible memory of the trenches in World War I and the tradition of frontier fortification that gave birth to the idea of the Maginot Line. There was an additional spur: the mesmerizing fear of a new war with Germany. The French had only to read what responsible Germans were writing to see that this fear was well grounded. Colonel General Hans von Seeckt, whom the French had come to know during the 1919 Paris Peace Conference (at which he was the military member of the German delegation) and who has been rightly regarded as the father of the new German army, wrote openly of the necessity for Germany, *in the next war,* to strike against France before England and America could mobilize. Frightened by this and other warnings of the probability of a revival of German military power, French military planners reacted by proposing a means to hold the enemy during the time required for its allies to march to its defense. That means was to be the Maginot Line.

Since the earlier French experiments with fortifications, two requirements had changed. On one hand, in the peace settlement at the end of World War I, France had regained all of the territory Germany had claimed, so that France's objective was defense rather than offense; on the other, improvements—particularly in artillery—had made fortification very much more expensive than ever before. Expense, in addition to diplomatic considerations, made the construction of a wall from the channel to the Mediterranean unacceptable. Even to build the shorter line from Belgium to Switzerland, M. Maginot had both to badger his parliamentary colleagues and to sell off a number of French military sites. His parliamentary victory was only partial, but work finally began on an experimental basis in February 1928.

The "wall" was constructed on a strip of land averaging 12 kilometers (7.5 miles) deep. At the frontier itself what military planners would later call a trip wire was composed of *maisons fortes,* which were simply the fortified barracks of the frontier police. Roughly a kilometer and a half (one mile) further back were bunkers embedded in a mass of barbed wire, tank traps, and antitank mines. These were manned by lightly armed troops. Still further back was the main barrier, composed of partially buried structures designed to house artillery, soldiers, and supplies. The smaller structures were for units of platoon strength, whereas the larger fortifications, placed at intervals of roughly five kilometers (three miles), were huge, mainly underground structures linked to the rear by tunnels in some of which narrow-gauge railways operated. These forts might be best thought of as buried battleships, servicing whole regiments with ammunition storage facilities, electrical generating equipment, dormitories, kitchens, canteens, sewage plants, hospitals, and mortuaries.

Only parts of this mammoth undertaking were completed by 1936, when the first major crisis in Franco-German relations occurred; that crisis, although now viewed more as a test of the will and foresightedness of the French government, was also rightly seen as a step toward neutralizing French strategy. The commander-in-chief of the French army, General Maurice Gamelin, understood its importance; in January 1936 he warned his government that if Hitler were not stopped from moving troops back into the Rhineland, a move that would violate two clauses of the 1919 peace treaty, he would "neutralize the French Army by constructing . . . a fortified barrier comparable to our own."[33] A German defensive line would enable the German army to ignore the French and free it for operations elsewhere. That is exactly what happened in the "phony war" of 1939–40.

Not only did the French not manage to prevent German reoccupation of the Rhineland and rearmament, but they also failed to carry their own defense plans to fruition. Because of technical problems, structural defects, cost overruns, and money shortages, much remained undone or was scaled back to inadequate levels. A critical point was the employment of cannon: by the time war broke out, only 344 cannon were mounted on the whole line, which meant that at any given point of attack fewer than 20 cannon could be brought to bear on an attacker. The French defender would always be inferior to the German attacker, whose well-known tactic involved the *Schwerpunkt* (concentrated assault).

In the event, it was even worse than the French had anticipated. The main attack, a *blitzkrieg* through the Ardennes forest in 1940, bypassed the line. France then collapsed. That is the quite valid interpretation of the events, but, although overshadowed by the main action, there is another story: the German army units attacking the line were halted, and its French defenders did not surrender until the French government conceded defeat.

So, although "Maginot Line complex" has come to mean something like burying one's head in the sand, the line was not wholly wrong in concept. Moreover, although there is no indication that its planners were aware of them, there were a number of successful historical precedents for it (and for its German counterpart). The massive fortress-building programs of the Byzantine emperor Justinian and his Sasanian Persian foe, Khusrau I, in the middle of the sixth century did actually stabilize their frontier for nearly a century. It was at least a reasonable gamble that, pushed to its logical conclusion and put in the context of a firm Allied policy against Hitler's early moves, the Maginot Line *might* have kept the peace.

The French were not alone in reaching their assessment of the value of building walls: in addition to the Czechs, who started to copy the Maginot Line only in 1937 and were almost immediately stopped by the sellout of their country in the Munich agreement and the subsequent German takeover in the spring of 1939, the Poles and others set about building comparable frontier defenses. But the nearest analogy to the Maginot Line is the fortification known as the Siegfried Line, which the Germans built, as General Gamelin had anticipated, facing the Maginot Line. Less elaborate than the Maginot Line, it was perhaps militarily sounder, being both deeper—up to thirty-two kilometers (twenty miles)—in some places and longer—indeed almost double the length—running from the Swiss frontier parallel to the Maginot Line and continuing to a point about twenty kilometers (twelve miles) from Arnhem in the Netherlands. Final work on the project was under the supervision of the *Organisation Todt,* which had constructed the German highway network. One-third of the German construction industry and half a million men were put to work on it. When completed in 1940, it consisted of more than fourteen thousand bunkers and incorporated twenty-one million cubic yards of concrete.[34]

After 1940, as its army smashed its way across Europe, Germany saw little need for defense, but in August 1942 an otherwise ineffectual and costly raid by Canadian forces on Dieppe caused the Germans to begin a project that ultimately would become the greatest defensive barrier Europe had ever seen: the attempt to create "Fortress Europe" through the construction of the Atlantic Wall. Dwarfed only by the Great Wall of China, it was to be composed of pillboxes, forts, glacises, minefields, and other obstacles and to stretch some 2,600 kilometers (1,612 miles) from Norway to the Spanish frontier. At first work went slowly, but it speeded up when Marshal Erwin Rommel became Inspector General of Defenses in October 1943. Thereafter, Albert Speer's *Organisation Todt* built some 30,000 individual fortifications out of 17.3 million cubic yards of concrete and 1.2 million metric tons of iron. In addition, the Germans laid more than

6 million land mines. Tens of thousands of antitank and antilandingcraft obstacles, described as "sharp tetrahedra, jagged hedgehogs, concrete dragon's teeth and stout logs loaded with spikes,"[35] were placed between high and low tide while potential landing fields for gliders within seven miles of the coast were similarly blocked. Antitank ditches and thousands of kilometers of barbed wire ran between the pillboxes and gun emplacements. For a nation under constant aerial bombardment and blockade, these figures represent an almost unbearable expenditure of resources.

Concrete and steel were in short supply, but even more scarce was German manpower, particularly after the huge losses on the Russian front, so increased use was made of foreign labor forcibly recruited from the occupied zones and from among prisoners of war. In an internal German government document from the fall of 1944, Speer said that he then had 850,000 workers inside Germany[36] and that work on the wall took about a third of the total work force. Even that staggering expenditure was not enough, so, desperate for additional manpower, the government tried to recruit 1 million additional French workers, of whom 900,000 were to be deported to Germany along with 500,000 from Holland and Belgium, 1.5 million from Italy, and 600,000 from the Baltic states.[37] When quotas were not being met, particularly for work on the Atlantic Wall, raids were carried out by police and military units. By one means or another some 85,000 Frenchmen were added to the work force.

Despite this vast outlay, the Atlantic Wall suffered from a fatal weakness: once breached anywhere it was of no value everywhere. As American and British troops punched through in Normandy, what had been done along the Atlantic was largely irrelevant. So Germany found itself fighting on two fronts in what became a war of movement, with its forces almost constantly in retreat toward their ultimate defeat.

Defeated Germany emerged from World War II divided into four zones occupied by the Soviet Union, Great Britain, France, and the United States. The old capital, Berlin, was similarly divided among the victors. Four years later, in September 1949, the three Western powers allowed their zones to be amalgamated into the Federal Republic of Germany while the Soviet Union fostered the emergence of the German Democratic Republic. Berlin, however, remained an occupied and divided city. And this set of divisions gave rise to the most famous fortification of our time, the Berlin Wall.

From 1958 Soviet leader Nikita Khrushchev pressed for a peace treaty making the East-West division permanent, and in June 1961, in his meeting with President John F. Kennedy in Vienna, Khrushchev escalated his demands for a peace treaty that would end the rights of access by Western powers to Berlin across East German territory by threatening to sign a separate peace treaty with East Germany and to defend the East German closure of Western routes of access. To signal their determination, the Soviets arranged two months later that the East German authorities begin to impose various legal and physical barriers to movement between East and West Berlin. Special permits were required for vehicles and for pedestrians, some crossing points were periodically closed, and West Berliners were prohibited from working in East Berlin. Almost immediately construction began on watch towers (which subsequently numbered 189) with sentries manning searchlights. These were the early moves that led to the construction of the Berlin Wall.

Ironically, however, what seems to have forced the building of the wall was the very opposite of all historical wall building programs: it was to keep inhabitants *in* rather than to keep enemies *out*. And, rather than creating a sense of "us" as distinct from "them," moves toward the construction of the wall stampeded East Germans into emigration. Fearing that they would be cut off from access to the West, they began streaming across the frontier into Western-controlled areas. By the end of the summer of 1961, some 3.5 million people had moved into West Berlin, and because many were young and educated, their flight virtually crippled the East German economy. Consequently, although there was no sympathy for the East German dilemma in the West, there was some understanding of it. Even the chairman of the U.S. Senate Foreign Relations Committee spoke publicly in July 1961 about the reasonableness, from the East German point of view, of closing the frontier. President Kennedy privately commented that he understood that the Soviets and their East German allies "will have to do something to stop the flow of refugees. Perhaps a wall." He went on to say, "And we won't be able to prevent it. I can hold the Alliance together to defend West Berlin, but I cannot act to keep East Berlin open."[38] Kennedy was prescient: the Soviets and the East Germans found the wall their best answer to the "hemorrhaging" of the East German labor force, and he was also right that he could do nothing about it. Therefore, although in time both the Soviet Union and the United States pulled back from their confrontation at the "brink," the wall was built and remained in place for a generation.

Since the concept of what came to be called the Ulbricht barrier was not defensive but restrictive, it more resembled walls around prisons than those I have discussed. From 1963, as various refinements were added, this became more evident: observation posts equipped with sophisticated electronic surveillance equipment were manned by fourteen thousand border police, who had orders to shoot to kill any unauthorized person in identified "death strips"; attack dogs were placed in some 185 corridors through which escapees would have to pass; barbed-wire entanglements were laid with elaborate minefields and underwater barricades were placed in waterways; nearby houses were demolished; and 184 roads were cut.

The wall served its purpose: the flood of emigres slowed to a trickle, but the cost was prohibitive and unsustainable. The cost was to be measured not in money, manpower, tons of steel, or cubic meters of concrete but in politics: loyalty to the East German regime was sapped so that its destruction in November 1989 was greeted with wild and equal delight by both "us" and "them."

. . .

Of necessity, I have omitted discussion of thousands of other walls.[39] Enough has been said, however, to prove that the task of keeping enemies at bay has been a perennial occupation of societies throughout the world for as long as men have lived in cities and have accumulated wealth. Moreover, wall-building has played a major role in defining the nature of the "in" group and enhancing the organizational and technical capacity of its members. The winners in history were those who rose to meet the challenge and succeeded in keeping *them* outside.

In short, over the past ten thousand years, the frontier barrier is perhaps the most fundamental and pervasive, and certainly the most tangible, manifestation of the problem of dealing with neighbors and strangers. Is it merely a relic of the past whose abandoned battlements are picturesque sites for picnics? I do not believe so. As tensions among ethnic groups periodically wax into strife, warfare, and "ethnic cleansing," as I will discuss in part 7, I think that governments and communities will fall back on this most ancient and most unambiguous tool of foreign affairs and that our children and their children are likely to have to endure a world of compartments in which walls will rarely be far from view.

PART III   ARMIES AND WARFARE

· · · · · · ·

7 THE FIRST ARMIES

As we saw in part 2, the people of Jericho began what has become an unending search for security by building walls. But the historical record has shown us that no society ever grew so large as to encompass all the strangers who were its neighbors. No matter how much the walls took in, there were always actual or potential enemies beyond. Consequently, much of history is filled with accounts of the race between those who would defend themselves and those who would attack, making history, as Edward Gibbon put it, "little more than the register of the crimes, follies, and misfortunes of mankind."[1]

As technology improved, walls and other means of defense, as we have seen, became more massive, more sophisticated, longer, better defended; but, in tandem, now getting ahead, now falling behind, the means of attack also grew apace. As both were improved, the costs of each rose ever higher. And, of course, walls needed to employ soldiers since, as Niccolò Machiavelli observed, fortresses "are useless to those that do not have good armies."[2]

Who first made war on Jericho is unknown, but the construction of its walls indicates that the inhabitants thought that the danger was clear and present. And, just as Jericho was not the first society that tried to build a barrier against invaders, those who frightened the people there were probably not the first aggressors.

In this bloody twentieth century, armies are so much a part of our lives that we take for granted their enormous scale, cost, and impact. In peacetime, we resent their drain on our hard-won resources, their diversion of our youth, and, in many parts of the world, their potential for political disruption. Those are serious tolls, but in wartime their effects are far more costly. Yet, since men have accumulated property and lived in settled societies, investment in armies has been regarded as at worst a necessary evil and at best a source of excitement, pride, education, and economic stimulation. In short, warfare and armies constitute not a single but a manifold aspect of foreign relations.

In order to understand them we must consider their various aspects. Yet the subject garners more heat than light. At the most basic emotional level, we are apt to retreat into patriotic shibboleths about *our* just defense while reacting to *their* unjust aggression with fear, outrage, or disgust. Such emotions do not help to minimize risks. But the task of understanding is not easy, especially since even those who would lead us toward an appreciation of armies and warfare often do so in narrow or misleading ways. At their head is warfare's most famous analyst, Carl von Clausewitz, who is best known for his statement that "war is a mere continuation of policy by other means."[3]

It is a memorable remark, but like many apothegms it does not really get us very far. Like all of us, Clausewitz was a child of his times, and his insights, necessarily, are a reflection on late-eighteenth-century Europe. By looking at the wider, long-term experience, we can see that although actual or potential warfare is often best seen as an instrument of foreign relations, as Clausewitz thought and as his successors have echoed, it is highly complex in cause, form, and process. Armies, its instruments, are correspondingly manifold: always bureaucracies, they are often the embodiment of national myth, sometimes armed political parties, occasionally virtual states. In these various roles there is much that Clausewitz neglected.

Clausewitz thought of the role of the military as a chess game, aloof from the sordid play of politics and emotion, and thus his analysis does not illuminate most of world history and is certainly misleading today. His best students, the German general staff, as we shall see in chapter 10, paid a fearful price for their ignorance of politics. Far from the arid refinements of chess, armies are blunt instruments, often wielded by the blind to bring about what was neither expected nor desired and, being wielded, transform those who think they are in control. Indeed, their very existence creates temptations, objectives, and emotions that, defying logic, policy, or interest, often precipitate self-destructive conflict. So it behooves us to analyze armies and warfare as completely as possible. Failure to do so will certainly prevent us from reaching a full understanding of foreign relations and could include us among their victims.

In this part of the book, therefore, I begin with warfare in its simplest forms and show how it evolved during three great episodes: first, the formation in China of the Qin dynasty from the warring states; second, the conquest of western Asia by the Assyrians; and third, the domination and collapse of the Roman Empire. The diversity of these examples will, I believe, serve to bring out neglected aspects of armies and warfare. Next, I discuss the main kinds of soldiery including guerrillas, mercenaries, colonial troops, and armed citizens. Because they affect not only the soldier's capacities and his enemies but also his society, I sketch the development of weapons; finally, I deal with modern armies, emphasizing the evolution of the Prussian army as it turned into the Imperial German army and then into the powerful instrument that nearly won World War II. In the course of this account, I show how political leadership was (and is) often formed and sometimes controlled by involvement in military affairs and bring out some aspects the impact on statecraft of changes in technology, finance, and attitudes.

My aim is not a history of warfare or, indeed, of any of the episodes I recount; rather, I selectively use aspects of them to highlight the nature of this facet of foreign affairs and to relate it to the larger pattern I am unfolding. I start with an irony: as much a part of our lives as warfare has become and as laden with warfare as is the historical record, the question of how armies arose is one of the many things about the past that we do not know. Therefore, I begin, as I did in chapter 2, with a few things we can observe among contemporary primitive peoples and social animals.

♦ ♦ ♦

In New Guinea's Baliem valley, two tribes, known as the Kurelu and the Wittaria, live side by side and presumably have so lived for centuries or even millennia. In both, virtually the entire adult male population forms an "army" to engage in periodic "warfare." I put these two words in quotation marks because what is meant by them here is different from what we usually mean today. In the sense that Thomas Hobbes used the term, the relationship of the Kurelu to the Wittaria is, indeed, one of "Warre," yet neither group appears to have made any attempt to supplant or capture the other. Rather, fighting is a process whose purpose is immaterial and whose action is treated as theater. Elaborate in costume and restricted in action, it ends when passions are satisfied by someone on the guilty side's being seriously wounded or killed. Both sides then decamp to their villages for the evening meal without fear of further hostile action. This ritual warfare is a violent masque limited in duration, scope, and geography.

Similar to the warfare of the Kurelu and Wittaria was the American Indian practice of "counting coups." Before the last desperate days, when starvation and fury distorted their way of life beyond endurance, the Comanche, like the other Plains Indians, usually engaged in stylized hostilities, primarily to win prestige. Feats of bravery, particularly striking or touching an enemy with a symbolic weapon, usually a decorated stick, were reckoned as what the French trappers called *coups*. For each coup an Indian brave won the right to wear a symbol, usually a feather, much as a white soldier might wear a medal. Combat was nearly as stylized as a medieval European knights' tournament. There were rewards for winning and penalties for being captured, but the original purpose was not to kill the opponent or capture his goods or land.

Implicit in this violent theater are concepts that are deeply embedded in warfare as it has evolved all over the world: everywhere rulers and soldiers have tried to make war a pageant with colorful flags, elaborate uniforms, and martial music, an occasion of drama, dash, and derring-do, a controlled performance that could be terminated without unacceptable losses. This was certainly the view of war that dominated the thinking of the statesmen and generals who led their peoples into World War I and, torn, bloodied, and crippled as it was by that war, the image has survived into the late twentieth century. So, returning to the simple model given us by the primitive Kurelu and Wittaria, let us introduce the uglier side of warfare.

Much more deadly was what happened between these two peoples outside of ritual war. In "nonwar" all contacts, even those casual and peaceful in intent (as when an unarmed person from one village strayed into the territory of the other), were lethal. Then no prisoners were taken and, unless the intruder could escape, he or she was usually killed. This is not a local peculiarity: among primitive (and not-so-primitive) peoples such conduct is common.

Among social animals, particularly carnivores, parallels are evident: when groups encounter one another along their boundaries, they often (like the Kurelu and the Wittaria) posture and threaten but are usually content to test one another's determination and, after a suitable display, avoid serious hostilities. In part 6 I will deal with this as an early form of negotiation or diplomacy. When a stray or lone intruder enters the territory of another group, however, he is nearly always attacked by the home pack. Then the customary signs of submission are disregarded, and if caught the stranger is usually killed.

This conduct suggests a fundamental division in conflict—that between war, which is a formal encounter, and which we today treat as a legal status, and prewar or extra-war hostilities, which are essentially formless and, therefore, are often conducted without rules. That distinction is neither arcane nor antiquarian—we observe it in our times and in ways not entirely different from the actions of primitive peoples and animals. In twentieth-century war, the uniformed soldier is usually allowed to surrender and subsequently, when a prisoner, has certain limited rights, whereas the out-of-uniform partisan or guerrilla, even if he is or considers himself to be a soldier, has virtually no rights and is rarely saved by surrender.

All forms of war involve combat; so, always implicit, even in ceremonial warfare, is the possibility of violent death. This harsh reality cannot be completely disguised, although both soldiers and statesmen often try, by what Shakespeare called the "pride, pomp, and circumstance of glorious war." The inherent ugliness of war becomes most visible when its aim is to seize territory or people. That is the stage in the progression from "ceremonial war" to true combat that is exemplified by another primitive New Guinea people, the Maring.

The Maring have passed beyond display into the form of conflict we observe in the earliest recorded history: when hostilities end in the rout of one side and no truce is made, the winning side tries to destroy the war potential of its enemy completely. "The victors, in such instances," writes Roy Rappaport of the Maring, "after killing every man, woman and child unfortunate enough to be caught, laid waste the territory of the vanquished."[4] We shall see similar conduct in the examples I cite from China, Assyria, and Rome, and we know it best in modern warfare, especially that between ethnic groups, as in the Bosnian-Serbian and Tutsi-Hutu conflicts.[5]

The distinction between limited war and total war is sometimes drawn in kinship or neighborhood terms. I have mentioned the "dear enemy" effect discovered among birds. A similar kind of muted hostility is evident in the customs of some African tribes. For example, when the Sudanese Nuer fought culturally allied groups, they limited their actions so that women and children were safe, huts and byres were not destroyed, and captives were not slaughtered. But against such alien groups as their neighbors the Dinka, whom the Nuer regarded as strangers or even as "natural prey," they engaged in total war.[6] The Bantu, similarly, recognized no rules or ritual of war with their non-Bantu neighbors; rather, they aimed to terrorize their neighbors into surrendering pasture lands to them.[7]

Shifting toward more sophisticated societies, we find a parallel to the evolution from the Kurelu and Wittaria to the warfare of the Bantu and the Maring in two periods of Chinese history known as "Spring and Autumn" and "Warring States."

As I briefly discussed in part 2, the Chou dynasty slowly collapsed in the ninth century B.C.E. and, invaded by nomads in 770 B.C.E., it abandoned its capital. Seizing their opportunities, governors of provinces and districts formed more than a hundred petty states. Five centuries of turmoil and war followed. Divided by Chinese scholars into the *Ch'un Qin* (Spring and Autumn) and *Chan Kuo* (Warring States) periods, these centuries were a time of intense military, diplomatic, and economic activity among the states and, under the increasing pressure each exerted on the others, of major structural changes in government and society. During this time there were fewer than twenty years without hostilities.

During the Spring and Autumn period, from roughly 722 to 481 B.C.E., "wars" among the states were mostly just one-day ceremonial battles to which the lords rode in decorated carriages and whose outcomes were often determined by individual duels. Governed by elaborate rules, they were fought in quest of honor in a sort of order of chivalry.[8] In fact, none of the petty states was organized for war: each had only primitive means to collect supplies; the rulers and aristocrats wished to be seen in glorious array but not to take undue risks; and their troops were simply temporarily impressed peasants, "straight from the marketplace" as one contemporary strategist put it,[9] who, driven out of their villages, hungry, ill-equipped, and unpaid, sullenly did the minimum required to escape punishment.

These wars-as-theater might have continued indefinitely—as they did among the Kurelu and Wittaria—except for the existence of barbarian tribes outside of the "Chinese" system who wanted in. Fighting them was more like the warfare between the Nuer and the Dinka or the Bantu and their neighbors—deadly serious—so, while they continued to joust among themselves, some states, particularly those on the frontier, ceased to play by the ceremonial rules for the symbolic rewards but began to engage in more violent combat and even adopted the tactics of barbarians.

Toward the end of the Ch'un Qin some of the smaller states disappeared, whereas others, recognizing the growing cost of failure, struggled to transform themselves. Had they known the term, contemporaries might have referred to Darwin's survival of the fittest. To be "fit" in the intensifying competition meant to grow in size, gain technological competence— particularly in the arts of warfare—and to improve agriculture, manufacture, and transportation in order to become rich enough to support or rent an army and to bribe enemies or buy allies.

By roughly the middle of the fifth century B.C.E., China had entered what the chronicles term the *Chan Kuo* (Warring States) period. By then, the weaker, smaller, and less progressive states had been weeded out, and the survivors desperately struggled to find and control the mechanisms of power. The survivors were those who realized that power was not just a matter of arms or even of soldiers (although in desperation each state procured new weapons, learned new tactics, and enrolled ever-larger armies). What distinguished winners from losers was more fundamental change, so old norms of status and relationship were replaced by a single-minded emphasis on efficiency. Wise rulers prided themselves on being able to attract talented men even from among the barbarian tribes while capable but desocialized individuals whom the Chinese called *yu-shui*, "itinerant strategists," moved from court to court peddling their skills.

In order to mobilize capital more efficiently, the states began to replace barter with money. Getting money into the government coffers was then, as it has been ever since, a prime interest of rulers. The state of Lu led the way in 594 B.C.E. in levying the first known tax on land. But because land without farmers was obviously worthless, the more ruthless states returned to the old Shang dynasty custom of raiding their neighbors to abduct peasants. When that was neither feasible nor profitable, some sought to lure peasants with promises of houses, land, and even exception from military service.

Engorged with the remains of the other petty states, the few survivors in the middle of the Warring States period had become major powers: their combined population probably numbered at least fifty million—about the same as the Roman Empire at its height. The more able—or more fearful—rulers realized that, in the increasingly desperate struggle, their fundamental resource was the common people; old rulers had merely milked them for taxes, but the new rulers forced them to become soldiers. Conscription of males between fifteen and sixty became common and made possible armies of upwards of a million men.

Even at rudimentary levels of organization and logistics, the challenge of feeding and arming such vast hosts required the growth of a highly competent class of managers. This group had a variety of tasks thrust on it. Because the states monopolized the manufacture of the new iron weapons required by the armies, a sort of "military-industrial complex" came into being. Those who had industrial capacity sought to prevent others from getting it. So the new bureaucracies were expanded to monitor domestic production, acquire foreign produce, and control or embargo the exportation of war materials, particularly iron. Increasingly the states relied on massed infantry and so armed their soldiers with the

crossbow (a revolutionary weapon they borrowed from the southern barbarians) and instituted the horse cavalry (which they copied from the
northern barbarians).

In the new style of warfare, no quarter was given. Surrender no
longer brought salvation: when, for example, the soldiers of the state of
Chao laid down their arms in defeat, half a million of them were sum-
marily slaughtered. And, as the victors raped and burned what remained
of the devastated countryside of the defeated, whole societies perished.

Finally, one of the warring states, Qin, whose northwestern location
left it open to attack both from its Chinese rivals and from the northern
frontier, became particularly adept in military and diplomatic skills.
Driven by the imperative of its foreign relations, Qin underwent a revolutionary internal transformation: it reorganized its army to emphasize cavalry, rigidly stratified its society, replaced the feudal gentry with a tightly
organized bureaucracy, campaigned to entice alien settlers, and gave title
to lands to the peasantry. These developments raised it out of the class of
its rivals. Despite their attempts to defend themselves by banding together
in a confederation, Qin was able to pick them off one by one until in
221 B.C.E. it had finally mastered them all, and its king, Shih Huan Ti,
proclaimed himself emperor.

In this story are, I suggest, two important themes: the first is that
limited warfare is a luxury that is unlikely to be sustained as the costs of
defeat escalate, and the victor is usually the party that most completely
understands and exploits the possibilities of the use of force. Perhaps at
some remote time the primitive Maring had undergone a similar transformation from a Kurelu kind of theatrical warfare. In our times, military
thinkers drew a comparable distinction between "conventional" and nuclear war in the hope that one side would accept defeat rather than employ
its nuclear force. As between the Soviet Union and the United States, this
hope was fortunately not tested; as between the Arabs and the Israelis, the
issue was never in doubt: Israel planned for the "Samson" option.

The second theme, which is clearly brought out in the Chinese
chronicle by Sima Qian, is that the very process of warfare forces major
changes in the cultural and social orientation of the participants.[10] Two
thousand years later, both the Ottoman Empire and the Egypt of Mehmet
Ali underwent a remarkably similar (and deeply unpopular) transformation with the introduction of Western uniforms, drill, tactics, and weapons
when forced to do so to avoid certain defeat. Many societies in between
and others since have been comparably and radically transformed, as was
the American society in the 1940s, by war. In short, although warfare is
certainly an aspect of foreign affairs, as is implicit in Clausewitz's analysis,

it often transcends this definition to reshape the state and the society that engages in it.

We can see this impact of warfare in stark relief in primitive societies' selection of rulers and shaping of ruling institutions. Among all primitive peoples, whatever else wars were about, they provided occasions in which warriors could prove their heroism. And in proving themselves, successful warriors would gain in domestic status, acquire rights over women and treasure, and in certain circumstances achieve control over the property or even the lives of their fellows.[11] What we see in this simple form becomes, of course, more elaborate and less evident in sophisticated societies. As I will point out, we see this process clearly in Rome, where the road to power usually was military. A triumph, the ultimate accolade of Roman civic life, could be won only in combat abroad. So war with neighbors and strangers was the natural pursuit of ambitious Roman men. It followed that when given a post where honor, fame, and riches might be won, the men we know best in history provoked hostilities in order to win the rewards.

Such conduct was not a Roman innovation: in many parts of the world from very ancient times, something like the following must have happened. As the transition began to be made from kinship-defined clans and small villages to geographically defined towns and cities, the problem of leadership became acute. People in the first towns probably acted as though they were still kindred, but various new criteria of leadership must have been tested. Where we have any means to observe, as in contemporary primitive communities where rudimentary warfare has come into being, we observe that leadership usually comes about through demonstrated valor in combat.

In the first sophisticated civilization we know, the cities of Sumer, we find the elements of the change already present: the riveting fear of the neighbor enthroned the war leader, a *lugal* (big man), which is exactly the translation of the New Guinea Maring *yu maiwai*. The analogy is even closer in Aztec Mexico, where the *tlatoque* (city-state rulers), whom the Spanish conquistadors called *señores supremos,* also began as warriors of renown.[12] Eventually, the task of the *lugal* outgrew personality and took on the aspects of a separate profession. By at least 2800 B.C.E. the *institution* of kingship—what the Sumerians called *nam-lugal,* the "existence of the great man"—was firmly established.

During the time in which the growing cities were investing in walls and irrigation and flood-control projects, they must naturally have turned to labor gangs to perform military service. These men would have become rudimentary militias. As a next step, cities regimented their citizens into conscripted military units supported by corvée labor brigades. The city rulers, however, probably soon became aware of a conflict between their objectives: if men were taken away from constructing flood-control dikes or digging irrigation canals, the city might starve. Similarly, since trade had already come to be recognized as a source of wealth, to demand militia service from artisans could be seen to take them away from making goods for export. Moreover, warfare itself became increasingly demanding. Technically advanced in warfare as in other fields, the Sumerian cities developed a tactical formation that was a forerunner of the later Greek phalanx, sophisticated siege techniques, and a variety of new weapons. So, at some point, the Sumerians began to do in the military what they were doing in all other aspects of their lives: they specialized. From that time on, some men would always plow, others would always work at crafts, and others would always bear arms.

. . . .

8 ASSYRIA AND ROME

Inspired by this early linkage between military action and political power was one of history's purest examples of the state as a military machine. Forged in the bitter clashes of tribe against tribe, town against town, and city-state against city-state in the turmoil at the end of the second millennium B.C.E., the Assyrians were to become the first great empire of the ancient world. Like the Macedonia of Alexander and the Rome of the Caesars, Assyria's later majesty almost blinds us to its beginnings, which were unpromising, its rivals, who were many, and its natural endowments, which were few. Like those two later powers, but far less well known, its achievements were astonishing.

The core of the Assyrian Empire was a small area, roughly the size of Delaware, occupying part of what is today Kurdistan. Like Macedonia in the century before the rise of Alexander the Great, it was a "melting pot" in which diverse and primitive tribesmen were gathered, given a sense of nationality, and schooled for war. There, buffeted by a harsh climate and remote from the centers of civilization, grew a hardy, enduring population of peasant farmers. With little to sustain or hold them at home, the early Assyrians engaged in commerce with distant areas. As they became

proficient soldiers and conquered an empire, they applied their knowledge of commerce to imperial exploitation.[13]

Over time, the Assyrian kings developed a national purpose that may
be taken as the first thrust toward world domination. The aim of each
ruler was to push his frontiers to the ends of the world.[14] War became for
Assyria, as thousands of years later it would become for Prussia, the "national industry": its deeds and victories were relished with a passion that
makes the Norse sagas appear pacific by comparison.[15] But in those ruthless times, it was not the taste for gore that set the Assyrians apart, because
that was widely shared (as we learn from Deuteronomy 20:10); rather it
was the calculation and thoroughness of their policy.

To the Assyrians, the gods embodied political legitimacy: without
the approval of the gods, which could be verified by worldly success, civil
authority was in some sense crippled, deformed, and outlawed. Military
success was thus not only an article of faith but the very proof of the validity
of faith. It followed that the gods of the defeated were themselves part of
the spoil of war. This explains why the Assyrians carried off the religious
vessels of the Jewish temple in Jerusalem: since they could find no statues
of gods, they took the things associated with the Israeli god.

As important as was their ideology, however, the Assyrians put trust
in their weapons, formations, and tactics: they were pioneers in the use
of iron and "steeled" weapons and in recognizing the value of terror. Even
before the first arrow struck or the first battering ram reached the enemy's
gate, they had numbed, overawed, and immobilized him by a deluge of
propaganda. These things the Assyrians backed with superb military organization. Universal conscription fed men first into the standing army and
then into a national militia. Each governor commanded a garrison,
whereas the king commanded a highly mobile strike force. In a remarkable innovation, the central command was organized according to arms—
not by tribes or towns or ethnic groups as was customary among other
states—with separate formations for horse cavalry (which was first employed in the ninth century B.C.E. and was an Assyrian innovation), light
infantry, and sappers. More than in any other field, the Assyrians excelled
in siege warfare. They approached war professionally, even (like the Persians) academically. They studied the terrain on which battles were to be
fought, planned tactics in advance, and carefully designed and manufactured appropriate military equipment. Constant drill enabled the army to
deploy so rapidly that it often caught enemies before they were ready to
fight or, if the enemy had prepared, the Assyrians engaged in complex
maneuvers to confuse his dispositions.

Because the rulers rewarded their soldiers generously with the spoils of battle, a peasant-farmer-soldier could gain more from a single campaign than from years of hard work on the thin soils of the homeland. Risks were reduced for each soldier by his (and his enemies') awareness of Assyrian military superiority. Moreover, his government—uniquely in that age—provided care for widows and orphans. If a married soldier was reported missing in action, his widow was required to wait two years before remarrying, but during that period she was provided with a house and a plot of land. Thereafter she was free to marry whomever she wanted. If, subsequently, the soldier was found alive and returned home, he could take back his wife and could claim the land and house she had been given. No other ancient or medieval army was so well treated. Not surprisingly, morale was high.

Driven by their hunger for mastery, sustained by their certainty of divine favor, and organized to project their force with maximum effect, the Assyrians smashed their way to power. By 708 B.C.E., they ruled an empire stretching from the shores of the Caspian westward to the Mediterranean and from near the Black Sea to the Persian Gulf. More was to come. Having taken Cyprus, they invaded Egypt in 675 B.C.E. Four years later it was all theirs. For a state whose original inhabitants had probably numbered only about a hundred thousand, the empire was an almost unbelievable achievement.

Yet, foreign success produced a domestic cancer: the very benefits of imperialism were lethal to the free farmer-soldiers on whom the whole structure rested. Lured away from the land and stimulated to a new standard of luxury, they became vulnerable. In bad years, they mortgaged their lands to city merchants. When they defaulted, the impoverished farmers were replaced by alien prisoners of war and drifted into an urban proletariat. Then, no longer hardy peasants, they proved also no longer to be reliable soldiers, so the state soon came to rely on foreign mercenaries. With military service thus made servile and the preserve of foreigners, the old elite sought to avoid it, with fatal consequences.[16]

Like China and Rome, Assyria was hard pressed by its alien neighbors and against them mounted frequent "search and destroy" operations; it showed no pity but could not succeed because, inevitably, it left some people alive. Time after time, the survivors rose against their overlords. And time after horrifying time, the Assyrians struck them down. (In 820 B.C.E., for example, an Assyrian king boasted of having ravaged twelve hundred inhabited places.) Often, those who were not massacred or abducted were mutilated. But no amount of ferocity brought peace. The most powerful empire of its time could no more than its successors find secure frontiers. It would ultimately be poor mountaineers, a people much like the ancestors of the Assyrians, who would destroy their empire.

The fall of Assyria teaches us that imperialism begets a shared sense of humiliation and anger among its victims, who gradually come to realize their common aim: to break free. Enlightened imperialism, toward which Assyria had been evolving from its brutal and destructive middle period, appears, to the outsider, less likely to stir either a bitter hatred or a sense of desperation. Yet, ironically, in seeking to spread the benefits of its culture and to rule its empire economically, it draws its subjects into the secrets of its power and makes less acceptable, because less obviously necessary, their own powerlessness. So it was in the Assyrian experience. So it has been also in our century.

* * *

In chapter 4 we saw that the early Romans learned from their bitter defeat by the Gauls in 391 B.C.E. the cost of not having an effective military establishment and that they set about remedying their deficiency. They adopted new weapons and armor, borrowed from the Etruscans elements of their military organization, substituted for the traditional Greek phalanx a more flexible formation, and virtually re-created their city-state in the form of an army: votes were assigned by military unit, political authority was apportioned according to military service, and citizens were obligated to complete a number of military campaigns before they could hold political office. So far did this process go that Rome has been called "a community of warriors."[17] Even more than these formal military and governmental changes, the leaders used the army as a school of public order to discipline the citizenry. Infantry was always the queen of Roman battle and, in the formation adopted by the Romans, discipline was vital: to break ranks, even if to perform conspicuous acts of bravery, was to imperil the safety of all. From military tactics, order was thus enshrined as the prime civic virtue.

Early Rome prided itself on its citizen army and, indeed, linked military service to citizenship. But it was only a small town, so no matter how competent its military commanders or how patriotic its soldiers, it had little to distinguish itself from the scores of similar city-states in the Italian peninsula. As in Warring States China, competition among the more aggressive led to the reduction of independent tribes and towns so that by 350 B.C.E. the sixty or so Latin ministates had been reduced to about twenty. As William Harris has written,[18] Rome was so obsessed with war that "almost every year the legions went out and did massive violence to someone." Indeed, there was "an almost biological necessity about the event. . . . During the first eighty-six years from 327 [B.C.E.] onwards there were, as far as can be seen from defective sources, at most four or five years without war." Hostilities, however, were merely the sharp edge of a weapon that was to win the empire: as they moved against their neighbors, the Romans transformed *them* into Romans. Assimilation would be the key to Roman military power.

I will discuss this issue more fully in part 7, but here it is useful to mention that it was Rome's greatly increased population that enabled it to establish colonies at strategic sites and to settle virgin lands, each of which added new resources that in turn encouraged further population expansion. So, when the Romans were forced to fight a coalition of the remnants of their old enemies and rivals in 295 B.C.E., their population-citizenship policy had so raised the state's strength above that of its rivals that, even combined, they were no match for it. Shortly thereafter, Polybius reported that Roman manpower had reached more than 750,000. To put this figure into context, consider that such classical city-states as Sparta and Athens rarely could field a citizen force of 10,000: Rome had moved into a new class of world powers.

In its great wars with Carthage, Rome exploited its military population policy to the full: as a city-state, Carthage relied on a foreign mercenary army to fight its wars, so Rome sought to weaken it by closing its recruiting grounds. One condition of the peace settlement in the First Punic War was that Carthage would no longer recruit soldiers in Italy. Shortly after peace was established, Rome occupied Sardinia in order to prevent the Carthaginians from recruiting its "goatskins," as the Romans called the Sardinians.[19] Later, when the Romans met the forces of Hannibal, Hannibal commanded what amounted to detached fragments of a league of nations, or, as Livy commented, "an army composed of men who shared neither language, customs, laws, weapons, dress, appearance, nor even a common reason for serving." Against it, and *outnumbering* it, were only Romans.

Making foreigners into Romans proved very effective overseas, but it created severe problems for Roman society and overwhelming temptations for Roman politicians. Like many later peoples, the Romans resented the new converts and sought to keep them apart. Temporarily they won in the so-called social war, but their leaders found cause to overturn their victory. Beginning with Cornelius Sulla (138–78 B.C.E.), each victorious general, fearing for his own safety and ambitious for power, brought his army to be his partisans and protectors. And the price of the mainly foreign soldiers' loyalty was land on which to settle *in Italy*. Sulla thus opened the floodgates on what became under Caesar and his successors a torrent of immigration and reallocation of lands that virtually washed away the old Italy.[20] Foreign soldiers soon dominated Roman politics, and, under weak emperors, Rome became the plaything of the alien Praetorian guard.

Whatever distinctions we choose to draw between the Caesars, they agreed that Rome should rule the world. And for centuries the reality of their domain nearly fulfilled their ambition: covering at its height an area of 4.5 million square kilometers (roughly 1.75 million square miles), or half the size of the United States, numbering more than 50 million inhabitants, surrounded by 10,000 kilometers (6,000 miles) of frontier, a giant towering over the lesser states of the West, Rome seemed a world apart. No other Western state was able for so long to dominate the neighbor and keep away the stranger.

Not just the Caesars but the Romans as a people were certain of their right to rule the earth—in Cicero's phrase they were the *princeps gentium* (lords of peoples). Pliny the Elder quipped that "the [alien] peoples pay taxes even for [the] shade [of our trees]." Increasingly, even for the common citizen, Rome was the world. A schoolmaster is quoted as having remarked that "it is a pleasure to look at a map of the world as we see nothing on it that is not Roman."[21] So vast and imposing did this empire become that even members of subordinate societies agreed with the Roman view of their destiny and not only vied to become accepted by the Romans but also devoted themselves to convincing their fellow countrymen of the inevitability of Rome. This attitude permeates the writings of the Greek Polybius and the Jew Josephus. It led even to the astonishing acts of client kings of non-Roman societies *bequeathing* their kingdoms to the people of Rome. Even Rome's enemies saw an inevitability in its majesty.

Polybius ascribed this inevitability in part to the violence with which Rome approached its enemies—and allies. In this we may compare Rome to Assyria. In both empires, the litany of brutality was not only long and numbing but essentially unchanging: what changed for both was that in the days of their might violence commanded respect, whereas in their decline it incited hatred. In campaign after campaign, whole cities were slaughtered, rebels were crucified, victims raped and enslaved, and these actions were performed not by drunken soldiers in fits of passion but by disciplined soldiers acting under orders.

In Gaul, Caesar used the ten legions he raised, primarily of "barbar-

ian" Gauls, to carry out a "pacification" program that amounted to genocide. His proud and graphic account establishes the record: even dis-
counting for the usual exaggerations of military commanders, his "body
count" is horrifying. Often, as in the seizure of the town of Avaricum
(Bourges), he killed every man, woman, and child. Even animals were
hacked to pieces. Terror was his eleventh legion. Back home, the laconic
and grim Romans were so shocked that some senators suggested that Caesar be handed over to the Gauls as a war criminal. But the policy worked,
and most Romans liked the results.

What did the military establishment cost? Chester Starr has estimated
an average state budget at about 3.5 percent of gross national product
and military expenditure at roughly 60 percent of the budget. The government as a whole thus was cheaper than those of most premodern European states—about 65 percent of the price government cost the English
in the seventeenth century—and the military component was substantially
less than that of most seventeenth- and eighteenth-century European
states.[22]

Viewed from another angle, military action stimulated the national
economy. For example, in the war against Hannibal, when the army exploded from four to twenty legions, requirements for arms, clothing, and
food could not be met by the Senate. To equip the new forces, the Senate
let *ultro tributa* (contracts) to merchants and bankers who in turn bought
or organized the manufacture of the required items and delivered them
to the designated places. In the process, what essentially became a new
class of capitalists was created. And unlike most states, Rome made money
on many of its wars, so much treasure was introduced into Rome from
abroad.

But there was a price to pay. As in Assyria earlier and later even in
Nazi Germany (where "racial purity" was the principal article of faith),
war and occupation of foreign areas increasingly "alienized" the army.
Sulla's Asian troops were followed by Caesar's Gauls and soon by Germans,
Thracians, Huns, and various Celtic groups. Moreover, even Roman citizens serving as soldiers abroad kept foreign mistresses and produced half-
breed children who could become Roman citizens only by serving in the
army. Thus, over time, the army came to be an asynartetic force of self-
perpetuating, legally Roman but ethnically distinct legions. More alien yet
were the two hundred thousand or so tribesmen who served in the *auxilia*
under their own chiefs. While Rome and its leaders were strong, they controlled the balance of alien versus citizen power, but by the fifth century
C.E. both the western and the eastern divisions of the old empire had lost
this balance. This was in part because "Romans" no longer were willing

to serve in the military forces. Those with influence or money evaded service and did so most successfully when Rome most needed them.

And need them it did. Even with armies of six hundred thousand men, by the fourth century it could no longer protect its European frontiers. Along the exposed northeastern frontier, attacking barbarians, although fewer and less organized, could pick their targets, whereas the defenders were tied to more or less static defense of towns and agricultural areas. The very size of the empire that had so delighted earlier Romans proved a weakness, enabling attackers to achieve local tactical superiority.

Rome occupies such a central role in our concept of history that we tend to think of its decline and fall as virtually unique; yet, there is much in these events that is paralleled in the experiences of other great empires. As it weakened, Rome sought to divide and exclude its barbarian enemies. This policy was to remain the mainstay of its eastern division, Byzantium, for centuries. And it was precisely the policy that evolved in China during the Han dynasty, where it was known as *i-i-fa-i*, "using barbarians to fight barbarians."

Even more impressive was the infusion of foreigners into empires. If we substitute Turks for Rome's Huns, Germans, and Celts, the Roman experience was largely duplicated by the Abbasid caliphate. The Abbasids first brought in their Turks, but gradually, like the Romans, they were forced to rely on tribal groups, who owed them no allegiance. In both empires, the move was tactically wise, because tribal auxiliaries were often effective fighting forces, but strategically ruinous because the warriors brought along their families and settled permanently. Moreover, as the tribesmen learned the extent of the weakness of their hosts and began to taste power, they moved toward dominion. Rome thus ceased to be Roman and splintered into Vandal, Gallic, German, and Hunish states, whereas the Abbasid Empire ceased to be Arab and evolved into the Seljuk Turkish empire and other states.

Despite its recognition of the danger and the violent public hatred of the foreigners, so desperate was the Roman government for troops that it even "bred Germans on Roman soil by the system of *laeti* . . . corporations (*corpora publica*) with a special obligation of furnishing recruits."[23] But at a critical point some thirty thousand barbarian auxiliaries went over to the Gothic side and urged another man of barbarian ancestry, Alaric, who had served as a Roman general under the emperor Theodosius, to turn against Rome. Alaric first tried to invade the east but was rebuffed by the walls of Constantinople; turning west, he conquered Greece and around 400 C.E. invaded Italy. By 408, he and his auxiliaries were camped outside Rome. Temporarily stopped by the twenty-one miles of Roman walls, they settled down to a siege. First bought off by a ransom, they seized the city in 410. This is what we know as the fall of the Roman Empire.

. . . .

9 SOLDIERS, MERCENARIES, AND GUERRILLAS

I now turn to the "instruments" that statesmen and aspirants to power seek to use: soldiers. History tells us that their life is dangerous, uncomfortable, frustrating, and often short. So what motivates men to become soldiers? A "policy" answer is that they do it to extend the tribal territory or to protect their nations; we see examples of this motivation from the most primitive tribes down to sophisticated societies in our own times. But this answer only scratches the surface. I have already discussed another motivation—military service as the road to political power—a prominent theme in the history of societies from Sumer through Rome to modern times. But that cannot have been the hope of most of those who did the actual fighting in history's thousands of wars. Many of them did not always have a choice, and even for those who did there were often imperatives that could not be denied. Poverty was certainly high among them. Yet, after one assigns due weight to these and other reasons, one is left with a single thread that seems to run through the entire historical experience. It is, as Günter Wagner put it after a long field study of African tribesmen, "the thrill or 'sport' which warfare furnishes and the fame and prestige which the display of courage and daring bestows upon a warrior."[24]

The literature of virtually every culture is full of paeans to war. So we may assume that some men have always found it attractive and have wanted to become soldiers. Indeed, when no war was convenient, men either went in search of one (as did the Norman knights in the Crusades, and the samurai and *rônin* in fourteenth-century Japan) or created a local substitute in the tournament, which in medieval Europe embodied the "heroic dream" of the nobility.[25] The tournament certainly had some function as a training ground for cavalry, but, as Barbara Tuchman writes, "though justified as training exercises, the impulse was the love of fighting."[26] Some societies used sports as a means to inculcate martial ardor and discipline. The Mongols blended hunting with military campaigns, usually beginning a campaign with a massive hunt. In his *Yasa,* or edicts,

Chingis Khan ordered that "when there is no war raging against the enemy, there shall be hunting; the young shall be taught how to kill wild
animals, so that they become accustomed to fighting, and acquire strength
and endurance, and will subsequently fight, without sparing themselves,
against the enemy as though against wild animals."[27] In a controversial
passage, Richard Lee and Irven DeVore virtually echoed great Mongol
when they wrote, "Men enjoy hunting and killing, and these activities are
continued as sports even when they are no longer economically necessary.
. . . And until recently war was viewed in much the same way as hunting.
Other human beings were simply the most dangerous game. War has been
far too important in human history to be other than pleasurable for the
males involved."[28]

Then there was the issue of boredom. The outbreak of World War
I, for instance, was greeted ecstatically everywhere; contemporary photographs show smiling faces on crowds dancing in the streets. Suddenly the
harassing petty concerns of life faded away and people were caught up in
the excitement of the great events, filled with a new and grand purpose.
Similar emotions are reported in many early wars. As W. W. Tarn wrote,
"The warfare of the little states of classical Greece had once been a kind
of seasonal occupation; the harvest was reaped early, and there was little
to do for the rest of the summer: there were not many amusements, so
you fought somebody. This phase was assisted by the shortage of agricultural land in Greece; even a few farms made a difference, and there was
a constant temptation to start early and reap your enemy's harvest."[29]

◆ ◆ ◆

That passage introduces yet another element in the quest for war: the
"push" of poverty must usually have supplemented the "pull" of adventure
to start some men down the road to war, often for the benefit of others.
The mercenary thus appears in warfare. Unfortunately, we know almost
nothing about him. Where we have information, we hear that mercenaries
were "wasted" at prodigious rates. Their lives must have been hard, thank-
less, and short. But some, at least, were volunteers, so hopes or images of
their life must have appealed to poorer peoples on the fringes of the settled states.

Already in the ancient world, we begin to hear of armies in the thousands, larger than the total populations of the towns of the pre-Sumerian
period. Not only were native men also needed for other purposes, but the
level of military threat escalated as societies grew and became more efficient. So soldiers themselves became a sort of commodity, to be imported

as needed. They came—and still come—as the troops of allies, defeated enemies, colonial peoples, and mercenaries. They figure in what appears to be the first recorded international treaty, in which the king of the northern Syrian city of Ebla addresses the king of the northwestern Iranian city of Khamazi as "my brother" and asks for the supply of mercenary soldiers.

In the long war focused on the battle of Kadesh, 1286–85 B.C.E., when both of the great empires of that era—the Egyptian and the Hittite—exhausted themselves, they went to the ends of their known earth to augment their forces. In their turn the fiercely separatist Greeks came closest to achieving nationhood in their common service to foreign rulers. Alexander's invasion of the Persian east pitted his Macedonians and their Greeks against the Persians and their Greeks. But it was Carthage that made more extensive use of mercenaries than any other state.

A typical city-state, Carthage was never large, occupying only about 1,000 square kilometers (385 square miles), or about one-third the size of Rhode Island, in what is today Tunisia, and even in that small area, the Carthaginians themselves were always a minority, so wherever their merchants traveled recruiting agents were to be found. The Carthaginian experience illustrates both the utility and the dangers of reliance on mercenaries.

Among the mercenary's attributes were the considerations that if he were killed, died of disease, or were captured, his service cost nothing. Then, as Plutarch commented, "the loss was borne by other nations."[30] And if he was successful, he could be compensated at the expense of his victims. Far from his home, he could not evade his duties by running away as easily as the native could. Nor had he anything to gain, even his life, in surrender because the victor would probably simply kill him. Coming from uncouth, poor, and "barbarian" peoples, he was assumed to be a natural fighter and, if chosen with care, he might bring a special military skill that his employers lacked. So we hear of the Indian elephant handler, the Scyth archer, the Balearic slinger, and the Greek heavy infantryman.

The mercenary's main drawback was that he was dangerous. Those societies weak enough to need to employ him might not be strong enough to control him. Occasionally, we can see the danger he posed: the "other side" of the story Xenophon tells us in the *Anabasis* of the valiant fighting retreat of "the Ten Thousand" from Persia is of a government trying to get rid of its predatory "dogs of war." But it was Carthage where the danger is most evident: after the First Punic War, Carthage economized by not rewarding its hard-fighting mercenaries, and, feeling cheated, they revolted. Suppressing them was exceptionally costly and bitter. So frightened were governments of mercenaries that enemies sometimes paused in their hostilities toward one another to make common cause against them, as Rome and Carthage did after the First Punic War.

Much later, in medieval and Renaissance Italy, the city-states recruited soldiers from everywhere—some even from among the Muslim Turks and Arabs. Religious differences, even hostilities, mattered little since the mercenary of whatever venue or persuasion was hated, feared, and exploited in equal measure. The city-states had little choice. Despite the dangers mercenaries posed—particularly when they were disbanded, as they often were, with their pay in arrears, hungry and desperate—and despite the fear that they might switch sides in the midst of a campaign, medieval and Renaissance states were slow in creating citizen armies.[31] So, in the troubled seventeenth century, scores of thousands of mercenaries crossed national frontiers to make up as much as 25 percent of the armies of the major European states. A Bavarian regiment in 1644 is said to have included, along with fourteen Muslim Turks, men of some sixteen nationalities.[32] Some went freely, but many were impressed criminals or those we would today call "the homeless." Rounded up forcibly, they were frequently told that they faced the death penalty if they tried to return home. Most did not have a chance to test the prohibition: those the bullets missed, disease was apt to get. So the traffic in mercenaries was a convenient means, and one often lucrative to officials, to get rid of undesirables.

Mercenary service remains a feature of our times—sometimes in the most unlikely circumstances. Consider the Nazi Schutz Staffeln (SS) of World War II: planned as a racially "pure" organization, the SS was established in 1933. By the start of the Russian campaign, the Waffen-SS, as it was then known, had grown to more than 160,000 men, almost none non-Germans. By February 1942, however, the Wehrmacht had suffered more than 1 million casualties, and the SS began to try to make up losses by recruiting non-Germans. By the end of the war, it contained about 500,000 non-Germans, including members of such "despised races" as Slavic Ukrainians, Russians, and Serbs. Indeed, none of the 38 Waffen-SS divisions in service at the end of the war was entirely German, and half were mainly foreign, including British, French, Dutch, Norwegian, Ukrainian, Romanian, Hungarian, Serbian, Albanian, Bulgarian, and Croatian units.[33] Ironically, the SS had returned the German army to the condition before Gerhard von Scharnhorst's reforms a century and a half before, when foreigners made up more than one-third of all troops. So the mercenary is clearly still with us. It would be fair to regard him as Necessity's second child.

Surprisingly, however, instances of mercenaries "going over" to the enemy have always been rare. Even where the mercenaries were fighting against their fellow countrymen, they generally remained loyal to their employers. In our times, it is noteworthy that the troops that fought hardest to protect Hitler at the end of World War II were the foreigners, many of them despised *Untermenschen,* in the Waffen-SS.

In addition to foreign mercenaries, states often enrolled the armies of their allies and clients. An early instance occurred during the Assyrian invasion of Egypt in 675 B.C.E., when both sides employed tribal militias and city-state armies, often under their own leaders—the king of Judah and some twenty-two other "kings" marched with the Assyrian army against Egypt. But the most impressive such army in ancient times was the force under Xerxes that invaded Greece in 480. Herodotus, never one to miss a good story, gives us a graphic account,[34] nation by nation, uniform by uniform, of this league of nations under arms; almost every known people, including Greeks, was there.

The Persians had internalized most of the world as they knew it, but later peoples, having to mobilize comparable diverse forces, suffered acutely from divided command, conflicting pride, differing objectives, linguistic misunderstandings, and opportunism. Such dangers were very much on the minds of both Soviet and Western strategists during the Cold War. What both sides needed to know was what the armies of the Soviet client states, particularly the German Democratic Republic, would do in a military confrontation between the Soviet Union and the United States. Fortunately, we never had to find out.

Similar to the foreign auxiliary and the mercenary in some respects is the undercover soldier, or "volunteer," a man sent by one country to fight for its interest in another country. The aim of his sponsor is to harm the enemy without incurring responsibility for his action. Perhaps the first known precedent was in Greece in 432 B.C.E., when the city-state of Corinth mobilized a force to thwart Athenian policy in a third city-state. Many states have since donned this thin veil. In our century, the Russians, the Germans, the Italians, and others organized "volunteer" armies to fight the Spanish Civil War while Americans "allowed" serving army pilots to fly for the Chinese against the Japanese on the eve of World War II. Where direct involvement in fighting is deemed politically too risky, volunteers may serve only as technicians or trainers, as Americans did against Russians in Afghanistan.

◆ ◆ ◆

Different from the mercenary or the volunteer is another military figure who emerges early in history and remains with us today—the guerrilla. The word itself comes from Spanish and was used by the Duke of Wellington to denote small parties of irregular Spanish fighters. The guerrilla may be considered the polar opposite of the mercenary since he (or she) is a person who fights for a cause, usually apart from armies and often without pay.

Under article 1b of the 1899 Hague War Regulations, the guerrilla should be accorded the same treatment as a regular soldier, but this protection applies only if he is wearing "a fixed distinctive emblem recognizable at a distance." Since practically none have done so in any recent war, guerrillas are customarily considered *francs-tireurs* (bandits). It pays to be on the winning side, however: after World War II, the American military tribunals in Nuremberg held that some partisan units in Yugoslavia and Greece who were certainly not in any sort of uniform, were covered by the Hague War Regulations, although, when these same people opposed British policy, Winston Churchill referred to some of them as "miserable Greek banditti" who were not to be treated as prisoners of war if captured.

As defined by the U.S. government in 1863 for the Civil War, what we today call guerrillas were

> men or squads of men who commit hostilities, whether by fighting or inroads for destruction or plunder, or by raids of any kind, without commission, without being part and portion of the organized hostile army, and without sharing continuously in the war, but who do so with intermitting returns to their homes and avocation, or with the occasional assumption of the semblance of peaceful pursuits, divesting themselves of the character or appearance of soldiers—such men or squads of men are not public enemies, and therefore, if captured, are not entitled to the privilege of prisoners of war, but shall be treated summarily as highway robbers or pirates.

Even if conventions and regulations that attempt to define him are relatively recent, the guerrilla is not. We already find his description, quaint to be sure, in ancient Egyptian sources: he is a *drdrw* (stranger)— a word that also implies "strange doings," irregularities, hostilities. The Sumerians called their guerrilla opponents, Amorites, nomads "who know not grain." Unpredictable as enemies, unreliable as allies, and impossible as subjects, always engaged in hostilities to no conclusion, the nomad did not fight in the approved manner, with formally declared war or standing forces, but darted about, stealing supplies and cutting off stragglers. This is the "classical" notion of the guerrilla, and it was applied in our century to partisans. The best known of these was T. E. Lawrence (Lawrence of

Arabia), who during World War I raised a Bedouin force to harass Ottoman troops. The modern guerrilla has evolved a more complex style of operations, and these in turn have given rise to ever more complex ways of fighting against him. These now deserve our attention.

In modern guerrilla warfare, almost every aspect of what may be termed strategic or conventional warfare is reversed. Indeed, guerrilla warfare re-creates the conditions of social insecurity that we saw in primitive warfare. Men, women, and children alike are seen as combatants and are treated as spoil; combat is often conducted by stealth; actions are small, made up of raids, forays, and alarms in the night. But these are only the tactics. The strategy is more complex. The guerrilla has essentially three aims. The first is political: to identify himself with a popular cause (usually, in recent years, nationalism); the second is administrative: to provide an alternative state structure (schools, hospitals, police); the third is military: to use his relatively puny armed force both to terrorize his opponents and the uncommitted and to draw a reaction from his opponents that will divide them from the people. In broad outline, this was the strategy first laid out by Mao Tse-tung in China in the late 1930s and followed by most successful guerrilla movements ever since.

Probably the earliest account of a counterinsurgency operation is recorded by Herodotus, who says that when the Persians were putting down Greek resistance in the Aegean, they formed a "drag net" of soldiers who joined hands, making a chain that stretched right across each island so that no one could hide from them. Although this is not possible in modern counterinsurgency operations, a similar result has often been sought by the regrouping of populations so that areas in which guerillas operate are turned into no-man's-lands.[35]

As the Egyptians and Sumerians had found four thousand years earlier, it is not usually possible to fight guerrillas successfully in the same manner as conventional forces. Just as the guerrilla cannot hope to win with conventional tactics, neither can his opponent. This simple fact will out, regardless of military doctrine, culture, religion, law, or national style. Whether or not commanders wish to fight in this manner, their soldiers' exposure to the apparently random violence of guerrilla tactics will affect, even shape, their actions and attitudes.

From the bitter experience of the Indochina war, a number of French officers, primarily in the elite paratroop formations, evolved a new doctrine that they sought to apply to the conflict they faced in Algeria and that influenced Americans in Vietnam, Israelis in the occupied territories, and Russians in the Chechen campaign. The French concluded that the guerrilla must be deprived of secrecy, cut off from safe havens, isolated from his supporters, and hunted down. It was Algeria that evoked the doctrine of torture as the means of destroying secrecy. Paratroop colonel Roger Trinquier wrote that torture was to "modern war" what the machine gun had been to trench war. In Algeria also it became routine to "liquidate" suspects, to "pacify" areas where guerrillas were thought to lurk, to "regroup" those who might support them to internment camps, and to terrorize would-be sympathizers. The French experience was to influence the American "Phoenix" program and other military and intelligence operations in Vietnam and Latin America.[36]

This "modern" warfare was hardly new. Internment, torture, "pacification," and summary execution of suspects had been practiced by the French in Algeria and other colonial areas for more than a century. Such tactics were described as early as the end of the sixteenth century in what has been called the first manual on fighting guerillas.[37] What was new was the politicization of the native population: in the revolt that began in 1954, Algerians of all classes and persuasions were determined to shake off French rule. Politicization came in reaction not only to acts of savage suppression, of which there were many, but also to loss of land, social humiliation, apartheid, and the attempt to stamp out local culture.

In their emphasis on the tactics of the conflict, the French never understood the politics. Indeed, the issues agitating the Algerians either were not perceived or were not credited even by humane and socially sensitive Frenchmen such as Albert Camus or Socialist politicians such as François Mitterrand, both of whom had reacted against comparable (if much milder and briefer) anti-French policies during the German occupation in World War II. Rather, the French, smarting from their defeat in Indochina, which many regarded as a national humiliation ranking with their defeat in World War II, were determined not to be defeated again. So for eight years, nearly half a million Frenchmen and perhaps twenty thousand Algerians fought one of the most ferocious wars of modern times.

In the last stages of the war, moreover, a second, quasi-guerrilla force arose. Convinced that the French government was not prepared to fight to the end to preserve their position, many Europeans (including members of the French armed forces) joined a terrorist organization known as L'Organisation de l'Armée Secrète (OAS) that began to attack the French government as well as the Algerians. Units of the French army revolted, and, had it not been for the reputation and firm stance of General de Gaulle, it is likely that France would itself have been plunged into civil war. As it was, the home government had to block the roads and airports of Paris, to place anti-aircraft guns around the presidential palace and other key buildings, and to prepare for an attack by its own army. When they were defeated, the members of the OAS engaged in a reign of random terror that gradually faded into criminal activity inside France, just as the Vietnam conflict spawned much of the drug-related crime in America and the Afghanistan conflict gave rise to a variety of Mafia-like activities in Russia.

In Algeria, the nature of the fighting has left deep and as yet unhealed scars on both French and Algerian society.[38] It left many issues unresolved and also taught a whole generation to argue with the gun and the bomb. No one has yet found a way to heal the wounds, resolve the issues, or pacify the new gunmen—neither aid from France nor internal development, neither success in the national revolution nor multiparty democracy. Many Algerians today seek to break the mold that Europe has imposed on them by reverting to Islamic fundamentalism.

A similar story can be told of Lebanon as it was torn apart over the issue of Palestine and of Afghanistan as it was torn apart by the Russian invasion. Is a return to peace and stability any more likely in Northern Ireland, Cambodia, Sri Lanka, Bosnia, or Chechnya? Guerrilla wars leave residues that poison societies for decades or even generations. And it is not just the society caught in the war that suffers. What begins in one country spills over into others. Not only weapons that are easily and profitably exported but also personnel and doctrines are widely disseminated. From the Algerian conflict, both guerrillas and counterguerrillas scattered throughout Africa. From Afghanistan, those trained and equipped (partly by the Americans) to fight the Russians went on to fight the Saudi Arabian and Egyptian governments and the Bosnian Serbs and even to attack targets in America.

Guerrillas do not need expensive equipment. Most of the killing is done with land mines (which can be purchased for as little as $3) or with light weapons. The United Nations estimates that more than 100 million mines have been laid in 62 countries, 20 million hand grenades are in the hands of unknown persons or groups, and hundreds of thousands of other weapons are in circulation. In many cases these have been provided free, and in others they are sold at or below cost. Their cumulative effect can be seen in the horrors of Rwanda, Bosnia, Somalia, Sri Lanka, and other trouble spots where they have added massively to the roughly 30 million people who have died in warfare since 1945.

Yet for all the terrible costs to the innocent and however much governments inveigh against guerrillas and their methods when they are the targets, guerrilla warfare is probably here to stay. The reasons are mainly political—in many situations dissidents believe they have no alternative means to redress what they see as insupportable grievances. Support of guerrilla warfare is also sometimes attractive to foreign powers since war by proxy in another country against one's enemies is relatively cheap and often effective. Thus, the Soviet Union was as willing to help the Vietnamese against the Americans as Americans were to help the Afghans against the Russians. Tragically, but not surprisingly, therefore, since the end of World War II perhaps twice as much has been spent on giving people in the poorer countries the means of killing one another as on assisting them to make life more tolerable.

In the years ahead, if what I predict in part 7 proves correct—that many existing state structures will come to be regarded as tyrannies and ethnic groups will seek, often by violent measures, to achieve national self-determination—the guerrilla will probably come to be an even more significant figure than he has been throughout history.

. . . .

10 THE COLONIAL AUXILIARY

Not all soldiers are on the side of their "nations." An important role in history has been played by those who side with the foreign invader. I have already alluded to the fact that Caesar raised a force of about fifty thousand Gauls to conquer their homeland. They were not the first. In the glorious epic that has come down to us as the Greek defense of liberty against the dark forces of Asian tyranny, it is sobering to learn that a former king of Sparta rode with Xerxes and that a former leader of Athens had encouraged the invasion. In fact, the majority of the Greek city-states either helped the Persians or stood aside during the invasion, and many of the "Persian" troops were Greek.

In recent times, all of the major imperial powers have relied heavily, some almost exclusively, on natives (usually minority groups or tribal factions) to establish and uphold their rule. I take as an example the British in India, although much the same could be said of the French in Morocco and other parts of Africa and, indeed, in India itself. In the middle of the nineteenth century, Britain ruled an empire almost the size of Europe with only 40,000 English troops supplemented by 232,000 *sepoys* (native troops).[39] Why did the sepoys help the British conquer their country, why did they fire on their own people when ordered, and why did they not overwhelm the foreign invaders? To answer such questions, it will be necessary to discuss some aspects of Indian history.

The India into which the British had come in the eighteenth century was the wreck of the great Mughal Empire, in its heyday a vast multinational state whose ruling elite was drawn from Turks, Arabs, Persians, Afghans, Rajputs, and Mongols. Cohesion among these groups depended on the vitality and dedication of a single man, the sultan-shah-emperor. A weak ruler caused a decline of the state; a succession of weak rulers spelled ruin. This was the first "genetic defect" of the state.

The second was that the state rested on diverse traditional societies without either fully replacing them or completely integrating them. As we would say, it failed to "nationalize" both them and itself. Indeed, to an extreme degree, India exemplified the most significant weakness, vis-à-vis the European powers, of many third-world countries: its society was separated into mutually hostile groups along myriad religious, ethnic, linguistic, and caste distinctions. In the eighteenth century, the 180 million Indians (then about one-fifth of the world's total population) were divided among speakers of nearly 200 separate languages and more than 500 distinct dialects. Many of these were not only mutually unintelligible but also carried cultural traditions and religions that either were not recognized or were regarded with opprobrium by others. Moreover, each of the major religious sects (Hindus, Muslims, Sikhs, Jains, and Jews) was internally subdivided into castes in the Indian fashion. Even after the British wars of conquest and confiscations of native territories, India was still, at the middle of the nineteenth century, divided into more than 600 states. And within states, differences of wealth, social status, and caste created or explained hostilities that were easily exploited by enemies. These divisions made Indians willing to act against one another and overshadowed any sense of a common interest or bond.[40] Consequently, it was easy for the British (and the French) to find Indians willing to help them dominate other Indians.

Such auxiliaries were attractive because they were cheaper than Europeans. This was particularly crucial to the British, who became involved in India as a commercial venture. John Maynard Keynes, perhaps with tongue in cheek, explained where the East India Company (the de facto ruler of India) fit in the grand sweep of English history: "The booty brought back by [Sir Francis] Drake in the *Golden Hind* may fairly be considered the fountain and origin of British Foreign Investment. Elizabeth paid off out of the proceeds the whole of her foreign debt and invested a part of the balance (about £42,000) in the Levant Company; largely out of the profits of the Levant Company there was formed the East India

Company, the profits of which during the seventeenth and eighteenth centuries were the main foundation of England's foreign connections."[41]

The original use of the native soldiers by the company was simply to guard the trading stations that the Mughals allowed them to establish before 1750. Meanwhile, in the interior, area after area, "nation" after nation, split away from Mughal authority. The Sikhs, the first to rebel, were suppressed, but the Mughals were unable to defeat the central Indian Maratha states, with whom they fought repeated wars while Sind, Surat, Gujarat, Oudh, and Bengal—each the size of a major European state—became autonomous. This anarchy provided an opening for the British.

Their opportunity came in an otherwise undistinguished minor engagement, the so-called battle of Plassey, where Robert Clive commanded a force of fewer than a thousand Europeans and about three times that many Indians against a much larger force of Mughal troops. The battle became part of the myth of the (British) Indian Empire, but in fact it was hardly even a battle. The Mughal force that Clive defeated was split into mutually hostile groups some of which had been bribed not to fight. Indeed, Plassey has been convincingly described as more of a commercial transaction than a battle.[42]

Having seized Bengal, the company became an Indian territorial power, a *state,* almost as big as France. Reflecting on these events in far-off Edinburgh, Adam Smith shrewdly warned in 1776 that a "company of merchants . . . [is] a profession no doubt extremely respectable, but which in no country in the world carries along with it that sort of authority which naturally over-awes the people, and without force commands their willing obedience. Such a council can command obedience only by the military force with which they are accompanied, and their government is therefore necessarily military and despotic. . . . Such exclusive companies, therefore, are nuisances in every respect; always more or less inconvenient to the countries in which they are established, and destructive to those which have the misfortune to fall under their government."[43]

With the home government responsible for the expenditures, managing the new territory economically became crucial. A series of compromises evolved, the first of which was to reduce the already-low pay of native workers and to restrict the numbers of Europeans.[44] But the British-controlled area kept growing, and so did the cost of the military establishment; soon it was absorbing half of the British India's revenues. Enrollment of less expensive native troops thus became an urgent priority. The 18,000 sepoys enrolled in 1763 grew in the early years of the nineteenth century to 150,000 and to nearly 350,000 by about 1820. Without them, there could have been no British India.

For decades there was little evidence that these troops had any feeling against their masters or any idea of interests or objectives of their own. Under the surface, however, changes were taking place that would lead directly to the great rebellion of 1857. The first was the rise of apartheid. From the freewheeling days of the eighteenth century, when Englishmen consorted with Indians, often dressed in Indian clothes, and kept "Anglo-Indian" households complete with *zenanas* (harems), a glacial shift in attitudes began. As increasing numbers of Englishmen and women arrived in India to staff the new administration, the English community developed the critical mass to exist as a separate society. The advent of English women created, as in the American experience with black slavery, a *reverse* sexual overtone. Whereas earlier white men had enjoyed sexual relations with Indian women, suddenly there was a perceived threat that white women might be violated by the dark men. This attitude—a Freudian might term it a projected attitude—permeated the British society.[45] Given this view, which rapidly became that of the entire English community, various social and physical barriers were erected to divide the rulers from the ruled.

The second glacial change was the extension of apartheid to social humiliation. As it developed, this new segregation took bizarre and childish forms. When Indian notables had to call on English officers, many of whom were still teenagers, they were required to obtain "certificates of respectability," especially if they expected to be granted a chair on which to sit during their audiences; they had to call on British officials on foot; and in the law courts no seats were provided even for Indian government officials. Resentment against what Indians perceived as loss of dignity would grow into a major cause of the great revolt.

The third major change was in the attitude toward Indian religions. In early years the administration, not keen to have its tasks complicated by missionaries, had sought to keep them away from India, but in 1813, under pressure from London, it allowed them to come. They immediately found in both Hinduism and Islam sinister forces that were beyond redemption. Worse, they believed, both religions so affected their followers as to make them nearly subhuman. So, they concluded, both must be suppressed. Not unreasonably, Indians began to fear loss of their religion as they had already lost their freedom.

These concerns affected the military in practical ways. We see it first clearly in relations between the English officers and sepoys during the 1824 campaign to conquer Burma. Most of the troops were Brahmans for whom travel across the sea was an anathema embedded in the Hindu religion, yet a Bengal sepoy regiment was ordered aboard ship for a voyage that would have defiled them. The regiment refused the order. Without hesitation, the British brought up artillery and opened fire on the troops. The 1824 massacre was a precursor of much worse to come.

The fourth underlying cause of the rebellion was cultural. Imperfect clay though they thought the Indians were, the English decided that they would have to be reformed into Asian Englishmen. This policy was set forth by Thomas Macaulay, who later would become a widely read historian, a member of Parliament, and an adviser to successive governments. In a paper on education for Governor General Bentinck in 1835, he laid out a revolutionary new cultural policy in simple and stark terms: make the Indians forget their past, their culture, and their language.[46] It was Bentinck, advised by Macaulay, who thus turned Indians in a direction that would at least partially denationalize them and would turn their society into the largest mass of English speakers in the world today but that also would threaten their very identity.

Finally, Britain was also creating anxieties and enemies on the commercial front: when restrictions on English imports were lifted, the factories of Manchester and Birmingham swept the hand looms of Dacca and Benares out of the market. I will discuss this aspect of imperialism more fully in part 4, but I mention it here to show that merchants and artisans along with the other groups, as diverse and mutually opposed as they were, were alienated, humiliated, and frightened by the British. Like a miasma, hostility spread through the body politic of India, and group after group was smothered until finally India was convulsed by the revolt of 1857.

The revolt was triggered by what seemed a minor technological change—a new rifle was issued to the sepoys. The Enfield could be fired faster and had a longer range than earlier rifles. Using it, however, involved biting off the tip of each bullet before loading. To prevent deterioration in humidity, the wrappers had been smeared with animal fat. Given the climate of India, this was a sensible procedure. The Indian troops for whom the rifles were intended, however, were either Muslims (who feared that the fat that would touch their lips came from pigs, forbidden by Islam) or Hindus (who feared that it came from cows, sacred in Hinduism). Both immediately concluded that this was no innocent technological change but yet another diabolical plot to subvert their religions and was further proof of the contempt with which they were regarded by the English.

Instead of recalling the rifles or changing the drill, or even explaining the reason for the grease and its composition, the British made their order to use the rifles as prescribed—that is, after biting the bullet— a test of loyalty. Regiment after regiment of sepoys was drawn up on its parade ground, which was then surrounded by English artillery. If any sepoy refused the order to load, he was stripped of his uniform on the spot, dismissed, and sent home penniless. Often the "ringleaders" were arrested, imprisoned, and hanged or blasted off of cannon. The trigger of revolt was pulled at the Meerut garrison near Delhi, where some eighty-five men, many of whom had served the British with distinction for years, were condemned.

The resentment that had grown for half a century exploded in violent hatred. After liberating their fellow soldiers and killing some of their English officers, the sepoys at the garrison marched to Delhi to "liberate" the Mughal emperor. Unfortunately for them, the incumbent was an eighty-two-year-old man little interested in the politics of this world and to whom there were no identified alternatives. Without central leadership, no one could turn the tactical successes into a strategic victory.[47] Like the Mughal Empire itself, lethargic without a strong central figure, the rebellion was stymied.

The fundamental weakness of the rebels was that as yet there was no "India"—indeed, many doubt that even today India can be regarded as a nation-state. Then the only unity among the sepoys arose from their army affiliation. Even that affiliation was not general. Wisely, the British had created three separate sepoy armies—those of Madras, Bombay, and Bengal—of which only the Bengal sepoys revolted. Most of the quasi-independent Indian states either did nothing or supported the British, while the Sikhs and the sepoy armies of Bombay and Madras fought for the British.

The British troops were the first to determine what to do, and, when they moved, they struck with a savagery unknown even in the bitter wars of the past. The killings of European officers and civilians, particularly of women, by the "nigger natives" evoked a primal hatred that was multiplied by fear. Some company officers actually recommended that Indian prisoners be flayed alive. Large numbers were strapped over the breeches of cannon and blown to pieces—preferably in sight of an Indian audience. Whole villages were burned for the crime of being near centers of revolt or convenient to a route of march. Contemporary English accounts graphically and often happily describe the mass murder and the torture that frequently preceded the burning. Tens of thousands of Indians were killed.

The official history proclaims the "retaliation not excessive, it did not exceed the bounds necessary to ensure the safety of the conquerors. But beyond the deaths he inflicted in fair fight, the British soldier perpetrated no unnecessary slaughter."[48] Even far from the hysteria of the action, Prime Minister Lord Palmerston was in favor of razing Delhi, an act already partly accomplished by the shelling during the British siege; former governor-general Ellenborough spoke of the desirability of castrating all the mutineers and renaming Delhi "Eunuchabad." But generations of English schoolboys were thrilled by the accounts of the heroism of the English. The Indians simply fade from the pages of history.

The rebellion thus proved a turning point in the relations between the English and the Indians. Trends toward apartheid that had begun earlier hardened into what amounted to a new caste system. Indians were treated as inferior beings who could understand, and deserved, only an iron fist. But, at the same time and with great skill, the English quickly set about creating a new ethos that might be characterized as "separate but respectable." This new ethos rebuilt the sepoy's self-respect and loyalty by dressing him in colorful uniforms, parading him in military splendor, and denoting him the upholder of the new empress of India, a kind of latter-day Mughal who also happened to be the queen of England.[49]

Only thus can one explain the negative role the sepoys played in the march toward Indian independence. At the end of World War I, when nationalist sentiment had grown among civilians, Indians began gathering in informal groups throughout the country to be harangued by their leaders. At Amritsar an English general, imbued by years of service in India with the racial hatred that had become the norm, ordered his Indian sepoy troops to fire into one crowd of 5,000 men, women, and children. Without any compunction—humanitarian or national—the sepoys obeyed, killing 379 and wounding more than 1,000. They stopped firing only when they ran out of ammunition.

The Indian experience calls to mind two reflections: first, the way the British indoctrinated sepoy troops was a variation on what earlier empires had done with their foreign troops. The Ottoman Empire enrolled in its armed forces as janissaries (Turkish *yeniçeri*, new troops) Greeks and other Christian young men, while various other Turkish and Arab states enrolled as *mamluks* (possessed ones or slaves) a variety of peoples from the Caucasus, Russia, Central Asia, and Africa. To render these aliens useful and trustworthy, they were converted to Islam before being taught the profession of arms. In their turn, the British "converted" the Indians they made into sepoys not by making them Christians but by denationalizing them and giving them a new sense of culture. So successful were the British that the sepoys continued to serve under British command, fighting ably and long during two world wars, far from their homelands; and in India itself they would continue to fight to the very end for the British against their countrymen.

Second, in the new states of Africa and Asia where the heirs of comparable military formations have emerged as the only coherent institutions, they are as prepared to use force today for their own ends as their fathers were for their European masters. Themselves partly denationalized by the culture of military technology and organization, they thus constitute a part of the unresolved legacy of the imperial era with which those who seek stability, representative government, and development must contend.

. . . .

11 WEAPONS

From the soldier I turn to his weapons and their impact on warfare and society. The weapons range from the horse (first domesticated about 4500 B.C.E.) through the chariot to cavalry to the tank; from the spear through the crossbow to the arquebus to the musket to the rifle to the machine gun; from gunpowder to field artillery to the hydrogen bomb; and from the balloon through the airplane to the rocket. It would be tedious and unproductive to discuss them all, but I want to mention aspects of a few that affect my account. I begin with the source of mobility, the horse.

No one knows how the horse was first used, but sometime early in the second millennium B.C.E., as I will discuss in chapter 28, the Indo-Europeans who had first tamed it acquired light, two-wheeled chariots that gave them the overwhelming advantages of mobility and shock in their invasions of Greece and the Indus River civilization. Borrowed by many peoples, the chariot became a major weapon among the Egyptians and the Hittites, primarily as a platform for archers and spearmen, and was deployed as a sort of flying wedge, rather as tanks were in World War II.

Among the petty states of Spring and Autumn China the horse-drawn chariot was used extensively, but in their clashes with the northern nomadic "barbarians," some of the Chinese states learned that massed horsemen were more efficient, less constrained by terrain, and more flexible than charioteers. China did not produce enough horses of sufficient quality to match the nomads, however, so the Chinese began a quest for horses that drew them, during the Han dynasty, across Central Asia into what had been the eastern limit of Alexander the Great's empire, Sogdiana.

Meanwhile, in the Middle East, horse cavalry and chariot warfare both were being developed. Both the Achaemenian and the Parthian Persians experimented with a form of chariot to which scythes were attached. Probably never a very effective weapon, it appears, however, to have terrorized foot soldiers; for this reason, the Romans considered bringing it back into service against their barbarian invaders.[50] But the future lay with the horse rather than with the chariot.

Horse cavalry was not new. As I mentioned, it had been employed by the Assyrians, who even experimented with armored or protected cavalry, but their pioneering efforts appear not to have been taken up by their successors the Achaemenian Persians, whom Alexander found too lightly armed to be able to hold their own against disciplined infantry. The Parthian Persians remedied this failure: their cavalry adopted the nomad's composite bow in place of the lance and javelin and were fitted out with metal armor. When Gaius Crassus and Mark Antony unwisely met them on their own terrain, the Romans were soundly defeated. The Roman response (already tried by Crassus) was to incorporate auxiliary native troops with their horses and weapons. This was the origin of the Roman heavy cavalry, which in turn formed the model for the medieval heavy cavalry of Byzantium and inspired the lighter and differently armed cavalry later adopted in western Europe.

Among the Arabs, use of the camel spread toward the end of the first millennium B.C.E. It was always the preferred animal in the desert, but the horse was the animal of prestige and played a significant role in the Muslim conquests. The Arabs and their Berber allies relied more on speed than on shock, so their cavalry was always "light." But it was highly effective, particularly when employed in a tactic the Arabs called *karr wa farr* (wheel and flee), used while discharging missiles and in lightning raids. Those tactics so impressed the Franks, who were then all foot soldiers, that Charles Martel decided to adopt cavalry as his main battle arm in 730 C.E. That was too late to affect the most famous clash with the Muslims, the battle of Tours in 733, but it forced on early medieval Europeans a thorough reorganization of their society. If horsemen were to be available, they had to be freed from other chores. The answer that Charles Martel and his successors devised was the complex of economic, social, and military arrangements we call feudalism.

The European mounted soldier, the knight, did not use the bow and arrow; his preferred weapons were the lance and the sword or the battle-ax. So he had to engage his opponent at close quarters, and for that he wanted a big, heavy horse (the *destrier*) rather than the pony or quarter-horse favored by the nomads. Initially, however, the knight did not become the steel-encased figure we picture; at first his "armor" was leather with occasional bits of chain mail. Heavy metal armor came only in the thirteenth century in response to the introduction into Europe of the crossbow.

Cavalry was then the "queen of battle." In an echo of the Parthian defeat of the Roman legions under Crassus and Antony, but with far more dramatic and lasting consequences, the mounted archers of the great Chagatai Mongol conqueror Timur met and crushed the janissary infantry troops of the Ottoman sultan Bayezid, which had been poised to conquer Constantinople, at the Battle of Ankara in 1402. In a similar campaign, Timur virtually annihilated the forces of the Golden Horde in the Crimea, which had controlled Russia for more than a century. Ironically, although Timur was both a pious Muslim and a staunch believer in the Mongol right to world dominion, his cavalry saved Christian Byzantium for nearly half a century and enabled Russia to throw off the Mongol yoke.

"Without cavalry," Napoleon said, "battles are without result." But the increasing use of artillery and such tactics as the infantry square reduced the opportunities for cavalry. Nevertheless, armies continued to utilize horse cavalry not only in Europe but also in the New World, Asia, and Africa, and it was still employed, mainly for scouting, by the Germans, the Russians, and the Japanese in World War II. The inherent weakness of cavalry is that the combination of rider and horse presents a large target. Encasing that target in armor offered some protection against the bow and arrow but none against the rifle, machine gun, and cannon. So military thinkers sought some means to keep its virtues (speed and flexibility) while overcoming its defects (vulnerability). The answer was the tank.

Ironically, the tank was conceived not by a military man but by the novelist H. G. Wells in his 1903 story "The Land Ironclads."[51] When trenches became common after the battle of the Marne in September 1914, both horse cavalry and the newly introduced armored car proved ineffective. In the following year, various suggestions were made on how to create a machine that could cross trenches. Winston Churchill's suggestion was to

> fit up a number of steam tractors with small armoured shelters, in which men and machine guns could be placed, which would be bullet-proof. Used at night, they would not be affected by

artillery fire to any extent. The caterpillar system would enable trenches to be crossed quite easily and the weight of the machine would destroy all wire entanglements.[52]

This was the beginning of the machine that has virtually dominated warfare in the twentieth century. It was first used in August 1916 at the battle of the Somme, and its first major success came in the battle of Amiens in August 1918, a battle that broke the German will to continue the war and has been called "the most decisive battle of the First World War."[53]

How to use the tank as the main battle weapon in a mixed force of motorized infantry and aircraft was essentially the concept of a young British officer, Major J. F. C. Fuller, whose writing was regarded as the "bible" of tank warfare by such later practitioners as General Heinz Guderian and Marshal Edwin Rommel. Meanwhile, the tank profited from advances in the design of diesel and gasoline engines and automotive suspension systems. The principal designer during the postwar years was an American by the name of Walter Christie, whose M-1931 (or T-3) inspired most of the tanks used in World War II.

I turn now to missile weapons, and I begin with the bow. The crossbow, as I have already mentioned, was probably borrowed by the Chinese from the area around modern Vietnam. The Chinese developed it to fire multiple bolts; for them, it was primarily an infantry weapon to enable foot soldiers to stand up against horsemen. Everywhere it was taken, it was regarded for almost two thousand years as war's most lethal weapon, so lethal, in fact, that when it was introduced into Europe in the twelfth century, it was banned by the church for wars among Christians. It was much easier to aim and shoot accurately than the famous long bow, and it projected missiles with far more power. For these reasons, it was often used by ship's companies to repel boarding parties and to defend town walls. Not until 1490 did the Venetian Republic take the lead in what became a general move to replace the crossbow with the firearm.

A number of larger projectile-throwing devices were developed in western Asia in classical times. The first catapults were said to have been made in 399 B.C.E. during the siege of Syracuse, from which their use spread. The most important of these devices were the *ballistae*, which the Greeks, the Romans, and the Carthaginians used to hurl boulders or logs against the walls or gates of cities. *Trébuchets* (or mangonels) were similarly used to project stones by the action of a counterweight and ropes under tension. Adopted by the Arabs, such machines were taken across Central

Asia to China. As with crossbows and handguns, so catapults existed side by side with artillery for more than two centuries after the introduction of explosive propellants about 1290.

The first true gun, a sort of vase-shaped cannon made to fire arrows, seems to have been introduced simultaneously in Europe and in China. We know the Song dynasty employed firearms as well as *trébuchets* in 1132 against invading Jürchen tribesmen. Shortly thereafter the Chinese developed what seems to have been a sort of land mine and equipped soldiers with a kind of blunderbuss. But, as today, military technology easily crossed frontiers and spanned long distances. In 1272, after the Mongol conquest, an Arab brought to the Mongol court from the Middle East the first true cannon seen there, and somewhat later European firearms began to appear. Then, in 1523, the Chinese captured two Portuguese ships whose cannon they immediately began to copy.

As Carlo Cipolla writes, the first battles won by artillery took place in the first part of the sixteenth century, but Europeans were using cannon in warfare two centuries earlier. "Florentine official documents refer to the acquisition of 'pilas seu palloctas ferreas et canones de mettallo' in 1326 thus indicating that by that date bronze guns shooting iron balls were already in use."[54] Ironically, the same casting technology that produced church bells proved useful in the making of cannon, which at first were made of bronze. Iron was much cheaper but more difficult to work and, with a variable chemical composition not then understood, often burst under pressure. Reliable iron cannon were made only after 1543. At roughly the same time, manufacture of cannonballs shifted from stone to iron because iron, being denser, made a more powerful impact and was easier to fashion. It was these changes, as I mentioned in part 2, that forced the rebuilding of the walls of medieval fortifications and set off another phase in the contest between defensive and offensive weaponry.

Handguns were much slower to be introduced, but in 1536 and 1537 the Chinese are known to have distributed about five thousand blunderbusses (along with some three thousand brass cannon) manufactured in newly opened factories to the elite regiments of their army. They appear, however, to have remained hostile to this form of military technology (as indeed to the military in general) until the Manchu invasion early in the seventeenth century convinced the Ming dynasty that only through firearms was there a chance to save itself.

At about the same time as in China, around 1530, matchlocks came into common military use in Europe. The next step was to standardize both the firearm and the way in which it was used. For Europe, this was the contribution of Prince Maurice of Orange, who "liberated" much of

Holland from the Spaniards. In Japan the sixteenth century was known as *Sengoku Jidai* (the Age of the Country at War). The Japanese, who already made the world's best swords and steel armor, now began to copy Chinese handguns. Within a few years, handguns were common, and a generation later they were the decisive element in a major battle. With the flair for which they are still known, the Japanese improved the arquebus (equipping it with a small lacquer box to protect its match and powder from the rain). They were the first to overcome its inherent weakness (slow reloading) by arranging the soldiers who used it in ranks so that as one group reloaded a second was firing.

But the social effect of the use of the gun was abhorrent to the Japanese aristocracy. Any peasant could be taught in a few hours—and in the sixteenth century often was—to kill the greatest Samurai swordsman, even clad in full armor. So warriors, who then made up about 8 percent of the Japanese population (in contrast to only about one-half of 1 percent in England), concluded that the gun put not only them but also their ethos and privilege in mortal danger. The ruling shoguns began to curtail the manufacture of guns and to confiscate those already in use. That policy was solidified when the 1637 Shimabara rebellion painfully taught the government the potential for sedition in the possession of guns. Thereafter, guns disappeared from Japan, and the samurai continued using the sword and the bow.

Sporadic attempts were made at roughly the same time to ban firearms in Europe, but, whereas Japan had virtually no foreign enemies, each European state feared its neighbors too much to give up this military advantage. For example, in England in 1523, Henry VIII restricted ownership of guns to the wealthy gentry, but in 1543, again at war with France, he encouraged all his subjects to acquire and practice with guns.[55] The Europeans found, as the Japanese had, that the gun "democratized" warfare. But in Europe this made the gun attractive to those states that were centralizing power and suppressing their wayward aristocracy—the *noblesse de l'épée*—so they eagerly embraced and tried to monopolize the new technology.

We see this perhaps most clearly in the professionalization of naval warfare. In the third century C.E., during the "Three Kingdoms" period, the Chinese built significant river fleets for service on the Yangtze. The tradition of this fleet passed into the T'ang and from it into the Song dynasty. Driven south by the Jürchen "barbarians" in 1126, the Song dynasty built a fleet of huge floating fortresses on the rivers and canals. These armor-plated "ships" were propelled by treadmills that ran paddle wheels and were armed with *trébuchets* that fired gunpowder bombs. It was there and then, wrote Joseph Needham, that "the rise of a permanent navy first took place. China must now, wrote Chang I in +1131, regard the Sea and the River as her Great Wall, and substitute warships for watch-towers."[56] The first admiralty was established near Shanghai a year later and grew over the next century to a force of twenty squadrons with fifty-two thousand men.

In its turn, the Yuan (Mongol) dynasty was able to mount enormous naval forces in the Pacific. The fleet Kublai Khan sent against Japan in 1274 is said to have numbered 900 ships, its successor in 1281, 4,400 ships. It is probable that ship-borne artillery was first used in the latter expedition. The expedition was largely destroyed by storm, but, astonishingly, the Mongols were able to send more than 1,000 ships to invade Java a decade later.[57] By comparison, the Spanish Armada was composed of only 132 ships, of which at least a third were small and of which fewer than half reached English waters.

The first mention of actual naval engagements with cannon was in 1362. What is significant about this trend is that it drew navies apart from armies: ships were no longer to be regarded just as means to transport soldiers or as platforms on which they could fight. The cannon in effect liberated the sailor from the soldier.[58] This is what makes the 1571 battle of Lepanto a watershed in military history: the winning side relied on cannon, whereas the losers treated their ships as mere personnel carriers.

Lepanto also showed that the light and relatively fragile oar-powered "Mediterranean"-style boats were obsolete. The future lay not with them but with the heavier boats built to withstand the Atlantic. They were able to carry more cannon than galleys and galleasses and, because of the experiment of a Frenchman in 1501 — cutting ports in the hull—far heavier guns could be mounted lower to the water on the main deck. These were the ships that were to fight in the Spanish Armada.

In the battle of the armada in 1588, the English ships were more maneuverable than the Spanish, but what appears to have given them their decisive advantage was the way the cannon were mounted. Most of the 2,431 Spanish cannon were placed on two-wheeled carriages. Those supporting the larger guns were of massive proportions. Including the "trail," which rested on the deck, some were nearly as long as the ships were wide so that they could not be "run in" for reloading. The English cannon, being mounted on four-wheeled carriages (without the cumbersome trail), could be relatively easily pulled back to be serviced. Consequently, the English were able to fire far more often than the Spaniards.

The demands of both navies and armies for firearms enormously stimulated the arms industry. Shortly after the middle of the sixteenth century, for example, the Italian city of Brescia was manufacturing about twenty-five thousand guns a year, of which many were destined for export. And the sources of supply were international. As J. R. Hale has noted, Dutch bronze cannon were being cast by a multinational migrant work force from Swedish or Japanese copper (which was alloyed with English or German tin) and were being fired with Italian sulfur and saltpeter from the East Indies.[59]

To get a weight of fire, both the English and the Prussians equipped their troops with muskets without sights. Troops were not to take aim but merely to fire straight ahead. Although "rifled" guns were known, they were not regarded as military arms since forcing the lead bullet down the barrel took too long in battle in mass formations. (It was not until about the time of the American Civil War that accuracy became a major objective.) And it was in this tradition that the machine gun was developed: there was no way to aim each bullet, so the target was to be saturated in the expectation that some rounds would hit. The machine gun came into its own in the trenches of World War I, where it was used to mow down attacking waves of infantry when they were slowed by barbed-wire entanglements.

Meanwhile, the British experimented with a very old form of propelled explosive, known to the Chinese in medieval times—the rocket. Their Congreve had the advantage of not requiring a heavy platform or carriage, as conventional artillery did; although not very accurate or powerful, it was in service from 1805 through the Crimean War. In a sense, we may take it as the direct ancestor of the missile technology re-created by the Germans during World War II and that in turn gave birth to the massive deployment of long-range and nuclear-armed missiles by the United States and the Soviet Union during the Cold War.

Somewhere between aircraft and rockets are cruise missiles, which have been called the "poor man's air force." For an expenditure even underdeveloped nations can afford, it is possible to buy hundreds of cruise missiles. Even more attractive to many third-world governments, neither the weapons nor the bureaucracies that control them can be so easily employed in coups d'etat as conventional air forces manning fighter-bombers.

What is happening in the missile field is shaping military doctrine in the advanced countries. Whereas hundreds of thousands of young men were sacrificed in the trenches in World War I, military planners are today trying to substitute high technology and massive power for the soldier. The 1991 Persian Gulf War is a stunning recent example: in that war, 210,000 conventional bombs, 93,000 "smart" bombs, and more than 300 cruise missiles were hurled against the Iraqi army, with the result that casualties among the attacking forces were extremely small and many of those were probably due to friendly fire.

Finally, despite repeated patriotic calls for preparedness, it must be said that the availability of arms has probably never prevented the outbreak of war (at least not until the advent of nuclear arms, and on this the question is still open), but there is solid historical evidence that many wars have been started in the quest for security. Thus, the irony arises on the level of great societies, as it does within the individual body, that the pursuit of security can itself prove lethal.

＊ ＊ ＊ ＊ ＊ ＊ ＊

12 MODERN ARMIES

With peasant soldiers armed with guns, actually counting for more than obstructions to the movement of enemy forces and able to hold their own against elite noblemen, armies multiplied rapidly in size. During the seventeenth century, 10 to 12 million Europeans served as soldiers; economic stress, indeed large-scale starvation, made recruitment easy, with a high portion coming from beyond the frontiers of each country. Soldiers were an international commodity whose own states often were glad to get rid of them because many, as in previous centuries, were the equivalent of the homeless of modern times. And, as armies grew on hopes of food and plunder, or "the comparative security of being the robber and not the robbed," the numbers of camp followers also multiplied, to as many as five for each soldier, so that even relatively small *armies* became large *societies* on the move, often dwarfing sizable towns and creating a huge demand for food. To recruit the soldiers, at least a thousand men acted as agents, and to feed them hundreds of jobbers and suppliers went to work for the various governments. The war business was creating a whole new society.

As John Nef has pointed out, however, despite the fact that "expansion by conquest is one of the oldest and most elemental of human passions," in the century after about 1660 rulers were constrained by various considerations.[60] First, there was a severe shortage of war materials, notably iron and timber and the cash to acquire them; second, and more subtly, there was a cultural inhibition, not unlike that operating in Japan, which emphasized an aesthetics of restraint. After the end of the religious wars in the seventeenth century, Europeans were not motivated by any grand ideology to kill one another. Paradoxically, the major innovation in infantry weaponry, the bayonet—which was originally used by hunters to "close" with dangerous animals and so to enhance the thrill of the sport—was introduced just when soldiers no longer were motivated to inflict grievous pain face-to-face. Even Louis XV, the heir to that great warlord Louis XIV, refused to issue to his armies an improved gunpowder because he deemed it too lethal. Weapons, particularly warships and cannon, were transformed into works of art even when doing so diminished their effectiveness.

The great new ships built in the early sixteenth century show this emphasis on aesthetics. As Carlo Cipolla writes of the English *Harry Grace à Dieu,* built in 1514, and its French, Portuguese, and Swedish counterparts, "With their colourful flags and their fantastically ornate castles they diffused an aura of grandeur and pageantry. They were magnificent as well as formidable but they were very clumsy to manoeuvre. . . . The great ship had become a sea-fortress rather than a manoeuverable weapon of war."[61] And this style carried over into land weapons. Cipolla also mentions "the extravagance of some contemporary Italians who for the sake of beauty were engraving and decorating not only the guns but even the balls, knowing perfectly well that this was detrimental to the efficiency of artillery." Not until the industrial revolution had altered all these concepts would total war again be possible.

As a beneficiary of both that revolution and the social revolution in France, Napoleon may be regarded as the first modern military commander. The contrast between revolutionary France and the conservative Hapsburg military establishment is brought out in the battles of October 1805. In a campaign lasting only twelve days and culminating in the Battle of Ulm, Napoleon trapped the main Austrian army and killed or captured about sixty thousand men, or approximately 1 percent of Austria's militarily effective adult male population. For Napoleon, war had become a mobile slaughterhouse. For the Austrians, it was still a gentlemanly joust. The apotheosis of the (to the French) quaint Austrian approach to war may be seen in the (to the French) pathetic appeal of a senior Austrian general to Napoleon's cavalry commander, Marshal Joachim Murat, not to press too hard because the Austrian soldiers were badly in need of a rest.[62]

Of such niceties, little remained in the American Civil War, although correspondence between northern and southern generals, most of whom had been schooled together at the United States Military Academy at West

Point and had served together, was often chivalrous. Generals Grant and Polk, for example, arranged various truces, exchanged prisoners, cared for wounded, allowed wives to visit the sick and, in their correspondence, each signed himself, "I am, general, very respectfully, your obedient servant . . ."[63] Such sentiments did not, however, prevent either side from dealing extremely harshly with prisoners of war, starving or burning out civilian populations, and, in the final campaign by General Sherman, using scorched-earth tactics. Proportionally, the Civil War produced more casualties than any war fought by the United States.

The most impressive military machine of modern times, the German army grew out of the Prussian tradition. At its heart was the officer corps, which in turn was deeply intertwined with a still-medieval social and ethical order. The officer corps saw its duty as dual: defend the "warlord," the kaiser, from his foreign foes and prevent internal sedition.[64] Noble families were expected to send at least one son into the army, whereas the despised bourgeoisie was effectively excluded from military service. Prussia, as Geoffrey Best has written, was "a society hand-made for war," or as an eighteenth-century Frenchman said, "La guerre est l'industrie nationale de la Prusse." In the eighteenth century the Prussian army absorbed a larger proportion of the population and gross national product than that of any European state—one in each four young men and 90 percent of government revenues.

After the Prussian defeat by Napoleon at the battle of Jena in 1806, Gerhard von Scharnhorst formed a group of mainly non-Prussian officers (including Carl von Clausewitz) to modernize the army. They saw that change was necessary and would have to involve not only tactics and arms but the "spirit" of the army. This was rejected as too radical until the defeat of Napoleon in Russia in 1813 made possible the introduction of the very concept that the conservative forces of Europe had long opposed: nationalism. A nationalist sentiment was already being popularized by such publicists, poets, and philosophers as Schiller, Herder, Luden, and, above all, Fichte, whose 1807 Berlin lectures (later published as *Addresses to the German Nation*) electrified German youth. As interpreted by the military reformers, nationalism found its expression in the introduction of conscription for the regular army and compulsory service in the Landwehr, a sort of national guard. These two changes made it possible for Prussia to assemble a military force of more than half a million men, or twice what Frederick the Great had at the height of his powers. It was the first units of this new force (together with the British under Wellington) that destroyed Napoleon's army at Waterloo.

For roughly the next half-century, the new Prussian officer corps had to content itself with war games rather than war, but it used the time to develop the meticulous planning and academic analysis that made its general staff the exemplar for all modern armies. A leading student of the German army called the introduction of the general staff concept "an event in military science comparable in importance to the innovation of the ironclad and of aerial and mechanized warfare." He also quotes the great German general Alfred von Schlieffen as believing that the lack of such an organization had been the ultimate cause of Napoleon's defeat.[65]

Finally, in 1866, the Prussian army was able to try out its new skills in the war against the Hapsburg Empire, where its stunning victory swung the smaller German states into the Prussian orbit. The Prussian army then overwhelmed France in a new-style campaign, a precursor of the later blitzkrieg, taking Paris and forcing an abject French surrender in 1870. In two short campaigns, the army had made possible the empire that Bismarck had been working for a generation to create.

Around the turn of the century, Europe divided itself into two heavily armed camps. The trigger was pulled by others, but for many, particularly among the Germans, war had become *eine innere Notwendigkeit* (a spiritual necessity). Germany declared war on Russia on August 1, 1914. That brought France into the war as Russia's ally, whereupon, implementing its "Schlieffen Plan," the German army plunged into Belgium, and that brought Britain into the war. It was in large part the rigidity of the military plan that forced war on both Britain and France. In a reverse of Clausewitz, war (or at least war planning) was setting policy rather than implementing it.

Five German armies then poured into northern France through Belgium (just as their successors were to do in 1940) and ran head-on into also-attacking French forces. Both officer corps thought that the war would be short—the German estimate was six weeks—glorious and only sufficiently painful to bring out deeds of heroism. Up to that point, they were right: the war began with pomp and circumstance, gorgeous uniforms, jaunty parades, and uplifting sermons. Safely ensconced in their ministries, statesmen pondered what to do with the spoils of victory.

Reality, like a noxious fog, soon obscured that sunny day as the armies shed their dress uniforms and slithered into the mud of the trenches. Under the incessant pounding of artillery, rats and vermin proved to be the best equipped to survive. Barbed wire and poison gas had not figured in the ringing proclamations of the leaders. Grand ideas of strategy collapsed, but the generals, like punch-drunk boxers, continued to pound one another, inflicting and incurring catastrophic losses without hope of victory. Every attack was a slaughter; every retreat, a rout; every day of immobility, an execution.

From at least 1916 the specter of defeat was manifest to both sides. A whole generation of Englishmen, Frenchmen, Russians, and Germans was being slaughtered in the trenches along the western front. More soldiers were killed in actions of a single day than had even been present in most of the greatest battles of the nineteenth century. Britain lost 60,000 men in one day in 1916 at the battle of the Somme. France suffered even more than Britain; at Verdun in the spring of 1916, the French army lost more than 350,000 men. Russia suffered worst of all—its losses were so large as to be counted not by men but by whole armies.

But war was not only about men. It was also about food, raw materials, and energy. These were "wasted" at prodigious rates. The cost of the war could never be fully reckoned. Perhaps 37 million soldiers and 10 million civilians were killed or wounded; about the same number died of disease or starvation; France, where most of the fighting took place, had 8,000 square miles of agricultural land, nearly 2,000 square miles of forest, and about 250,000 buildings literally ripped apart. The money figure, often put at nearly $400 billion, is perhaps meaningless, but the British Empire and Germany were both bankrupted.

Yet, the German army, as distinct from the economy that supported it, came out of the war relatively intact, and this gave rise to the myth, later exploited by Hitler and believed by many Germans, that Germany was sold out by its civilian politicians. No responsible German military officer ever admitted the truth, and almost immediately the German army began to rebuild itself.

Both the civilian government of the Weimar Republic and the high command of the army were caught between two pressures: on the one hand, the Allies imposed on Germany stringent restrictions on the size of its army. The army was limited to one hundred thousand men—about double what Napoleon had allowed Prussia a century earlier—including four thousand officers. It was to have no tanks, aircraft, or offensive weapons, and the general staff was to be abolished. On the other hand, domestically, the radical right, which ultimately coalesced behind Hitler as the Nazi Party, pressed for rearming. So the government vacillated. Hardly was the ink dry on the peace treaty before a commission was established to re-create the army.[66] To head this group, in effect a new general staff, came one of the most distinguished and highly decorated members of the old general staff, General Hans von Seeckt.

Seeckt knew exactly what he was about and quickly carved out a position for himself among the warring parties in German politics: he made himself indispensable to the civilians by using his troops to smash their left-wing opponents and to control the right. His single-minded objective was to keep the army united so he could rebuild it. (Like Scharnhorst a century earlier, he set about evading the restrictions on the army, but the means he chose were remarkably different: despite the horror the German army had created in Russia and the implacable hatred its conservative officers felt toward Communism, Seeckt arranged for the retreating German forces in Russia to help the Communists take over each area they evacuated. What Seeckt banked on happened. In 1921 Lenin requested German military help in building the Red Army.)

"Military assistance," as both sides realized, was only a cover for rearmament and reconstruction. Almost immediately a Junkers factory was established near Moscow to build new aircraft; another was set up to manufacture poison gas; and a third, artillery shells. Training establishments were also set up for crews of tanks and aircraft. For fifteen years, until Hitler abrogated the Versailles Treaty and clandestine activity was no longer required, Russia was to be the secret training ground for the German army. Lenin and Stalin thus cooperated in building the machine that would nearly destroy Russia in World War II.

At the same time, Seeckt set up what he called a *Rüstungsamt* (economic general staff) to design standardized equipment and to prepare plans for industrial support of a modern army of sixty-three divisions. This group also was empowered to seek alliances with industrial firms in a number of European countries to manufacture forbidden equipment. German industry rose to the challenge, and by 1928 tanks and even U-boats were being constructed in plants owned by German industrial firms in Holland, Spain, Turkey, and Finland. When he came to power, Hitler mobilized the thousands of out-of-work Germans into Nazi Party paramilitary groups and in March 1935 reintroduced conscription to the Wehrmacht. At the same time, he ordered the formation under the command of Heinrich Himmler of the SS Verfügungstruppe, the nucleus of the first SS division. Two months later he bragged that the Luftwaffe, created in secret in Russia, was already larger than the R.A.F. In 1936, plans were set for a wartime army of forty-one regular divisions together with a reserve of twenty-five cadre divisions, and shortly thereafter the Spanish Civil War provided an occasion for equipment testing and live-ammunition training.

The Wehrmacht high command and the Nazis had somewhat different interpretations of their roles. General Seeckt, having met Hitler in 1923, wrote, "We were one in our aim; only our paths were different."[67] Seeckt's successors in the 1930s began to grow wary of Hitler, however, and they despised his lower-class followers. Moreover, they regarded the army as their preserve and insisted that it remain the only organized German military force. So they resisted the formation of the Nazi Party army, the SS. Hitler initially promised to honor their position, but, taking advantage of a trumped-up scandal in the general staff, in February 1938 he took over command of the armed forces and initiated the first of three purges of the general officer corps.[68] Thus, when the Germans moved into Austria in the *Anschluss,* the Wehrmacht emerged from the shadows not only as a powerful, modern force but also one firmly under Nazi control. Germany was ready for World War II.

The events of the war are beyond the scope of this book; it is remarkable, however, that for all its military planning, Germany repeated crucial mistakes of World War I: fighting a war on two fronts, failing to implement its plan of attack in the west (by letting the British army escape at Dunkirk), allowing itself to lose its mobility (particularly on the Russian front), failing to stockpile for a long war, and, perhaps unnecessarily, forcing America into the war. Defeat shattered the German army but, in a very different form, it began to be reconstituted a few years later and is again the most powerful military force in Europe.

· · ·

Finally, I turn to the mobilization and finance of armies, particularly as influenced by the growth of technology and changes in emotional commitment. Most of what I have to say here concerns the period since World War II, but I begin with early examples in order to put recent developments into context.

As we have seen, the most primitive armies were essentially entire societies that were motivated either by the "sport" or drama of conflict or by the stark terror of extermination; because their conflicts were of short duration, each warrior cared for himself. It was not until the rise of the great empires that soldiers expected to be paid and cared for. Ancient Assyria led the way, closely followed by Persia, which relied increasingly on alien mercenary troops. Greek armies were small and popular, so pay was not a significant issue until the protracted wars between Athens and Sparta. The big transformation came in the Far East in the Warring States period when first Lu in 594 B.C.E. and then other Chinese states began to levy taxes to pay for their armies and military industries. In the West, Rome went through the whole process during its long history, moving from unpaid militia to citizen soldiers who were compensated primarily by booty and to foreign mercenary soldiers who often received land grants.

In the early medieval period, the small "states" of the West hardly used money; soldiers were treated as retainers of lords from whom they received grants of land and serfs sufficient to maintain their equipment and supplies. Then, beginning in Italy, intense competition among states together with the transformation of commerce re-created money economies. It has been estimated that, on average, about 80 percent of the income of the states went to pay for the military during peacetime and that some campaigns cost as much as ten times the yearly income. As increasing use was made of both gunpowder and mercenaries, particularly of mercenary cavalry, warfare escalated in cost. A military unit called a "lance," that is, two men-at-arms and a page, cost every day as much as a skilled artisan earned in a week. These expenses forced Florence, as they had the Chinese state of Lu two thousand years earlier, to institute a comprehensive tax system, the *catasto,* and also promoted the rise of what became the great banking houses—those who could raise money and lend it to the state. As Carlo Cipolla has written, "Public debt was an invention of the Italian city-states of the Middle Ages . . . following the series of wars in which Florence became involved in the 1330s."[69] And this process quickly escalated: as the Italian city-states became unable to afford their armies, the mercenary armies themselves grew into virtual states. The *condottiere* became less employees of the states than their masters.

In England, the problem was the same but the solution was different. Because the monarchy had to get Parliament to raise and allocate funds, Parliament began the process that eventually would turn England into a constitutional monarchy. It was this tradition that became embedded in the United States Constitution and remains a key element in the separation of powers, with the executive controlling the army (and other bureaucracies) but the legislature controlling the funds. So, in contrast to Italy and other European states, inflation of military budgets played a role both in England and America in the coming to power of representative institutions.

Involvement of citizens in the military has grown steadily in recent centuries. It has been estimated that in the eighteenth century only about thirty-three in each one thousand citizens could be mobilized; this is roughly the same as in many third-world countries today. And, at least in part, the reasons are probably the same—lack of social cohesion and emotional engagement: war was regarded as the sport of kings in which the common man was merely a pawn. This attitude began to change under the impact of the French Revolution and the rise of nationalism. Consequently, as mentioned above, by the time of World War I the citizens of both sides greeted its outbreak ecstatically and made it (at least at first) a national cause. We can see the transformation in a single statistic: in that war, as many as one hundred forty in a thousand Europeans were mobilized. And although those who remembered the horror of World War I were perhaps less enthusiastic about participating in World War II, they joined in their millions not only as soldiers but also as "war workers" in even greater numbers.

The figures are astounding. First, the armed forces: the Soviet Union, 22 million; the United States, 15 million; the British Empire, 12 million; Germany, 17 million. But it was American industrial output that more than any other feature put World War II in a class unique to history. Ship production went from 1 million tons a year at the start of the war to 19 million tons a year; aircraft production, from 6,000 to 96,000 for an aggregate of 275,000 planes; tank production went from virtually nothing to 21,000, and landing craft, similarly, from zero to an aggregate of 64,000. America was able to supply the Russians with more than half a million trucks, more than 2,000 locomotives, 11,000 freight cars, and more than half a million tons of rails and to supply the British with 86,000 Jeeps and thousands of tanks and aircraft and related equipment. The U.S. federal budget rose from $13 billion in 1939 to $71 billion in 1944, and the labor force increased by nearly 20 million.

After a brief hiatus, the American economy geared up again for the Cold War and the Korean, Vietnamese, and Persian Gulf wars. The expenditures are most impressive for the Americans, but by 1959 the United States had fallen to seventeenth place among world states in terms of the percentage of the population engaged in the military.[70] At that time, Jordan was spending almost 26 percent of its GNP on defense, the USSR about 12 percent, and the United States just short of 10 percent. During the 1980s, the United States spent more than $3 trillion, three-quarters of the current national debt, on its military.

In 1995, after the Russian threat was deemed to have ended, the U.S. defense budget stood at $262 billion; but this represented a smaller proportion of GNP than any military budget since America entered World War II—4 percent; this 4 percent, however, aggregated to an outlay approximately three times as much as any other country and more than all potential enemies and neutrals combined. Indeed, more than $1 in each $3 spent anywhere in the world was spent by the United States, with the former Soviet Union spending less than one-quarter of the U.S. budget.

And, what the major powers are doing is being widely copied. In fact, the major industrial powers, especially the United States, Russia, the United Kingdom, and France, actively promote their arms exports to developing countries; in 1995, Russia moved into first place with sales amounting to 39 percent of international arms sales, as compared to 25 percent for the United States. The countries of the Middle East alone have ordered about $600 billion worth of arms in the last twenty years. The biggest customers are the members of the Gulf Cooperation Council, of which the largest has been Saudi Arabia, but now even the tiny United Arab Emirates has moved into the same league. Fresh from concluding a tank deal with France worth approximately $3 billion, the U.A.E. has indicated its desire to buy $6 billion worth of long-range strike aircraft (which it does not have the capacity to employ). What is interesting about the latter deal is that the U.A.E. has made the purchase conditional on the conclusion of a defensive alliance with the supplying country. Bluntly put, it was buying a defensive alliance by subsidizing Western industry.

So important to the defense industries of Europe, the United States, and the former Soviet Union do such contracts appear that not only industries but national governments compete to become the supplier of choice. The reason is simple: defense accounted for international sales of $64 billion in 1984, and although the market is shrinking it was still nearly $40 billion in 1995. The three largest American companies had sales in 1994 of approximately $41 billion and employed tens of thousands of workers. The two largest British firms produced sales of nearly $12 billion, and the two largest French firms, about $8 billion.

So massive has the arms industry become that it has been built into national—and international—economies to such an extent that it has developed, for perhaps the first time in history, a momentum and a constituency that have little to do with the traditional role of the military or even with war. Thus it seems reasonable to predict that, although the danger of war has certainly not ended and although military activities are probably even more pervasive than in the past, we are today moving into a new dimension of military-industrial international commerce.

If we consider the amounts of energy, resources, and time devoted to warfare throughout history, in virtually all known societies and in every form of ecology, we must conclude that there is no discontinuity between what we observed in part 1 on the "micro" level within our bodies and on the "macro" level among societies. The struggle against the alien and therefore the enemy has always been nearly constant. However hard we try to avoid it, as we surely must, warfare appears to be a "natural" aspect of our lives. But it is important to realize that, just as our bodies manage to find means of accommodation with aliens, so, on the social level, do we. It is to one such form of accommodation that I now turn.

PART IV NONGOVERNMENTAL RELATIONS

· · · · · · ·

13 TRADE

Trade is a peculiarly human activity. Unlike the other aspects of the lives of early man—protecting territory, organizing societies, hunting and gathering, and even practicing rudimentary agriculture—it is unknown among animals. But among people it began early, is practiced in virtually every known society, and is one of mankind's strongest habits. Consequently, as Edward O. Wilson has observed, "only man has an economy. His high intelligence and symbolizing ability make true barter possible. Intelligence also permits the exchanges to be stretched out in time, converting them into acts of reciprocal altruism."[1]

Using other words, this was more or less what Adam Smith wrote more than two centuries ago in *The Wealth of Nations*. He found the cause of the division of labor, "from which so many advantages are derived," to be "the necessary, though very slow and gradual, consequence of a certain propensity to truck, barter, and exchange one thing for another." It was everywhere evident, but where it came from baffled Smith: "Whether this propensity be one of those original principles in human nature, of which no further account can be given; or whether, as seems more probable, it be the necessary consequence of the faculties of reason and speech . . . [i]t is common to all men, and to be found in no other race of animals."[2]

So important is this "propensity to truck, barter, and exchange one thing for another" and yet so little understood or appreciated has it traditionally been by those who concern themselves with foreign affairs that it is often shoved aside as "just economics" and is rarely accorded a serious place in foreign offices and departments of state. Therefore, in this part of the book I will speculate on how trade came about, show how its agents— merchants—have been treated, illustrate the routes it took and the ties it created, discuss the goods traded, analyze the impact they had on the societies concerned, and, finally, bring the story up to our times with some thoughts on currencies, commodities, development, and free trade. First, the way trade began.

As I pointed out in chapter 2, hunters and gatherers, living on the edge of subsistence, had few "needs" and even fewer exchangeable items. With little to go on, we imagine that trade began when there was something to be shared. Probably that would have been the carcass of a wild animal, newly killed in a joint hunt, that was too large for a single group to handle or consume: then portions of it might have been given to kinsmen or neighbors in the hope that they would reciprocate at some future time. Experiences of this sort, repeated frequently, would have gradually suggested the idea and formed a pattern of gift exchange.

Exchanging gifts is common among a few "modern" primitive peoples whose practices have been analyzed by the French sociologist Marcel Mauss. *Gift*, he observes, is to some extent a misnomer since the transaction imposes known, accepted, and often severe obligations. The giver must give and the receiver must repay. The things exchanged, moreover, take on a sort of magical power sanctifying the exchange. The occasion is thus lifted above the commonplace. Those who take part are bound together and protected by observance of the ritual.[3] Gift giving transmutes what might have been a violent act—the seizure of goods—into a ritually controlled new relationship between the giver and the recipient. Indeed, Marshall Sahlins goes so far as to argue that the "gift is the primitive way of achieving the peace that in civil society is secured by the State. . . . The primitive analogue of social contract is not the State, but the gift."[4]

Hobbes identified greed, self-protection ("diffidence," he called it), and the quest for glory as major causes of hostilities. Exchange of gifts assuages or satisfies each. Greed is satisfied because the desired object is obtained; self-protection, because the sanctions that surround the transaction create a "peace of the marketplace." And finally, both the giver and the recipient, who must eventually return the favor, gain in stature in the eyes of their colleagues. On the surface, mutual gift giving would appear to be the ideal interpersonal relationship; yet, as we shall see, it is not an easy one.

The !Kung Bushmen show us how structured and how obligatory is the "gift." Elizabeth Thomas reports in *The Harmless People* that when a gift-giving situation arises Bushmen use the occasion to relieve tensions severe enough to precipitate hostilities. The ceremony of "potlatch" among the Indians of the American northwest, as Mauss observed, even links the apparently conflicting ideas and vocabulary of food, exchange, and vengeance.[5] In ancient Mesopotamia, the giving of gifts among rulers, as among the !Kung Bushmen, was precisely measured and exact reciprocity was expected. A clay tablet found at Mari puts it as bluntly as possible: "This matter is unspeakable," wrote the ruler of Qatna to the new king of Assyria, "yet I must speak and give vent to my feeling. You are a great king; you asked me for two horses, and I sent them to you. And you sent me two minas of tin. Don't you want to deal fairly with me? This is a paltry amount of tin that you sent me! . . . If you had sent no tin at all, by the god of my father! I would not have been so angry! You are no great king."[6]

Gifts were not always welcomed by the recipients. This is because they were not precisely gifts but merged into concepts we differentiate as trade and tribute. Among the Japanese, *giri*, the "gift" of either goods or deeds, imposes an obligation on the recipient and so may cause him to fear the donation and to resent the donor. For this reason, the Japanese describe *giri* as the thing "hardest to bear."[7] This theme runs through the remarkable filigree of the patterns we can see among widely divergent cultures.

In any form, gift, trade, or tribute, interplay with others through the medium of goods has always been tense, touching as it does on fundamental needs for food or those things symbolizing food, evoking hunger or desires and envies that gnaw at a person and that, even in being satisfied, impose obligations that threaten the person's well-being in the future. As hard as these things are to bear among close kindred, they often descend quickly into violence when practiced with the stranger.

We can observe both the violence-causing and peace-making aspects of the exchange of goods as animals share food. When one acquires a particularly attractive article, others will beg or attempt to steal what he has. Fights often break out, but occasionally the owner will give or allow others to take part of the spoils. From apparent chaos, a sequence or process emerges in which tensions mount when one has control and the others are driven by their desires; then, apparently inevitably, comes a moment in which there is danger of violence. This can be eased only by the disappearance of the object (as the owner hurriedly eats it or runs away with it), a fight (after which the loser withdraws), or by sharing.

We see both the process and various solutions in human societies. Since most small primitive societies ate around a common pot there was little to distinguish the "rich" from the "poor," but since there was often little to share, all contended for enough to satisfy hunger. As societies became larger, more elaborate, and less directly based on kinship, opportunities for social distinctions also grew and naturally exacerbated anxieties and angers. In some ancient Greek cities, the less fortunate learned how to *ostracize* those they envied.[8] In other societies, for example, the Cheyenne, social unrest was eased by the toleration of a high incidence of theft.[9] In whatever form it took, sharing was the norm and hoarding the exception.

Early trade probably began, as among the !Kung, with the sharing of a large kill among clans that had only recently split off from one another. From there the logical (but not easy) step would have been to share certain difficult-to-obtain necessities such as salt with neighbors. They, in turn, would deal with others further from the source of supply. And so on, in a chain of groups each interlocked by kinship or neighborhood with those nearby but perhaps unaware of the distant participants. Herodotus mentions just such a practice when he speaks of the Scythians as taking their goods "to their neighbors to see them conveyed to their destination by a process of relay, from one nation to another." And he comments that he knew of similar practices in his own time.[10] In this fashion, no group would have had to deal with completely alien peoples. All that mattered was that each link in the chain be able to join the next. Since salt leaves no traces, we cannot reconstruct this chain for very early trade, but we can at least get hold of the two ends of the chain, as I will show, when the exchanges came to involve durable and identifiable items such as flint, lapis, amber, and obsidian.

It was when trade came to involve true strangers that it became more dangerous and required the creation of a more abstract mechanism. We get some indication of what may have happened from what is known of trade among hunter-gatherers and nomads of two widely separated areas. In the first, an Arab geographer of the fourteenth century C.E. has described the trade among primitive fur hunters of the north of Russia. There, he said, exchange was transacted without any contact or even sighting by the two partners. As Abu'l-Fida' observed,[11] those who had objects to exchange went to an identified site. Possibly this was a local sanctuary—if Abu'l-Fida' knew, he does not tell us. But we know that sanctuaries are common among most primitive peoples. Among the American Indian tribes and peoples of the ancient Near East, for example, various religious taboos protected those within identified areas from one another and from outsiders.

Once at the agreed spot, the newcomers laid out the goods they wished to exchange and left. Then the natives approached and displayed their goods and retired. Next, the foreigners returned and, if satisfied, took the goods of the natives. If not satisfied, they reclaimed their own goods and departed. Presumably, those who were not satisfied tried again at another time or went to another settlement.

The second area is the Atlantic coast of Africa, where Herodotus describes Carthaginian trade. There, sailors would unload their wares and arrange them on the beach. Then they would make a smoke signal to alert the natives and reboard their ships. The natives would then approach to lay out what they judged a fair amount of gold and withdraw. The sailors would disembark in order to inspect the gold. If they were not satisfied, they would go back to their boats and wait. When, finally, both sides were satisfied, the Carthaginians would gather up the gold and depart. Perhaps unrealistically, Herodotus comments, "neither side deals unfairly by the other: for they themselves never touch the gold till it comes up to the worth of their goods, nor do the natives carry off the goods till the gold is taken away."[12] Since these two groups of peoples were so widely separated in time and place, there seems no possibility of one group's "learning" about trade from the others. What Walter Goldschmidt writes of the Nomlaki Indians of the Pacific northwest in the twentieth century differs little from what Herodotus wrote of the West Africans twenty-five hundred years ago. And Captain James Cook, certainly not aware of these practices elsewhere, employed the same techniques successfully during a visit to New Zealand in 1773. Aptly termed "the silent trade," this widely practiced form of interaction with the feared stranger whose goods were coveted must often have not worked—when those too greedy or strong abused it—yet it was constantly reemployed or reinvented as the appetite for exotic goods grew.

The next step in the evolution of trade must have been taken when experience of mutual benefit, in reasonable security, had led to confidence. This stage was observed by Bronislaw Malinowski in the Trobriand Islands. There, he said, the natives wishing to make *kula* (intertribal trade), like the traders described by Herodotus, laid their items out on the beach, but they stayed with their goods. That created new dangers for the traders, who now had to meet face-to-face those who coveted the goods. Consequently, "every movement of the Kula articles, every detail of the transactions is . . . rooted in myth, backed by traditional law, and surrounded with magical rites. All its main transactions are public and ceremonial, and carried out according to definite rules. It is not done on the spur of the moment, but happens periodically, at dates settled in advance and is carried on along definite trade routes, which must lead to fixed trysting places."[13]

Putting this together with the previous examples, we observe that so widespread have been these forms of exchange for at least the past four thousand years that they must have formed a "natural" response to perceived needs. Trade was here to stay.

But trade, as I have observed, was more complex than mere acquisition of goods; it involved the establishment of a process leading to other results. Adam Smith, who doubtless heard stories of how ships' captains had begun trade with hostile natives, correctly perceived trading as a force to build society. No individual, he pointed out, lived long enough to form associations of any magnitude, nor could he rely on the benevolence of strangers to get what he might need. The mechanisms of trade accomplished both desires. Smith might have been surprised to discover, however, that *economics* (improving or lessening one's relative position) or even *acquisition* (getting some *thing* one wanted) often played a minor role in trading transactions. For example, in the Trobriand Islands, Malinowski found that many of the items traded were useless to those receiving them or were soon given away. Similarly, among the South American Yanomamö, Napoleon Chagnon observed that each village was capable of being self-sufficient and each produced essentially identical goods. To form an alliance based on trade, each group had to give up making certain items in order to create the need to acquire them from its partner. If the alliance failed, each then began again to produce the items it had given up making. Yanomamö trade is thus not only not "economic" but is in fact *countereconomic.*[14]

Trade and raid both accomplish the acquisition of goods. The difference in the means and the result is obvious, but what may be more interesting is that they often follow different routes and occur, structurally or conceptually, between different groups. Among the Maring agricultural peoples of New Guinea, whose warfare I discussed in part 3, hostilities always occur between neighbors, whereas trade occurs between distant groups.[15] That was true also in Jericho. Why is this a common pattern? On the surface, the reason appears simple: those nearby share an essentially similar ecology so that at least the economic aspects of trade are not satisfied by dealings with them. Also significant is the fact that near neighbors may pose a danger because they can quickly attack. Remote peoples are precisely the reverse in each regard: they produce different goods and so are attractive trading partners but, being distant, pose little military threat. For these reasons, the Hebrew prophets advised their people to slaughter their nearer enemies while entering into mutually beneficial economic ties with those further afield. Similar advice was given in the first great treatise on strategy by an Indian "politico-military" expert: Vishnugupta advises his prince to enlist distant peoples against the nearer enemies.[16]

Did people always become (relatively) friendly with distant peoples while regarding their neighbors with more hostility? It does not appear so. In both animal societies and small primitive human groups, distance, by increasing strangeness, normally intensifies hostility. But it seems that a change took place at some time, perhaps coincident with the Neolithic revolution when people acquired goods to protect and trade; at least since then societies often evince less hostility to the distant alien than to the nearer neighbor. Attitudes toward the immediate neighbor remained constant: he was dangerous.

At least to rulers if not to merchants, trade was often linked to other or, as they would have thought, "larger" interests. Consequently, rulers often sought to manage it. In one of the earliest Sumerian documents, we can see in mythic terms the attempt by Uruk to buy goods under what we would call a tributary relationship from the town of Aratta.[17] In a heavy-handed way Uruk tried to force Aratta to build a temple in territory controlled by Uruk. The temple was to be filled with valuable and, in Uruk, unobtainable, items. From our rather more materialistic point of view, that was the key element; but to contemporaries, perhaps equally important was the calculation that when Aratta put the statues of its gods in Uruk territory, Uruk could hold them "hostage" as the Sumerian cities often did to one another's gods. Materialist or symbolist, the ruler of Aratta refused. So the king of Uruk sent an ambassador—our first documentation of this role—to demand retribution in the form of precious metals. In reply, Aratta agreed to provide the metals against a reciprocal gift. After a certain amount of haggling and threatening display, both common in early international trade, the deal was made.

State-to-state relations between the Phoenicians and the Hebrews are set out in the Bible. In 1 Kings 9–14 we are told that Solomon sent to Hiram king of Tyre requesting timber to build "an house unto the name of the Lord his God." Apparently, the trading relationship that grew out of this request was so successful that the Phoenicians and Hebrews established a joint trading station at the head of the Gulf of Aqaba from which they sent a mission to the still-unidentified land of Ophir. And closer to home, the two monarchs entered into a remarkable exchange of goods for territory in what must have been the first international multi-year aid program.

Perhaps the most sophisticated early use of trade was in Han China, where, beset by constant warfare on the northern frontier, the emperor Wen cast about for a means to tame the wild nomads. A policy planner named Chia I recommended the use of trade to accomplish what arms had failed to do: lure the Xiongnu into a way of life that would politically emasculate them. He proposed, in what he called the "five baits," the sale or provision of Chinese luxuries to change the way of life of the nomads.[18] As a coherent plan, Chia I's suggestion was not acted on. (Few grand plans ever are.) It was too long-range and subtle. Yet it did shape thought, and, as the individual desires and needs of the participants shaped their actions, it did forecast events. Rather than spending vast treasure on trying to keep the nomads beyond the barrier, it would be better, Chia I had argued, to bring them, at least psychologically and customarily, into China. That much happened. Trade turned out to be profitable and merchants on each side of the Wall established contacts; tastes changed; religion was challenged, altered, and even replaced; and at least temporarily warfare ceased to be a major threat.

About two thousand years later and far across Asia, the Ottoman government embarked on a comparable policy, forcing or luring into settlement the nomadic Arab tribes of Mesopotamia and Syria. Its policy was continued by British Mandate Government and the independent kingdom in Iraq and by the French Mandate Government and the independent republic in Syria.[19]

From obscure beginnings trade was itself traded back and forth between those who would use it for other purposes and those who saw it merely as a means of passing goods between producers and consumers. Rarely was it the sole preserve of either side; even in times of strong state control, there were areas of freedom, and even in times of apparent freedom, there were (and are today) significant areas of state control. The archaeology of the modern town of Maadi shows us a different Egypt from that of dynastic times. For several hundred years before the first dynasty, Maadi supported a vigorous commercial community. Located on the main route to the copper mines of the Sinai Peninsula, it not only imported ore but, apparently, also processed it and marketed it over a wide area. From the form of houses uncovered there, contacts with the Levant appear to have been intimate. Maadi may even have had a resident alien merchant community.[20] And Maadi was probably not unique. According to Michael Hoffman, at about the same time, further to the east, along the Red Sea, other merchants and shippers were "linking various economies of the ancient Middle East in a vast superexchange network that revolved around symbolically prestigious, exotic goods increasingly in demand by the emergent social and political elite from Egypt to India."[21]

In that still-fluid time before the first dynasty, Egypt appeared to be on the way toward a diverse, open, and commercial society. Political authority was apparently segmented, each town walled against its rivals. In short, predynastic Egypt must have resembled Sumerian Mesopotamia and the China of the Warring States period; then, whoever it was who unified Egypt sought to dominate internal life, extirpate commercialism, and keep the foreigner as far away as possible. By early dynastic times, private initiative was viewed as little better than sedition. But in Mesopotamia, even when the Semite conqueror Sargon in the twenty-fourth century B.C.E.

suppressed the particularism of the Sumerian cities, the merchant tradition remained strong. Indeed, Sargon may have been the first of a long line of rulers who made it state policy to protect merchants, trooping the flag after trade. Elsewhere and time after time, the goods themselves— their cost, their accessibility, their potential to endanger the provider or enrich the user—determined which way the balance between state control and free enterprise would shift. So now I turn to what was traded.

In addition to mates, space, and food, modern primitive peoples learned to need things they could not produce. How old a habit this is is not known. However, Ice Age hunter-gatherers from at least 35,000 B.C.E. have left evidence of importation of seashells and flint from sites hundreds of kilometers away. Later, in Jericho, as we have seen, improved technology for gathering and processing food made it possible for the inhabitants to gather more than they consumed. In turn, being less mobile, they could accumulate and store the surplus. This gave them, for the first time in the human experience, what we might think of as *strategic* items, mainly food, both to exchange and to protect from others. Increased contact with foreigners got them involved in trade with relatively distant groups. The presence of seashells and hematite (a reddish iron oxide) shows that Jericho was in touch with people who lived near the Gulf of Aqaba, but the people of Jericho could not have bought their goods with what appears to have been the only thing they had to offer—salt from the nearby Dead Sea; rather, they had to offer what the people living near the Red Sea did not have. So, at some point they sought out other trading partners. In short, they assumed, indeed we may say created, the sophisticated role of middleman for the goods of others.

One of these other trading partners can be pinpointed by pieces of obsidian found at the ruins of Jericho. Obsidian is a volcanic glass whose chemical composition varies enough to determine which volcano it came from, and this enables archaeologists to plot trading patterns radiating from the obsidian's source. The obsidian buried in Jericho about 9,000 years ago was mined at a location roughly 800 kilometers (500 miles) away, near modern Ankara in Anatolia.[22] But it does not necessarily follow that the pieces we find today were delivered directly from Anatolia to Jericho. Probably, the movement of goods was not only along an interlocking chain as described above but was also a process taking years, decades, or even generations. One point stands out in relief, however: those who produced the obsidian could have done so only in anticipation of trading it. They were thus making a leap of imagination of startling dimensions: theretofore, in all human affairs, people had consumed or immediately used what they gathered or made. But in Anatolia, those who mined obsidian were expending their labor to get something that, in bulk, they could not have used. Then they shaped the raw materials into objects that they thought unknown peoples might find desirable. After they had done this, they had to carry the objects to some place where, they hoped, travelers would come peacefully offering in exchange objects they would want.

Behind the obsidian blade is thus not just an odyssey but a remarkable "international" process, a true revolution in foreign relations, involving at least two, and probably several, groups of people in work, anticipation, trust, and long-distance movement. Even more remarkable, in Jericho, the goods and services of a third—also absent—trading partner were involved: Jericho, itself producing little or nothing, used the produce of Anatolia to buy the seashells and hematite of the southern Jordan valley and those products to buy obsidian from Anatolia.[23]

As obsidian also shows us, for centuries or even millennia before the advent of the great, relatively well-policed civilizations of Mesopotamia, Egypt, Anatolia, and the Aegean, goods were regularly transferred over vast distances. There were no pack animals as yet, and the "boats" were probably, as in northern Europe, just some form of canoe. No true boat is in evidence for at least four thousand years after long-distance trade is known to have begun. Later, in the more developed civilizations, we see dozens of new items of exchange: in Harappan India, turquoise was brought from Turkmenia, lapis lazuli from Badakshan (in modern Afghanistan), and conch shells from the Arabian Sea. Jade beads hint at contacts with China or Chinese Turkistan. And even the earliest known pottery shows affinities with Mesopotamia. Mesopotamia brought ivory from India, lapis lazuli from Afghanistan, copper from Oman, and stone from the Anatolian and Iranian mountains. Indeed, what we find today reveals only a part of the story: metals, for example, were so expensive that, when worn or broken, they were recycled; so we find relatively few metal objects from the many that certainly were in use. But where records exist, as in the northern cities of Mari and Ebla, they indicate a profusion of goods imported from afar on a remarkably widespread network of trading relationships in western, southern, and eastern Asia and in western and northern Africa.[24]

As the urban centers in Mesopotamia, the Indus valley, and Egypt grew, the volume and kind of trade rapidly changed. No longer confined to luxury goods, traders exchanged foodstuffs and textiles from Mesopotamia for copper, timber, stones, ivory, silver, and pigments from the Indus valley. Some of these goods began to be measured in tons. At one site in Oman, an estimated one hundred thousand tons of slag show the vast extent of the copper trade. And, both in Mesopotamia and in the Indus valley, there is evidence not only of long-distance but also of vigorous inter-urban trade.

Sometime around 2500 B.C.E., relating the exchanged items to one another became too complex: some form of intermediary had to found. Although coins were as yet unknown, copper first and then tin and silver, often formed into rings, drinking vessels, or ceremonial ax heads, were used as mediums of exchange. Banking was already a recognized occupation, and the factoring of goods was commonplace. From the archives at Ebla, we know that the city stored tons of silver and large amounts of gold (which it apparently imported through Egypt). Its merchants even learned how to establish a stable price ratio between gold and other metals. Thus, profiting from countless generations of experimentation, the trader now emerges onto the world stage as a major new actor. It is to him that I now turn.

. . . .

14 THE TRADER

For millennia, the only means of transport of goods was the back of the trader, because pack animals had not yet been domesticated. But transport was not his major problem: rather, it was a combination of lack of knowledge and a lack of convention. The trader had often to venture into the territory of an alien people whose language he could not have known, whose customs and religion were strange, and who probably had no surplus food to give or exchange.[25] Every settlement was a law unto itself, so the stranger was, by definition, an outlaw. Finally, weighed down, as he had to be, with desirable goods, the merchant would have been the target of the envy or craving of everyone he met. Yet, already by 8000 B.C.E., as obsidian shows us, some men found the gamble of life and limb worth taking. And, despite what must have been frequent miscalculations, losses, and deaths, they never gave up.

Their descendants took a giant step sometime late in the third millennium as they became better organized and were joined by bankers and venture capitalists. We get our first reasonably clear picture of the new international merchants about 1900 B.C.E., when Ur was the port of entry for the Indian trade. The temple documents that illuminate this trade list offerings made by returning sailors and merchants. Their "offerings" may have constituted some sort of tax, but the documents make clear that while abroad the merchants were acting in their private capacities rather than as state agents. And they specifically differentiate venture capitalists (who assumed overseas risks) from mere moneylenders.

When Uruk, Ebla, and various walled cities in Egypt and India were built, neighborhood had long since replaced kinship as the basis of social and civic responsibility. The urban environment coagulated not only kindred but people of diverse languages and cultures. Even more striking, in Uruk we can see that aliens settled down to live more or less permanently; there, merchants from the faraway Indus valley lived outside the city walls in the area of the port, the *kâru*, with their own administration and law. This appears to be the first example known of what we now call "extraterritoriality" and which we generally treat as a prerogative of diplomats. It was probably a matter of convenience and public order rather than privilege, although presumably those who offered it and those who demanded it made it part of the bargain of trade. This arrangement was not unique: evidence seems to indicate that Indus merchants had at least six colonies on the Oxus River, far to the north. Whether they had similar privileges is not known, but certainly other, more or less contemporary merchants did; it was beneficial to trade to keep the merchants reasonably happy. In fact, sometimes the local merchants and even rulers adopted the customs and habits of the foreigners.

The requirements of trade also fostered technological change. The Indians were world leaders in the development of deep sea navigation. By inventing boats that could utilize the monsoon winds, they made a breakthrough that ranks with the domestication of the donkey and the camel in the growth of trade. Their achievement is the more remarkable when we consider that, to take advantage of the winds and to avoid the waterless desolation of the south Persian coast, they had to sail directly across the Arabian Sea. Nowhere else in the world, for thousands of years, were such voyages undertaken; in the Mediterranean, even as late as the fourth century B.C.E., Greek sailors hugged the coast and pulled their boats ashore at sunset. The skills and the equipment thus developed by the Indians probably enabled them to make even more venturesome voyages to the Far East.[26]

How merchant venturers fared when they visited villages in distant lands is unknown, but we can draw inferences both from contemporary accounts of such dry-land trading centers as Ebla and also from later seafarers.

Trade appears always to have been central to Ebla's "national purposes." Not only did it fight to protect its trading interests but, in a remarkable treaty with the city of Ashur, it set out to define both citizenship and taxation—both of which are issues that have filled the dockets of international courts ever since. The treaty specified that nonresident merchants were to be treated by both parties as citizens of their original countries and that each expatriate was to be subject to taxes of both states. Indeed, legal problems began early. Almost everywhere, the trader probably required a local sponsor. Even in the classical world, when trade was relatively well established, he was sure to lose his cargo, probably his freedom, and perhaps his life if he ran aground or landed where he was not known. This, as has been suggested, may be the reality behind the legend of Iphigenia and Odysseus's encounter with the Laestrygonians.[27] But, even if he had a sponsor, that was only the first step.

Disputes over the value of items traded must have been common. In the ancestor of trade, reciprocal gift giving, both parties, as I pointed out in chapter 13, regarded a disproportion in the value of goods exchanged as fraud. Perhaps that fact played a role in the creation of arbitration, which is known in the most primitive contemporary societies. From this source could have come, ultimately, our concepts of abstract authority and law. In pre-Islamic Arabian society, for example, the root from which the word *government* is derived, *hkm,* originally meant "arbitration." In pre-Islamic poetry one frequently encounters scenes in which respected elders are praised for "laying out the claims side by side and scaling them down" so that they could be satisfied.[28]

Even in such sophisticated and well-ordered societies as ancient Rome, the existence of legal penalties tells us that regulation of trade was difficult. In Roman practice, as Mauss points out, "the first trader, *tradens,* shows his property, detaches himself from it, hands it over and thus buys the *accipiens* . . . the person who receives the thing . . . does not merely recognize that he has received it, but realizes that he himself is 'bought' until it is paid for."[29] In Greek practice, a borrower, similarly, owed himself and his family, bodily, to the lender; he could be sold into foreign slavery for nonpayment. The pound of flesh in Shakespeare's *The Merchant of Venice* thus echoes an ancient reality.

Those who stole the salt of the primitive trader might not have understood all of the ritual embodied in tribal customs and certainly would not have understood Greek practice or Roman law, but they would have made the connection between bad behavior and the absence of the trader. Over time, the advantages of a minimum standard of fairness became evident.

Some ancient states declined the risk and treated trade as a state monopoly or relied on foreigners to provide what was needed. Dynastic

Egypt gives us an example of both practices. Much of the Levant trade (in which the major item was timber) was carried in non-Egyptian boats and handled by Levantine merchants. In the Red Sea, on the contrary, trade was essentially government-controlled. On her expeditions to Punt, Queen Hatshepsut spent in relative terms far more of Egypt's treasure than Queen Isabella was to spend on Columbus's voyages.

The Egyptians did not, apparently, plant colonies, but the Assyrians did, and they have left a fairly detailed account of them. The merchants, like most emigres, may have felt exposed, although Tahsin Özgüç has found evidence that for two centuries from about 1950 B.C.E., Assyrian traders lived peacefully and profitably in the Anatolian town of Kültepe (Kanesh). During the fourteenth century B.C.E., it seems, colonies both multiplied and became more formal; nine have been identified although only one has been located. The picture that emerges from it is startlingly sophisticated. The merchants seem to have engaged in several kinds of trade. Perhaps on the government account, they secured and shipped back to the Assyrian capital gold, silver, and precious stones. They imported, probably also as agents of their government, tin or an alloy of tin, but, since this was not produced in Assyria, either the Assyrian government or their partners must have procured it for them from another area. Probably for their own account, they bartered tin and textiles for silver.[30] Since coined money had not yet been invented, they used gold, silver, and copper as mediums of exchange with outsiders, while among themselves they also made extensive use of credit, for which they developed a system of personal collateral.

In their foreign residences, these "expatriates" even created quasi governments, or what we should today call chambers of commerce. Elected by the merchants, these bodies not only settled disputes but also negotiated on the merchants' behalf with the Hittite state. This is the first known example of a nongovernmental organization operating in international relations. The Assyrians lived in a *karum,* or what we now call, from its use in a quarter of medieval Venice, a ghetto. In their sheltered neighborhood, cut off from the society in which they were physically present, they governed themselves, used their own language, and worshipped their own gods. (Like a number of international practices, forms, and offices, the extraterritorial ghetto was invented and reinvented by peoples who had no knowledge of its use elsewhere or in prior ages.)

Of course, to his own country, the wandering or foreign-based merchant was valuable. Probably largely as a result of their venturesome merchants, who often doubled as spies, the Mesopotamians were comparatively well informed about the world. They had a notion of world geography and even of ethnography. The Assyrians became experts at judging the exploitable talents of foreign peoples and, in their period of imperialism, imported not only foreign goods but also skilled craftsmen. Much later, the principal "booty" of such "world conquerors" as Chingis Khan, Timur (Tamerlane), and Sultan Suleiman also consisted of people, whom they virtually had inventoried by merchants and other travelers. Thus, from very early times to modern times, although emigres and travelers spent much of their time apart from their societies, they were still at least partly under protection. Démarches provoked by attacks on merchants fill the earliest diplomatic correspondence. Listen to one from the ruler of Babylon to Pharaoh Amenophis IV protesting the ambush of a caravan: "Canaan is your land . . . and in your land have I been outraged. Arrest [the brigands and] make good the money they plundered, slay those who slew my servants and avenge their blood!"[31]

Despite attempts by governments to give protection, the practice of killing merchants was so widespread that treaties began to include provisions setting out reparations to be paid to the relatives of the deceased. Dangerous though his life certainly was, it was both too important to his society and too profitable for the merchant to abandon. So profitable, indeed, was it to become that a whole people was to cast itself in the merchant's image. These people are the *Kinahu*, or Canaanites. We know them, courtesy of the Greeks, as the *Phoenikes* (Phoenicians) and, from Roman records, as the *Poeni* (Punic peoples).

The Phoenicians lived on the fringe of the Asian landmass, almost surrounded by powerful neighbors. They could not compete with the land-based empires of Mesopotamia, Anatolia, or Egypt, but they could serve these empires—and profit from them—by providing goods and services that the powerful could not obtain for themselves. They took to the sea and gradually shifted their international trade from raw materials (primarily the cedar of their mountains) to fine luxury commodities that they manufactured or acquired from others.

The decline of the Mycenaean confederation of cities in the twelfth century B.C.E. gave the Phoenicians their opportunity; the timing was opportune because the Phoenicians were then being crowded out of their homeland, Palestine, by the newly arrived Hebrews. So, increasingly, it was to the sea that they turned in order to become the navy and the merchant marine to the non-Greek world. The port was where we see the Phoenician way of life at its most characteristic. Just north of the modern Syrian city of Latakia, Ugarit became the first great cosmopolitan port and the ancestor of the Alexandria, Beirut, Marseilles, and Barcelona of later ages. It was ideally placed for the commercial and diplomatic opportunities of the

Mediterranean. Near the timber of the Lebanese and Turkish mountains (which Egypt avidly sought), it drew animal products from the steppes south of Aleppo and agricultural produce from its fertile littoral. The copper mines of Cyprus were within a two-day sail, and the city was a natural terminus for the Euphrates River traffic.

Ugarit might best be described as a sort of ancient Venice in which the ruler himself was a merchant and ran his state as a commercial center. Artisans and merchants had an unusual degree of freedom to determine their affairs. They used the state for enrichment rather than allowing it to use them for glory or dominion; this was relatively easy since the state hardly existed, especially where it mattered most to traders—abroad. Where they were accustomed to travel, they were on their own, so why, they would have thought, should they share their profits or cater to the vanity of any ruler? Indeed, so congenial was the Ugarit environment to traders that even foreign merchants flocked to it, finding there security, relative freedom, and riches. But, as little as they liked government per se, they (like many later businessmen) were quite happy to use the state to further their own interests. So, while firmly committed to free enterprise (when *they* practiced it) the people of Ugarit also practiced protectionism to be sure that they were not overwhelmed by foreigners (whom they confined to a ghetto).

The individualistic Phoenicians never thought of themselves as a single people or formed a single state. Tyre, Sidon, Byblos, Ugarit, and, above all, Carthage never developed interurban institutions or concepts. Indeed, there appears to have been no recognition even of a sense of "Phoenicia" as a cultural unit, as the Greeks, however divided, thought of themselves as fellow Hellenes. Perhaps this was because the Phoenician city was itself the reverse image of the cohesive ancient town—being rather an international polyglot emporium.

Having little to protect, they had much to venture. And venture they did. Herodotus tells us, with obvious disbelief, of one of their great voyages of exploration: the circumnavigation of Africa. In it, they played the Genoese to Egypt's Castile. Unfortunately, we do not know the name of their Columbus, but we do know that the Egyptian pharaoh Necho in about 600 B.C.E.

> sent to sea a number of ships manned by Phoenicians, with orders to make for the Pillars of Heracles, and return to Egypt through them, and by the Mediterranean. The Phoenicians took their departure from Egypt by way of the Red Sea, and so sailed into the southern ocean. When autumn came, they went

ashore, wherever they might happen to be, and having sown a tract of land with corn, waited until the grain was fit to cut. Having reaped it, they again set sail and thus it came to pass that two whole years went by, and it was not till the third year that they doubled the Pillars of Heracles, and made good their voyage home. On their return, they declared—I for one do not believe them, but perhaps others may—that in sailing round Libya [Africa] they had the sun upon their right hand.

Some years later, an expedition from Carthage reported sailing down the west coast of Africa to a point at which they discovered "a dwarfish race, who wore a dress made from the palm-tree." So the very details that made Herodotus scoff make the tales believable to us: of course the sun would appear on the right of sailors going west around southern Africa—and we now know of the existence of pygmies. We know also that a Phoenician in the fifth century B.C.E. wrote a sailing guide to Africa, the so-called *Periplus of Africa*, which was translated into Greek in ancient times.

Evidently, it was on the sea that the Phoenicians found their element. Their mountains gave them cedar, and with designs learned from the Greeks, they built their boats. Having no navigational equipment, they (unlike the Indian Ocean mariners) hugged the coast and hauled their boats ashore each night. When they had to sail at night, they used Ursa Minor, which the Greeks, in a compliment to them, called "the Phoenician." Recovered wrecks show that Phoenician boats resembled the peddlers' carts still common in the Levant. Little floating shops, they coasted from village to village, their masters selling pots and hammering out tools and weapons. Months of sailing and rowing away from rulers, judges, or officials, each Phoenician had to be trader-tinker-soldier-sailor.[32]

On long voyages, inevitably, accidents and sickness took their tolls. From time to time, bands of Phoenicians began to stay behind, setting up trading posts or, perhaps, occasionally serving as hostages to prevent their compatriots from raiding and kidnapping the natives. These trading posts march along the southern Mediterranean coast. Carthage was the greatest, but Spain was Phoenicia's Eldorado: from there came the silver that underwrote their Near Eastern trade and enriched their cities. For nearly five hundred years, they made the Mediterranean nearly a Phoenician lake.

More than explorers or colonists, the Phoenicians were also gifted entrepreneurs. When they saw the chance for profit, they entered local industry. Even on the Greek island of Rhodes they joined in producing "Greek" perfume flasks; in Egypt they made "Egyptian" faience; and in the western Mediterranean, they went into joint ventures to produce luxury goods from bronze, gold, and amber. And they carried ideas and motifs and styles, some of which they invented or modified, from one area to the next so that their goods are found today from the Atlantic to the Persian Gulf and from southern Russia to Nubia.

From the freewheeling Phoenicians, I move to Rome where officials regarded trade much as the ancient Egyptians and the Chinese had: as a necessary evil. The road network, which stretched about fifty thousand miles in the time of Augustus, was a marvel, but it was designed for military rather than commercial use. It rarely connected areas of production and markets, so most goods had to be carried inland on the backs of pack animals at a cost that often doubled their price every hundred miles. Roman policy was not to stimulate trade but rather to encourage citizens to moderate their needs since, above all, Rome was determined not to become dependent on the foreigner. Grain was generally an exception, as Rome could not feed itself. Grain thus was not so much a commodity as a strategic resource, and, over long periods of time, the city of Rome had to import perhaps as much as two hundred thousand tons yearly.[33] This trade was too important to the safety of the government to be left to market forces or the whims of merchants; rather, it was secured mainly by "government to government" purchasing missions, much as weapons sales are usually managed today.

But private Roman merchants did penetrate into southern Russia for slaves and grain, to northern Europe for amber, and deep into Africa for slaves, ivory, gold, and animals. Indeed, so massive was the Roman appetite for animals for the arena—sometimes thousands were slaughtered in a single spectacle—that they virtually destroyed the wildlife of northwest Africa. Conversely, throughout the Roman empire, foreign merchants left signs—frequently graffiti—of their passage or residence. Europe was not to be so welcoming to foreign travelers again until modern times.

As Rome was overrun by Celts, Germans, and others from the fourth century onward, the western empire fell to pieces. In many, the only coherent remaining institution was the church, which struggled to maintain something like the old commercial system. But it was a losing battle: by the eighth century, northwestern Europe had reverted to an essentially agricultural economy. Even that was severely damaged by the invasions of the Norsemen and the Magyars. Long-distance commercial activity was confined to the East, where Byzantium remained a major urban center, and the Mediterranean. Familiarity with the larger world declined as merchants no longer plied their trade; a moderately informed Roman would have been astonished to find how ignorant of geography were his descendants. What they knew was what was summarized about 1410 by Cardinal Pierre d'Ailly in his *Imago Mundi,* the book on which Columbus relied for his concept of the earth.

During the long centuries after the fall of Rome, there was one kind of trade that flourished: as life became more insecure, belief in the supernatural power of relics grew, and people avidly sought them. A "piece of the true cross" was deemed to have a value beyond compare. Everyone realized that it was unobtainable, but the bones or pieces of clothing of saints occasioned a lively contraband commerce that was fueled by thefts from graves and churches. Exhumation and theft reached such proportions that in 817 Pope Paschal I had more than two thousand corpses, thought to be the remains of Christian martyrs, dug up and moved into safe quarters in the center of Rome. But nothing stopped the underground trade because people believed that possession of a holy relic brought health and fertility. And, above all, a relic was a physical symbol of a mystical union of the believer with the godhead. It was both tangible *and* incorruptible. Moreover, as we saw in chapter 5, people believed that a relic might protect a whole city from the ravages of barbarian invaders and pirates. Each church and each city had to have at least one. In the ninth century, Venice got from Egypt by "hook or by crook" what was claimed to be the body of the man who was to become its patron, Saint Mark.

Being few people themselves, the Venetians welcomed not only dead saints but live foreigners; however, they shrewdly used Venice as a combination market and barrier. Merchants from Italy and Germany were sanctioned to come to trade but they were not allowed to go beyond Venice into the sea, whereas the Greeks, Syrians, and Egyptians who came across the sea from the East were welcomed in the same way but were prevented from venturing beyond Venice toward the interior.

Like the Phoenicians before them, the Venetians were above all opportunistic traders. Generally, their rulers maintained a reasonably tight control over their actions abroad, so that, in the wars with the Muslims, they often attempted to enforce embargoes, particularly on the export of slaves, iron, and timber, all necessary for galleys. So lucrative was this trade, however, that bans were ineffective. Other Italian cities hardly bothered to pretend. Naples and Amalfi, for example, not only carried on an active trade with Muslims but also actively aided them against the papacy despite the threat of excommunication.

In order to handle the more regular (and legal) influx of foreign traders, Venice also reinvented the ghetto (and, as I mentioned, gave us the word). Venice was, in part, only following the lead of its early patron, the Byzantine Empire, in allotting districts to foreigners. Generally, visiting merchants were allowed to stay for only a limited time, often as little as three months. While in residence, they had to report to local authorities and were rarely allowed to move about freely. Some "outlandish" visitors, such as the Russians, were lodged outside the city gates and were allowed inside only under police escort. Even the more civilized Christians were required to lodge in special "hotels." German merchants set up perhaps the most famous of them, the *fondaco dei Tedeschi,* where, presumably anxious to prove themselves good neighbors, they hired not only Albrecht Dürer (who had gone to Venice in 1494) to decorate the altar of their chapel but also the local artists Giorgione and Titian to decorate the facade.

From the Mediterranean, the custom of giving foreigners a place to live under their own control spread to northern Europe. German merchants set up housing similar to the *fondaci* in London and other English ports, and these were recognized in the Great Charter of 1303. Such warehouse-cum-residences were later known as factories—places where factors or traders dwelled and traded. So convenient were they that they spread all over Europe and even into Russia.

Outside Europe, trade continued to be as active as in classical times. Although in the Muslim countries minorities lived in their own quarters, at least in Egypt Jews and Christians were able to move freely; Jews, in fact, occasionally became business partners of resident Muslims. Yet, although segregation in the European sense was not practiced, groups of visiting European merchants lived and traded in *caravanserais,* where a representative of the merchants (in Arabic, *wakilu'l-tujjar*) functioned more or less as a modern consul, representing the merchants to the authorities and handling their documents.

Meanwhile, the countries around the Indian Ocean remained a great market, with the sea, its "highway," largely the preserve of Arab and other Muslim seafarers, whom we see vividly if imaginatively through the tale of that Oriental Odysseus, Sindabad the Sailor. Like the Greek, the Arab was probably a composite of many sailors' yarns. The real Sindabads not only explored the east coast of Africa and the Indonesian islands, they also established colonies in China, converted large sections of the native populations of southern Asia to Islam, and created a trading network that linked this whole vast area into one market. We learn this from Jewish sources, because the Jews were not only traders and bankers but intermediaries among Muslims and Christians.[34]

The scale of medieval travel has been grossly underestimated. As many as eight thousand merchants and others traveled the Tunisia-Sicily-Egypt route in a normal year in the eleventh century; while land caravans, often numbering five hundred camels, were frequent. So frequent were their journeys that merchants found it inconvenient to handle money and invented (or reinvented, because there seems to be some precedent even in ancient Babylonia) a form of bank transfer or "check" called *suftaja,* defined in Islamic law as the "loan of money in order to avoid the risk of transport."[35]

Egypt and India traded with the band of societies stretching from Genoa in the east to Barcelona in the west, an area that in medieval times was culturally and commercially virtually homogeneous. The western part was adjacent to the rich and advanced society of Muslim Spain, *al-Andalus.* There, during the last quarter of the tenth century, a lively trade began. It drew angry comments from true believers on both sides. As they became more affluent, the Christians became more broad-minded and more venturesome, shedding some of the uncouth ways that had drawn the barbs of Jewish and Muslim writers.

Trade fairs began to be regularly held at St.-Gilles, Muret, Carcassonne, and other towns increasingly visited by Muslims and Christians from the south and the east. Generally, the records only mention such people when they got into trouble or when the way they were taxed or treated threatened trade. In the twelfth century, Cairo Jews maintained particularly close contact with Jews in Narbonne, Lunel, Montpellier, Arles, and Marseilles, although only Marseilles is mentioned as being in regular sailing contact with Egypt. Even in those days, Jewish fundraising for community projects was significant. The Cairo Geniza documents (see note 34) mention contributions sent from Narbonne and Montpellier to schools in Baghdad and Jerusalem. The western Jews also submitted to these schools their questions on law, ritual, and civil affairs and accepted men appointed by Easterners as judges and rabbis, but, until the end of the twelfth century, there is no record of a visit by an Egyptian Jew to Narbonne or Marseilles. Western Europeans were thought still to be dangerous hosts.

Trade contacts with Italy and Byzantium are less well documented. We have no records comparable to the Geniza for non-Jews, but we do know that extensive trade was carried on by Muslims, Jews, and Christians from the Italian cities with Catalonia and Provence. This traffic was almost entirely by sea. From the west, they made short passages between Almeria, which was the jumping-off place for the North African ports, northward to Valencia and Barcelona; then they touched at Narbonne, Montpellier, and Marseilles before going on to Genoa, Pisa, and Amalfi or Naples, from which some sailed to Palermo. From Palermo some sailed to Tunis and made their way to Alexandria, while others went through the Straits of Messina to the Adriatic or on to Cyprus. From Cyprus, ships sailed to Byzantium, Antioch, or Alexandria. Thus, shipping partook of the nature of both a coastal and a long-distance traffic, intimately linking the whole Mediterranean into one complex.

In northern Europe, beginning in the tenth century, a similar network of trading ties known as the Hansa linked a huge area stretching from Novgorod in Russia to Portugal and involving some two hundred towns and cities. So successful was the organization that it lasted about five hundred years, until competition with England and the Netherlands sapped its prosperity.

In the Pacific and Indian Oceans, the Chinese had sailed for many centuries. China, like ancient Egypt and Rome, distrusted private enterprise, which it equated with disorder, barbarian chaos, and piracy (which it usually blamed on foreigners). But also like Egypt and Rome, its rulers had a taste for exotic products, so successive dynasties not only encouraged the establishment of foreign merchants in China but favored the activities of Chinese merchants abroad. When in 1271 the Mongols conquered China, the whole of northern Asia became one vast empire. True, it had been won by appalling violence, but once their conquest was secure, the Mongols fostered a relatively open, tolerant, expansive, and eclectic approach to the world. Particularly in the port cities of China little colonies of missionaries, traders, scholars, and soldiers of fortune congregated. Most were Arabs or other Muslims, about whom we know a good deal thanks to the redoubtable fourteenth-century traveler Mohammed ibn Abdullah ibn Battuta. Having visited much of central Africa, the lands of the Mediterranean, India, the Maldive Islands, and the East Indies, Ibn Battuta sailed for China. En route he found everywhere well-established colonies of Muslims and Chinese who engaged in a long-range commerce by ship. He marveled at the sophistication of the Chinese junks in comparison to the ships of the Mediterranean. Some, he noted with delight, carried up to a thousand passengers and crew. And, when few European ships were decked at all, the seagoing junks had as many as four decks divided into spacious quarters with private lavatories—unheard of in Western ships—for the traveling merchants. Indian Ocean ships, Ibn Battuta found, even had facilities that enabled the crew to "cultivate green stuffs, vegetables and ginger in wooden tanks." Thus, although he does not mention it, we may presume that scurvy, that great killer of the Western explorers, was not so severe a problem in the East. He mentions in passing a juxtaposition of nations that brings out the tolerant and international nature of this commerce—the agent for the Chinese ship on which he, a Moroccan, was traveling from India was a Syrian Arab. And, when he reached China, he found that in every city "there is a quarter for Muslims in which they live by themselves, and in which they have mosques."[36]

Among the Western merchants who profited from the relative openness of the Yuan (Mongol) period were a score or so known to us by name. The Venetian merchant family of the Polos, Nicolò, Maffeo, and Marco, are the most famous since, on his return from twenty years in Yuan China, Marco found a good ghostwriter, a Pisan by the name of Rustichello, who secured for Marco immortality. But the Polos were not alone.[37] Indeed, before the end of the thirteenth century, a commercial handbook, the *Pratica della Mercatura* of Francesco Balducci Pegolotti, described the Central Asian route as "quite safe."

Keen not to be left out of the exciting and lucrative trade with the rich East, sailors began to seek alternatives to the Central Asian land route. That would become the consuming passion of the Portuguese and the Spanish for the next two centuries. Marco Polo's account must have deeply influenced Columbus, whose marked-up copy still survives.

During the Yuan dynasty, foreign trade—as with all forms of foreign contacts—was allowed or even stimulated, but, after the fall of the Mongols, the new Ming dynasty drastically cut back on foreign contacts. Even the relatively xenophobic Ming, however, did not lose the traditional Chinese taste for exotic products. Probably this taste was a significant motive behind the earliest and greatest venture in exploration in the fifteenth century, the seven voyages of Grand Eunuch Cheng Ho. The first of these, in 1405, was said to have been composed of sixty-three ships manned by thousands of soldiers, sailors, and officials. Cheng Ho led his fleets all over the Indian Ocean and probably sailed around the Cape of Good Hope into the Atlantic.[38]

Some ships of the Ming dynasty "Treasure Fleet" were giants of their era, probably nearly 150 meters (about 450 feet) long and more than 45 meters (150 feet) wide. Even more impressive was the advanced technology they demonstrated: the ships were fitted with floating stabilizers, adjustable and balanced rudders that acted as extra keels, and watertight bulkheads. Few of these innovations would be tried on European ships for the next four hundred years. To put these features into perspective, consider that even as late as the end of the sixteenth century, European ships were relatively tiny. In 1582, Englishmen owned only twenty ships of more than two hundred tons. Moreover, European ships were both sluggish and hard to sail. The hulls were lined with tar and goat hair and quickly got fouled with barnacles and weeds; it took as much as eight months to sail from England to South Africa.[39]

Remarkable achievements the Chinese voyages were, and in scale they quite dwarfed the efforts of the Portuguese and the Spaniards in that century, but suddenly in 1433, just as the Europeans were setting out from the opposite direction, the Chinese tied up their ships to rot. Apparently, the government decided that there was little to be gained, and perhaps much to be lost, by contact with foreigners. Although this government policy destroyed a grand venture that might have changed world history, it did not completely end Chinese overseas trade because private entrepreneurs, many of whom were considered by their government to be outlaws, even "Japanese" outlaws,[40] continued to call at all the ports from Indonesia to eastern Africa. But China would never again rival the Western powers in their quest for foreign trade and empire.

. . . .

15 EUROPEAN TRADE AND FINANCE

As Europe began to revive, partly under the impact of increased commerce, the Europeans rediscovered forms (such as banking and insurance) that had been practiced for centuries and were still in use in the East. As the fifteenth century opened, the major European merchant fleets were those of Venice and Genoa. Venice is thought to have had then about three hundred ships capable of carrying more than a hundred tons of cargo. Some of its ships were as large as four hundred tons. Genoa, which did not suffer from Venice's shallow port and sandbars, profited by building even larger ships. While none approached the Chinese in size or technical sophistication, they were serviceable and generally safe. Any of the larger ships could have sailed around Africa or across the Atlantic—but they did not. It may be illuminating to ask why.

Probably the main reason was simply that the Venetians and the Genoese were content with the existing trade routes, but there were other factors as well. The first was intellectual: their navigational technique was, we might say, tactical rather than strategic, insular rather than global. Although sailors in the Mediterranean had some form of magnetic compass as early as the twelfth century, they used it primarily to move from point to point in fog; that limited use enabled them to accomplish their objective, that is, to extend the sailing season in the Mediterranean beyond the summer months. A longer sailing season was commercially important because it made round trips possible even between distant points and cut shipping costs. But practically no one considered the compass as a tool for long-range voyaging. The second reason was technical: their ships were designed for the Mediterranean. Needing to sail close to shore, they were typified by a very shallow draft. The bottom was often curved so that, if the vessel ran aground, it could be "rocked" backward and forward (by moving men and cargo) until it floated free. The crew slept on deck or, in bad weather, on the cargo in the hold. Most of these boats were driven by triangular or "lateen" sails that were very efficient for sailing across or against the wind but not well adapted for running steadily with the wind. That was the job of a square sail. So when, much later, sailing into the Atlantic became important, Mediterranean boatbuilders developed the caravel, the hybrid rig we see in imaginative reconstructions of Columbus's *Niña*. The third reason was commercial: European trade was carried on by private merchants who would not invest in risky ventures. When Europeans did venture onto the ocean, it was usually under government patronage, and then usually only for high-profit goods (gold and slaves being the most common) or for piracy. Thus, although the Italians were the most competent sailors and merchants in Europe, they found their way into the Atlantic under the patronage and in the ships of the Spanish and the Portuguese.

Despite these handicaps, sailors and merchants in the fifteenth century began actively to seek foreign trade. This is particularly surprising when we consider that Europe was suffering from plague and other epidemics and frequent famines that, together with endemic warfare, caused a severe decline in its already (in comparison to China and India) small and scattered population. Probably only Venice and Milan had 200,000 inhabitants, while the other major Italian cities and Paris had between 50,000 and 100,000. London was then little more than a town with a population of about 40,000; Antwerp was half that size. In the Iberian peninsula only four towns—Barcelona, Cordoba, Sevilla, and Granada—had 35,000 people. Lisbon was smaller still. Moreover, much of the population lived at or barely above a subsistence level. Consequently, demand was limited. And so were items of trade suitable for the East: the Chinese and the Indians would have scoffed at shoddy European produce, so most of what could be sold abroad consisted of "primary products" (nonmanufactured goods). Consequently, the Europeans suffered that painful problem, a balance of payments deficit (which we wrongly think is unique to our age), and made up for it by exporting gold and silver when nothing else would do. The facts that Europe was deficient in gold and that the silver mines of Central Europe were then in decline put a high premium on acquisition of precious metals from foreign lands.

The best source for gold was then Africa.[41] So, what the Polos and others did in Asia was, in a limited way, tried in Africa. Not content with buying gold dust from Muslim middlemen in the northern African ports, which they had to do by selling goods that were either illegal there (such as wine) or embargoed in Europe (such as timber, ships and ships' supplies, and arms), some more venturesome traders tried to find the source of the gold dust. Benedetto Dei, a Florentine merchant, seems to have visited Timbuktu in 1470. Such journeys, however, were not only exhausting, expensive and dangerous but were also commercially futile. And Italian merchants were, above all, practical men.

Africa offered not only gold but also slaves, and for them as well Europeans had begun to develop a taste. In fact, many of the travelers of medieval Europe had been slave dealers. We get the word *slave* from the fact that they often traveled to Russia for Slavs. In the wars between the Christians and the Muslims in the Mediterranean, both sides engaged in huge hunts for captives. From the taste for servile and alien household helpers we get the word *blackamoor* (originally meaning "a dark-skinned Muslim"). In Renaissance Italy, the wealthy all had their pages, maids, mistresses, porters, and cooks from Asia and Africa. What raised slaving to a massive enterprise was the growth of sugar, tobacco, and cotton plantations, but it was always profitable and could be combined, in attacks on the Muslims, with religious mission. That is how it began for the Portuguese. Their first overseas venture was their attack on the (African) Mediterranean port of Ceuta.

The fifteenth-century Portuguese were lured by slaves, but they were also driven by hunger. From very early times they engaged in fishing to supplement their meager crops. And, in this endeavor, they were favored by the closest Atlantic equivalent to the monsoon winds—the prevailing winds in the North Atlantic, which moved in a rough circular pattern. Sailing southwest, ships caught the winds out into the Atlantic, and returning northeast, they caught the winds back. Wind and current made it possible virtually to drift down to the Canary Islands. We know that a Genovese merchant got a group of Portuguese to do just that in the fourteenth century in order to establish the first overseas colony in those islands. And, catching the winds for the return voyage would or could land them on the Madeira Islands. This apparently is what happened about 1420 when two Portuguese and one Italian—the father-in-law of Columbus—began a colony there. Madeira became a major producer of sugar for Europe and, having brought over the Malvoisie grape from Crete, began to export that wine for which Madeira has been famous ever since.

The first great leap southward—toward the presumed source of gold—by the Portuguese came in 1434 when a small, undecked sailing boat equipped with oars rounded Cape Bojador, just eight hundred miles downwind. In 1441 Portuguese sailors and merchants carried out what may have been the first Portuguese amphibious slave raid on the Atlantic coast. Four years later, Prince Henry the Navigator ordered the erection of the first barracoon (slave prison) on Arguim Island, and over the next three years, some fifty Portuguese ships brought back to Europe about one thousand slaves.

Along the way, in the Gulf of Guinea the Portuguese found natives who were willing to sell them gold. For a while, Africa became literally a golden land from which the Portuguese were able to extract an average of perhaps seven hundred kilograms a year. Gradually the source dried up, but it lasted long enough to encourage French and English privateers to begin to raid Portuguese shipping. That, in turn, certainly stimulated the growth of North European sailing and exploration. More important, as costs rose and trade declined, the Portuguese redoubled their efforts to reach India.

The history of the Portuguese ventures toward India is shrouded in mystery. The conventional story is that the first voyage aimed at India was made in 1482 by Diogo Cão, who was said to have discovered the Congo River but not to have reached the tip of Africa, and that five years later, Bartolomeu Dias rounded the Cape. Our history would probably be very different except for two influences: first, at the time, the Portuguese regarded all materials relating to their voyages as state secrets; and, second, when they were no longer a security threat, their archives were destroyed in the great Lisbon earthquake and fire of 1755. Other information suggests a different sequence. First, a Portuguese ambassador informed the Pope three years before Dias's trip that Portuguese ships had reached almost to the Arabian Gulf; and, second, an Arab book of sailing instructions reports that "a frankish [Portuguese] expedition had been shipwrecked near Sofala as early as +1495, three years before the coming of da Gama."[42] The Portuguese must have felt themselves on the brink of success in the race to India, and it was in part that assessment that caused them to turn down Columbus's project.

When Columbus returned, he stopped first in Portugal, and the incensed Portuguese immediately planned a voyage across the Atlantic. But they were too late. The Spanish Crown got the Papacy to support its new claims, and in June 1494 the two sides negotiated the Treaty of Tordesillas, which effectively divided the rest of the world between them. However envious the Portuguese were, Columbus's Spanish backers were profoundly disappointed because by 1496 they realized that he had not reached Asia. The race was still to be won or at least publicly proclaimed. The latter task was performed in 1497 by Vasco da Gama. In the Indian Ocean, he picked up an Arab or Indian pilot and so was able to sail, with the monsoon winds, directly across the ocean to a point just north of the minor Hindu city-state of Calicut. He had done what Columbus wanted to do with his discovery of the vast Old World; into that world the Portuguese plunged with enthusiasm, greed, and ferocity.

Rightly, da Gama's feat is celebrated in the history books, but little known is perhaps the most astonishing event in the trip: on a sandy beach in the Anjedivas Islands, just south of Goa, the Portuguese came across an Italian who had somehow made his way there. Thinking him a spy, the Portuguese tortured him and took him along with them on the return voyage to Portugal, where he was given the name of his "benefactor," da Gama. Whatever Gaspar's means of traveling, surely his trek, from somewhere in Europe to a remote fishing village along the Indian Ghats, must rank as one of the most remarkable "expeditions" in that age of exploration. We know of him only by accident, because he turned up in that unlikely place just when the first Western boats ever to go there were being careened. How many more such men—merchants, explorers, and just victims—have disappeared, voiceless, down the corridors of history?

Right on the heels of the Portuguese, in deeper-draft, hybrid-rigged carracks and square-rigged, ocean-going galleons, were the Spaniards, the Dutch, the English, and the French.

Both luring and restraining pre-industrial Europeans in their thrust outward toward Asia was their desperate shortage of specie. It has been estimated that just after Columbus's first voyage, Europe as a whole had about 3,500 tons of gold and 37,500 tons of silver.[43] It had a small internal production of silver, but this hardly made up for wear on coins as they moved from hand to hand,[44] hoarding, and satisfaction of such newly acquired "needs" as jewelry and table silver, which, after the middle of the seventeenth century, had become almost a mania in the West. (The new pattern of eating with forks instead of fingers had been set by the Italians, who themselves had copied the habit from a Byzantine princess who had married a Venetian doge centuries before.)[45] And, as European commerce expanded, the need for specie expanded apace.

The problem could be crippling, as a Spanish episode shows. In 1543, and on many subsequent occasions, the great trade fair at Medina de Campo had to be postponed for lack of currency.[46] The Spaniards tried to solve their part of the problem by despoiling and destroying the native societies of Latin America, which, sadly for them, had supplies of gold and silver. It has been estimated that from 1500 to 1650 the Spanish government brought back from the New World 181 tons of gold and nearly 17,000 tons of silver—and these figures do not include the amount brought in by contraband merchants, privateers, and pirates. But this inflow of gold and silver quickly poured out again and did Spain little good in promoting its economy. A shrewd contemporary observer, the Venetian ambassador Vendramin, said, "This gold that comes from the Indies does on Spain as rain does on a roof—it pours on her and it flows away."[47] The government was well aware of the problem. In the 1580s the *Cortes* of Castile lamented, "Experience has shown that within a month or two of the arrival of a fleet from the [West] Indies, not a farthing is to be seen." But the government did not know what to do.

The causes for the Spanish problem were more complex than was then realized. When it expelled the Moriscos (the descendants of the former Muslims), who constituted about 3 percent of its population, it lost a far larger proportion of its productive labor force because the Moriscos were Spain's best farmers and among its best artisans. Furthermore, such industry as it retained was priced out of competition with northern Europe because of the inflation stimulated by, among other causes, the massive influx of bullion.[48]

Bullion was Europe's obsession; Columbus wrote from Jamaica in 1503, "Gold is a wonderful thing! Whoever possesses it is master of everything he desires. With gold, one can even get souls into paradise."[49] Less concerned with paradise, the Spanish not only poured the produce of the Americas into Europe to buy the goods they could not make for themselves but sent a second river of bullion westward across the Pacific to their entrepôt at Manila to buy silks, porcelain, and spices from Pacific basin countries for shipment to Acapulco. This trade route, opened in 1572, was to remain significant for more than two hundred and fifty years.[50] And it wasn't only the Spaniards. All of western Europe was guided by the mercantilist notion that specie exactly equated to wealth and power. The English reaction to Clive's conquest of Bengal in 1757 was delight more at the discovery of the hoard of gold and silver in its treasury than at the vastly more valuable dominion over that rich country. Even as late as 1831, when they seized Algiers, the French felt justified in their aggression when they discovered that the treasury contained more than seven thousand kilograms of gold and one hundred thousand kilograms of silver. As spectacular as was the flow of bullion into Europe, it did not, could not, meet the growing demand. This shortfall was to play a key role in the development and spread of European banking and various kinds of credit facilities, including what has been called "ink money," or fractional reserves.

The second critical problem for all pre-industrial Europeans was that they had little that was attractive to offer in exchange for the Asian goods they so avidly sought. Neither the Indians nor the Chinese wanted the woolens that then amounted to about 80 percent of all English exports. In fact, toward the end of the eighteenth century, a Chinese emperor told a British trade mission that there was nothing the Chinese wanted from the "foreign devils." A European visitor half a century later commented, "One excellent reason why the Chinese care little about foreign commerce is that their internal trade is so extensive. . . . China is a country so vast, so rich, so varied, that its internal trade alone would suffice abundantly to occupy that part of the nation that can be devoted to mercantile operations."[51] So Europeans, particularly the English, were forced to buy what they wanted with silver. Indeed, silver was virtually the only thing Europe had to offer those civilizations it could not conquer in the Indian Ocean and the Pacific. In 1601, for example, three-quarters of British exports to the East had been simply silver bullion. Each year, European traders spent about 80,000 kilograms (176,000 pounds) of silver in the East. In some years bullion was the only export. It was apposite that the emperor of China referred to his Spanish counterpart as "the king of silver."[52]

But, needing silver at home and being inspired by mercantilist ideas (which held that bullion was the bedrock of national as well as personal prosperity), Europeans were anxious to sell rather than buy goods—they shared the modern obsession with acquiring a "positive" balance of trade (a phrase, incidentally, that was first used in 1622). Their objective was not, or at least not originally, to stimulate the domestic economy to produce goods but rather simply to acquire bullion. Where possible, the Spaniards, the British, and the French accomplished this by theft—in the form of either imperialism in Asia and Africa or piracy among one another's merchant marines. Where they engaged in trade, it was thus the foreign rather than domestic activity that was attractive to them. Indeed, a prominent mercantilist, writing just at the end of the seventeenth century, "argued that in domestic trade the nation in general did not grow richer, only a change in the relative amounts of wealth of individuals took place; but foreign trade made a net addition to a country's wealth."[53]

This line of argument was carried forward in perhaps the most famous of the mercantilist tracts, *England's Treasure by Forraign Trade*, written in 1630 by Thomas Mun, a director of the East India Company. Like other mercantilists, Mun was keen to acquire bullion abroad, but, reflecting on the fact that the flow of bullion *through* Spain had done that country little good while enriching the manufacturers whose products Spain bought with the gold and silver looted in the New World, he argued for permission to export bullion to buy goods for reexport as (unknown to him) Jericho had done at the dawn of foreign trade and as England, Portugal, and Holland were then doing successfully in the Pacific. But his was not an argument for free trade: the ideal situation, he argued, was an Asian area dominated by England and closed to foreign competition that could supply both cheap primary products and cheap native labor. Indeed, Mun got the basis of his argument right: it was only where and when a European power was dominant that its trade would be satisfactory for the next two centuries.[54]

Where possible, the European powers tried to create monopolies so that they could control prices and direct the flow of goods. Cocoa was an early example. Spain developed the production in South America and tried to funnel cocoa beans through its markets to Europe. Had the system worked, it would have been ideal. Given the limited technology of the times, however, it could not prevent contraband and steadily lost control; it has been estimated[55] that less than one-third of the South American cocoa was legally exported in the seventeenth century, and by the beginning of the eighteenth century none was. We see many similar examples today, particularly in the narcotics trade. Even with 1990s technology, trade is almost impossible to control where profits are large.

Meanwhile, the Europeans and particularly the English had developed a taste for the exotica of the East. Silks and porcelain were significant but, during the eighteenth century, China tea became an English addiction; the yearly importation increased from 122,000 to 16 million pounds.[56] In the absence of a suitable exchange product, the drain on English silver reached crisis proportions. In desperation, toward the end of the eighteenth century the East India Company, with the agreement of the British government, sent a diplomatic mission to the Chinese emperor to demand an opening of ports for free trade, but, as I have mentioned, the Chinese insisted that they neither wanted nor needed anything from abroad.[57] Britain could not and did not have to accept this rebuff. The answer it hit on a few years later was opium.

Opium offered a potential refinement on the strategy Thomas Mun had put forward in 1620: it could be grown in an area of Asia—India— where Britain had created a closed zone and then used to penetrate another zone that Britain had not dominated. The problem was that the Chinese did not want opium and had not used it before the end of the eighteenth century. So, the British justified their venture not as luring the Chinese into buying opium but as opening China to "free trade," a slogan of immense power and prestige. And they backed up the slogan by using Indian troops (sepoys, as discussed in part 3) as the strong arm of their policy. Finally, they increased the profit by using Indian indentured labor to plant and gather the item of trade.

Chinese government officials reacted as government officials might today. Some accepted bribes to turn a blind eye toward the smuggling, while others struggled to prevent the destruction of their productive society by opium traffickers. Striking a very modern note, the Mandarin official Lin Tse-hsü wrote a touching and pathetic letter to Queen Victoria begging her to apply English standards of legality to her overseas trade and offering to work with Britain to end the trade—"[w]e in this land forbidding the use of it, and you, in the nations of your dominion, forbidding its manufacture."[58] Angered by Chinese intransigence, the British, using sepoy troops, fought two wars (1839–42 and 1856–60) to force the Chinese to allow "free trade."

Meanwhile, during the seventeenth and eighteenth centuries in the Middle East, England and France dueled for dominance in the commerce of the Ottoman Empire under a system of favored commercial terms and partial extraterritoriality known as the Capitulations. Begun in 1352 in order to encourage Genoa to fight with the empire against Venice, capitulations were extended to France (primarily for military purposes) in 1569. Within a few years, the Ottoman Empire accounted for half of France's overseas trade. Because the intent of the Ottomans was to encourage European competition, the same terms were subsequently granted to the Austrians in 1567 and to the English in 1592.

By the middle of the seventeenth century, the English had achieved dominance in "the Turkey trade"; they accomplished this partly through the transactions of merchants in their Levant Company, which had been founded in 1581. But even that peaceful trade was founded on violence. I drew on John Maynard Keynes (in chapter 10) for the story of how Queen Elizabeth invested part of her share of the proceeds from Sir Francis Drake's piracy to set up the Levant Company. Drake's was but one instance of a common practice: as a well-informed Venetian observer commented in 1659, "The English would be a fine and praiseworthy race if they were not so given to robbing the ships of Christian merchants."[59] There is no doubt that the trading venture was based on British armed power, but it is also true that in the Levant as in India the critical factor was the *relative* decline in the capacity of the local power.

By a combination of hard work, main force, and (later) industrial capacity, foreign merchants dominated the local market, acquired more privileges than are today accorded even to diplomats, and enjoyed tax incentives and protection not available to their native counterparts. The system was to reach its apex in the Commercial Treaty of 1838, to implement which Britain went to war with Egypt and destroyed Egypt's attempt at industrialization.[60]

An English traveler commented after the Commercial Treaty took effect that "the current of precious metals, which a few years ago carried £5,000,000 toward the east, is now drawn backwards by the spinning mules and power looms of England." In the Ottoman Empire, as elsewhere, local manufacture was driven out of the market; the only local produce that remained "economic" consisted, as a writer commented in 1856, "in raw material, which it hands over to Europe, and which the latter returns to Turkey in a manufactured form." A modern Turkish author has pointed to the fact that social or cultural "reforms" in one sphere sometimes undercut economic or political "reforms" in another:

> The people not only preferred European dress but also gradually showed a preference for European furnishings. These changes narrowed the market for products of the old industry and struck a heavy blow against these institutions exactly at a time when they were in great distress because of the keen competition of European factories. . . . The fundamental point, which is bewildering and regrettable, is the following: whereas in the European countries it had been possible to replace the old declining industrial forms with an advanced system, in our country, with the decline of old forms of industry, almost all important industrial activity also ceased, and the country's economy lost all the major branches of industry; it was then necessary to import even the most basic products.[61]

And it was not only in manufactured goods that local activities were swamped; by 1838 soldiers (on orders) and the more affluent civilians (by fashion) had put aside the cumbersome and time-consuming, but Asian-made, turban in favor of the fez, which by then they imported from France, and were drinking Indian tea out of glasses made in Bohemia. Coffee drinkers began to buy their beans from France rather than from Yemen, while the Kashmiri shawl, a virtual necessity for the well-dressed man in previous generations, went out of style. The Baghdad-to-Damascus caravan made its last trip in 1857. If Middle Easterners traveled by sea they did so on English or French steamers because these modern ships, in the words of a British consul, had "annihilated the local coasting trade."[62]

The "local coasting trade" was, indeed, one of the most important aspects of European relations with Asia. In the days when sailing ships were the only means of transport, a round trip from England to India was rarely less than sixteen months and often as much as two years. Just as the Spaniards had found two centuries earlier in the Pacific basin so the British found in India that the only way to make such long-distance, and long-term, gambles pay off commercially was by penetrating into the local market, cutting out middlemen, buying directly from producers, and selling to villages and towns upriver or along the coasts. Associated with this direct intervention was the need to find locally produced goods that could be traded within Asia. This was the origin of the "triangular" trade, which in Asia took several forms. Much of the trade between Japan, China, Indonesia, and India came to be the province of the European merchants. But that did not suffice to pay for the goods Europe wanted from the East. So new production was stimulated. The most widely practiced was the shipping of precious metals (until the conquest of Bengal made it possible to levy local taxes) to buy opium grown in India to be shipped to China to exchange for tea to be shipped to England. To succeed, one had to dominate at all levels.

And markets had to be opened. It appeared immoral to Europeans that Asians and Africans would try to prevent free trade or would refuse to buy European goods. The major answer to this was force: I have mentioned that Britain destroyed the Egyptian attempt to create a protected zone where native industry could develop and, of course, did not allow the Indians or other colonial peoples to develop in competition. The Russians acted similarly in the areas they conquered in Central Asia, pulling them into the Russian economic sphere and using them to produce only primary products. The Russians also made repeated attempts from about 1792 to force the Japanese to open their land to foreign commerce, and in 1808 a Royal Navy warship forced its way into Nagasaki, but the Japanese resolutely manned their defenses. Then in 1842 the Japanese *bakufu* (shogun) eased the restrictions somewhat and in the process precipitated the most profound social transformation in Japanese history. The mission of Commodore Matthew Perry of the U.S. Navy in 1853–54 that "opened" Japan was the culmination of a series of actions dating back more than half a century.

In those areas in which they did not become politically and militarily dominant, the European powers sought to carve out for themselves economic enclaves. The two, interlocking, activities that figure most prominently in the nineteenth and early twentieth centuries are the building of railways and the provision of finance. The two have a very modern ring:

in our times, the provision of large-scale public works projects with the necessary finance are comparable ventures. The major difference is that today, the finance is apt to be provided at concessionary rates, at least initially, or sometimes even as a gift, whereas in the heyday of imperialism it came at often ruinous rates. For the Suez Canal and other projects Egypt paid as much as 26 percent interest, and that on what, at least by today's standards, constituted fraudulent capital. In the Ottoman Empire, primarily for railway construction, European bankers lent a nominal amount of $900 million, of which at least a third never reached the Turks. When the inevitable failure to meet the debt requirements became evident, Egypt, the Ottoman Empire, and Iran were treated as though they were public companies registered in England or France—they were effectively declared bankrupt and were put under debt administrations so that, regardless of their policies or responsibilities, the European creditors could be fully repaid.

Where the Asian trading partner had enough power or sophistication to insist on it, trade was, from time to time, linked with various forms of subsidies or with financial or technical assistance. This was an old pattern, much used outside of Europe. Traders in sixteenth-century Japan, for example, engaged in what today we would call technology transfer, primarily in weapons, in order to secure access to markets. And in many areas, both aid and trade were often regarded as arms of statecraft. The Chinese always regarded them in this light. Indeed, they generally denied that they engaged in "trade" but regarded relations with their neighbors as a form of reciprocal gift giving—the tribute system—in which their superiority and hegemony were explicitly acknowledged. In the West, it was the Italian city-states that pioneered the use of aid as a means of influencing policy,[63] but it became much more common in the seventeenth and eighteenth centuries when both the British and the French subsidized their allies and even rented armies or bought support for their policies.[64]

In the nineteenth century, the French government created a new form of subsidy/pressure by controlling the listing of foreign bonds on the *Bourse* (Paris Stock Exchange). By this means it could effectively grant or withhold access to capital. Thus, just before World War I, the French facilitated the lending of funds to the Russians in return for assurances that the Russians would remain anti-German and would build railways toward their Western frontier to enable them to mobilize more rapidly against Germany.

The French experience points up a lesson that donor nations have repeatedly forgotten and painfully relearned ever since: once an aid program, in whatever form, or a government-to-government commercial relationship is established, terminating it is very difficult because for the recipient a cessation is tantamount to an act of aggression. Had the French stopped their loans to Russia, for example, regardless of any criteria they might have adduced, the whole structure of their national defense policy might have been subverted. In 1956 the U.S. secretary of state, John Foster Dulles, undercut his policy for the Middle East by similar moves: he made and then withdrew an offer of aid to Egypt to build its High Dam. The consequences were predictable: the Egyptians turned against the very policy Dulles had been trying to promote by the grant of aid, and, temporarily at least, placed themselves on the side of the Soviet Union in the Cold War.

Recipient countries often point out that aid, trade, and strategy are not so separate as the donors like to say. Most civil aid involves purchasing goods and services in the donor country; for example, virtually all aid from England, France, and Germany has been restricted to their products, while American aid has averaged more than 80 percent, and sometimes reaches 94 percent, from U.S. sources. For military aid, this figure reaches nearly 100 percent. And in that field today, America's share has grown from 25 percent in 1987 to 52 percent in 1996. Much of this aid is, bluntly, purely political in purpose: it cannot improve the capacity of the recipient and, having been given, often can be seen to increase political instability and repression. At the very least, to judge from the last generation in Africa and Asia, it has promoted authoritarian forces despite the avowed intent of the United States and Western European countries to help societies evolve toward openness and freedom. Yet it has developed such a constituency, not only among the recipients but also among the work forces and capitalists in the producer countries, as to become the "sacred cow" of late-twentieth-century trade. So intent on passing out arms to the Third World is America (and until recently the Soviet Union) that when countries cannot afford them, they can get them free.

Donor countries naturally emphasize their benevolence and, at minimum, expect gratitude. Yet, the contrast between yesterday's greed and today's generosity is not so sharp as it appears to them. The scale is certainly greater than in the past, but consider the following: in the decade from 1956 to 1965, a period of massive capital transfers from the rich nations (especially the United States) to the poor nations, transfers averaging about $6.7 billion yearly, $1.3 billion was in military equipment, which benefited the donor countries' industries rather than adding to the productive capacity of the recipients, while interest and principal repayment rose (depending on the area) to between 12 percent and 50 percent. Private investment averaged about two-thirds of the aid package and by the end of that decade amounted to about $100 billion—aggregating to a "virtual" economy larger than any single state except for the United States and the Soviet Union. As has been pointed out, however, the major output of the Third World is in primary products whose average market value has steadily fallen. When weighed in this scale, aid has not only not given rise to a higher level of productivity but has failed to make up for the fall in income of poor nations and has not offset the approximately $50 billion they pay annually to the rich in interest on loans and other forms of capital transfer.

Failure to take these facts into account has played a role in the decline of interest in—indeed, in the belief in the very use of—overseas assistance. The United States, which led the way in seeking to apply the lessons learned in its recovery from the Great Depression to the Marshall Plan and then to Third World aid programs, has now slipped to the lowest per capita contribution among the twenty-seven major industrial powers and in 1996 gave only about one-tenth of 1 percent of its GNP to improving the world's economic health. After nearly half a century of assistance programs, then, a large proportion of the world's population lives well below the "poverty level." The implications of this are clear. Leaving aside the humanitarian issues, others, instances of which are reported almost daily in the world press, speak directly to the self-interest of the rich: in an age of increased travel, poverty in one area enormously increases the risk of the outbreak and spread to other areas of lethal diseases; poverty and attendant overcrowding is one of the major causes of the deepening environmental crisis; low standards of living effectively remove a large portion of the world's population from the market for the goods and services of the advanced economies; finally, the fact that a large portion of the world's population lives below a decent minimum standard of living inevitably undercuts, indeed in some sectors virtually destroys, the labor market on which the political and social health of the advanced countries depends.

. . . .

16 THE AMATEURS

Few things disturb professional diplomats more than "a bunch of amateurs running around trying to set policy." That remark came from a career diplomat in reaction to a huge assembly of representatives of dozens of nongovernmental organizations (NGOs) that were attempting to influence the way governments treat laws on the environment. But it might be repeated with respect to issues ranging from women's rights to endangered species of animals, from trade practices through nuclear weapons policies, from population control through coping with refugees.

Governments often try to contain or prohibit the activities of NGOs, occasionally violently, as the French government did in two commando attacks on Greenpeace ships in 1992 in New Zealand and at the site of a French nuclear test, and as the United States has done in restricting access to travel permits, freezing assets, or embargoing export of goods. In 1948, the U.S. Congress even passed a law—the Logan Act—that makes it a criminal offense for American citizens to correspond with representatives of foreign governments to try to influence them in disputes with the United States. Even despotic governments have seldom managed to achieve a monopoly of foreign affairs, however, despite their efforts. At least in times of relative peace, and at least in our times, their actions have usually been ineffective. Whether the professionals like it or not, amateurs are here to stay.

The most powerful and pervasive NGOs today are, in fact, not even classified as such: they are the multinational corporations, some of which dispose of funds far larger than many states and employ more specialists in "foreign affairs" than their governments.

These facts are evident to any reader of the press. What is perhaps less known is how ancient is the role played today by NGOs and how often throughout history have they been active. The first "NGOs" on which we have information were (as mentioned above) associations of Assyrian merchants resident in foreign cities. Many others—merchants, churches, trade associations, special interest groups, various kinds of "brotherhoods" by the thousands—have followed them. Whereas today the line between NGOs and states seems clear, it was not always so. Both in antiquity and in modern times we have examples of NGOs turning themselves into states. The example most familiar to Americans (and which I discuss briefly in chapter 29) is the Mayflower Compact. Today, there is such a profusion of NGOs that a list of them would fill this book. Without going into excessive detail, I will here attempt to do two things: differentiate three kinds of organization and take an example of each to illustrate their roles. First, sports.

. . .

Certainly the most famous nongovernmental activity in the world today is the Olympic Games. Originally begun in the eighth century B.C.E., they were foreshadowed by games from very ancient times in Egypt and other parts of the Mediterranean.[65] Like the earlier events, the Greek games grew out of religious festivals and were convoked on sacred sites: Olympia was a shrine dedicated to the god Zeus. What set the Olympic Games (and, ultimately, several hundred other Greek games) apart from their ancestors was that they were a contest among states. Previous games had been domestic events usually glorifying a ruler, but the Olympic Games were not under state control. Indeed, Olympia itself was not a city-state but was a territory open, at least theoretically, to all Greeks and, ultimately, in Roman times, to all inhabitants of the vast empire. Athletes competed as representatives of their cities.

The Olympic Games were held every four years for nearly a millennium until they were abolished as pagan events, probably in 393 C.E., when the Christian Roman emperor Theodosius closed all shrines associated with pagan cults. For that long sweep of time, they were perhaps the greatest of all international events. Then, for fifteen centuries, the only people who thought about the Olympic Games were classicists in their libraries. Like so much of the classical world, they were just recondite memories. Ironically, as access to the classical world through a knowledge of Latin and Greek was declining, the games got a new lease on life when, in the last years of the nineteenth century, the French sports enthusiast Pierre de Coubertin mounted a campaign to resurrect them. His efforts led to the first modern Olympic Games, which were held in Athens in 1896 among 285 athletes from 12 European countries and the United States to "propagate the principles of amateurism."

In the centenary celebration of games, held in Atlanta, Georgia, 83,000 spectators attended the opening—more people than lived in the largest of the Greek city-states—and 10,000 competitors represented 197 countries. But this was just the tip of the iceberg because television and radio carried the spectacle throughout the world to audiences estimated in the billions. Today, without a doubt, the Olympic Games and their various spinoffs are the largest nongovernmental activities in the world. The media, advertisers, promoters, and the host authorities are determined that virtually no one alive today will be unaware of them.

From sports, I move to business enterprises. So common today is the movement of personnel, money, factories, and whole companies into the world market, across national frontiers and even into "multinational cyberspace," that we often are surprised to see how recent is this trend. Although, as I have set forth, trade took place among nations from very early times, and colonies of merchants or factors were often established in distant parts, the massiveness and depth of the modern transformation is on such a scale as to force a redefinition of "private" business: it is a truism that some modern companies have economies (and in some cases populations) larger than those of most members of the United Nations.

A pioneer in this development and fairly typical of the current members is ITT, the International Telephone and Telegraph Company, which at its height employed a work force of nearly half a million people in seventy countries. Operating on so massive a scale and able to shift production and sales more or less at will among "its" countries, such a giant necessarily transcends commerce and enters diplomacy and politics. Indeed, ITT had its own "foreign policy," one that played a significant role in the rise of Nazism to power in Germany and played an even more pervasive role in the events surrounding the fall of the Allende government in Chile.[66] Sometimes, its pursuit of profit led the company into actions directly opposed to the policy of its principal host country, the United States. The most obvious occurred just on the eve of World War II when ITT became a major stockholder in Germany's Focke-Wulf aircraft company, which produced bombers and fighters that subsequently killed many American and Allied troops and destroyed Allied cities and equipment. Yet, so powerful had the company become that, by astute lobbying, it persuaded the American government to pay it $26 million for having bombed the German factories during the war. In 1970, through John McCone, then a director and the former head of the CIA, the company offered the CIA a sort of partnership, to which ITT would contribute $1 million, to mount a campaign of "destabilization" against President Allende in Chile.

The importance of these events is not only in their political direction, although the involvement with Nazi Germany at least was directly and violently opposed to U.S. policy, but also in their demonstration of the supranational political role of such large enterprises. So deep is the investment in a given country that the company often believes it cannot afford to be merely a passive recipient of the government's largess or punishment. Yet, at its height, ITT was only the tenth largest multinational and today is dwarfed by such older members as General Motors and such newcomers as Sony. As Richard J. Barnet and John Cavanaugh have written, "The emerging global order is spearheaded by a few hundred corporate giants, many of them bigger than most sovereign nations. Ford's economy is larger than Saudi Arabia's and Norway's. Philip Morris' annual sales exceed New Zealand's gross domestic product. . . . In the 1990s large business enterprises, even some smaller ones . . . are becoming the world empires of the twenty-first century."[67]

These facts have obviously alarmed many of the smaller states, some of which are beginning to fight to recover their sovereign powers, not only through international organizations but by means of manipulation of exchange rates through the actions of central banks and international agreements and through national regulations designed to shape investment of profits made by trade. This is particularly evident in the arms and the aircraft industries, where the size of deals enables governments to negotiate contracts requiring at least some local manufacture, transfer of technology, and "offset" investments. It is, naturally, only the richer of the small states, such as Saudi Arabia, the United Arab Emirates, Kuwait, and some of the Asian "tigers" that have this leverage. China is a heavyweight in this new balance. But the issue is increasingly sharply drawn everywhere. Thus, in the decades ahead, we are apt to see a seesaw battle between the multinationals and the states.

Third, I turn to the hundreds of NGOs that have been established to promote or protect special groups or to further shared causes. Some of the better-known today include Amnesty International, Greenpeace, the Red Cross and Red Crescent, Pugwash, Doctors for a Sane Nuclear Policy, Médecins sans Frontières, Asia Watch, the World Wildlife Federation, and Human Rights Watch. In addition, many organizations including churches and labor unions maintain international programs. Some of these are now going into their third century. Particularly active have been the American Presbyterians[68]—who throughout the nineteenth century founded missions, schools, and hospitals among the American Indians and throughout Africa, the Middle East, and Asia—but Buddhists, Muslims, Catholics, Mormons, Seventh-Day Adventists, and others have engaged in large-scale foreign activities. A number of the major American foundations, notably the Rockefeller, Ford, Guggenheim, and Carnegie Foundations, but including dozens of others, have sponsored programs throughout the world to promote, as the Rockefeller Foundation motto puts it, "the well-being of mankind." Although they have, for the most part, tried to stay out of political and social controversy, they have undertaken projects, trained people, and encouraged trends that have profoundly affected the societies in which they operate.

Since the end of World War II, American and British labor unions, somewhat like older labor movements in these countries and others, including the Soviet Union, have maintained quasi-diplomatic relations with their counterparts in other countries and have directly intervened to promote workers' causes throughout the world. And their work has been paralleled by various trade, industry, and professional associations.

Of quite a different order are organizations designed to promote international understanding. One of these, Pugwash, founded by a group of nuclear scientists after World War II to promote discussion among professional but mainly nongovernmental men and women, has recently been awarded the Nobel Peace Prize. It is unique in that it is composed of and sponsored by the academies of science of a number of countries. It has provided a forum for the testing of ideas that governments might be loath to raise for fear of engaging in lost or unpopular causes or of committing themselves to programs that might turn out to be detrimental to their interests. Although naturally it is difficult to gauge Pugwash's impact, I believe that in some instances it has profoundly influenced the course of recent history and, at least as important, has built a cadre of informed, professional, and active private citizens across national frontiers.

Human Rights Watch is an example of an entirely different kind of transnational group. It is a private organization devoted to the protection and furtherance of fundamental civil liberties throughout the world. Founded in 1978 as Helsinki Watch, its original aim was to support groups set up in Moscow, Warsaw, and Prague to monitor compliance with the Helsinki accords. It is now the largest of the civil liberties organizations, placing observer teams in more than seventy countries in 1995–96 and actively engaging in press and political campaigns and in contacts with governments.

Again different are numerous transnational organizations of which some were established by the League of Nations, or even before the formation of the league, and of which many operate under the umbrella of the United Nations. Many of these are what have been termed intergovernmental organizations, as, for example, the International Postal Union. Many newer organizations are regional or trade- or commodity-oriented and are outside of the United Nations orbit. So, from time to time, governments have established multinational organizations to control trade, such as the Organization of Petroleum Exporting Countries (OPEC) in our times and the international steel cartel formed in 1926 to stabilize prices and halt overproduction.

Loosely associated with the United Nations is the largest and arguably the most important of all international organizations, the International Bank for Reconstruction and Development (the World Bank), which is the principal "motor" of development throughout the world's poorer areas. Directly, the World Bank helps to conceive and formulate projects, to finance them, to train the key personnel, and to work with national and regional organizations, and to serve as an advanced training program for the national personnel who in the future will increasingly take responsibility for these activities. Moreover, the World Bank coordinates a family of related institutions, among them the International Monetary Fund, which interfaces with the central banks of member countries.

Thus, in a variety of ways undreamed of half a century ago, international relations have increasingly transcended the frontiers that divide states and have moved far outside of the jurisdiction and even the oversight of individual states. Probably never again can governments impose on world affairs the sort of coherent system managed by their officials that was regarded as the proper order in nineteenth-century Europe. Adapting to this often chaotic parallel system will challenge governments and public bodies in the decades to come.

PART V INTELLIGENCE AND ESPIONAGE

. . . .

17 GETTING TO KNOW *THEM*

Spying has been called "the second oldest profession."[1] But, actually, that is not true. Whether prostitution is the oldest can be debated, but the historical record makes it certain that the roles of both diplomats and spies were initially mere adjuncts to the role of merchant. He, poor fellow, burdened with coveted goods, beset by fears for his safety, exposed among strangers who often were not discriminating in their means of acquiring what he carried and who sometimes even considered his body as part of the loot, was often charged by his government with conveying diplomatic messages—many of which were thinly veiled threats—and with collecting intelligence. So anxious was he to avoid these extra duties that the merchant usually did everything in his power to avoid fulfilling them. Often the merchant was threatened with fines, imprisonment, or death if he did not accept his foreign assignment. It may be because the task was considered so burdensome and dangerous that spying (and diplomacy) evolved into separate professions in modern times. That may have been a relief to the merchant, but the line drawn between the spy and the diplomat remained thin. Particularly when relations between two states are strained, each usually regards the diplomats of the other as "spies with credentials" or merely as "honorable spies."[2] The difference is primarily in their methods.

And for most of their work, the methods differ little because most of contemporary intelligence gathering is "open"[3]—the sort of activity in which we all engage every day, that is, reading the newspapers, listening to radio broadcasts, and watching television or talking to people and observing what they do. There is nothing esoteric or recondite about it. A normal part of daily life, such activity is available to everyone who wishes to participate in it. In "civilian" life, those who go beyond what is socially acceptable, prying into other people's private lives, are often called busybodies and treated with suspicion as amateur spies; indeed, much of what they do is similar to what professional spies do.

But, astoundingly, the simple, overt part of intelligence is often overlooked. It is a truism that the sure way to avoid having anyone read your mail is to write on a postcard. We are seldom excited by the obvious. Even sophisticated statesmen—among them former U.S. secretary of state Dean Rusk—are known to have preferred to read reports from secret sources even when they were poorer than publicly available press reports.

We often rather casually cut ourselves off from what is readily available, little esteeming its value until some crisis makes us wish we had it. A famous example comes out of America in the 1930s. As an economy measure during the depression, the Library of Congress cut down on subscriptions to Japanese publications. Among those available in any Tokyo bookstore was the yearbook of the Japanese electrical industry, a book that described the national power grid. What American reader, after all, would be likely to want that? But after Pearl Harbor, a large team of experts was to spend over a year trying to reconstruct what could have been learned in that one freely available book. Similarly, it is said, nowhere in America was there a collection of simple street maps of Asian cities of the kind that every gasoline station provides. That lesson was apparently learned, as I found on an inspection trip to a small U.S. Tactical Air Force base in Turkey in 1964. Although the base supported only a single squadron of F-100 fighter-bombers with limited range, it housed a library that included 250,000 maps.

If roughly 90 percent of intelligence is completely open, what about the other 10 percent? First, in many societies there really is no other 10 percent. In perhaps the most famous war in ancient history, the attack by the mighty Persian Empire of Xerxes on Athens and Sparta, it would have been difficult to locate a Greek secret. In the bustling little world of the Greek city-states, everything was done in the open. Espionage was hardly worth undertaking. To build a wall or launch a ship was a community project.[4] Indeed, one did not even need to go and watch: so bitter and long-lasting were the internal feuds that wracked the little states that angry or fearful citizens would come running with the latest information damaging to their domestic foes. Consequently, no spies were needed: everything was visible, loudly discussed, well advertised.

But the Persians employed spies anyway. Some countries engage in espionage whether they need it or not, just as some people always eavesdrop. In ancient Persia espionage was a national style set by the kings. Perhaps in part because of their seclusion, the Persian kings lived in a "covert" world and relied heavily on espionage. What the "great king," as their ruler was styled, could not see for himself, he sent spies—charmingly called "eyes"—to examine for him. From Herodotus we learn that, in preparation for his invasion of Greece, Xerxes dispatched a fifteen-man survey mission (including a Greek who had been "turned") to scout the coast. Herodotus believed that this was the first intelligence mission to come to Greece from Asia, and with them, as A. R. Burn has remarked, "The era of intelligence missions . . . had thus fully arrived."[5] Doubtless, the Greeks did not think of their coastline, which had been sailed for hundreds of years by itinerant merchants, as a state secret, but the Persians obviously did. So, we may say that the definition of that residual 10 percent is what the parties think it is. Permit a personal anecdote to make this point: as a young student I was stopped in 1954 by Syrian police for photographing a little village bridge. I took the snapshot because of the picturesque market scene around the bridge, but the police thought I was collecting military information. To my interrogator I pointed out that the bridge had been built by the French thirty years earlier and that one could buy a postcard showing it in a local shop. To me, it was obviously open. To him, my action seemed like spying.

Sometimes what is freely available is not accessed because those who want to know are too far away, lack the necessary knowledge, or do not know the required languages. Perhaps the most ambitious intelligence-gathering mission ever mounted was an attempt to overcome these three problems.

During the Han dynasty in China, in an attempt to find nomadic allies to attack the Xiongnu, its northern "barbarian" neighbors, an emperor sent a mission westward across Asia. After an appalling series of misadventures and dangers, including captivity by the Xiongnu, the agent eventually reached a place he called Dayan and that is believed to be Ferghana. There he managed to convince the ruler that he was indeed the representative of what must have seemed to the natives a mythical kingdom, and he was given supplies and guides to take him to look for the nomads he sought. He finally found the Yuezhi people near the Sea of Aral. Zhang Qian spent a year with the Yuezhi tribes trying to convince them to join the Han in an attack on the Xiongnu, but they had long since come to terms with their defeat and exile. Thwarted in his main purpose, Zhang spent his time learning about the other peoples and places of Central Asia. After an adventurous return trip, he brought the Chinese their first "hard" intelligence on the geography and politics of Central Asia. Even more intriguing than what he had personally observed were the hearsay accounts he provided of lands with advanced civilizations—the first like theirs ever discovered by the Chinese.[6] Discovery of what are thought to be the Indus valley, Parthia, and Mesopotamia was an electrifying event, comparable to Columbus's discovery of the New World.

Less dramatic was the American discovery of exotic cultures during World War II. Rather suddenly, a large group of Americans, most of whose immigrant parents had made sure that they had not learned the languages of the old country, had to become proficient in German, Italian, and Japanese in order to translate intercepted radio messages, interrogate prisoners, and man military governments. So successful was this effort that during the Cold War it was applied to a much wider range of cultures. Finding that, for example, fewer than a dozen Americans of non-Arab descent knew Arabic, the academic community was given massive government support to set up scores of programs to teach virtually all of the world's languages. These subjects had always been freely available in at least some universities, always open, but it took an unprecedented act to get Americans to become literate in them. It was not that they were hidden but rather that Americans were blind.

Now to the other, the less open 10 percent. It is customary to think of intelligence operations in several more or less distinct categories, based on the means of collection. Like many aspects of espionage, these are given quaint, or quasi-codeword, designations. What results from the activities of a spy is often called "human intelligence," or "humint," whereas "communications intelligence" ("comint") is the interception and, if necessary, decoding of messages; "signals intelligence" ("sigint") is the interception by directional finder or receiver of a radio wave that is then analyzed to show the location, the frequency of transmission, and the identity of the sender. Various other kinds of collection are done with seismic, chemical, and photographic apparatus (to name a few) and have acquired even more bizarre names. "Cratology," for example, is the study of shipping crates in order to guess what might be inside! But I believe it serves my present purpose better to discuss intelligence in terms of the "target" rather than the means. I begin with what is paradoxically perhaps the most common, least reliable, and most questionable object of intelligence gathering—the private thoughts and actions of other people.

Here, the intelligence gatherer comes close to what the common busybody does. The difference between what private persons and government agencies do is largely in the methods available to the government-sponsored professional: he may have access to the mails, bug telephone lines, and sneak into locations in what, if ascribed to a private person, would be called burglary.[7] Also, governments can afford to assign many people to amass and analyze large amounts of detailed information, whereas the private person gets only an impression, or discovers a good story, from just a few incidents. In governmental as in private intelligence gathering, much of what is produced is mere gossip; occasionally amusing, sometimes salacious, often financially compromising, it usually yields materials that might be useful for blackmail but are seldom of political importance. Statesmen love to read information on the lechery and avarice of their opposite numbers, so it commands an avid if necessarily restricted audience.

From such materials, supplemented by others of a more general nature, however, analysts attempt to derive an appreciation of how politicians and statesmen "on the other side" are likely to act or react. So, in recent times, intelligence organizations have spent much time, money, and effort to construct "unvarnished" profiles of major figures, often submitting them to psychiatrists, in order to make better guesses about their conduct. In this way, vast amounts of information have been accumulated on virtually every politician in the world. The picture that emerges is not edifying. Few world leaders turn out to be made of other than the common clay; it is questionable how cost-effective it is to use these methods to learn what a cursory reading of history could have taught: the flesh is weak, and when one has nearly unlimited power to indulge, he usually does.

Sometimes, as in the chance overhearing of a remark by a supposed friend, the information derived can be deranging. Just after the end of World War I, the British statesman Lord Curzon found it impossible any longer to deal with French premier Raymond Poincaré after reading what Poincaré had said about him in an intercepted secret French dispatch. "I can't bear that horrid little man," he hissed as he walked out of their last meeting.[8] Poincaré, one imagines, might have had the same reaction had he known what Curzon thought of him. Sometimes it is better not to know.

At the other end of the intelligence spectrum is simple military or tactical intelligence: learning, for example, where a gun emplacement or a missile silo is located. This form of intelligence is of major interest to all armies and, from the time armies were first used, it was ordinarily acquired by someone going out and looking. In the heat of battle that someone was usually a soldier; in times of tension but not actual conflict, the person was usually a spy.

The ancient Assyrians, the greatest conquerors of their times, were highly proficient in this business and routinely required their provincial governors to gather information on the areas at their frontiers, bribing foreign officials where useful, but always keeping an eye "on anything of remotest political or military interest going on in their area."[9] Failure to keep informed in this way was a recipe for disaster, as the Byzantine historian Procopius warned in his *Secret History*.[10] Numbers of secret agents had formerly gone regularly into Persian territory:

> Then after making careful note of everything they came back to Roman territory and were in a position to acquaint the Emperor's ministers with all the secrets of the enemy. The ministers, warned in advance, kept a sharp look-out and were never taken unawares . . . [whereas Justinian by refusing to spend a penny on them] blotted out [the very] name of spies from the dominions of Rome. This folly was the cause of many mistakes . . . the Romans being completely in the dark as to the whereabouts of the Persian king and his army.

Procopius was probably excessively critical in this passage since Justinian, who effectively ruled Byzantium from about 518 to 565, successfully checkmated his many foreign foes and is known to have conducted a very clever game of espionage that included bringing all of his allies and would-be enemies to his capital to overawe them and drain them of information in order to turn them against one another.

The Byzantines fell back on espionage because of their military weakness, but others embraced it as a part of their strength. Prior to the unparalleled blitzkrieg in which they conquered all the vast lands of inner Asia, Chingis Khan's Mongols prepared their campaigns by sending spies ahead to ascertain how cities were fortified, what stocks of food and weapons they had, whether they would fight or surrender, and where the Mongols could get food and water. Most of the information was acquired by merchants (whom Chingis Khan called "my golden bridle") as they hawked their wares in bazaars.[11] Meanwhile, in Europe, as J. R. Hale has written, "Merchants and bankers were used particularly by the Italians, and the Medici were often better informed by their branch at Lyons, with its contacts at the court, than by their ambassadors. Venice favored doctors, who were likely to be near monarchs at their least guarded moments. Charles V used members of religious orders as spies, and under Francis I a staff of secret agents was built up which comprised noblemen and women as well as obscure clerics and adventurers."[12]

Because of the extensive network of secret agents he maintained in Italy, Spain, and the Spanish Netherlands, the great spymaster of Elizabethan England, Francis Walsingham, was able to give the government "almost as accurate an account of [the Spanish Armada's] equipment and of its plans as the Spanish Admiral himself could have furnished. [Indeed]

Elizabeth . . . was informed month by month of the completeness of his preparations." So thorough and widespread were his activities that it was said of Walsingham that "not a mouse could creep out of any ambassador's chamber but Mr. Secretary would have one of his whiskers."[13]

Why all this activity? The great eighteenth-century student of international affairs François de Callières summed up the prevailing answer succinctly when he wrote, "It frequently happens in negotiations as in war that well-chosen spies contribute more than any other agency to the success of great plans, and indeed it is clear that there is nothing so well adapted to upset the best design as the sudden and premature revelation of an important secret upon which it depends."[14] That, at least, is what most statesmen believe, and those who do not are usually unwilling to take a chance by testing their skepticism.

Of course, information is of little value if there is no means to get it to the central authority, so from very early times, aggressive empires created postal services whose purpose was clearly shown by the fact that they doubled as intelligence services. The Romans and the Byzantines had elaborate systems of couriers conveying messages from all over their empires. So did the Sasanian Persians and the Chinese. In their turn, the Arabs created a similar system called the *barîd*, which was copied—and greatly extended and elaborated—by Turks and Mongols, among whom it was known as the *yam*. In England, the 1711 Post Office Act confirmed an already existing approach to the mails whereby "correspondence from or to named diplomatists resident in London was regularly intercepted, deciphered, and submitted to the secretaries."[15] In the Public Record Office in London there are today some twenty-seven volumes of intercepted diplomatic correspondence just for the eight years from 1756 to 1763.

Ironically but practically, the English post office found a way to make those on whom it spied fund the compromise of their own correspondence: it provided them a convenient service. By gathering communications into one channel and delivering them by post riders and stage coaches, it encouraged ambassadors, spies, and their local contacts to entrust their messages to it. Because these messages were enciphered and sealed the senders presumed them to be secure. And they were delighted to save money by using the bulk service of the post office rather than hiring a rider each time they had a message to send. The post office made a profit, and this profit was used to pay the salaries of the spymasters. But the real value to the English government was that, having steamed open and deciphered the messages, they were able both to keep their fingers on the pulse of their own, deeply divided nation and also to keep tabs on what foreign agents were saying and doing. Further, knowing how such a system could work, and assuming that others would also figure it would, the British devised what today would be called a dead letter drop for their agents abroad. Enter the merchant again. To confuse their European rivals, the British pressed their merchants living abroad to allow their postal addresses to be used for intelligence collection. In this way, they hoped to avoid having their spies' reports intercepted. In the American Revolution, George Washington used a similar ploy.

During the 1814–15 Congress of Vienna, when the statesmen of the victorious powers gathered to establish the shape of Europe after the fall of Napoleon, the Austrians were obviously anxious to know what their allies were saying and planning, so they bribed the couriers to lend them incoming and outgoing dispatches to be opened and transcribed. They also made sure that the cleaning women employed by each embassy gathered and passed along to the authorities the contents of wastebaskets. It was in this way that they found out about a plan to kidnap Napoleon from Elba. In more recent times, it was from the same fertile source that plans on the projected German invasion of Russia in World War II began on their way to Stalin.

* * * * * * *

18 SPIES AND SPYMASTERS

The value of this form of tactical intelligence depended ultimately on the skill and daring of a person. In whatever guise—envoy, merchant, postman, or cleaning woman—the spy was the source of the information and, to get it, he usually had to go and find it. In doing so, he frequently had to go where he was not allowed, at great risk. Far from his own people, often alone and unprotected by even the usually vague notions of diplomatic immunity, he was truly an outlaw. If his sponsor acknowledged him at all, that worthy (and safe) gentleman might lament his fate or even take revenge, as Chingis Khan did for the murder of his "golden bridle," but revenge did the hapless agent no good. So how did an agent go about his task? Consider the story of an Ottoman spy in Europe at the end of the fifteenth century.

In May 1481, just as he began what was to be a great assault on Italy, the Ottoman sultan Mehmet II, "the Conqueror," suddenly died after a reign of thirty years. His two surviving sons, each the governor of a province, raced toward Istanbul, each planning to proclaim himself the rightful successor. The elder of the two, Bayezid, reached the capital first and with the support of the commander of the army assumed office. The younger, Jem, knowing that he would be imprisoned or strangled if he did not overcome his brother, rebelled. Defeated in battle, he fled to Egypt, tried to return, was defeated again, and fled to Rhodes, where he was imprisoned by the Knights of St. John.

The knights realized that Jem was of immense value. If they released him, the empire might be wracked by civil war. Bayezid knew this because his (and Jem's) uncle, Prince Orhan, had posed exactly this threat to the reign of their father, Mehmet. Then, Orhan's captors, the Byzantines, had used him to win concessions from the Ottoman state. The knights decided to play the same game. So Jem found that he had escaped death only to become a pampered prisoner, indeed a strategic asset. So great was his value (or danger) that the knights feared that Bayezid would invade Rhodes to capture or kill him. Prudently, they shipped him off to France to be immured in various castles belonging to the order. Meanwhile, the knights made contact with Bayezid and arranged a sort of reverse hostage deal: they would promise not to release Jem if Bayezid paid them a huge yearly subsidy. The Ottoman government paid up, but determined to find and kill him.

For twelve years Jem was carted around Italy and France, hidden, sometimes treated as a guest, always kept as a prisoner, sold or donated by the knights to the pope, and finally taken as booty by the king of France. During that period, the Ottomans apparently made many attempts to kidnap or assassinate him, one of which was documented when the agent was "debriefed" at the end of his mission.[16]

For an Ottoman agent to travel around western Europe in the fifteenth century required great courage, skill, and luck. Far from his base, not knowing the local languages, customs, or even geography, always at risk of being denounced, robbed, sold into slavery, or merely lynched by xenophobic mobs, he had to find a way on his own. The way he did this both gives us a remarkable instance of espionage and shows us a little-known picture of Western society.

After making his way up the Adriatic, the agent we know only as Barak landed in Italy, accompanied by a Genoese; crossing Italy, the pair arrived in Genoese territory after nearly being apprehended by a representative of the knights of Rhodes. Saved by "an Italian friend" whom he had known in Ottoman territory, Barak was sent to the city of Genoa, where he was taken in, fed, given money and (later) provided with a safe conduct document by merchants. In short, he was able to tap into a network of people whose commercial ties with Byzantium had survived into the Ottoman period.[17] Some of his Genoese helpers operated a trading station on the island of Chios and apparently sold military uniforms to the Ottoman army. Through them, Barak met a member of the Grimaldi family, well-known opportunists and soldiers of fortune, who put him in touch with the duke of Savoy.

On the face of it, that would seem to have been a fatal move: to identify oneself is hardly what we think secret agents should do. But the duke did not take action against him, and at the duke's palace he met a Christian priest who also was said to have been an agent of the Ottomans. (This man even offered to take off his clerical garb and go with Barak to find Jem.) He met another man who was a sort of ambassador-at-large and confidential agent in the Ottoman Empire for the Florentine ruler Lorenzo de Medici. None of these men seemed to think it odd to find Barak in northern Italy, nor were they outraged when they learned of his mission. The fact was that the European powers were so caught up in their hostilities one with another that they cared only formally about their hostility to the Ottoman Empire.[18]

The duke closely questioned Barak, showing a surprising grasp of the organization of the Ottoman state, and he demanded proof of his relationship to the Ottoman government, but was not hostile. When Barak finally was able to satisfy the duke, the duke said to him, "Well, now that we know that you are the servant of the Sultan, we will give you a man to go with you, but you must attend to his expenses." Obviously, there was no way that Barak could get money from his office, and he was unable to get more from his merchant contacts; so he had decided to abort his mission when, by chance, he learned the whereabouts of Jem's latest hiding place. Jem was then in France, so Barak returned to the duke of Savoy, who allowed him to travel through his territory; he reached the little village of Bourganeuf, where, pretending to go to the castle church to pray, he spied the hapless Jem. Mission accomplished, Barak rushed back to Savoy, thanked the duke, went down to Genoa to get a new safe conduct from his commercial allies, and made his way back to Istanbul, where, he hints, he expected that orders would be issued for a hit man or a commando squad to attempt the assassination of the prince.

As in so many grand adventures of espionage, nothing then happened. Apparently, various agents followed Barak's trail, but Jem was shipped off to Rome to be held in the Vatican, where he was seized by Charles VIII of France. Unlike those of fictional accounts of espionage, the end of the story was prosaic: Jem died in his bed in Naples, apparently of natural causes, ten years after Barak's mission.

Barak's story is unusual, but, although the methods and the motivations of spies varied somewhat from place to place and culture to culture over the centuries, in many ways they were similar. Few have left us their own accounts. But among them is a curious period piece by Lt.-Gen. Sir Robert Baden-Powell called *My Adventures as a Spy*. In it Baden-Powell gives us a picture of the "classical" English idea of espionage: the spy had to be an athletic man, capable of climbing mountains or clambering over high fences, but one, above all, who could pose as an eccentric naturalist or artist. His sketch pad of butterflies—his "hobby" cover—is made to conceal drawings of fortifications while his butterfly net allows him to wander unhindered through forbidden zones. "Even in the neighborhood of the forts . . . one was on fairly safe ground in that way, and they [the natives] thoroughly sympathised with the mad Englishman who was hunting these insects." Hunting butterflies, he made his way over some of the ground covered by Barak four centuries earlier. Barak's disguise had been, as far as one can infer, merely Western clothes, but Baden-Powell tells us in touching detail how he affected mustaches and beards, taught himself to amble in a slovenly way (as English gentlemen assumed that Europeans did), and even to dress like a construction worker.

What is one to make of this? If we did not know that many Englishmen did, in fact, masquerade in disguise through Europe and Asia, his account might pass as a joke. It seems highly unlikely that his disguises would have fooled any sober person, but a number of other Englishmen, notably Capt. Sir Richard Burton, Col. Sir Alexander Burnes, Col. F. M. Bailey, Lt. Arthur Conolly, Col. Gerald Leachman, and Maj. E. B. Soane, did pass undetected (or at least thought they did) among Arabs, Kurds, Persians, Afghans, and Turcomans. As General Baden-Powell recounts, one could rely on a rather casual attitude toward spying. And why not? The natives probably thought they had little or nothing to hide and, as the English tended to view it, spying was really just a more serious version, with higher stakes, of the game of hide and seek. "Undoubtedly spying would be an intensely interesting sport," Baden-Powell wrote, "even if no great results were obtainable from it. There is a fascination which gets hold of anyone who has tried the art. Each day brings fresh situations and conditions requiring quick change of action and originality to meet them."[19] And, indeed, that was more or less how the British played "the Great Game" against Russia in High Asia.

There is a genre of English literature (to which Kipling contributed with his novel *Kim*) that has partially created but largely honored the beau ideal of this calling, the man who knew Asian languages so well that he passed easily into native society, scorned danger, loved the wild and disdained the tame, respected the noble savage and despised his city cousin, and, above all, marched to the distant drum of empire. The real-life counterparts are surely as extraordinary a collection of men as ever served a country. These were the men who fought and spied in the Great Game. Although it is unlikely that the Great Game accomplished anything of significance for either the British or the Russians, and certainly caused both great losses, it left an indelible stamp of romance on "the sport." Playing it, Russians and Englishmen had glorious adventures, riding out on horseback into the mountains and deserts of Central Asia, much as Chingis Khan's "golden bridle" had done centuries before.[20]

That is as may be in the distant parts of Central Asia and in less sophisticated times, one may rejoin, but surely it is not the sort of thing one would do in the late twentieth century. Really? It might have been a granddaughter of Baden-Powell who wrote the following in an internal CIA publication about her time in Russia as a CIA agent under the cover of an attaché at the American embassy:

> To go native one needs first of all to look and dress more or less like a Russian, or at least someone from one of the other republics. I managed to take on the drab appearance of the average Soviet woman by wearing a tacky outfit consisting of grey-green skirt, nondescript tan blouse, much-worn brown loafers, and of course head scarf. . . . Attired in my sloppy and deteriorating outfit and equipped with the required language skills plus a willingness to rough it for the sake of learning something, I spent almost all of my free time in Moscow wandering about the city.[21]

Ms. Schroeder may well have fooled the Russians or, just possibly, the Russians did not really care whether she shopped for bread, fruit, and shoes in her tacky outfit.

Parallel to this form of active penetration of territory (or today the airspace over a neighbor) is the passive receipt of his communications. We tend to think of this is as a very modern development, but in fact it also is of great antiquity. One of the earliest intercepted diplomatic documents of which we have a record comes from Egypt. During the seventeenth dynasty, roughly 1600 B.C.E., when much of Egypt was under the control of alien forces, Pharaoh Kamose was attempting to expel one group, the Hyksos, from the Egyptian delta when he learned of a planned attack on his rear from another group, the Nubians. At this point, caught between the two invaders at the oasis of Bahriyah, his fears were substantiated by the interception of a message from the Hyksos king to the Nubian king urging him to attack the Egyptians. The document has a modern ring: "Come, journey downstream! Fear not! He [the pharaoh] is here with me, and there is no one [else] who will stand up against you in that part of Egypt. Behold, I will allow him no road until you have arrived. Then shall we divide up the towns of that part of Egypt and [Nubia] shall thrive in joy."[22] With this in hand, Kamose no doubt knew just how to align his forces.

A thousand years later, the great conflict between Rome and Carthage offers another fateful example of an intercept. It happened like this: belatedly, the still bitterly divided Greeks had begun to realize that their principal danger was not one another, as they had always thought, but the "superpowers," Rome and Carthage. Prudence required that the Greeks and particularly their most powerful ruler, Philip V of Macedonia, try to keep a mutually destructive balance between Rome and Carthage so that neither was free to attack Greece. Rome then seemed the more dangerous, so Philip dispatched an ambassador to Hannibal with an offer to help him against Rome. Along the way to Hannibal's camp in Italy, the ambassador was captured by Roman troops but, with admirable *sangfroid*, talked himself free. When he finally arrived at the camp, he and Hannibal negotiated a sort of letter of intent in which Hannibal offered to cede Roman Italy to Philip if Philip attacked the Romans along the Adriatic coast. That seems clear enough, but the draft is so full of the oaths of the negotiators as to make it appear that Hannibal had come to doubt the Macedonian envoy. Perhaps he thought that the envoy, himself not a Macedonian but an Athenian, had been "turned" by the Romans while he was detained. Hannibal must also have doubted that the envoy could commit the Macedonians; so he delegated three Carthaginians to return with the ambassador to Philip's court. Almost immediately, they were captured by a Roman ship. They were at first merely detained because they were accorded diplomatic immunity; but their attendants were taken aside and "interrogated." When they revealed what they knew, the Romans searched the ambassadors and found the draft treaty.[23] The treaty showed that the ambassadors had "stepped outside of the sanctuary of the gods." At that, their protection was considered to be voided and they were arrested and treated as spies.

Episodes similar to the interception and compromise of the Greco-Carthaginian documents must often have happened in the following centuries. As written communications became more common, those sending them sought to protect them by making them unreadable. Thus, the use of cipher and codes grew apace. At first they were quite elementary. For example, the code that Caesar employed in his correspondence merely transposed each letter for the third following letter (d for a, e for b, and so on). His efforts appear to us quaint and archaic, but in this century an even more obvious form of deception was used by President Woodrow Wilson. He naively thought he had disguised references to his secretary of war by referring to him as Mars and to his secretary of the navy by calling him Neptune.

Between Caesar and Wilson, governments gradually employed increasingly elaborate codes. The Persians and the Arabs led the way at a time in which any written message was effectively encrypted for illiterate Europeans, but as Europeans awoke in the late Middle Ages, it was the Venetians, early masters of diplomacy, who in the thirteenth century began to lay the basis for modern cryptology. In the following century, as each tumultuous Italian city-state put agents in the neighboring cities and sought to subvert or bribe their leaders, their reports became potential causes of war, so keeping them confidential was vital. Thus, as David Kahn has written, "The growth of cryptology resulted directly from the flowering of modern diplomacy."[24]

Obviously, the shrewd, worldly, ambitious princes of the Renaissance states were not prepared to let such deceptions go uncovered. So, wherever they could, they stole or bought the dispatches of their rivals (and allies), copied them, and set about figuring out what the garbled text might mean. By the end of the fifteenth century, several states had small bureaucracies whose functions were to think up new codes for themselves and to decipher those of others. It was not long before their practices spread across Europe. The most famous office, and the one that left its name to the practice, was the *cabinet noir* of Cardinal Richelieu in early seventeenth-century France. The leading cryptanalyst of the time, Antoine Rossignol, was in fact installed in a small room off the private study of Louis XIV at Versailles. Louis's "Black Chamber" was widely copied among the courts of Europe.

But it was not the first. During the reign of Queen Elizabeth, sophisticated intelligence and counterintelligence activities including code breaking had been employed. At that time, the domestic struggles for power between the Catholics and the Protestants were enormously complicated by dynastic and foreign policy issues. The heir apparent to the Protestant Elizabeth was the Catholic Mary, Queen of Scots; Philip II of Spain had marital and martial designs on both; he in turn was opposed to the ambitions of the French royal house and deeply involved in a civil war in the Netherlands, whose rebels were from time to time assisted by England. All of western Europe had come to resemble the Italian city-states, with similar results in espionage and intelligence gathering. A central, if usually passive, figure in all this was Mary, and Elizabeth's great chief of intelligence, Sir Francis Walsingham, used a variety of means, including employing a mole in her entourage and using double agents and cryptanalysis, to trap her.

Elizabeth's agents were generally circumspect, but it is surprising to observe how often in the past, even when they could not get lucrative book contracts, intelligence agents could not resist bragging. Secrets, after all, are no fun if they cannot be revealed, and few people can resist showing that they are "in the know"—even when the costs are high. Thus, the clever cryptographer of King Henry IV of France boasted to the Venetian ambassador that he could read all Venice's secret dispatches; the horrified but more sober ambassador immediately reported the claim to his government, which of course speedily changed its code.[25] And, lest this seem merely a quaint episode from an age of amateurs, consider a modern French version.

In 1911, the French premier had established a confidential channel of communication with the German government through the German embassy in Paris. Wisely or not (but like many other heads of government)[26] the premier chose not to inform his foreign minister. But the latter found out about this channel by reading German embassy telegrams that the *cabinet noir* of the foreign ministry had intercepted and decrypted. The foreign minister may have suspected treason or may just have been miffed at being "cut out of the loop." In any event, he confronted the premier and, unsatisfied in their stormy encounter, acted in a way that led the premier to believe that he had spread rumors denigrating the premier's patriotism. Naturally disturbed, the premier indiscreetly told a confidant what had happened, and this man, in turn, injudiciously warned the Germans to be more circumspect in what they telegraphed. Thus alerted, the Germans quickly changed their codes so that the French, who had profited from access to much confidential information, became "intelligence blind" in the midst of the dangerous events that presaged the outbreak of World War I.[27]

These two episodes point up the central dilemma of intercepted information: revealing it (which is irresponsible) and using it (which may be necessary and is, after all, why it is acquired) are both likely to destroy the source. This dilemma was illustrated by the British in the 1920s when they caught the Russians in acts of subversion and espionage in England. Angry, the government decided to break diplomatic relations. But it could not just act; it had to explain. So in May 1927 Prime Minister Baldwin and his colleagues read out in Parliament several secret Russian messages that they had decoded with the help of a former Tsarist officer. Taking heed, the Russians naturally altered their system so that thereafter none of their messages could be read for at least a decade. Logically, no source of information is valuable unless it can be used, but the decision to use it and so compromise it, unless some believable alternative source of the information is available, is at best a very close call. The British made that decision in two crucial interventions in American politics. The first was in the infancy of the republic: having intercepted French dispatches that appeared to implicate Secretary of State Edmund Randolph in pro-French activities and even suggested that he was in French pay, the British made them available to President Washington. Predictably, and to the delight of the British, Washington forced Randolph to resign.[28] But the most famous example of a decision to use very secret intercepts of this kind came in World War I. The British had had some success in reading encoded German messages. Many were of little value, but one turned out to be of supreme value. This was the "Zimmermann telegram," which has been credited with bringing America into the war.

In 1916, the chief of the German naval staff had predicted that if the war continued Germany would collapse by August 1917; at the same time, leaders of the English government also privately prepared themselves for the possibility of defeat. In desperation, each side sought to produce some magic device or policy to snatch victory from looming defeat. For the Germans, this hoped-for magic was the submarine—by sinking supply ships, the German underseas fleet would starve Britain into surrender or negotiated settlement. For Britain and France, the hoped-for magic was America. America had to be induced to keep on advancing credits for food and weapons and ultimately to send an army to Europe. Only thus would Germany be defeated. These were the grand strategic ideas that came to dominate the two sides as the horror and futility of the war in the trenches became evident even to those standing aloof in distant safety.

Meanwhile, President Wilson, who had campaigned on keeping America out of the war, was determined to honor his pledge. But, as it happened, the Germans and the British took the decision out of his hands. Acting on the demand of his military commanders, the kaiser decided on January 9, 1917, to allow the German navy to conduct an all-out submarine campaign. Even neutral ships, which supplied one-third of Britain's imports, would be attacked. Fears that this act would cause America to enter the war on the Allied side were discounted because, the military chiefs assured the kaiser, England would be starved into a negotiated peace within five months and during that period the ill-prepared and ill-armed Americans could not affect the outcome of the war.

Wilson did not know of the kaiser's decision when he made his "peace without victory" speech to the Senate on January 22, 1917; he learned of it only on January 31. The knowledge was devastating. Afterward, he could barely justify or sustain his peace effort. So, three days later, the U.S. government reluctantly broke diplomatic relations with Germany. The brink of war had been reached—but not exceeded. That had not solved the British problem: America was still *nearly* neutral.

Three weeks later, the British government handed over to the American government the text of German foreign minister Arthur Zimmermann's telegram to the president of Mexico urging the Mexicans to begin hostilities against America. Wilson was enraged. Because of his own deep involvement in Mexican affairs, a theme that ran like a dark thread through his administration, he had been hit at his most vulnerable point. If the submarine warfare was the "cause," the Zimmermann telegram was the trigger. The United States declared war on Germany on April 6, 1917. At the price of violating the secrecy of its code breaking, the British government had achieved its supreme strategic objective.

How was this done? The answer is both complex and tangled. From modest beginnings, the decoding of messages of friends, rivals, and enemies has become one of the great government activities of modern times. But several governments, at least, found the activity distasteful and either did not take it up or discontinued it. The British were among them. When the British Foreign Office was established in 1782, it inherited from the royal office a small staff of code breakers, but in 1844 it abolished the service and did not replace it until the eve of World War I. The effort was initially not only modest in size but also without impressive technical resources. So, not surprisingly, much of the success of the British even as late as World War I resulted less from sophisticated deciphering of messages than from the retrieval of codebooks from sunken ships by divers and through the activities of agents. But, increasingly, the British developed a capacity to decode radio and telegraphic messages. The greatest opportunity this gave the Royal Navy was at the Battle of Jutland, where knowledge of German tactics enabled it to damage the German battle fleet so severely as to put it out of action for the remainder of the war.

But the British were fairly evenly matched by German efforts in this field. The German destruction of the Russian Imperial Army may be reasonably credited to message interception. Indeed, access to this information saved them from disaster. In their first encounter with the Russians in 1914, the German army had panicked and fled, leaving the Russians poised to crash into Prussia. But then everything began to go wrong for the Russians. Wherever they moved or whatever tactics they adopted, the Germans were ready for them. What happened, we now know, was simply that the Russians rarely bothered to encode their messages, so Generals Hindenburg and Ludendorff were able to plan their destruction in the certain knowledge of the Russian dispositions and timetable. Defeat after Russian defeat followed, and the army finally collapsed, paving the way for the 1917 revolution.

In addition to encrypting messages, governments can sometimes restrict the access to the messages. This is routinely done in all government headquarters. Papers are delivered by trustworthy agents, or held in separate locations for "cleared" officials to read, and then are often destroyed. But where the messages must be transported over distances, such precautions are not always possible. Many examples might be cited, but my personal favorite is a run of British documents from India and the Middle East dating from the 1830s and 1840s. The original messages are in London in the Public Record Office. Reading them, I was puzzled to find that each page of each document was punched through with an irregular pattern of holes. When a document was returned to the original fold, the holes matched. The cause of this strange configuration was that the British couriers from the Persian Gulf and Damascus were forced to stop and deliver their sealed messages to be fumigated, allegedly to prevent the spread of cholera. Holes were punched in each packet to enable "purifying" smoke to enter. But, when the documents disappeared into the front door of the smoke house, they were immediately rushed out the back door, opened, and copied. And, in that era of venal government, the copies not only were sent to the Ottoman capital but were also sold to the Austrians, who in turn sold copies to the French. So, instead of the usual fragmentary records with which he must deal, the historian of this period can choose among four complete sets.

Putting messages in locked coffers sounds reliable, yet just such a procedure gave rise to one of the great spy stories of World War II. In Ankara, which was then neutral and a pivotal point in German, Russian, British, and American activities, British ambassador Sir Hughe Knatchbull-Hugessen was routinely provided with highly classified documents from London on the strategy and politics of the war. Like most British embassies at the time, his staff paid less attention to security than to the personal convenience of the ambassador, who liked to take files home with him to read at night. In a rather refreshing example of the old-fashioned notion of spying, his butler, an expatriate Albanian jack-of-all-trades who was familiar with the embassy circuit, borrowed the keys to Sir Hughe's bedroom safe while Sir Hughe was in his bath and made a copy. Then, at his leisure during Sir Hughe's absence, he photographed a few of the incoming dispatches. Having previously worked for an official of the German embassy, he visited his former employer and offered a deal: he would photograph all of the top-secret documents as soon as the ambassador received them in return for money. Naturally, the Germans were suspicious but, after some hesitation, they agreed to the deal. So, as he delivered each batch the Germans paid him and forwarded them to Berlin.

The irony of the story is that "Cicero," as the Germans called their new spy, gained nothing because the Sterling notes he received in payment were counterfeit, the Germans gained nothing because they decided that the information he supplied was bogus, and the British lost nothing because the Germans did not credit their incredible windfall.

Stories of this kind, which delight espionage buffs, are legion. And legend. It has been written that the great English spymaster of Elizabethan times, Sir Francis Walsingham, arranged to have an agent in the Vatican steal from the pocket of the sleeping pope the keys to his safe and extract a letter from King Philip of Spain detailing the plans for the Spanish Armada's attack on England. Probably that story is a canard,[29] but nothing in espionage ever seems to be totally new, unique, or preposterous: an almost exact duplicate of the Cicero story happened about the time of the American Revolution to a British ambassador at Constantinople whose correspondence and codebook were sold to the French by one of his Polish valets. And, at about the same time, the representatives of the new American republic in Paris were having theirs turned over to the British. That episode took the following course:

Just before the American Revolution, several members of the Continental Congress, led by John Adams, drafted a "model treaty" calling for a non-national approach to trade. Their real objective was not to create worldwide free trade, which they thought unlikely, but to involve France and England in hostilities by holding out a lure that the French could not resist but that the English must try to prevent. It was a well-aimed ploy, but the French foreign minister did not go for this bait without help; rather, he was pushed into action by one of the most unlikely secret agents ever known. The playwright Pierre de Beaumarchais, later and better known as the author of *The Marriage of Figaro* and *The Barber of Seville,* had been sent to London on a different mission. While in London, Beaumarchais met a charming, well-connected Virginian who, unusually for that time, had studied at Eton and at the University of Edinburgh. But what was really unusual about Arthur Lee was that he was a secret agent of the Continental Congress.

Whatever Lee may have thought important about his work in London, its historical significance arose from the chance encounter with Beaumarchais just when he had begun to despair of the American cause. Lee's pessimism alarmed Beaumarchais, who reported it to Paris, where it convinced the foreign minister and ultimately Louis XVI that a great opportunity to damage the British was about to be lost. This assessment played a crucial role in preparing a favorable reception for the mission Benjamin Franklin led to France to buy war supplies. Further alarmed by reports that the British were moving toward negotiations, the Americans were granted credits to buy, among other things, most of the ammunition with which the American colonists fought the War of Independence.

The Americans thought themselves very clever negotiators, but none of what they were doing or thinking escaped English notice.[30] The Americans were certainly naive and ill-equipped to play at espionage with the French and the British, who had been at the game for centuries, but still it is difficult to credit what the record reveals. Never, perhaps, has a mission been so completely compromised. One of the three American commissioners, Silas Deane, either already was or later became a British agent whose task was to provide information directly to the British on the Franco-American arms negotiations, and he did so—except, that is, when he tried to keep it for his own speculation. He wasn't very clever with his own security arrangements, however, since he probably thought he controlled the flow of information. The British found out exactly what he was doing, partly by intercepting and reading his mail and largely by employing *his* trusted assistant, Edward Bancroft, to report on his investments and arms-running ventures.

Bancroft was thus a mole employed against a mole. Yet, he was completely trusted not only by Deane but also by Benjamin Franklin, who wrote him a testimonial certifying his loyalty and, moreover, treated him virtually as a member of the family. But Bancroft was a very effective British agent even though the way he carried out his assignment seems too frivolous to be credited. To get his reports to the British, he disguised them as love letters and deposited them in a "dead drop" in a hollow tree right in the middle of the Tuileries garden. But the story does not end there. The other American representative, Arthur Lee, conveniently employed as his confidential clerks various other British moles. Whatever Bancroft did not provide from Deane, Lee's clerks were sure to supply. And, finally, so keen was Franklin on cutting an exciting, slightly mysterious figure in French society that he was unable to keep a secret; every Paris salon was entertained by his adventures. To us in a security-conscious age, so extraordinary (and in retrospect so amusing) is the whole episode as to appear like something out of a Keystone Cops comedy.

. . . .

19 TOOLS OF THE TRADE

The traditional tools of the spy's trade are rudimentary—maps and telescopes and, for map making, thermometers to estimate altitude. In the Great Game, the British also equipped their Central Asian native spies with modified versions of Buddhist prayer rosaries with the beads of which they could count their strides. Such devices have been used for centuries. Many "modern" primitive peoples employ symbolic maps, and representational maps were known at least as early as Babylonian times. The map as we know it was pioneered by the Chinese and the Greeks; the Romans, who were skilled surveyors, were particularly avid map makers. Probably many ancient military commanders had sent out scouts or used merchants to find sources of water and routes across difficult terrain. We know that in his invasion of Greece, Xerxes had somehow found out, probably from scouts he had sent ahead or questioning natives in his employ, that he could take his army across the allegedly trackless mountains west of Olympus. (It is a proof that nothing is ever really new that the German army similarly surprised the British and the Greeks by following the same route with tanks in 1941.) In their turn, the Romans employed, among others, the historian Polybius, whom they sent to explore the coasts of Africa and took along with their armies to Spain and the south of France to compile what today would be called a national intelligence survey.

For the Mediterranean, in or about 1250 c.e. the sailing instructions or guides that must have been in use for many years were brought together in a single collection. Then, within a generation, some unknown navigator or artist got the idea of making this information visual. He took a tanned ox hide and marked it off with a grid. On the lines of the grid he measured the distances given in the "port books" and simply plotted the locations of landfalls. The earliest extant such map, the *carta Pisana*, dates from about 1270. This information was probably too much "in the public domain" to be kept secret, but for more remote areas maps were regarded as major intelligence assets. In the Indian Ocean, for example, the Portuguese greatly profited from their purchase or theft of Arab maps and treated them as state secrets, jealously hiding them from other Europeans.

But maps derive their value from accuracy, and that depends on detailed surveys; someone had to go and take measurements. That might be a long, slow, expensive, and dangerous undertaking. So even in relatively recent times and even in Europe there were vast uncharted areas. In the Seven Years' War (1756–1763), as Geoffrey Parker remarks, armies "managed to march off their maps, and suffered defeats through ignorance of topography,"[31] and, even during the Napoleonic wars, no reliable maps were available for Egypt, Spain, Russia, or even the Netherlands. At Waterloo, some English units failed to find their assigned places through lack of maps, with occasionally disastrous results.[32]

Consequently, not only in Africa and High Asia, for the men playing the Great or lesser games, the making of maps was a prime objective of governments and quasi-public societies, an objective that led the bold, the curious, and the foolhardy further and further afield as the map was gradually filled in. Nonetheless, even as late as the 1970s, maps of Arabia, for example, contained large areas marked "terrain features unknown."[33]

The spy's other basic tool, the telescope, or the spyglass, was probably first used in the sixteenth century.[34] It greatly added to the safety of the observer by enabling him to conceal himself far from his target, but it was difficult, even with a telescope, to see enough to satisfy military commanders. In answer to their demands, the French army began in 1793 to employ hot-air balloons. Napoleon used them to good effect in his campaigns in Italy, but one of the casualties of Lord Nelson's destruction of the French fleet off Alexandria was the apparatus for filling the ones Napoleon had taken with him. In Egypt, in any event, a general hardly needed to rise above the flat lands, and Napoleon seems to have lost interest in them, perhaps to his great cost at Waterloo.

Later, in the American Civil War, some use was made of balloon observation by Union forces,[35] but balloons came into their own in World War I, when they were used extensively to enable observers to look down on the panorama of trenches. From such vantage points they could direct artillery barrages far more accurately than from the ground. So important was this aerial access to intelligence that one of the major tasks of the fledgling air forces of that conflict was to shoot down the balloons.

The balloon had obvious disadvantages: it could not be moved or, if set free, might not be retrievable. As airplanes became more reliable and were increasingly brought into use, they offered more flexible platforms for observation, but it was difficult for the pilot both to fly the plane and to watch the ground. Even when an observer was added, he had trouble seeing enough, especially as his first (and highly personal) priority must have been to look out for enemy aircraft. It was only when cameras were added to the equipment that the airplane became reliable.

Perhaps the most stunning early application of the airplane to intelligence gathering was in the vast and largely arid areas of the Middle East in the 1920s. The Italians were pioneers in their war against the Sanusi-led tribesmen of Libya, and what they had pioneered was used by the French to terrifying effect in their war against the Berber Rif. In Iraq and the Persian Gulf, the British broadened the scope from strafing and bombing to the collection of intelligence and guidance of motorized ground forces that spelled the end of tribal resistance. Under the impetus of Winston Churchill, the R.A.F. established bases from which a few patrols could cover virtually the entire British-dominated area. Pilots could then call ground troops in "armed Fords" to trouble spots. As the high commissioner of Iraq informed the League of Nations in his report for the year 1923,

> [i]n earlier times punitive columns would have to struggle towards their objectives across deserts or through difficult defiles, compelled by the necessities of their preparations and marching to give time for their opponents to gain strength. But now, almost before the would-be rebel has formulated his plans, the droning of the aeroplanes is heard overhead, and in the majorities of cases their mere appearance is enough.

These uses did not require cameras, but subsequently, mounted on ever-faster aircraft, the camera was ever more widely used. Beginning in 1930, flying the Junkers aircraft that then held the world's high altitude record, a German pilot began photographing Polish and French military installations. A few years later the Germans extended their flights into Russia and England. In an eerie foreshadowing of the later episode when Americans lost a number of aircraft over the Soviet Union, the Germans lost a plane over Russia and the Russians kept silent about it.[36] What the Germans had been doing for almost a decade, the British began doing on the eve of the war, using special American-made aircraft. Later, in the war itself, aerial photography enabled plotters to assess damage, plan new raids, and deploy troops. In the Cold War, a variety of American and British aircraft, including the B-47, the B-52, and the U-2, overflew restricted zones of the Soviet Union while Russian airplanes monitored the Arctic and the eastern coast of America; in them, the airborne camera came into its own. During the Cuban Missile Crisis, it triggered American action and virtually controlled developments. As cameras became more precise and could transmit to ground receivers the information they collected, drones could replace manned aircraft. Today, virtually the whole world is under surveillance from satellites: consequently, it is probable that there are no longer unidentified gun emplacements or missile sites anywhere. Indeed, as the camera has been fitted to armaments such as the "smart bomb," it has become both soldier and spy.

Ironically, after the explosion of technology that made possible high-flying and ultrasonic jets and satellites, some armies are again turning back to balloons for intelligence collection since they are much less expensive than manned aircraft, drones, and satellites and can provide continuous coverage of very large areas.[37]

Although the collection of intelligence has been vastly improved, the means of guarding what has been collected has not. Today, although "human intelligence" has lost some of its luster in competition with high technology—despite spectacular exceptions, especially in the Kim Philby and Aldrich Ames cases—it also has remained virtually impossible for any government to restrict access to its materials. Spies such as Philby and Ames and dozens of others have penetrated or absconded in surprising numbers, but more important, or at least more routinely, use of first the telegraph and then the telephone and the radio have made messages potentially vulnerable to compromise. In the never-ending struggle to protect them have come various devices to encode messages. Some of the most modern machines are technical and intellectual marvels, but, like virtually everything in espionage, they are adaptations of very old techniques.

The remote ancestor of the modern encoding machine is the Greek *scytale*, which is thus described by Plutarch:

> They prepare two cylindrical pieces of wood of exactly the same length and thickness. . . . One of these they keep themselves, the other being given to the departing officer, and these pieces of wood are known as *scytalae*. Then whenever they want to send some important message secretly, they make a long narrow strip of parchment, like a leather strap, and wind it round the cylinder with the edges touching, so that there is no space between the folds and the entire surface of the *scytale* is covered. Having done this, they write their message on the parch-

ment in the position in which it was wrapped round the cylinder, and then they unwind the parchment and send it without the cylinder to the commander . . . [who] has to take his own cylinder and wind the parchment round it. The spiral is then arranged in the correct sequence, the letters fall into their proper order, and he can read round the cylinder and understand the message.[38]

A more sophisticated version of the same sort of machine was designed by Thomas Jefferson, probably while he was secretary of state, about 1793. Jefferson's device looked rather like a rolling pin, about six inches long, made up of disks fixed on a central axle. Each numbered disk was inscribed with the alphabet in a random pattern so that when an encoded message was received, it could be plotted on the machine and the plain text would appear in one of the other positions.

The most famous encoding device in this century has been the Enigma machine, which played an unintended but critical role in the Allied victory in World War II. The prototype of the Enigma was designed by a Dutchman for businesses and was available on the public market. There it was not a success, but it soon was picked up by the Germans and became the standard machine of their armed forces. Combined with a sophisticated code, its flexible relocations of the disks or wheels led the Germans to believe it to be unbreakable. It has been calculated that each letter had 5×10^{87} possible positions. The story of how it was broken has filled many books since F. W. Winterbotham was allowed to publish *The Ultra Secret* in 1974.

What decipherment, code-named Ultra, effected was superb tactical intelligence. When General Montgomery in a gesture of nonchalance went peacefully to sleep the night before the battle of El Alamain, he had good reason: he knew from intercepted German reports almost as much about General Rommel's forces as Rommel himself since the Germans meticulously reported their dispositions, plans, and supplies to higher commands.[39] In addition, because the British had also profited from reading German reports on the sailing of supply ships and so were able to sink them, the British had starved Rommel's forces of fuel and ammunition.

One of the most valuable sources of intelligence for the invasion of Europe involved not only modern technology but a curious twist on an old theme. In an effort to impress the Japanese both with their capacity and with their friendship, the Germans invited the Japanese ambassador in Berlin on a tour of the Atlantic Wall in late 1943. The ambassador was delighted, and to show his own grasp of the situation, a motive not un-known among ambassadors, he reported in great detail to his home office what he had learned. His observations were transmitted to his government in code by radio and were intercepted by the British. They, together with a companion report by his military attaché on the German order of battle in the west, were of immense value in planning the D-Day invasion. So, unwittingly, the Japanese ambassador was turned into a sort of scout for the Allies.

In the Normandy campaign itself, information derived from Ultra played a major tactical role in repeated battles and in the ultimate Allied victory.[40] The enemy himself provided the reconnoitering that had been done in previous wars by other means.

And it is worth emphasizing that although the decipherment of Ultra was a remarkable, indeed a stunning, achievement, it rested in part on a bit of old-fashioned spying. In 1931, a German official turned over to the French, simply for money, information on the German codes and ciphers. But, even with this remarkable windfall, the French made no attempt to break into the German system, so, in disgust, the senior French officer of this service turned over copies of key documents to his Polish counterpart. Using this material, the Polish cryptanalysts broke the German code in 1933 but, probably fearing compromise, did not tell anyone they had done so until just before the outbreak of World War II. Thus, without the venality of a single German official, the anger of a single French official, and the brilliance of a small group of Polish mathematicians, the British might not have broken the code.[41] The story is the mirror image of the old jingle, "for want of a nail . . . the battle was lost": indeed, for the payment of a small bribe, one might say, the war was won.

The German interception and code-breaking effort was far more modest than the British. Yet the Germans managed to crack many of the Royal Navy codes. Relayed to the underseas fleet, the information thus obtained enabled the Germans to come close to blockading Britain. In the middle of March 1943, German submarines sank twenty-one ships with a total tonnage of 141,000 that had been precisely located for them. As David Kahn writes, "The Admiralty despaired. They considered abandoning the convoy system as ineffective, which was tantamount to an admission of defeat, since no alternative existed, the loss rate of single vessels being double that of ships in convoy."[42]

Meanwhile, both the U.S. navy and the U.S. army had quietly built up modest code-breaking operations. The civilian operation had been closed down when President Herbert Hoover came into office in 1928, and the 1934 Federal Communications Act banned interception of messages to and from foreign countries. Consequently, many of the telegraph companies refused to turn over the encoded texts they transmitted on behalf of foreign embassies to the federal agencies. But, relying primarily on intercepted radio signals, the army and the navy directed their small-scale efforts primarily against the Japanese. For several years they were able to read lower-level codes but it was not until August 1940 that they read their first message in the highly sophisticated diplomatic code known as Purple. Working backward from what they had learned, the Americans were able to build a machine like the one used by the Japanese. Materials from this source were given the code name Magic.

During the fall and winter of 1941, while the American secretary of state, Cordell Hull, was reading the dispatches sent between the Japanese government and its embassy in Washington, it was difficult for him to treat the Japanese ambassador civilly and to refrain from indicating that he knew about Japanese duplicity. Indeed, Hull excluded his senior adviser from the meetings because he feared that an outburst of the man's well-known temper might reveal what the Americans knew.[43]

Yet, for those overhearing hostile information it was difficult or impossible to estimate what the overheard party actually intended to do, where he might do it, or when. Decoding could not provide more than the messages contained and, in Purple, the Japanese did not identify Pearl Harbor as the target or December 7 as the date of attack. Arguably, the American military chiefs should have identified Pearl Harbor because it was the major American base in the middle of the Pacific and had been "war gamed" years before as a logical target in more or less the way the Japanese attacked it. So the controversy raged through contemporary congressional hearings and has ever since; the fact that some of the key documents are still restricted adds to the mystery.

What the public record shows is that when, on December 7, 1941, the chief of the U.S. Army General Staff, George Marshall, learned from Purple of the breaking of diplomatic relations (but not of the Japanese decision to go to war) he decided not to telephone his commands in Hawaii and Manila to warn of the probable Japanese attack because he had no "secure" means to do so. By 1940, the "scrambler" had come into use and promised to provide secure communications along telephone lines. But, as so often happens with technology, offense and defense played leapfrog. Marshall feared that offense was then ahead. He may have been right. At any rate, later in the war it became clear that the Germans had both tapped the transatlantic cable and learned how to unscramble conversations so that they were able to listen to conversations between President Roosevelt and Prime Minister Churchill.

The payoff for the American and British work on the codes and the silence about what they had learned came not at Pearl Harbor, where the Japanese caught the United States unaware, but at subsequent great naval battles. Access to the Japanese naval code enabled the Americans in the Coral Sea in May 1942 to surprise and sink part of the invasion force aimed at Australia and near Midway on June 3 to ambush and cripple the Japanese fleet. At Midway, Admiral Nimitz knew about as much about Admiral Yamamoto's fleet as General Montgomery had known about Rommel's Afrika Korps and for the same reason: he had read the complete Japanese battle plans. Midway, as Admiral Nimitz later said, "was essentially a victory of intelligence."[44]

These episodes offer a simple but important insight: reading the Japanese diplomatic materials could not provide complete insight into the Japanese plan at Pearl Harbor because the messages did not contain the key information. In contrast, the intercepts of Japanese battle plans (like those the British got before El Alamain) gave the Americans precise details on timing, location, and force size. When afterward we search for causes or clear warnings, we can often find them, but predicting on the basis of nearly always incomplete, faulty, or obscure information is the most elusive and difficult of all intelligence actions. The guess made before is rarely seen subsequently to have been satisfactory and, being subjective, is as likely to be formed by prejudice, anger, or ignorance as by logic and insight.

A powerful example is the CIA "appreciation" of Soviet intent on Cuba in 1962. The professional analysts, on the basis of the most complete information they could muster, opined that the Soviets would not put missiles in Cuba. They were wrong. Meanwhile, the director of the CIA, John McCone, also guessing and with access to the same information, came to the opposite conclusion. He was right, but, as he admitted, it was a judgment call. After the event, hundreds of people inside and outside the U.S. government and even in the Soviet establishment[45] mulled over the events leading up to the crisis in an effort to find patterns on which accurate prediction might have been based. They are still in the dark. And, since governments feel that they cannot afford to give up on the quest for certainty, both failures and successes have given rise to huge bureaucracies and vastly expensive new scientific devices: not only in the United States but also in England, France, Germany, Russia, and Israel billions of dollars are spent today on intelligence. We have reached a point at which it is likely that no single telephone call, fax, or telegram anywhere in the world goes unrecorded by someone. What was once the task of a soldier or a spy is now a passive presence in virtually every office and living room in the world.

* * * * * * *

20 ESPIONAGE AND COUNTERINTELLIGENCE

Different from intelligence collection but often accomplished by the same people are various sorts of "dirty tricks" that are intended to confuse, give an incorrect impression to, or frighten an adversary. The simplest and most benign are the intelligence counterparts to the military use of camouflage. There are many kinds, ranging from false messages that are allowed to fall into the hands of the opponent, sometimes in a code that is known to have been broken, to deliberately circulating false information. The Zimmermann telegram was genuine, but had it not existed, the British could have manufactured a fake, as they often did when in 1941 they were trying to stampede the American government into World War II.

Sometimes even more powerful than action is careful inaction: the British, for example, knew of the Japanese plans for their attack on China in 1937 but did not inform the Chinese. This was understandable because the British had little faith in the Chinese government. But it is considerably more painful to the British (and to the Americans) to discuss the possibility that the British (under direct orders from Prime Minister Churchill) withheld information on the Japanese attack on Pearl Harbor, which they had got from breaking the Japanese naval tactical code (JN-25). They intercepted at least twenty messages to and from the attacking fleet and did not pass along the information to the United States, presumably in an effort to force America into the war. If this is true, and it is disputed, it had the effect (although by opposite means) of the Zimmermann telegram: once Pearl Harbor was attacked, America had to declare war.[46]

In espionage, actions, inactions, half-truths, and falsehoods are not new. In his war with Rome, Hannibal used some of them. Although he then occupied southern Italy, he was essentially cut off from his base in Carthage. In between, invitingly, was Sicily, on which stood the ancient Greek city of Syracuse, where a generation of harsh Roman rule had created a strong anti-Roman sentiment. Hannibal's successes in Italy and his occupation of most of the south had allowed the Syracusans to achieve a quasi independence, but they were afraid to take sides against Rome. Carthage lacked the naval power to intervene militarily, but Hannibal realized that Syracusans offered a fertile field for covert action. If he could not win them over by a show of power, he could convince them that their only hope lay in a Carthaginian victory. Already they were half convinced because they knew what Rome had done to their cousins on the mainland and what it always did to those who tried to defect from alliances, so when their young king was given evidence that the Romans planned to assassinate him, he immediately sent envoys to Hannibal asking for assistance. Shortly thereafter he was in fact assassinated. That violent act and the fact that a pro-Roman faction used the ensuing disorder to seize power seemed to confirm the popular belief. In their turn, taking advantage of this assessment, Hannibal's agents circulated an allegedly intercepted but actually forged letter from the pro-Roman faction leaders urging the Romans to massacre Syracuse's troops. A superb piece of "black propaganda," the letter turned the public mood violently against the Romans and their local allies.[47]

A famous modern version of a similar trick was allegedly played on Stalin by German intelligence in 1937. The Germans arranged for Czech intelligence to acquire information that pointed to an anti-Stalin plot among the senior command of the Red Army. Thinking to help the Soviets, the Czechs passed along this information, which frightened Stalin into a massive purge of his general staff. The result was evident in the chaos that nearly overwhelmed the Red Army when the Germans attacked in 1941.

Agents can also play havoc with morale. During the "phony war" in 1939–40, the Germans tried to stimulate French fears of war by sending weeping women agents, apparently lamenting the loss of their sons or husbands, through the streets and subways of Paris. This also is a modern adaptation of a very old trick. In the Persian attack on ancient Greece, the Persians may have "turned" the Delphic oracle (as others are reputed to have done before them, perhaps by bribery) to prophesy Persian victory and to encourage Greek disunity.[48] Some years later, the Spartans adopted a pro-Delphic stance that won for them the powerful support of the oracle against Athens.

Few people today share the Greek belief in oracles, but many can be convinced by more tangible evidence. And that was exactly what the British used to confuse the Germans about the point of the Allied D-Day attack on the Continent: they created a "message" with the body of a drowned man, complete with incorrect invasion plans, which they arranged to have washed ashore in Portugal, where it was passed to the Germans.

If dead men can pass damaging information, live men can do better. Perhaps the most famous use of spies against their masters took place in the ancient world just before the Persian invasion of Greece. Having learned that Xerxes' army was on the move toward Greece, the Greeks sent three spies (as Herodotus tells us) to find out all they could about his army. They were caught and tortured and had been condemned to death when news of their exploit reached Xerxes. He immediately countermanded the order and set the spies on a further fact-finding tour of his forces. As he explained to his generals, "The killing of three men would not have done the enemy much harm; but if, on the other hand, the spies returned home, he was confident that their report on the magnitude of the Persian power would induce the Greeks to surrender their liberty before the actual invasion took place, so that there would be no need to go to the trouble of fighting a war at all."[49]

It is probably just a coincidence, but there is a striking modern parallel. On the eve of World War II, the Germans, who were avid students of the classics and whose officer corps had all read Herodotus and other Greek and Latin histories, "deliberately allowed French air force officers to admire the military installations—some of them Potemkin airfields—and had succeeded in depressing their guests. Military authorities all the way to the air minister were persuaded that the Germans had ten aircraft to their every one and that they could and would bomb Paris as they had Guernica [during the Spanish Civil War]."[50] Revealing overwhelming military capacity may not have accomplished all that Xerxes wanted, but it surely played a role in defeating the French before World War II began.

Today, the "mole" is a kind of agent we know best through the unmasking of Kim Philby, Guy Burgess, Donald McLean, Anthony Blunt (from England), Aldrich Ames, and, charged but not tried, Harold Nicholson and—allegedly—former French defense minister Charles Hernu. His aim is usually stealing protected information, but his role may be wider. In earlier times, he was apt to open the gates of besieged cities; from ancient Persia through the Middle Ages to relatively modern times, agents or disaffected local people played this destructive role.[51] Long after cities ceased to be walled and locked, information on their defenses was still crucial, and the means to get it was still the same—bribery. As we can now learn from private and public papers, European officials and even members of royal families were often in the pay of foreign embassies. In England, which was by no means unique, the Spanish ambassador had royal counselors, secretaries (those we call ministers today), the commander of the Royal Navy's home fleet, the head of counterintelligence, and even the queen of James I on his payroll.[52] One particularly useful mole in the seventeenth century was a royal mistress.

Where mistresses feared to tread, dervishes, priests, and labor leaders might go. The great fourteenth-century Turco-Mongol conqueror Timur regularly employed dervishes and itinerant monks to gather military intelligence because they could move easily across frontiers and often got support from members of their orders in foreign lands.[53] In our century, the Russian priest George Gapon, a police agent who was admired by Lenin, played a confused but destructive role in the revolution of 1905. Lenin, himself a beneficiary of German intelligence and a highly experienced denizen of that murky world, was hoodwinked by one of his close collaborators, Roman Malinovsky, who, as "head of the St. Petersburg metal-workers' union on the eve of the First World War [had] enjoyed Lenin's complete confidence but also had been a police agent."[54]

"Dirty tricks" can also be more direct, but because they are more dangerous and often have adverse consequences—particularly when they fail—they are rarer. However, occasionally one is dramatic. In November 1939, believing that the British Secret Intelligence Service (SIS) planned to assassinate Hitler, the German *Sicherheitsdienst* lured two British intelligence officers into an ambush at the Dutch frontier, kidnapped them, and forced them to tell what they knew about their organization. This was the so-called Venlo Incident. Other violent operations involving kidnap, attempted murder, or murder were carried out by both the CIA and Soviet intelligence. But one of the largest (and now most publicized) was undertaken by Israeli intelligence (*Mossad*) under the personal supervision of Prime Minister David Ben Gurion: it was the blowing up in 1954 of the United States Information Agency libraries in Cairo and Alexandria in an attempt to damage relations between Egypt and the United States. One of the Israeli agents was caught red-handed, and his arrest, and reports of an Israeli double agent who was secretly working for the Egyptians, led to the apprehension of other members of the group. The episode created a scandal in Israel that was named after Minister of Defense Pinchas Lavon as the Lavon Affair. Although Lavon was publicly blamed and forced to resign, the incident almost destroyed the government of Ben Gurion.

On a much larger scale is the organization of coups d'etat. Perhaps the most famous of these was the joint operation of MI6 and the CIA to overthrow the Iranian government of Mohammed Mossadegh in 1953. Although this operation, and others in Guatemala and Chile later, were counted as successes at the time, it is likely that the years of turmoil that followed might have been avoided, or at least moderated, had they not been undertaken. The American attempts to get rid of Fidel Castro, Gamal Abdel Nasser, Patrice Lumumba, and Moammar Qadhaffi were further proof of the dangers of governmental extralegal actions, and the overthrow of the Diem regime in Vietnam showed how hard it always must be to predict the result of outside intervention. Today's success may prepare tomorrow's disaster.

. . .

Detailed information on current intelligence organizations is, by its nature, difficult of access and, if obtained, suspect. Moreover, events in the last few years, particularly the end of the Cold War, but to a lesser extent the (temporary?) lowering of tensions in the Middle East and among the Far Eastern and North Atlantic powers have probably recast both absolute and relative figures. The following may, however, give some approximations. First, the Soviet Union.

The Soviet Union's intelligence apparatus has undergone the most frequent transformations, at least in official designations, although it seems likely that below the change of acronyms, old structures and key personnel were merely absorbed into the new. The Bolsheviks began in 1917 with The Extraordinary Commission for Combating Counterrevolution and Sabotage (CHEKA), which was formed under Felix Edmundovich Dzerzhinsky. This organization was supplemented in 1920 by a military intelligence office known as the GRU. Then, in 1922, CHEKA was "abolished" and replaced by the State Political Administration, whose name was changed in 1923 to the United State Political Administration. In 1934 this organization was absorbed by the People's Commissariat for Internal Affairs (NKVD), from which, in 1941, was split off the People's Commissariat for State Security (NKGB). The two were reunited after the German invasion but were again split in 1943. In 1946 the NKVD became the Ministry of Internal Affairs (MVD) while the NKGB became the Ministry of State Security. They were again merged after Stalin's death as the MVD. But the MVD was "abolished" in 1962, only to be reborn in 1966 as the All-Union Ministry for the Preservation of Public Order. The KGB (Committee of State Security, *Komitet Gosudarstvennoy Bezopasnosti*), set up in 1953, lasted until 1991.

Beginning in 1991, when Boris Yeltsin began to press for a larger Russian role within the Soviet Union, he found that alone among the fifteen republics, Russia did not have an independent intelligence organization, so he pushed for and got a new Russian service in May of that year. Following the involvement of the KGB in the attempted overthrow of Mikhail Gorbachev, the old KGB was broken up. Within the Russian republic, which inherited most of the former U.S.S.R. organization, many of the key figures were replaced, and it was split into a domestic service and a foreign intelligence operation. In the fall of 1991, the foreign intelligence organization was again split, into the Central Intelligence Service (*Tsentralnaya sluzhba razvedki*), which was given responsibility for foreign intelligence, and the Federal Security Agency (*Agentsvo federalnoy bezopasnosti*), responsible for counterintelligence.

Compared to this tumultuous bureaucratic history, British and American intelligence and counterintelligence appear relatively simple. The first rudimentary British intelligence service was set up under Queen Elizabeth by Francis Walsingham (on which see above), but it was not until 1886, in response to the Irish Republican rebellion, that Scotland Yard established the Special Branch, which, on the eve of World War I, became (and remains) MI5. At the same time, an overseas intelligence organization known as MI6 was created. These activities were supplemented in the aftermath of World War I by a special organization dealing with the interception and decoding of wireless communications.

Resembling the British system, which greatly influenced its formation and growth, is the substantially larger American intelligence establishment. Domestic intelligence, counterintelligence, and federal police work are primarily focused in the Federal Bureau of Investigation (FBI), which was formed in response to the so-called Red scare at the end of World War I. For personal, political, and historical reasons, the FBI operated not only in United States territory but also in Latin America and occasionally—particularly in matters relating to security and terrorism—all over the world.

Some overseas intelligence activity was and is carried on by the armed services, each of which maintains intelligence divisions. Code breaking, so vital in World War II, was the preserve of these divisions before being constituted as a separate organization, the National Security Agency (NSA). The Department of Defense, of which the NSA is legally and administratively a part, also maintains the Defense Intelligence Agency, which, among other functions, sends military attachés abroad to liaise with and report on foreign armies.

During World War II, a new organization known as the Office of Strategic Services (OSS) was created on the pattern of the British MI6. Although highly touted publicly, it served with indifferent success during the war. Bitterly opposed by the head of the FBI, J. Edgar Hoover, who saw it as an invasion of his territory, the OSS was made by William Donovan into a vehicle for his political ambitions. Being new and inexperienced, eager to "do something," the OSS worked out a deal with Vyacheslav Molotov to allow teams of Soviet intelligence agents to set up in Washington and made available to them highly sensitive communications intelligence information. After a series of confrontations among Hoover, Donovan, and General Marshall, President Roosevelt decided to deny the OSS personnel, including Donovan, access to most of the deciphered materials from Ultra and Magic and commissioned an investigation of the OSS by a senior officer in military intelligence. The result was devastating. As Curt Gentry has written, "In his fifty-four page report [Colonel Richard] Park listed more than 120 charges against the OSS and its personnel—including incompetence, corruption, orgies, nepotism, black-marketing, security lapses, and botched intelligence operations, some of which had cost dozens of lives. By contrast, Park found only seven OSS actions worth favorable mention."[55]

In September 1945, the OSS was legally abolished, but much of its staff was almost immediately put into transitional offices and ultimately folded into the Central Intelligence Agency, created two years later pursuant to a directive issued by the newly formed National Security Council. The 1949 Central Intelligence Agency Act gave the agency broad authority to disregard U.S. laws and to expend funds without accounting. These very powers were ultimately, in 1995, to lead to a demand that the agency be drastically reduced or even abolished. Indeed, long before the current outbreak of criticism, a number of men with personal experience in intelligence (including Somerset Maugham, Graham Greene, and John le Carré), as David Fromkin comments, had portrayed such activities as "morally corrupting, usually incompetent, and more likely to harm our friends than our enemies. We now know that this body of literature should not be classified as fiction."[56]

Although it is a small country, Israel plays a disproportionately large role in the intelligence world. Not only is its population extraordinarily able, but the wide geographic dispersion of Jews, their linguistic and cultural knowledge, and their sense of national and religious loyalty have been mobilized to give the Israeli intelligence agencies, particularly Mossad, great access. Throughout the half-century of the state's existence, Israeli intelligence has been a prime conduit of information from the former Soviet Union, where the Jewish community has been prominent in scientific and governmental affairs; from Africa, where Israel played a role in balancing Arab influence, in the Arab world, which for Israel has been a prime target; and in various international agencies and nongovernmental organizations. It has developed a "special relationship" with the British, the French, and the American military, intelligence, and industrial establishments and has been heavily subsidized and assisted by them.

These agencies, and the scores of smaller intelligence services, probably employ directly at least 150,000 people. Probably at least that many more people are employed indirectly or occasionally. And, when those who cater to or produce for the intelligence establishments are counted, the total number is probably not less than 1 million, on whom and on whose activities the world community probably spends $100 billion a year, of which the American budget in 1994 was at least $28 billion.

Today's massive statistics are not matched man for man or dollar for dollar in the past, but rarely have nations not devoted major resources to spying. Not surprisingly, therefore, governments throughout history have struggled to prevent spies or moles from infiltrating their establishments and to catch those who do. In America, this task has been allotted to the FBI and in England to MI5. Many other organizations in other governments occupy themselves with such matters. The Russians in particular have been fecund in spawning state security organs. The Tsarist Oprichnina, "Third Section," and Okhrana faded into the various Communist organs, today represented by the Federal Security Agency. The Germans operated several overlapping agencies to catch spies and, given the hostility of some Germans to Nazism, they had a big job—France alone claimed to have fifteen hundred agents in Germany in the late 1930s.[57]

Generally speaking, counterintelligence has proved more effective than spying. It is noteworthy that just before World War II the Germans had some twenty-five agents in Britain, none of whom remained in place when the war began, so that the Germans did not learn that the British had moved an expeditionary force to France until their troops ran into them. How clever the British were, one may say, but the reverse was also true. Within a few months of the outbreak of war, the Germans had captured or immobilized all the British agents in territory they held as well.[58] Pity the hapless spy. No wonder the merchant shunned the job. He is the object of a ruthless and determined search.

Ruthless or not, all governments assert the right to do whatever it takes to apprehend spies. And they always have. Even the great Mongol conqueror Chingis Khan, who had less reason than most to worry about effective enemies, established a sort of counterintelligence operation under one of his close associates, whom he called "the eyes I see with and the ears I hear with."[59] Those who faced more powerful enemies worried more and devoted more attention to their activities. The Indian strategist Vishnugupta warned his prince to begin his search in his own harem because princes "like crabs have a notorious tendency of eating up their begetter."[60] The Ottoman sultans and many European rulers were well aware of this danger. But, like spying itself, counterintelligence has a cost, sometimes a cost too heavy to bear. In a humane early recognition of this, the Seljuk Turkish ruler Alp-Arslan is said to have replied when asked why he did not appoint a *sahib-khabar* (chief of counterintelligence) to check on the loyalty of his associates,

> If I appoint a sahib-khabar those who are my sincere friends and enjoy my intimacy will not pay any attention to him nor bribe him, trusting in their fidelity, friendship, and intimacy. On the other hand my adversaries and enemies will make friends with him and give him money: it is clear that the sahib-khabar will be constantly bringing me bad reports of my friends and good reports of my enemies. Good and evil words are like arrows, if several are shot, at least one hits the target; every day my sympathy to my friends will diminish and that to my enemies increase. Within a short time my enemies will be nearer to me than my friends, and will finally take their place. No one will be in a position to repair the harm which will result from this.[61]

Such sentiments are rare because inherent in the intelligence establishment are two fundamental problems. The first, of which we have a modern example in the career of James Jesus Angleton of the Central Intelligence Agency, is the political version of paranoia. So immersed in a world of intrigue was Angleton that ultimately no one could pass his test for loyalty. The irony was that, paranoid or not, Angleton was right. There *was* subversion in the heart of his organization. "From the beginning [of the CIA] the Soviet Union knew every move [the CIA chiefs] made," writes David Fromkin. "In the beginning it was Kim Philby; in the middle it was the Walker ring; in the end, it was Aldrich Ames."[62] We now know that Ames was not the last mole. If the charges against Harold Nicholson are true, he was an even more damaging spy than any of these. But the unresolvable dilemma faced by any counterintelligence force is that completely to "purify" it involves killing the organization. It was the final realization of this that caused a subsequent director of the CIA to remove Angleton.

The second fundamental problem is that there is a tendency for practitioners to fall prey to the ambitions or hatreds of their sources where independent verification is more difficult than in less secret activities. An example with major consequences in our times is British intelligence in pre-independence India, where the very schisms in Indian society that facilitated the gathering of information also ensured its unreliability. Muslims, Hindus, and others were so driven by communal hatreds that they raced to denounce one another as dangerous agitators and fomenters of sedition. Meanwhile, landlords and merchants saw everywhere the hand of Communist agitators. And the political police, by training, inclination, or self-interest, added to the alarm by their employment of secret informers since the police officers' "continued employment in effect depended upon their ability to unearth or to fabricate sedition[, so they] sent in incredible tales of pending mutiny and an Afghan-Russian-Punjabi entente to seize the border districts."[63] We now know that these were fabrications, but "intelligence," like other forms of perception, is always automatically and unconsciously weighed in the scales of memory. And British administrators lived with the haunting memory of the great sepoy rebellion of 1857–58 and saw Indians as always ready to revolt.

To discount built-in prejudices, clichés, and presuppositions requires a major effort of imagination—and a good dash of old-fashioned skepticism—qualities that are not only always in short supply but that are frequently regarded with disfavor. The naysayer is seldom a popular player on any team. Evaluations of information are inherently subjective, and often are close calls. Since the penalties for overreacting are often less than those for underreacting, the natural propensity is for those who receive information to take a "worst case" view—"If they have the weapons, they will use them"; "If they are saying that, they will do it." Thus, inevitably, the most difficult aspect of intelligence is not collection but evaluation, a point that is often enunciated but seldom reflected in budgets or in the allocation of manpower. Almost worse, those who are charged with evaluation are themselves subjected to political pressures that are hard to resist. The propensity to be "patriotic," to "wave the flag" by affirming dislike of unpopular movements or figures, is present even in those whose "objectivity" is demanded by statute and who inhabit the most sacrosanct offices of state.

Moreover, we all have a natural propensity to avoid or overlook the things we regard as distracting, inconvenient, unpopular, or unimportant. A great practitioner of analysis, Thomas Hughes, recounts a classic example: when it became clear that World War I would drag into a long war of attrition, a German official recommended that a special organization be set up to run the economy, but he was admonished by General Helmuth von Moltke, "Don't bother me with economics. . . . I am busy conducting a war."[64]

Lest this seem arcane or archaic, it is significant that the American official who correctly perceived the conditions and movements that re-sulted in the revolution in Iran in 1979 was similarly admonished that he was wasting his time and government money on such obscure issues and unimportant religious figures and was "selected out" of the U.S. Foreign Service for his bad judgment. What he had to say, to borrow the motto of the *New York Times,* simply didn't "fit." The reception by senior civilians in the U.S. government of pessimistic reports on the Vietnam War from the CIA was similar; one cabinet officer even refused to be briefed any longer by the deputy director of the CIA because he did not want to hear the contrary view.

Finally, in intelligence, as in most other activities in this busy twenti-eth century, there is an "overload" of information. We are deluged, and there is intense competition for attention. Not so very long ago, statesmen could take days or even months to digest and reflect on information, but the advent of the telegraph made this an impossible luxury. Today, each significant actor is bombarded with hundreds of discrete pieces of infor-mation every day. He is often virtually deafened by the cacophony and must inevitably fail to hear much that is important. A very good example is the British reaction to intelligence reports on the eve of World War II. As Donald Cameron Watt has written, "In the spring and summer of 1938, the British government received so many different and conflicting signals as to Hitler's intentions that they seem to have resigned themselves to ignoring all indiscriminately."[65] We may rightly conclude that Say's Law— that bad money drives out good—is mirrored in government, where the urgent often drives out the important. Thus, even good intelligence may be and often is defeated by the weakest link in the policy of any govern-ment: the human mind.

PART VI DIPLOMACY

. . . .

21 PEACEFUL RELATIONS BETWEEN STATES

Diplomacy has been defined as "the conduct of business between states by peaceful means."[1] And, like many definitions, that is a reasonable generalization. However, it is only a generalization. For a fuller understanding, it will be useful to probe more deeply into the historical experience and to test the boundaries of contemporary practice. That is the purpose of this chapter.

The word *diplomacy,* like the practice itself, has a curious history. First used in English about three hundred and fifty years ago, in various other languages it was employed in medieval times to mean a document issued by a sovereign. It was then the practice to fold the parchment on which texts were written (in effect to make an envelope), and so they came to be called diplomas, from the Greek word *diplou,* meaning "something doubled." Naturally, the original meaning gave rise to innumerable puns: the English diplomat Sir Henry Wotton wrote that a diplomat is an honest man who is "sent to lie abroad for the good of his country."[2]

Although it is usual to start any discussion of diplomacy more or less when the word came into use in what historians term "early modern" times and to restrict the discussion to Europe, to do so is to neglect its ancient history and widespread use. In fact, diplomacy is one of the oldest and most common of human endeavors. To put it into context, we need first to examine how a sense of relationship arose among societies. Then I will show how kinship set the basis of an "international" system and provided the first of a long series of "worldviews." Next, I will examine how various states adapted strategies to fit their concepts of the world and their roles. Then I will discuss how diplomacy came to incorporate customs such as diplomatic immunity, neutrality, and treatment of prisoners into law. Then I will consider the role of rulers and their surrogates (agents, orators, negotiators, and ambassadors). And finally I will discuss the legal context of foreign relations. First, the "biology" of foreign affairs.

As we saw in chapter 2, the fundamental social fact in the life of early men is that "us" meant the immediate family. "Them" meant everyone else. If groups of kinsmen could have lived as they wished, they would seldom if ever have interacted with strangers, but the boundary between "us" and "them" was more of a smudge than a precise line separating neighboring groups. Clans were constantly splitting apart as they grew beyond their resources or as their resources contracted in times of drought or seasonal change, so some of "us" were periodically becoming "them."[3]

Contrariwise, our ancestors had to reach out to "them," among other reasons to acquire mates since the clans in which they lived were too small always to provide them. So some of them were always becoming the mothers of "us." As societies grew in size, the urgency of this quest receded, but acquisition of suitable mates has remained a persistent quest down to modern times, especially among those groups about whom history tells us the most—the rulers. Thus, ancient and medieval history is filled with the political results of marriage among aliens.

Mates apart, some societies have gone to almost any extreme to avoid having to deal with foreigners. The customs they have adopted include population control by enforced expulsion and infanticide to try to maintain a balance with available resources, but such a balance has always been difficult to achieve and impossible to maintain. Others, thwarted in the quest for alien mates, have practiced endogamy or even incest. But these were usually only partial or temporary solutions. And, as societies grew richer, people recognized "needs" for knowledge, goods, and services that were not always locally available. So, all over the world, from the most primitive to the most modern, from tiny villages or nomadic clans to huge cities and vast empires, people have been driven into contact. But aliens did not always march to their drumbeat or at least to the same tempo, so often the concepts of "alien" and "enemy" merged. American settlers, for example, learned to call two of the Great Plains Indian tribes—the Nemene and the Dine—the Comanche and the Apache, words that meant "enemy."[4]

Dealing with the alien-enemy often compressed each group. One of the first important thinkers to emphasize this was the great fourteenth-century North African Arab historian Abdur-Rahman Ibn Khaldun, who has been called the first sociologist. Reflecting on Arab and Berber tribal societies, he based his analysis on the concept of 'asabiyah, which I translate as "tightly bound together in groups." The groups that prevailed were those that stuck together, and the fundamental concept on which group cohesion rested was kinship. For Ibn Khaldun, the concept comes to mean "that emotional attachment to a group which causes men to overcome their selfish aims to act in the collective interest"; it comes about, he writes, only as the result of being of a single lineage (*ahlu nisbin wahidin*), "since the zealous devotion to the group and the absolute attachment to one's immediate group of relatives is the most important of the emotions that God put into the hearts of His creatures."[5]

In this essentially political sense, we may define kinship as the inherited and common memory of peaceful, cooperative, and intimate relationships with nearby persons. As I pointed out in chapter 2, so connected are these concepts that many peoples use the same words for them all. This is not just a quaint echo of primitive tribal peoples. Such English words as *gentle, generous, genial,* and *benign* derive from their ancestor language's word *gen,* "to give birth."

But, particularly as societies settled down and grew in size, the obviousness of kinship came to be supplemented—and in places replaced—by neighborhood. We can see this become effective in two ways: on the one hand, groups living near one another, as I discussed in chapter 2, almost certainly formed what biologists call (from the Greek) a *deme.* Although members of a deme do not necessarily count one another as close kin, they find in one another enough of "us" to dilute or soften the danger they would feel in the presence of the totally alien—"they" become "almost us." Among the Bedouin there is a saying: "My brother and I against the cousin; the cousin and I against the world." This saying finds expression, at least to the level of the cousin, in willingness to meet peacefully at appointed times, to settle feuds with honor, and to cooperate against the still more alien. On the other hand, where biological kinship does not exist but peaceful relations have been established with immigrants or neighbors, Arab tribal groups often fabricate a genealogy to explain or justify the political reality.

As groups interacted, it was natural—indeed, perhaps inevitable—that the common basis on which some form of modus vivendi could have arisen was kinship. Kinship was the one form of peaceful relationship that everyone understood. It not only set the pattern for peaceful relationships but also set an ideal toward which all nonhostile relationships were expected to evolve: coexistence. Indeed, from the time when we can first hear voices, what we hear suggests that many ancient and primitive people customarily extended to immigrants and near neighbors fictitious or "honorary" kinship. Like the Arab Bedouin, whom they resembled in many ways, the Comanche, the Berbers, the Tuwareg, the Turks, the Mongols, and others lived in self-governing bands in which most were kindred but in which kinship was not the only criterion, so that unrelated or distantly related groups might at least temporarily coalesce. It was on this biological-geographical basis that various extensions, mutations, or transfigurations—expressed in terms of marriage, geography, religion, language, ideology, way of earning a living, and so on—have been superimposed or elaborated to explain and justify that impermanent, anomalous, "artificial" condition we call peace.

So general are these feelings that we see them expressed in the Tigris-Euphrates complex, Anatolia, Egypt, and China, where rulers, those most exposed to extragroup contact and those who have left the most durable records, explained their nonwar relationships to one another in kinship terms. Our earliest records of this come from ancient Mesopotamia. There, at least by the beginning of the second millennium B.C.E., it was the custom of rulers to address one another as "brother." We see this first in what may be the earliest international treaty—that between the northern city-state of Ebla and a city in what is today northwestern Iran. The treaty demands our attention because in it we can already see elements that would typify diplomatic relations for thousands of years. Most important, the king of Elba refers to an already established "diplomatic" context, a comity of nations, in which relations were assumed to take place: kings are brothers and so should behave toward one another in a context of mutual respect and affection. "Let us swear between us," says one ruler to another in a roughly contemporary dispatch, "a mighty oath of the gods and, you and I, let us meet and establish brotherhood between us for ever."[6]

By ascription, the ruler was transforming the fundamental peaceful *intra*group relationship into a framework for a nonhostile *inter*group relationship. So obvious and so simple was this transfer that we find it repeatedly employed by both primitive tribes and sophisticated societies from China to Egypt.

Skipping down the centuries, consider the bipolar world of the thirteenth century B.C.E. in the eastern Mediterranean. There Egypt and the other superpower of the time, the Hittite empire of Anatolia, had long been locked in a wasting war. Finally, in 1270 B.C.E., the two powers negotiated a peace treaty.[7] Since treaties were proclaimed publicly, they were in part statements for "home consumption" (a pattern of international exchange that persists down to our times). Consequently, in their version the Egyptians chose to pose as conquerors, but the reality of the Egyptian-Hittite relationship was revealed in the use of the words *brother* and *brotherhood* to describe the ties of the two kings. The god-king of Egypt thus acquired not only a mortal but also an alien "brother" with whom he agreed to live in peace.

Peace, what the Hittites called *sulumu,* covered both the objective and the means necessary to secure it. The objective was not only tolerance of one another but active support in case of need. The means was assumed to be a relationship among rulers symbolized by and codified in a treaty. Friendly states were those ruled by brother monarchs. Diplomatic dispatches show us both how widespread the concept of "brotherhood" was and how carefully analogies to kinship were drawn. Subordinate or petty kings, often those defeated in battle but allowed to live, were relegated to the junior rank of "sons" and required to seek "fatherly" advice from the victor. The protocol was rigid and clear. When an upstart king of Ashur sued for great power status by addressing the Hittite great king as "brother," he was scathingly put in his place: "With what justification do you write about brotherhood? . . . As my [father] and my grandfather did not write to the king of Ashur [about brotherhood], even so must you not write [about brotherhood and] great-kingship to me."[8]

Indeed, so carefully used was the term *brotherhood* that some historians today believe they can assess the relative power of states by whether or not it applied. For example, a state known as Ahhiyawa (which is now believed to be preclassical Greek Mycenaea) is assumed to have been a significant power because its king was addressed as "my brother" by a Hittite great king.[9]

Nor was this just a convention of the eastern Mediterranean, as we can see from evidence from far across Asia. The first Chinese dynasty on which considerable information is available is the Chou, which ruled China at about the same time as the Hittites and the Egyptians were contending for power in western Asia. It conceptualized its state as a family: the ruler was said to have stood in a relationship to his subjects as a father to his children. To help him, he co-opted and granted posts and lands to men who were actual or ascribed "uncles." Governors with the same family name were addressed as "paternal uncle," whereas those either not related or related through the maternal line were addressed as "maternal uncle." Each grade of kinship was matched to a certain level of political power and over time became tantamount to a class as the members proliferated and the bonds of kinship were attenuated.[10] Two thousand years later, the Japanese similarly described and treated feudal relationships as ascribed kinship. Diplomatic usage followed this familial pattern: it was family ritual in eastern Asia as in western Asia that set the pattern of polite international intercourse—a visiting diplomat, for example, was regarded as a younger brother, whereas rulers of protected or dependent states were "sons."

Even "barbarian" rulers who were co-opted into the Chinese system were treated as distant kinsmen. Later, in the Han dynasty, when a barbarian kingdom in the north (the Xiongnu) acquired enough power, its ruler was "promoted"—he too was addressed as "brother"—and the relationship was "geneticized" (as it was so often to be in medieval Europe) by the grant of a princess from the ruling family so that the two rulers of the next generation would become actual kinsmen.[11] A Han emperor is quoted as saying, "We have united ourselves in bonds of brotherhood in order to preserve the multitudes of the world."[12] As Wolfram Eberhard has written, "From that period, the history of Far Eastern diplomacy began; forms and customs of international relations were developed, quite similar to those in the West. Down to about 130 B.C.E. Chinese and Hsiung-nu [Xiongnu] lived as neighbors, or, using the legal term of the time, as brothers."[13]

The surviving records of medieval and Renaissance Europe show us diplomats scurrying from court to court, arranging marriages among ruling families. These alliances are usually, and rightly, analyzed mainly for their impact on inheritance of title to lands, but they also were a principal means of solemnizing the ending of conflicts and a principal hope of solidifying peace.[14] Sadly for them, the bartered brides of Europe were usually (but not always) merely pawns in the international game; in Asian courts the role of women was rather different. It is customary in the West to think of them merely as odalisques (from the Turkish *odaluk,* meaning "appropriate to the [bed]room") but, at least in the Ottoman and Mughal Empires, the wives and mothers of kings were often powers behind the throne, sponsors of rival claimants. Coming from usually plebeian or foreign backgrounds, they were rarely, if ever, regarded merely as the nominal owners of coveted property.

The concept of the brotherhood of rulers has left a significant and occasionally formative heritage in modern diplomacy. In the nineteenth century, Metternich's conservative strategy against revolution—the Holy Alliance—was based on a treaty that began with an affirmation of "bonds of a true and indissoluble brotherhood" among the rulers of Russia, Austria, and Prussia; the same concept, renamed the "three emperors league," was later used by Bismarck in 1881 to head off war between Austria and Russia over the so-called eastern question. Today, kings are rarer and less important, but some of the old protocol that surrounded them remains. Even in circumstances of great hostility, rulers show themselves keen to establish at least collegial rapport with one another. The frequent summits that mark contemporary interstate relations are held not just to discuss policy (since such issues are normally thrashed out at lower levels of government in advance of the meetings) or just for publicity (although the leaders obviously crave it) but also to enable the rulers to establish personal, indeed virtually "kindred," ties. Even in the absence of such ties but at least in part in hope of creating them, rulers customarily go to great lengths to avoid embarrassing one another. During the Cold War, for example, both the Soviet and the American leaders withheld information not only from their own people but even from their own senior officials when the "leakage" of such information might embarrass the other ruler. For example, prior to the stunning exception — the shooting down of an American U-2 spy plane by a Soviet rocket, to the acute embarrassment of President Eisenhower—we now know that the Soviet armed forces had shot down a number of American aircraft over the preceding decade with no publicity of any kind.[15]

As records become available, it is amazing to see the number of incidents or conditions well known to both the Soviet and the U.S. governments (and often to allied governments) that were never made public even though doing so might have been a propaganda coup. The United States, for example, maintained at one point approximately 27,000 men in Turkey. Supposedly, their activities were among the most clandestine then undertaken by the super-secret National Security Agency. Knowledge of what they were doing or even of their existence was so restricted that even senior officers, including those responsible for the American aid program (whose allocations to Turkey were determined not by normal aid criteria but by the amount required to get Turkey to give America use of the facilities), were not cleared for information on them. But, through its own intelligence efforts, the Soviet government knew all about what the NSA was doing and even stationed surveillance ships within a few hundred meters of its bases along the Black Sea. At the same time, Soviet planes were flying along the eastern coast of America, shadowed, indeed escorted, by American fighter planes. Pictures of the Soviet planes were printed in internal U.S. government publications, but they were highly classified and were unavailable to the public.

The emphasis I have placed on the quasi-biological concept of international relationships, the brotherhood of rulers, the protocol to which it has given rise, and its extensions are thus properly to be seen as neither merely archaic nor bizarre, but, although largely forgotten in the original sense, still deeply influence the contemporary international system.

. . . .

22 WORLDVIEWS AND STRATEGY

From this biological-geographical foundation, we can trace three essentially distinct worldviews. To these I now turn. The first are *collections* of states in which members view one another as more or less equal. The earliest known aggregation was in Mesopotamia, but in the ancient world, the best known (to us) was in Greece. In medieval Europe, Italy, Germany, and Muslim Spain often were divided into similar city-states. In more modern times, the United States under the Articles of Confederation was a collection of virtually independent states and the Civil War was fought, in part, because the southern states thought it still was. We might be tempted to dismiss these as antique, but the member states of the European Community today struggle with similar problems and are affected by comparable influences.

The second category of worldview is made up of states that regarded themselves as *peerless.* Old Kingdom Egypt, Assyria, dynastic China, the Roman Empire, early Islam, and Inca Peru thought of themselves as— and to a degree were—unique. Today, we know the world (and ourselves) too well to believe in uniqueness, but nationalism, ideology, and worldly success have come close to convincing some states that they are at least superior to all others.

The third worldview evolves in a situation in which *two or more great powers* regard the world as divided between them, with their neighbors, what today we would call "the third world," more or less relegated, politically and militarily, to peripheral status. An early example, briefly discussed above, was the binary system of Middle Kingdom Egypt and the Hittite Empire. There are many medieval and early modern examples— Byzantium and the Abbasid caliphate, Renaissance France and Spain, and in our times, the United States and the Soviet Union.

Although it is neither possible nor useful to try to cover every aspect of these worldviews, I will say enough to bring out significant characteristics. First, to the "collections."

In ancient Mesopotamia, the Sumerian cities were at least theoretically members of a confederation, worshipping the same gods, living by the same rules, and enjoying the same culture. Periodically, reality accorded with the theory, but such coincidence was seldom and probably late. Usually, the Mesopotamian plain was divided into scores of mutually hostile petty kingdoms that formed coalitions in which one king would be regarded as paramount while the others, like feudal retainers, were obliged to pay tribute and acknowledge their subordination. This created a sense that the world, or at least that part of it which mattered to the Sumerians, was made up of all of them together. So powerful was their conviction of their importance that they managed to convince foreign powers that becoming significant meant joining their world, or at least their culture.

Far better known to us are the Greeks, who assume importance in an account of diplomacy, as in most other things, because of their vitality, turbulence, and creativity. Some of the importance we attach to them, however, comes about from the fact that we can hear their voices, whereas those of their predecessors and neighbors seldom reach our ears. But the Greeks spoke well and had much to talk about. They lived almost literally cheek-by-jowl with one another in tiny societies that fought desperately to get enough to eat from a poor, barren land.

By the eighth century B.C.E., hundreds of tiny societies had coalesced into self-governing *poleis* (city-states) of varying sizes and wealth. The city-state of Athens comprised about 2,600 square kilometers (1,000 square miles), or an area somewhat smaller than Rhode Island. Although smaller than Sparta, Athens was three times the size of Corinth. Some islands and valleys were remarkably subdivided. Crete's 8,600 square kilometers (3,300 square miles), an area only half again as large as Delaware, were apportioned among a hundred city-states. Some city-states occupied less than 26 square kilometers (10 square miles).

Ironically, as I wrote in part 3, the closest the fiercely separatist Greeks came to achieving nationhood was in their military service to foreign rulers. So bitter and so immediate were their quarrels with one another that the Greeks were usually unwilling or unable to unite against invaders. Foreign powers—first Persia, then the Macedonians, and finally Rome—found the Greeks eager to march to their drumbeat if only they promised to harm the brother Greek. When Xerxes led the Persians into Europe, most of the Greek city-states were on his side and former leaders of both Athens and Sparta had joined his procession; Athens' fleet, which played so crucial a role in saving "Greece," had been built to fight not Persians but Greeks. And, later, when Rome menaced what remained of Greek freedom, ambassadors of the city-states gathered to try to work out a common defense policy. We do not know all of what was said, but it must have been rancorous because one of the delegates, from the small state of Naupactus, arose to warn his colleagues that they could no longer *afford* to indulge their hatreds of one another. Then, sadly, he continued, "But if we have no hope of achieving such a degree of unity . . . I entreat you, put aside your differences with the Greeks and your campaigns against them until times have become more settled."[16] They could not, and for that Greece paid a fearful price.

Today, when we reflect on the trauma of a Germany divided into East and West and see how enthusiastically it reunited itself to become the industrial heart of Europe, it is difficult to imagine how fractured German society was in the past. There were 900 sovereign states in "Germany" at the end of the Thirty Years' War, when the 1648 Treaty of Westphalia, which ended that war, reduced them to 355; in 1803 Napoleon reduced the remaining states to about 150, and the more recent Germanic Confederation still numbered 36 sovereign members. But, as I set out in part 3, by the time of Napoleon, one German state—Prussia—had so managed to arrogate to itself the "German" role that men flocked to it from the other states, spurred or justified by Fichte's *Addresses to the German Nation,* to infuse nationalism into the new Prussian army and to build around that army, through conscription into the *Landwehr,* a nation in arms. So strong was this concept of unity that it was able to overcome, virtually to efface, the historical heritage of regional particularism and murderous religious division and to survive catastrophic defeats in World War I and World War II and half a century of enforced division during the Cold War to emerge as Europe's strongest state.

What the military did to bring a degree of unity to Germany, commerce did for the United States. Immediately after the American Revolution, the thirteen former colonies agreed to form only a loose confederation. They could not avoid living adjacent to one another, but they wanted as little contact as possible with Europeans. So, although they established a Congressional Committee for Foreign Affairs, it seldom met and had no staff to handle its records; later, after it realized that some sort of executive agency was required, the Congress established a Department of Foreign Affairs with a secretary and four employees. But when, in frustration, the secretary resigned, the post was left vacant for a year. Gradually and reluctantly the delegates realized that the lack of a unified approach to foreign relations harmed commerce, so, at Philadelphia in 1787, the founding fathers set out to shape a constitution that would give enough unity to command respect abroad.[17] But even after seeing the dangers of a weak government and experiencing the dangers of a Europe roused in revolution and convulsed with war, the Washington administration and the new Congress remained profoundly isolationist. No one expected the government to engage actively in foreign affairs,[18] but the predatory policies of the British and the French—particularly their seizing of more than a thousand American-owned cargo ships, their blockades, and the British firing on an American warship and impressing into the Royal Navy sailors from American ships—frightened Americans. Americans were also lured into foreign activities by the possibility of acquisition of territory from France, Spain, and Britain, particularly in the administrations of Jefferson, Madison, and Monroe. It was, in part, the demands of this more venturesome foreign policy that forced a tightening of domestic unity.

As Europeans and outsiders watch today's tortured moves in the quest for European unity, few, perhaps, remember or draw the comparison to the stumbling, inept, but ultimately successful similar moves of the early American republic. Then, although the most articulate Americans thought that they were embarked on a great experiment, most appear to have been mainly interested in acquiring wealth and land. Sophisticated Americans also realized that, although their resources were potentially immense, their reality was puny. Their army numbered fewer than one thousand at a time in which European armies were counted in the hundreds of thousands. And what little the Americans had, they jealously subdivided. Thus, even if the former colonies and the new states were not initially so bitterly divided as the city-states of ancient Greece, the potential for breakup was there from the beginning and would come to tragic fruition in the great Civil War of 1861–65.

* * *

China is the classic case of the second worldview: a state that viewed itself as unique. I discussed in part 2 the way it built an intangible or "virtual" wall around itself, the *chung-kuo* (central kingdom), with its language- and literature-based culture, in the Chou dynasty. This barrier both excluded aliens (until they became culturally Chinese) and compacted resident aliens into a mass whose identity has been strong enough to survive through nearly three thousand years of turbulent events.

As the Confucian scholars saw it, the world could be compared to an onion. At the center was the *tien-fu* (imperial domain), where the emperor ruled directly; the *t'in-ti* ("son of Heaven"), he had, uniquely, received the *t'in-ming* (mandate of heaven). The next outward layer, the *hou-fu*, was composed of states controlled by the central government. Still further from the center was the *sui-fu*, an alien area that was conceived as being in the process of becoming culturally Chinese. Next came the *yao-fu*, the area of "restraint." Rulers in this area were vassals and were required to perform minimal services and to pay tribute. Finally, there was the outer world, the *huang-fu* or *wai-i*, the "wild," where the light of (Chinese) civilization did not penetrate. So radically different were the outer realms of darkness considered that the names of peoples living in them were "often written in characters with animal radicals, for example, Ti, 'northern barbarians' with a dog radical . . . and Man for 'southern barbarians' with a worm radical."[19] *Untermenschen,* Chinese style.

Lest this seem merely "Oriental," compare the Roman concept of their empire. The emperor was similarly divine but was too tainted by sordid events, particularly after Augustus, to occupy the position of the Chinese emperor, and the Romans were too much the students of the Greeks to make their Latin culture be their "wall," but in foreign affairs the early Romans functioned in accord with an onion model. In the first ring out from Rome were the associated Latin cities; then came the allied cities with whom Rome had treaty relationships; then, beyond Italy, a circle of "friends," the *formula amicorum,* who, although free in domestic affairs, were bound to Rome in foreign affairs; next, the circle of civilized nations who were enemies but also potential members of the *formula amicorum;* then two rings of barbarians, of which the nearer were thought to be unformed clay from which inferior copies of Romans could be formed; and, finally, the complete savages—*feri*—who should be exterminated but who at all costs must be kept off Roman territory.

From states founded on or shaped by cultural unity, I turn to a community founded on a religious mission: Islam. From its inception in the seventh century C.E., Islam gives us another variant of the unitary system. The Arabia into which Muhammad was born about 570 C.E. was divided among hundreds of tribal groups. Some, as in his native and adopted towns, Mecca and Medina, were settled, but most were nomadic. I have called these societies "tribal" but, in fact, the effective social units were clans that generally numbered only a hundred or so individuals; clans did not congregate, so tribes had only a theoretical or conventional existence. And, among them all, feuds and warfare were endemic.

To this situation, Muhammad reacted in a highly innovative but adaptive way: he set forth the notion that in the new community he was building members were *ikhwan,* brothers, and therefore had the obligations of clansmen toward one another. The most significant of these obligations were (internally) not to fight one another and (externally) to defend one another; consequently, all the inherent warlike energies of the clans, which previously had balanced against one another in constant feuding, were turned outward against the still-pagan and still-divided Arab society. Thus, the "super-clan" or "nation" (in Arabic, *al-umma,* a term derived from the word for mother) of the adherents of Islam far outnumbered rival groups and threatened them with extinction. Unable to conceive of any basis on which to unite, they found their only salvation was to become part of the new community's *Daru'l-islam.* (domain of peace). And, as each new clan adhered, it added to its strength and so further increased pressure on those who remained outside, in the *Daru'l-harb* (domain of war). Like a desert sandstorm this movement surged across Arabia, gaining strength, and then, from 633, blasted into Sasanian Persian and Byzantine territory. Within a century, Muslim armies had triumphed from France to Central Asia.

Becoming a Muslim initially required only an affirmation of the unity of God and the prophecy of Muhammad. But, gradually, on this foundation grew an elaborate system of belief, ritual, and social organization. The very worldly success of Islam, achieved not only by the sword but through commerce and in reaction to social deprivation,[20] seemed, at least to Muslims, proof of the validity of their religion and speeded it toward becoming not only an internally coherent but also, in the eyes of Muslims, a peerless universal system.

. . .

The third worldview is an accommodation to the common reality that powerful alien states exist. Perhaps the earliest such accommodation is evident already in the Near East in the thirteenth century B.C.E., when eighteenth-dynasty Egypt and the Hittite Empire divided dominion between themselves. Like many successors, they postured, fought, and finally realized that they would benefit from a degree of peace. Between themselves, they might have accomplished this satisfactorily, but their efforts, like those of modern Russians and Americans, were complicated by their "third world," small in scale but nearly as complex as ours. The Egyptians and the Hittites thought they had to cope with, or try to control, three kinds of neighbors: first, between them were a number of petty kingdoms and more or less autonomous towns and tribes that for the most part had become their clients or allies. Second, around the periphery of this complex were less civilized and more warlike tribes and states: to the west were the scores of little kingdoms of the Mycenaean Greeks, to the east, Assyria, a small power but already an aggressive neighbor. Third, more or less beyond the reach of either diplomacy or military force, were the nomadic and seminomadic tribal peoples of Central Asia and Africa. To the Egyptians and the Hittites these peoples appeared as wolves lurking just beyond the campfires of civilization.

Both the Hittites and the Egyptians thought of themselves as the arbiters and guardians of the civilized world. Both sought to find means of accommodation between themselves but were torn by the ambitions of their rulers and their clients. Their experience taught them that "peace" was a floating series of adjustments. Moreover, both destabilizing and lubricating the international system was an active commerce. Neither great power then was, any more than are we today, willing to buy isolation at the price of a lower standard of living. The exotic luxury goods that the frequent travelers carried were almost frantically sought by the ruling elites of both states and their clients. To enable the merchants to convey their goods with enough safety and profit to ensure availability thus became a principal objective of each of the governments. With their patronage, the passage of merchants in caravans and aboard ships reached new levels of frequency, their settlement in enclaves or ghettos among alien peoples became more common, and problems raised by their wealth and weakness more urgently commanded the attention of diplomats.

In order to facilitate the flow of goods, they had to tolerate areas of ambiguity. By definition, the nomadic tribes of the Syrian steppe were neither states nor friends. Nor, precisely, were they enemies because it was on their backs that trade was carried. So when hostilities erupted among the powers, it was beneficial to minimize the damage to trade by leaving aside these commercially necessary but militarily irrelevant peoples. Thus, although the formal worldview was then, as it became in the period after World War II, bipolar, various shades of activity between friendship and enmity came to be tolerated and gradually incorporated into diplomatic practice.[21] This, I believe, is the origin of the idea of neutrality.

Neutrality also made possible the avoidance of issues that might have prevented cooperation between the powers. For example, the Hittites often argued over the definition of their joint frontier with the great entrepôt city of Ugarit, but both recognized that this issue paled in comparison with the need of each, separately, to cope with the challenge of the rising state of Assyria. Ugarit generally was anxious to profit from trade with Assyria and so was unwilling to combine with the Hittites against it, but Ugarit also feared the Assyrians and so wanted not to cut strategic ties with the Hittites. On their side, the Hittites could occasionally use Ugarit against the Assyrians and so were unwilling to risk offending it. The solution was to pull back from the contested area and treat it as a neutral zone.

Neutrality came to be not a single status but a spectrum: on the far end some states were virtually members of the enemy camp, whereas on the near end others were formally vassals. But given the primitive transport of that era, even a vassal was often virtually autonomous since he might be weeks of hard journey away from the metropole. Close control was usually impossible or excessively expensive. In practice, conquerors had to choose between slaughtering the natives or leaving them more or less autonomous. Frequently, they chose slaughter, but occasionally this was not an attractive option. So the idea of a status midway between utter ruin and independence arose: the subordinate state would be made to assume obligations in return for its survival. Obligations commonly included military assistance, tribute, and the closure of frontiers to enemies. In return, vassals were allowed to rule themselves in reasonable security.

I turn now to how states holding these diverse worldviews tried to evolve strategies to accomplish their objectives. First, India.

A millennium after invading Aryan tribes had looted, burned, and destroyed the Indus River valley civilization, northern India had become a vigorous, violent world composed of many petty kingdoms that jostled one another for power and prestige but whose peoples apparently were oblivious, at least politically, to the world beyond the subcontinent. It was in this world that the first of the Indian empires, the Mauryan, was forged by Chandragupta in the fourth century B.C.E. To help to guide that empire, an Indian scholar-statesman known as Kautilya (or Vishnugupta) wrote a remarkable work on strategy. His *Arthasastra* can be compared to Machiavelli's *The Prince* and Sun Tzu's *The Art of War*. Through the eyes of the first Greek ambassador who was sent by Alexander's successor Seleucus,[22] we see how Chandragupta was influenced by Kautilya. As in the works of the other great strategists, Kautilya's theme was power: how to get it, how to keep it, and how to increase it.[23] But Kautilya, living in a highly ritualized society, lays out in minute detail prescriptions for everything from the care and training of horses to the selection of spies. No issue, he emphasizes, should be above or below the prince's purview. Like the Chinese, he believed that a rigid formula, the political counterpart to the ceremony of religion, was the main line of defense of the state: like a tightrope walker, the ruler must strictly observe the rules or tumble to his doom.

As does Machiavelli, Kautilya eschews moralizing,[24] but to survive the ruler must win the support of the people, and since they are generally moral and imbued with a sense of propriety, he must wear a mask of morality. Because power brings immense rewards, every ruler can be assumed to be surrounded by actual or potential enemies. By the nature of their calling and regardless of their personalities, rulers must constantly weigh the risks and rewards of subverting or conquering their neighbors. War is thus seen to be the natural condition of foreign relations even when men are not actually fighting.

Kautilya approached international relations with the classifying zeal of a biologist. He delighted in the intricacies of the model he builds of international relations. In this *mandala* (sphere of influence) model, one's immediate neighbor is seen as the natural enemy: we want his territory and he wants ours; it follows that his neighbors who are further from us, being his enemies, are our friends, and so on. A state bordering on *both* "them and us" can be considered a *madyama,* or "mediatory" ruler, since his interests force him to try to live with or between both neighbors. Last, one situated far away but close enough to be capable of intervening is a neutral.

But "foreign affairs" are not so foreign. They begin in the palace with the ruler's relatives, who, urged on by their own partisans and by his foreign enemies, are his most dangerous potential rivals. This insight is amply substantiated in Indian, Iranian, Turkish, and Arab ruling families where multiple marriages produced half-brothers whose mothers pitted them against one another in what often resulted in vicious civil wars and whose fear of one another made them willing accomplices of foreigners. Princes, Kautilya quotes with approval, "like crabs have a notorious tendency of eating their begetter."

Enrichment of the state, the purpose of government, he wrote, can be accomplished best through interstate relations, but these can be successfully undertaken only if the ruler maintains his power. There is thus no real separation of domestic and foreign affairs: the ruler must keenly observe the most minute and secret thoughts and acts of both his subjects and his neighbors. Moreover, by the use of spies and agents provocateur, he must constantly test their loyalty and probe their weaknesses. He can be sure his neighbors are doing the same to his people, and he should similarly subvert and destabilize theirs whenever possible. Like the great Chinese strategist Sun Tzu, Kautilya favored a logical analysis of benefits and risks of war. In war, even in victory, there was no necessary benefit; each case must be judged on its merits. In general, he thought, the prosperity of the state is easier to maintain in peace because war is always chancy and costly, so, "when the advantages derivable from peace and war are of equal character, one should prefer peace." Therefore, Kautilya urged his prince to welcome and cultivate foreign merchants and provide them with preferential tax rates, port facilities, and even exemption from lawsuits. But, he said, experience showed that peace is both fragile and dependent on the threat or exercise of force.

To guide rulers in translating their worldviews into action, there is a considerable body of literature called "mirrors for princes." Early examples, to which I have alluded, are the works of Kautilya and Sun Tzu. In medieval times, the genre was vast, particularly in Arabic, Persian, and

Turkish, from which it spread into virtually all of the Western languages from Icelandic to Russian and from English to Castilian. One of the most interesting is also atypical of the genre; it is the *Yuan Ch'ao Pi Shih* (Secret history of the mongols).[25] Written shortly after the death of the great conqueror Chingis Khan in the thirteenth century, the work incorporates the myths of the Mongol ruling elite and then, in what must have been occasionally embarrassing detail, recounts the rise of Chingis. Although not exactly what we would term a revisionist history, it reads as though the author wished to be sure that what really happened was not obscured by later legend. As an "unvarnished" history, it apparently was restricted to the ruling family, which it sought to warn of the dangers of internal strife and to convince of its inherent right to rule. It was on the pattern laid down in the *Secret History* that the Mongol empire stretched across the vast expanses of Asia for two centuries.

Niccolò Machiavelli wrote what is undoubtedly the most famous of such works, but the genre is not dead today. Could it be true that "mirrors for princes" are being written and read now? Yes, ironically, there are probably more produced every year in America alone than were written everywhere in the world for all the centuries before World War II. What is different today is that the "prince" is now assumed to be not a single man but that group, numbering in the thousands, including presidents and secretaries of state and their actual or potential advisers. What the Mongol *Secret History* undertook is now the domain of "civics" textbooks that are read by millions of schoolchildren; what Machiavelli, Kautilya, and Sun Tzu touched on now has bloomed into a vast literature dealing with overall strategy, military affairs, intelligence, commerce, aid, propaganda, and related activities. Whole governmental and quasi-governmental agencies[26] and scores of private organizations[27] in addition to hundreds of institutes, centers, and committees in universities[28] and various journals[29] constitute a veritable industry of mirrors for princes.

. . . .

23 THE CONDUCT OF RELATIONS

Control of foreign affairs has always been considered a prerogative of the sovereign. Even today, when relations among states have become unmanageably complex, rulers often not only make major policy decisions personally but also often take into hand even mundane aspects of their relations with their peers. When, however, the "sovereign" is not an individual but an assembly, the management of relations takes on a distinct character. We see this first in ancient Greece, where diplomacy was more open than even Woodrow Wilson would have advocated. All citizens took part at least as audiences: "An assembly was convoked and the rival advocates appeared," we are repeatedly told.[30] To be denied this public access was unusual, even reprehensible. The members of an Athenian mission to Melos, for example, complained that they were not allowed to speak before the whole assembly but only before "the few."

Herodotus reports an instance that illustrates the alliance-making role of the popular assemblies. In their massive invasion, the Persians had been successful in winning or holding the allegiance of many Greek cities. City after city sent the tokens of submission, but the Persians' campaign had reached a stage at which they thought it essential to divide their two main enemies, Athens and Sparta. The moment they picked seemed ideal for their purpose: the Athenians, who had left their city to be sacked and burned, were furious at the Spartans, whom they accused of giving them little succor. So the Persians sent an embassy to offer the Athenians a separate peace. Leading the embassy was the king of Macedonia, who was both pro-Persian and also Athens' *proxenos* (honorary consul).

The Persian maneuver was what modern strategists would term a "win-win" gambit—if the Macedonian won over the Athenians, so much the better, but even if he failed, the mere fact that the Athenians had received him would make the Spartans suspicious. It was a shrewd ploy, but, more practiced than the Persians in the ways of the assemblies, the Athenians turned the tables and used the occasion to cement their relations with Sparta. They delayed the meeting until a delegation of Spartan ambassadors, who had heard of the Persian mission, could arrive. Then, in full public gaze, the Athenians told the Macedonian king, "never come to us again with a proposal like this . . . for it would be a pity if you were the victim of an unfortunate incident in Athens, when you are our friend and benefactor."[31]

Thucydides gives a brilliant picture of the diplomatic process at work in the congress of the Peloponnesian Confederacy half a century later, in 432 B.C.E., when Athens and Sparta were at war. At the congress, the Corinthians were complaining to their allies about the behavior of the Athenians in besieging Corinth's colony of Potidaea. It happened that Athenian envoys were in town on unrelated business. On hearing the speeches of the Corinthians, they came forward to speak in behalf of their city. Their right to speak, though they were uninvited and already virtually an enemy of most of the assembly, was apparently taken for granted. It was, at least as Thucydides reports, they who challenged the credentials of the assembly: "Indeed you are not the judges before whom either we or they can plead." The issue was not law—there being none beyond the city walls—but prudence: their aim was "to prevent your taking the wrong course on matters of great importance by yielding too readily to the persuasions of your allies."[32]

Groups such as these Athenian envoys must constantly have been present, if on other business, when matters large and small were ventilated in the hundreds of city assemblies. They would have been welcomed not only for the seriousness of their tasks but also because they were a part of the amusement of the Greeks in the theater of politics. Those who sought to circumvent the public displays and disclosures were regarded as somewhat sinister: thus, when some Spartan envoys in 425 B.C.E. suggested that the terms of a proposed treaty be thrashed out in committees before being submitted to the assembly, they drew a public reprimand.[33] Woodrow Wilson would have agreed.

Many centuries later, the founding fathers of the United States consciously patterned themselves on what they understood of Greek democracy. So it is not surprising that, like the Greek assembly, the Continental Congress expected to participate in all significant discussions of relations with foreign states. Although this soon proved impractical, and in July 1789 the Congress created a branch of the executive to deal with foreign affairs, the Constitution requires that the executive act with the "advice and consent" of the Senate. As Bradford Perkins has written, the founding fathers intended "advice" to mean "consultation before and during negotiations"; but already in the Washington administration, the Senate's advisory role had virtually lapsed: advice had come to mean "nothing more than 'consent,' post hoc approval of what the executive branch has decided."[34] Today, although the executive branch attempts to influence Congress to approve its funding requests and to consent to its senior appointments, it jealously guards against congressional interference in the implementation of policy. The power of the purse, however, provides today, as it did in English parliamentary practice, the means by which the legislature forces the executive to cooperate with it.

The first Congress did not think the office dealing with foreign affairs would have much to do. So a few months after it was created in the summer of 1789, its name was changed from the "Department of Foreign Affairs" to the more general "Department of State," and its duties were increased to cover such diverse tasks as taking the census, handling correspondence between the federal government and the state governments, overseeing the mint, and publishing laws. As Henry Kittredge Norton wrote, "An unusually prudent Congress felt that the mere existence of such an office might seem like an invitation to other countries to have dealings with us and, lest they accepted the implied invitation, the conduct of such foreign relations as were inescapable were assigned to a 'Secretary of State' whose principal duties were supposed to be of a domestic nature."[35] To accomplish these tasks, the incoming secretary, Thomas Jefferson (who reluctantly gave up his diplomatic post in Paris), was allowed a staff of five.

The new office was ill-starred. Not only was it small and inexperienced, but, as viewed by at least one observer, it was doomed by the nature of the government. Based on his nine-month tour of America in 1831–32, the twenty-six-year-old Alexis de Tocqueville concluded that a democracy was ill-fitted to conduct foreign policy since it can "only with great difficulty regulate the details of an important undertaking, persevere in a fixed design, and work out its execution in spite of serious obstacles. It cannot combine its measures with secrecy or await their consequences with patience." But, he concluded, this was not likely to affect Americans very much since American policy, as set out in Washington's farewell address and followed by Jefferson, was to avoid foreign activities.

What happened to the office thereafter is the common experience of modern government: many of the functions of the Department of State were separated into new departments, other government offices copied many of the functions that remained, and the staff began to multiply. From 5 in 1790, it rose to 52 in 1870, 202 in 1909, 622 in 1922 and to about 15,000 today. Moreover, today, although outsiders look to the State Department as the touchstone of American foreign relations, it is only one of a number of organizations that have grown up over the years and particularly during the Cold War. Practically every government organization, even the Department of the Interior, has its own office of foreign affairs, so that the Washington foreign affairs complex today numbers more than 50,000 officials. Thus, to effect virtually any coherent overseas program, it is necessary to assemble a large interagency "task force." But it is not just that other agencies have mirrored the State Department: it has also mirrored them by creating offices dealing with military, trade, cultural, intelligence, and other affairs. In consequence, it grew sevenfold from about 1945 to 1970 despite periodic attempts to find a means to trim its size.[36] Obviously, none of these has been able even to slow the growth.

. . .

Between the home offices, the ministries of foreign affairs, and agencies abroad, tension has always existed. Distrusted by those to whom they are accredited, expected to tread partly blindfolded along a thin line between acceptable and illegal activities, forced to put a good face on occasionally reprehensible actions, and often abused, disliked, or distrusted by their own governments, diplomats have rarely led easy lives. Worse, they rarely have much to do with the making of the policy they are asked to implement; often, indeed, they are treated more as lackeys than as collaborators. Disparagingly, but with considerable truth, their position was summed up by Zara Steiner when she wrote that diplomacy is the "metier of head-waiters who . . . are sometimes invited to sit down at the table."[37] How then did this difficult, little-appreciated, but apparently necessary profession arise, and how did it proliferate throughout the world?

In its first manifestations, diplomacy must have been the task of at least all the adult males in a clan. This is because in primitive societies, as among animals, "diplomacy" was carried out by what we think of as the very modern process of "signaling." Today, in international confrontations, states signal their resolve by deploying troops, flying aircraft, or maneuvering fleets. In simpler situations, groups "negotiated" over such strategic possessions as water holes by positioning themselves, gesturing or howling, and posturing to try to convince their rivals of the seriousness of their intent to stay and their willingness to fight. Usually, signals sufficed and deadly combat was avoided.

In such encounters, everyone became a "diplomat" or prospective warrior, but as groups grew in size, reached outward beyond the neighborhood, and began to engage in distant trade, it became impossible for everyone to participate. At that point, as the language of gesture gave way (at least partially and usually) to the language of word, the warrior role became more hidden and that of the negotiator came to the fore. And this brought about a series of changes that are still evolving in our day. I will now examine these.

The earliest diplomats we know anything about lived in the Near East roughly four thousand years ago and were primarily merchants. They were the people who knew the way, who had made contacts, and who knew how to communicate. As we saw in part 4, merchants were found everywhere. Constantly coming with the latest news as well as goods from exotic places, merchants constituted a veritable foreign service for cities such as Ebla, which knew and traded with scores of other cities over a vast area, so it was natural that rulers would have turned to them both to spy and to carry messages.

Probably many of these people were quasi strangers. Their work caused them to spend much of their time abroad, where many must have adopted alien customs or dress and married foreign women. A near-contemporary example from a primitive tribe in Africa, the Nuba, shows the opposite source of ambassadors—immigrants. Known as the "chief of the path," the Nuban ambassador was often a captive or former slave who knew the language, the customs, and perhaps some of the members of another tribe. That helped, but he could not rely upon these things for protection. Rather, he was protected by ritual status symbolized by a special spear. Carrying it, he could go inviolate into hostile villages to negotiate with his counterparts. When agreements were reached, the chiefs of the path sanctioned them with religious or magical rites and threatened truce violators with curses thought to produce leprosy. Like rulers, they recognized a common interest—what we think of as diplomatic immunity—which they conceptualized as a brotherhood. To that end, they "especially safeguarded [one another] by a sacrifice and blood ritual which established blood brothership (*tussol*) between the different Chiefs of the Path and their families and descendants. Thus the office became hereditary."[38] This is not an isolated example: men with roles similar to those of the Nuba chiefs of the path could be brought forward from a number of primitive tribes in various parts of the world, and the carrying of a staff, spear, or wand as a symbol of office appears nearly universal.[39]

In ancient Greece and throughout medieval Europe, the counterpart of the chief of the path was the herald. He too carried a staff as the symbol of his office. But his duties differed. In addition to ensuring that the man who actually carried the message of his sovereign was given diplomatic immunity, the herald also served as a spokesman or public announcer. It was never far from the mind of the Greek that he must have a commanding voice; indeed, the primitive meaning of the Greek word for "herald," *keryx,* as we know from Sanskrit, is "singer."[40] A part of that function is today performed by government spokesmen. Like the chief of the path, the *keryx* was a professional, usually serving for life, and, in Greece, often a descendant of heralds. His calling made him sacrosanct: his staff or scepter was not only symbolic but was also thought actually to confer on its holder an immunity sanctioned by the gods and looked after by Agamemnon's herald, Talthybius. The duties of the herald were not limited to diplomacy but also included the disposal of the spoils of battle, selling prisoners into slavery, retrieving defectors, arranging truces, and declaring war.[41] Occasionally, a city might signal its determination not to negotiate by refusing to receive a herald until its conditions were met, as Athens did in 431 B.C.E. and Sparta and Argos did in 417 B.C.E.[42]

The men the Greeks called *prebeis* (or, if they were foreigners, *angeloi*) were, by contrast, amateurs on short assignment; the diplomacy in which they were engaged usually involved presenting the case of their city-state in the assembly of another. So they were primarily to be considered as orators and, unless sent to the Persian court, they could function without interpreters. But because city assemblies were notoriously fickle and suspicious, they were rarely sent alone.

Both the task and the team carried over into medieval Europe. For example, King Louis XI sent a mission composed of eight ambassadors to Pope Sixtus IV in 1479. In the best Greek style, after privately presenting their credentials, the eight demanded a public meeting in the presence of the Sacred College, the closest papal equivalent of the Greek assembly, at which their orator, the jurist Antoine de Morlhon, harangued the assembly on the dangers of the Ottoman invasion of Europe and offered to arbitrate the differences between France and the Vatican. The custom of sending a team spread to the young United States, which sent three emissaries to Paris in 1776 to negotiate with the French government, five in 1779 to Europe to negotiate an end to the Revolutionary War, and five to negotiate the Treaty of Ghent to end to the War of 1812.

To the embarrassment and danger of diplomats, embassies were frequently manipulated or used in underhanded ways. Thucydides reports that the Spartans built a justification for their declaration of hostilities against Athens by sending emissaries on a mission they knew in advance would be unsuccessful.[43] And diplomats were usually given little or no discretionary powers. Only rarely could they negotiate binding treaties.[44] An example will show how narrow were their powers. In 490 B.C.E., the Spartans sent a mission to Argos to encourage it to join in the defense against the Persians, but even on the brink of that feared invasion, the ambassadors were not authorized to negotiate so much as a truce.[45]

City assemblies were jealous of their powers and were often bitterly split among factions. That accounts for much of the custom of limiting the powers of the envoys, but it also arose from the geopolitics of Greece: the "stage" was so small that nothing happened more than a few days' journey away from any city. So an ambassador did not absolutely need discretionary powers; when, centuries later, the role of the ambassador grew, it was in large part because, as the stage grew to be months-of-travel wide, the ambassador could not consult with his home office. In our own times, as a result of the telegraph and the airplane, we have reverted to the Greek and Chinese models, with ambassadors often acting as little more than messengers.

Who were these orators, ambassadors, messengers? Among the

Greeks, they were amateurs whose real callings were in other fields. It was important that they be able to defend themselves because they were personally blamed for failure and risked censure or worse even for success when, as occasionally happened, the assemblies changed their minds. Often roughly treated at home, they were always at risk abroad. Under the protection of heralds, they had limited immunity, but this was so fragile that they often negotiated special agreements to ensure it.[46] So it was better if they were men of substance or at least of note. Even then, especially in times of high tension, they might be molested or killed. Both Athens and Sparta, in a well-known example, violated the immunity of the Persian ambassadors of Darius in 492 B.C.E. even though they believed this was an affront to the gods and they knew it was likely to bring retribution.[47] Immunity, moreover, was effective only in the country to which the mission was being sent; there was no immunity against third parties. This could be lethal because, since forthcoming missions were discussed in public assemblies (with foreign merchants and representatives present), they were occasionally intercepted before reaching their destination. Thucydides reports on a mission to Persia of Spartan, Corinthian, and Tegean envoys that, being betrayed to Athens, was kidnapped and executed by the Athenians in 430 B.C.E.[48]

As necessity arose, the Greeks pressed into service the most able or available person. Generals often acted as envoys. When the Persians were moving toward Marathon, the Athenians even sent a professional long-distance runner off as an envoy to Sparta.[49] This Greek habit also carried into the Europe of the Middle Ages, where Louis XI of France once employed his barber as an ambassador and Florence sent an apothecary to Naples.[50] The position was clearly not held in high esteem or thought to require special skills. In contrast, about the same time, Chinese missions even to small countries of little importance to China "were in all cases men of high scholarly attainment . . . eminent historians and literary figures."[51]

In classical Greece, ambassadors were not in residence in the cities to which they were sent and so could not handle unexceptional commercial matters. Rather, the daily routine of interstate relations fell on the *proxenos,* who more or less equated to an "honorary consul." *Proxenoi* were citizens of a city-state who, for pay, honor, or trading privileges, served the interests of another city-state. Permanent in residence, *proxenoi* were expected not only to attend to trade and other interests of their sponsors but also to provide temporary hospitality for visiting ambassadors since such inns as existed were shunned by those who had alternatives. Presumably they shared ideological commitments with their sponsors and probably often covertly provided a link with native dissidents. Thus, their positions were, by definition, exposed and dangerous; consequently, the appointing states went to considerable trouble and expense to try to protect them through treaties, reciprocal treatment of their counterparts, and, in case of war or expulsion, by the grant of asylum. In Athens, the title was granted by the assembly, and the person so honored had his name inscribed on a marble stele much as a modern honorary consul might receive a decoration.

Although not precisely inherited, the position of proxenos tended to be associated with families, and naturally each state sought to employ a respected local figure from a powerful family. But in Greece, as in modern times, men moved in and out of roles. The Athenian Callias, for example, was not only a proxenos for Sparta but also, curiously by our standards, was sent three times to negotiate with the Spartans, for whom he also acted as an agent.[52]

As later empires did, the Athenians and the Spartans created a new kind of international official midway between an ambassador and a sort of viceroy. To collect tribute and otherwise oversee Athenian interests in its two hundred allied and subordinate cities, Athens sent some seven hundred officials called *episkopoi*. The Spartan counterpart was known as a *harmost*.[53] These officials were similar in functions and status to the T'ang dynasty *Chuan yün shih*, who sent tax revenues to the capital and, under the Sung, accumulated wide powers, and to the Mongol *posoly*, who carried instructions from the court at Serai to the Russian princes in the thirteenth and fourteenth centuries C.E. As I will later discuss, some ambassadors in the period of European ascendancy over Asia similarly moved from what we normally think of as diplomacy into comparable positions of influence or dominance.

Although some of the "honorary consuls" may have gotten rich off the interurban trade, diplomatic jobs were certainly not coveted. In Athens, ambassadors, while on a mission abroad, were paid about the same as stone masons. But it was probably not finance that dissuaded men so much as the danger that they would be repudiated or punished for their work—and the lack of comfort and protection in their travels. This was to be a constant lament of ambassadors down to our times.

Unlike Greece, which was a hothouse for diplomacy, Rome put little emphasis on negotiation or propaganda. For Rome, as I discussed in part 3, war was "an almost biological necessity," and therefore the role of the Roman ambassador was conceived as quite different from that of the Greek. As Titus Livius (Livy), the first-century B.C.E. historian who delighted in the ancient lore of Rome, resurrects the traditional role of a figure known as the *fetial*, he resembles the Greek herald in his function of announcing war.[54] The more crucial task of the *fetial*, however, is shown by the primitive meaning of the word: "to put something in its proper place (*fas*) in the spirit world to ensure divine authorization." If the *fetial* accomplished his ritual task, the decision of the Roman people was regarded as divinely authorized. Thus, like the Greek herald or *keryx*, the *fetial* mediated between gods and men.

After the early period when it was a small city-state among many others on the Italian peninsula, Rome rarely considered other states to be in any effective sense its equals and so generally sent officials to give orders rather than to negotiate arrangements. The one state with whom the Romans had to negotiate was Carthage. And in one encounter, they were the victims of what today we would call "gunboat diplomacy." It happened that during the invasion of Rome by the great Macedonian-Greek general Pyrrhus the Carthaginians realized that they had an opportunity to strike a bargain with Rome on favorable terms. This became particularly attractive because of their worry that Pyrrhus might lead his army to Carthaginian Sicily. So they sent an ambassador to Rome to negotiate a mutual-defense treaty between the two superpowers. And to emphasize their capacity, they sent the Carthaginian ambassador with the whole Carthaginian fleet. The Romans were impressed and agreed to make the two Western powers allies against the East. But, shrewdly, they exempted Sicily from the treaty: Rome could call on Carthaginian help against the Greeks in Italy and the Carthaginians could call for Roman help if Pyrrhus attacked Carthage, but Sicily was left as neutral ground. The result was what Rome wanted: Pyrrhus sailed for Sicily, where the Greek population proclaimed him king while, one by one, the Roman armies subdued the cities and tribes of the Italian south. Tarentum, the last major Italian Greek city, surrendered in 272 B.C.E.

Romans prided themselves on their *gravitas* and were not easily lured or pushed into actions they did not want. In the beginning of their conflict with Hannibal, however, is an illustration of how the small and weak can sometimes manipulate the mighty. This too is a timeless theme in international relations: we have seen it often in the twentieth century. Perhaps in genuine fear but always opportunistically, a weak power will sometimes stimulate a strong but less immediately dangerous state to act against a more immediately dangerous neighbor. The little ally, here the Greek city of Massilia (the ancestor of Marseilles), agitated to get the Romans to act against Hannibal. Ever cautious, the Romans at first stood aloof, but at last, in 219 B.C.E., the Romans sent a diplomatic mission first to Hannibal in Spain and then to Carthage.[55] In the traditional Greek way, the Roman ambassadors appeared before the Carthaginian Assembly. But in the entirely Roman way, they presented an ultimatum that no Carthaginian statesman could accept—to surrender the young hero Hannibal to Rome's tender mercies. The assembly was furious. What particularly strikes a modern reader is that it apparently never occurred to the Carthaginians to kill or detain the Roman ambassadors after their outrageous demand or even to restrict their travel within territory controlled by Carthage. Livy casually mentions that when they left Carthage, the envoys sailed, apparently unhindered, to Spain to try to incite a rebellion among Carthage's tribal subjects and allies.

✦ ✦ ✦ ✦ ✦ ✦ ✦

24 THE MEDIEVAL SCHOOL OF STATECRAFT

The international politics of the late medieval Mediterranean world were dominated by three great issues—the inheritance of Byzantium, the Christian reconquest of Muslim Spain, and the struggle for domination of Italy. Challenges and opportunities presented by these issues would transform diplomacy from its primitive and ancient beginnings into systems more akin to modern practice. Consider first Byzantium.

Even shrunken within the great battlements of its capital city, like an aged dowager in the wraps of old finery, Byzantium evoked memories of the grandeur of Rome so intoxicating as to appear a prize outshining all others. Not just a city among the drab villages of medieval Christendom, but the sole great metropolis of the world known to Europeans, it was the focal point of imperial ambitions. Indeed, for centuries it mesmerized those who waited beside its deathbed, successively the Venetians, the Genoese, and the Normans of western Europe; the Umayyads, the Abbasids, the Fatimids, the Seljuks, and the Ottomans among the Muslims; and, among the eastern Europeans, the Bulgarians, the Ukrainians, the Russians, and other Slavs. It outlived many of them. But as the disparity widened between the memory of its grandeur and the reality of its resources, it was less and less able to defend itself militarily. Not surprisingly, it came increasingly to rely on diplomacy. In fact, no other state known to history relied so completely or so long on diplomacy for its security. As Louis Bréhier wrote, "Diplomacy was the very foundation of the Byzantine state and contributed much more than its arms to assure its survival. Indeed, Byzantine history is nothing more than a long diplomatic negotiation interspersed with wars."[56]

The Byzantine concept of the world and of its centrality to that world was very similar to that of the much earlier Chinese. Standing aloof from turmoil and conflict, it was legitimated by divine manifestations into a single state, under a single ruler and held together by a single religion. Beyond its gates, often literally the gates of the city, were barbarians. Further away to the west were upstart states of lesser Christians; to the east were infidel empires. None could be either trusted or extirpated. So, Byzantine diplomacy aimed at keeping the various components divided into their appropriate concentric circles, much as our bodily immune system attempts to segregate pathogens when it cannot destroy them.

From time to time, relations with the Persian Sasanian empire and its Abbasid Muslim successor improved because both were trying to pacify or subjugate nomadic invaders from Central Asia, but often they fought one another over territory and religion. When it was strong, Byzantium regarded the "princes of the West" as cadet members of the Christian family, and so deserving of some fellow-feeling, but generally it despised them for their recent paganism (which in its view expressed itself in heresy or near-heresy) and for their current barbarianism. Distinct from both the "other" Christians and Muslims, the Khazars, a Turkish people who converted to Judaism in the ninth century, were for a time useful as a counterbalance.

Given their declining power and the diversity of their neighbors, the Byzantine rulers became remarkably inventive in strategies to fend off or incite, ally or divide, flatter or humiliate. Like their Roman predecessors, they took as hostages alien princes whom they reeducated and then promoted as rival candidates for succession and, more than the Romans, they encouraged marriage, sparingly by the imperial family but more generously by the aristocracy, with strategic partners and enemies.

Being usually weak, Byzantium could not afford a passive or defensive diplomacy; rather, it had to reach into the ruling families and governments of its neighbors to create for itself partisans, agents, and spies. Its "special forces" were often clerics (who could move easily and, as it were, under cover) and families that, for reasons of affinity, origin, or commercial contacts, had specialized in the target community. The normal procedure was to bring the aliens to Constantinople, where they received elaborate, indeed overwhelming, displays of hospitality, pomp, and ceremony through a sort of foreign office known as the "office of barbarians." To its preoccupation with ritual and protocol we may trace one of the influences of later Western diplomacy. Like the Chinese, the Byzantines adroitly used ceremony as a weapon of statecraft. Ingenious programs were devised to convince visitors that the great officials of the state, above all the emperor, were a different order of mortals who commanded not only vast riches but advanced technology and awesome power. And, in making their visits memorable, pleasant and, if possible, compromising, officials encouraged flattering reports to home rulers, smoothed the way for favorable treaties, or turned foreign ambassadors into double agents. When it was necessary to send Byzantine ambassadors abroad, they went only on short missions; this likely showed a lack of trust of those who had been tainted by contact with foreigners, a sentiment shared by governments to this day.

Like most governments, Byzantium delighted in titles and multiplied personnel. In early medieval times, an official known as *magister* served as, in effect, foreign minister. Over the following centuries, the title was assumed by increasing numbers of aspiring officials so that, by the middle of the tenth century, there were said to be two dozen holders of the title, and, as often happens, a new position was created to carry out the now-dissipated functions of the old. This fell, somewhat oddly to modern ears, to the post office. But there was a logic in the move since the postal service in contemporary Oriental and later Western states combined both resources (horsemen and outposts) and interests in foreign areas. In China, successive Persian empires and the Abbasid Arab Empire, the Mongol Empire, and still later in Renaissance England and France, as I mentioned in part 5, the postal service was a major intelligence collection agency.

By skillfully using the little it had and preventing those who had more from combining or using what they had to full advantage, Byzantium managed to delay the reading of its will until the Ottoman conquest of 1453, a thousand years after the fall of Rome.

◆ ◆ ◆

The second great foreign affairs issue of the Mediterranean world was the Muslim sweep into Europe. It came in two stages. The first was in the form of an Arab-led Berber army that burst on the western Mediterranean lands in the eighth century and more or less reached its high point in central France at the battle of Tours in 732. Had the Muslims, who were only a raiding party, not been weighted down with plunder and anxious to get back to the warm delights of newly conquered Spain, that encounter, so much discussed in European history, might have been more than a skirmish. Then Edward Gibbon's famous speculation on one of history's great "might have beens" might not have been so droll. As he wrote of the Islamic assault,

> A victorious line of march had been prolonged above a thousand miles from the rock of Gibraltar to the banks of the Loire; the repetition of an equal space would have carried the Saracens to the confines of Poland and the Highlands of Scotland; the Rhine is not more impassable than the Nile or Euphrates, and the Arabian fleet might have sailed without a naval combat into the mouth of the Thames. Perhaps the interpretation of the Koran would now be taught in the schools of Oxford, and her pulpits might demonstrate to a circumcised people the sanctity and truth of the revelation of Mohammed.[57]

As it was, Muslim rule was quickly established over most of Spain and in part lasted nearly eight hundred years. For centuries, the Goths, as the Christians thought of themselves, remained isolated in the far north while in most of the peninsula a new state arose and for several centuries was the greatest power of the western Mediterranean—the caliphate of Cordoba. But in the first decades of the eleventh century C.E., that state fell apart, rather like Chou China, into dozens of petty kingdoms known for their rulers the "party kings" (in Arabic, *muluk al-tawa'if*). The resultant division and anarchy facilitated the Christian advance toward the south, drew Europe increasingly into Spanish, North African, and Near Eastern affairs, and created a new area of active diplomacy.[58]

Diplomatic missions were apparently frequently exchanged between the Muslim and the Christian petty states, but of them we do not know much. From the fourteenth century we have more information. The great North African Muslim historian Ibn Khaldun was sent on a diplomatic mission in 1364 to the by-then Christian-controlled city of Seville, where the ruler, Pedro I, "the Cruel," of Castile, offered to take him into his service. If Ibn Khaldun did the research for which he was later famous, he would have learned that Pedro's court was riven by hatreds and ambitions. As king of Castile, Pedro I was also in bitter conflict with the king of Aragon, Pedro IV, and at daggers drawn with the king of France, whose daughter he had married, spurned, and imprisoned. Probably in these circumstances Pedro would have regarded a man from "the other side" as more trustworthy than a fellow Christian. Wisely, Ibn Khaldun declined the offer.

A second remarkable diplomatic mission was sent from Castile at the beginning of the fifteenth century. King Henry III, casting about for friends and allies, sent diplomatic missions both to the Ottoman sultan Bayezid and to Bayezid's nemesis, the great Central Asian conqueror Timur (Tamerlane). Flushed with his great victory over Bayezid at the battle of Ankara, Timur made no substantive response but sent back his idea of a princely gift to Henry: two beautiful maidens.[59] Even without them Henry's family life was complex enough, and their arrival occasioned no diplomatic result.

At the eastern end of the Mediterranean, the Muslim move into Europe also came in stages. In an explosion of conquest, the Muslims seized nearly all of the Byzantine provinces south of Anatolia, and for centuries Byzantium and the successive Muslim caliphates raided and fought along that border. Then events far off in Central Asia pushed tribes of Turks and Mongols westward. In the eleventh century a confederation known as the Seljuks wrested power from other groups in what is now Iran. In 1055 they took control of the great metropolis of the Islamic world, Baghdad. Moving steadily westward, they seized Jerusalem from the (by then) more easygoing Fatimid dynasty of Egypt.

With the Fatimids, who were the middlemen in the trade between the Indian Ocean and Europe, western Europeans had developed stable if limited relations, both commercial and diplomatic. What they faced with the incoming Seljuks was entirely different. Not only were the Seljuks, as recent converts, less tolerant, but also their political and military organization was diffuse. Put simply, the Seljuks, like the German tribes who had invaded the Roman Empire in the fourth and fifth centuries, were not a state or an "army" but a collection of tribal groups each of which operated under its own leaders and according its own view of opportunities and dangers. The result was not so much a conquest as a glacial movement of peoples. Around 1060 they spilled into the settled Greek lands beyond the old frontier. There, they cut communications among towns, ravaged villages, seized and razed eight major cities, and yet presented no convenient military target to the Byzantine army and no coherent leadership with which Byzantine diplomats could negotiate. Like guerrilla and partisan warriors of our century, they appeared, terrorized, and melted away.

Faced with this frustrating situation, the Byzantine emperor Romanus IV Diogenes, like some modern statesmen, decided to strike at what he thought to be their sanctuary. The outcome was the great battle of Manzikert in 1071, where the Turks ambushed the only army Byzantium had and captured the emperor. Within a decade, Turks had taken over the Anatolian peninsula and were virtually within sight of Constantinople.[60] Alarmed at the loss of Jerusalem and little trusting the Byzantines, Pope Urban II summoned the bishops of the church to Clermont, where in

November 1095 he called for all Christendom to join in a crusade to rescue the East from the Muslims. The First Crusade is surely one of the most remarkable international undertakings of history, but, unlike the westward migration of the Turkish tribes, it (and its successors) involved relatively few people and so could not permanently change the balance of power in the Middle East. Over a century the venture lost the attention of Europe and, under the blows of Muslim armies, began to fail. In response to these alarming developments, Europeans, particularly those under the leadership of the pope, began to look for some counterpoise to Islam. Desire was the mother of invention of the myth of "Prester John," an anti-Muslim Asian who could attack the Muslims in the rear. To find this savior, the first ambassador, a physician in the service of the pope, was sent eastward in 1177. He was never heard of again. But the Western states and the papacy were unwilling to give up. Particularly after the Crusaders and their Venetian allies had fatally weakened Byzantium in the Fourth Crusade in 1204 and the Tatars or Mongols under Chingis Khan had been identified, the various European states and the papacy began to send embassies into unknown Asia.[61]

In retrospect, it is difficult to understand the basis of the European expectations. After all, the Mongols had conquered most of Russia, seized Kiev, virtually annihilated an army of German knights, and crushed the Hungarian king. Westerners who had met or talked with those who had seen the Mongols showed their terror by misunderstanding their name: they heard the word *Tatar,* by which the Mongols were known, as *Tar*tar, or the fiends of Tartarus (hell). Presumably, the pope assumed that Mongol atrocities were committed in ignorance of their common interest in overthrowing the Muslims. He certainly hoped to convert them. In any event, twenty-five years before the better-known Polos made their first trip in 1271, Pope Innocent IV (who was elected in 1243) sent the Franciscan friar John of Pian del Càrpine as his ambassador to the Mongol Khan— wherever he might be in the vast expanses of eastern Asia.

After a long trip across Poland and Russia, Friar John reached the camp of Batu, a grandson of Chingis Khan and commander of one of the Mongol armies, the Golden Horde. From its camp on the lower Volga, Friar John rode eastward for four months before he finally arrived in July 1246 at the Mongol royal camp near Karakorum. He arrived just in time to witness the election of Küyük, another grandson of Chingis, to become the Great Khan. Küyük received and questioned the ambassador, read the papal démarche, and prepared a written reply (which is preserved in the Vatican archives). After four months in the Mongol camp, Friar John returned to Lyons, where the pope was then staying. He recounted his remarkable adventure, without the usual fantasies so beloved of travelers, in his *Historia Mongalorum.*

Wisely, Friar John tried to discourage the Mongols from sending ambassadors to Europe, fearing that they would observe how divided it was and that this information might encourage them to attack Christians rather than Muslims.[62] Soon, however, Mongol ambassadors were being sent to the West while other Westerners followed in the footsteps of Friar John. A 1246 letter from Küyük Khan showed how wise Friar John had been and should have disabused Pope Innocent IV of any remaining illusion that the Mongols could be the saviors of Christendom.[63] In his message, Küyük Khan says that the envoys of the pope requested that he be allowed to surrender to the world conqueror, so, "If you act according to your word, then come: you, the Great Pope, and the Kings, all in person, to pay homage to us. . . . You personally, at the head of the Kings, you shall come, one and all, to pay homage to me, and to serve me. Then, we shall take note of your submission." But the pope would not, perhaps felt he could not, be disillusioned and shortly sent another ambassador, the French-Flemish priest William of Rubruck, who carried with him a letter of recommendation from Louis IX, who had already sent his own ambassador, also a Dominican friar. Several other priests were sent to the commanders of the Mongol armies near Europe—all to no avail. But finally, after thirty years of diplomacy, it appeared in 1289 that what Innocent had begun was about to bear fruit. King Philip IV, "the Fair," of France sent a priest to the Buddhist great-grandson of Chingis Khan, Arghun Khan—the ruler of the Ilkhans of Persia and so the most accessible of the Mongol leaders—proposing a joint attack on Muslim Egypt. Arghun (through a Mongol ambassador) agreed and offered to turn Jerusalem over to the Franks. It seemed that perhaps, after all, there *was* something to the Prester John idea. By the time of Arghun's offer, however, Philip could no longer fulfill his part of the deal, and the venture into which so much effort had been poured for so many years simply faded away.[64]

In this string of events are an irony and a lesson for our times. First, the lesson: while outsiders were trying to manipulate Asian politics to their advantage, they deluded themselves into thinking that those with whom they sought to deal were what they wanted them to be: not Mongols bent on conquering the world but "Prester John," who, although far away and out of touch, really was one of "us," at least in spirit. Ever since, statesmen and diplomats have similarly imposed on other regimes their wishes rather than soberly assessing what motivated "them." Delusion has resulted in failure after failure, but the lesson is far from having been learned. The irony is that long after the Europeans had given up, and for reasons with which they were unacquainted, a "Prester John" did, more or less, accomplish their objective. They would have been horrified by him, his state, and his objectives, which did not differ qualitatively from those of Chingis Khan, but, mercifully, they were spared this intimacy. On his side, Timur would probably have been hugely amused if he had known anything about the "Prester John" image. His own self-image and ambitions were drawn from the legacy of Chingis Khan (to whom he proudly related himself in the title he took—Kūrgān, Mongol for "son-in-law"). It happened that in the course of fulfilling his own plans he was blocked by the rising power of the new Ottoman state. The fact that the Ottomans had just routed a European crusader army (in 1396) and were poised to take Constantinople, the greatest city of Christendom, was of no interest to him. He was marching to his own drumbeat, and the Ottomans were in his way. At the battle of Ankara in 1402, he nearly destroyed them. Following that catastrophic defeat, in which the sultan Bayezid was taken prisoner, much of the Ottoman army defected to Timur. Bayezid's sons then began a succession struggle that engaged the former provinces in civil war. Consequently, the Ottomans were not able to mount a major attack on Christendom for half a century. In short, the objectives prayed for so long and so eagerly were unrelated to the Christian's grand strategy. In this irony there may also be a lesson: the "Prester John" story is not the last time statesmen ascribed *cause* to what is merely *sequence*.

Meanwhile, Europe, particularly Venice, had been building strong commercial ties with the East, and these required an active diplomacy. In the late Middle Ages, Egypt was the main conduit to the East, and by the beginning of the sixteenth century Venice had negotiated twenty commercial treaties with its Mamluk sultans.[65] With Byzantium's successor, the Ottoman Empire, relations were much more complex, involving as they did not only trade but former Byzantine areas under Venetian control that were claimed by the sultan, trading posts in the Aegean islands and along the Black Sea coast, and tangled interests (involving also the Holy Roman Empire and other European states) over the Balkan territories. For these reasons, Venice maintained an active embassy in Constantinople.

Sometimes, the Europeans sought simply to cut the Islamic world off, trying to embargo trade, particularly in war materials. But such measures were so hard to enforce that trade, and even military cooperation, continued. Italians sold military uniforms to the Ottoman state and mercenaries traveled easily to Muslim areas. That hero of American romance, Captain John Smith, served as a mercenary in the Ottoman army before his exploits in the New World and, later, a significant part of the "Barbary" pirate fleet that raided Europe was manned by Christian Europeans. Such restraint as existed was removed when the European rulers fell out with one another. Thus, Francis I encouraged Ottoman attack on the Hapsburg empire and, when Elizabeth I was condemned by the pope, she leaped at the chance to work with the Turks. On their side, the Ottomans were avid customers. After the disastrous battle of Lepanto in 1571, the Turks set about reconstituting their fleet and bought not only tin and powder but "the scrap-metal resulting from the upheavals of the Reformation—lead from the roofs of ecclesiastical buildings, old bells [from churches,] and broken metal statuary."[66]

In the middle of such complex events, inheriting the experience and lore of Byzantium and led by an active, cosmopolitan oligarchy, Venice was well placed to lead Europe into a new age of diplomacy. Beginning in the thirteenth century, the Venetians began to require their ambassadors to submit written reports on what they had learned at the termination of their missions. It seems an obvious requirement but it was revolutionary because, alerting them that they would have to present a comprehensive account, it caused them to take a more ordered and systematic approach to their missions. And, if well used by their successors, their reports converted what had been merely episodic ventures into a continuous process. Two kinds of reports have been identified. One was similar to what some intelligence agencies began to prepare during World War I, a sort of encyclopedic "survey" of a country. The second kind of report, known as a *relazione*, was a lecture before the Senate in which the returning ambassador discussed candidly and in detail the context and results of his mission.

Lamentably, this is one of the models governments and diplomats have not retained from the past. Earlier in this century, British, French, American, and probably other ambassadors periodically prepared essays on their missions, not quite *relazione*, perhaps, but thoughtful and unhurried reflections on what their jobs were all about, what they were trying to accomplish, what was worth accomplishing and how it might be done, what stood in the way, what was happening in the societies to which they were accredited, and so on.

Two famous dispatches, one American and one Soviet, illustrate this genre. In 1946, George Kennan sent what came to be called his "long telegram." The term itself may serve as a commentary on how unusual it was becoming for diplomats to write essays rather than the "I saw the foreign minister and I said to him . . . and he said to me" sort of messages. In his thoughtful and provocative message, Kennan set out his ideas on the shape of Soviet-American relations with the germ of what came to be called "containment," a strategy that underlay American policy for the next two generations. At roughly the same time, the Soviet ambassador to Washington, Nikolai Novikov, cabled his government with what might be regarded as the mirror image of Kennan's message, describing how the American political system functioned and what the Soviets could expect from it.[67]

We are not yet privy to the fate of such analyses in the Soviet, British, or Russian systems, but in the American government, they fade away in the 1950s. In part, no doubt, this resulted from Secretary of State John Foster Dulles's unwillingness to read more than a single page on any topic. But a more worrisome cause was the climate of fear of foreigners and those associated with them that was partly created and largely stimulated by the attack by the radical right led by Senator Joseph McCarthy on the State Department. Thereafter, the prudent foreign service officer kept his head down and his opinions to himself. Even in the inner sanctum of the principal advisory group to the secretary of state, comments by senior officers were not to be attributed. Minutes state, "It was said that . . ." rather than "So-and-so said . . ." In 1961, even in the privacy of the Policy Planning Council, where every possible aspect of American overseas policy was supposed to be discussed in complete candor, the chairman advised members that it was dangerous even to consider the recognition of Communist China.[68] But it seems, also, that reflective analysis has been a casualty of the telegraph. In the deluge of reportage of events, no one took the time to write or read extended analysis; so what at least aspired to wisdom has been replaced by news.

* * * * * * *

25 DIPLOMATS AND THEIR MASTERS

Up to the fifteenth century, most European ambassadors had been sent on limited missions and expected to return to "civilian" life on their completion. Many were actually little more than *nuncios* (messengers) whose task was simply to deliver a message or to take part in a ceremony. As the political and military conflicts among the Italian city-states intensified, however, it began to seem useful to some rulers to maintain their agents for long periods in the courts of their allies and enemies. It was, after all, cheaper to deal with one another by means of ambassadors, who were also probably relatively loyal, than through mercenaries, who were neither loyal nor inexpensive. By the middle of the fifteenth century, the sta-

tioning of resident ambassadors in key capitals had become a regular practice in Italy and, as France and the Hapsburg Empire became embroiled
in Italy, it quickly spread.[69]

For centuries no European state had what we would today consider
a professional diplomatic corps. In times of serious crises or when a ruler
wished to discuss marriage ties, which were often thought to "profoundly
affect the whole course of his foreign relations,"[70] he usually sent a high
nobleman or relative to call on his "brother," but most of the "meat and
potatoes" of diplomacy was the dish of lower-ranking men and women. It
was their task to listen to the gossip of the courts to which they were
attached and to employ informers to overhear what was withheld from
them. Consequently, as Donald Queller has written, "The suspicion that
an ambassador was a legalized spy was never far from men's minds."[71] They
also had boring, worrisome, and expensive protocol duties to perform and
frequently had to wait on the great men from the home country who from
time to time appeared at their posts.

Often diplomats were not citizens of the countries they represented.
Like the petty gentry of Europe, from whom they tended to be recruited,
they were divided—scattered is perhaps a more accurate term—among
territories, fiefs, and independent territories of the complex European
world. Class and religion are better guides to who they were and whom
they served than "nationality"; many were the diplomatic equivalent of
soldiers of fortune. The Ottomans often utilized Greeks, the Swedes occasionally engaged Poles, the English (particularly under King William)
made use of Dutchmen, and the Austrians drew on all the resources of
their polyglot empire. Everyone had recourse to Italians, who, in the Renaissance at least, were considered the most subtle practitioners. Little
states, which could not afford to play the larger game, furnished talented
individuals to the larger states. The Italian city-states, particularly, were a
seedbed of courtiers who faded easily into the diplomatic world.[72] And the
Swiss were everywhere. Cosmopolitanism was made easier by agreement
on a lingua franca: first Latin, then, particularly around the Mediterranean, Italian, and finally all over Europe, French.

Diplomats usually supplemented their meager allowances by moonlighting, sometimes even for the government to which they were accredited. Many worked part time as merchants. In places this activity took on
such proportions as to require warehouses for their contraband.[73] In the
Mediterranean, most padded out their stipends with the fees they got for
assisting travelers and merchants, and sale of *barats*—letters of protection
for members of religious minorities—was a major source of income for
diplomats in the Ottoman Empire and Morocco.[74] Pay was not only low

but usually so much in arrears that British diplomats commonly hired government clerks in London to process their expense accounts and salaries at a 1 percent fee. Others in both England and France avoided the diplomatic service as an uncomfortable and financially destructive form of exile.[75] Not a few ambassadors blithely traded in official secrets to the highest bidder, while even those who did not actually peddle their wares expected (and performed in such a way as to get) valuable presents from those to whom they were accredited. Not surprisingly, few men who had other options were eager for this insecure life.

The reasons to avoid serving were many. In addition to low and irregular pay, boredom, trivial tasks, and the heavy costs, it was always uncomfortable and frequently dangerous to travel. Public transport by land meant sitting for days or even weeks in springless carriages on roads that were usually just slightly improved trails, being soaked by rain (against which there was no waterproof clothing), fording swollen rivers, being savaged by bugs in filthy inns, and getting sick on rotten food. Then there was the constant fear of bandits.

Bandits were not all ambassadors had to fear. Humiliation, physical abuse, imprisonment, or worse by rulers to whom they were accredited was widely noted. Hardly the conduct an aristocrat might expect, but, as Ragnar Numelin has noted, in the early days few were aristocrats. The Celtic word *ambactus,* from which our word *ambassador* is derived, meant simply "servant" or "serf."[76] In late medieval and Renaissance Europe, the least expensive and most expendable *ambaxadeurs* or envoys were clerics, and European rulers made extensive use of them. But they were not always welcome. This was not so much for religious reasons—although a Christian priest must have been something of an anomaly in a Muslim court—as because they were assumed not to have the ear of their own ruler—a consideration that still today often determines the way an incoming ambassador is treated. Giving voice to this feeling, the great Persian emperor Shah Abbas sent word in 1614 to Emperor Philip III of Spain that he was "tired of receiving friars as envoys and that he would prefer 'some gentleman of note.' "[77]

Even if he was a gentleman of note in his own society, the ritual of the court to which the envoy was sent might be, by his lights, degrading. When Western ambassadors went to China before the middle of the nineteenth century, they "often complained that they were ill-handled by their hosts."[78] In part, this reflected the Chinese reverence for written texts: in the Chinese system, it was the credentials and the documents rather than the person of the ambassadors that merited respect. The protocol of the Chinese court was so different—indeed, to the Westerner so degrading—

as to wound by humiliation. The best-remembered today was the Chinese custom of kowtowing, which, from the time of the first British ambassador, Lord Macartney, in 1792, envoys from the West mostly refused to perform. Little did they know that much sterner protocol had been required of Chinese ambassadors to the great nomadic emperors of Central Asia. To gain admittance to the tent of the *Shanyu* of the Xiongnu, they had to allow their faces to be tattooed in black. Much later, Muscovite tsars, drawing on the Mongol precedent, required envoys to present themselves on their knees.

Outrages such as these or the violation of diplomatic immunity might be made pretexts for war. Although the Xiongnu were themselves hard on ambassadors, their ruler charged the Chinese emperor, who had detained a Xiongnu ambassador, with rupturing "the bonds of brotherhood that joined us" and breaking off peaceful relations. Francis I regarded Charles V's violation of diplomatic immunity—probably having a French ambassador murdered[79]—as a cause of their war. Sometimes, moreover, ill-treatment of diplomats was provoked in order to justify military action, as the French did in 1827 when a French consul deliberately insulted the religion of the *dey* of Algiers. But retaliation, justified or not, was of little solace to the diplomat who had been treated as an expendable pawn.

Isolation of foreign ambassadors is something we today usually associate with the Soviet Union under Stalin; however, it was quite common in earlier times. Venetians, for example, were not allowed to speak to or visit the homes of foreign ambassadors. An early British ambassador wrote that "the nobles of my acquaintance avoid me and their law is so rigorous that they will hardly converse with any[one] that comes to me."[80] Even more strict was the treatment of European ambassadors by the Ottoman government in its heyday. Ogier Ghiselin de Busbecq, one of the early writers on life in Turkey,[81] lived virtually under house arrest and had to make his observations from the window of his house. "If I wished from time to time to take a ride through the city with my custodian, permission would probably not be refused," he wrote plaintively.[82] In that age, the Ottoman Empire and Venice were perhaps excessive, although Japan and China were also highly restrictive. Elsewhere, especially in wartime, ambassadors could expect to have their access reduced, although, surprisingly, this often did not happen in Europe. Even during the bitter wars of the seventeenth century, ambassadors of warring nations often continued to function normally and to travel without restriction. In more modern times, this openness has largely disappeared. On the outbreak of World War II, embassy staffs were closely supervised. When exchange was delayed, as it was for the staff of the American embassy in Tokyo after Pearl Harbor, the staff was locked inside the embassy grounds under guard.

Historically, however, although they were not well supported by their own governments and were often ill-treated and sometimes virtually made prisoner by others, ambassadors were expected to report frequently and in detail on what they saw or heard or managed to find out. Many wrote dispatches daily or even more often. Niccolò Machiavelli, who was used as badly as any of them, is said to have "sent back forty-nine dispatches in fifty days on his first legation at Rome, and though this is exceptional at least one a week was looked for, even from residents of long standing."[83]

Worse, although he was expected to report, the ambassador rarely had a secure means of doing so. The mails were not only slow, they were also routinely tampered with by all the states; special couriers were occasionally "turned," robbed, or even murdered and were, even in the most tranquil of times, expensive. Moreover, what seemed important or even vital to the resident ambassador might seem irrelevant or trivial to his employer, who, in any case, was apt to discount his report as being colored by his identification with his host, a failing that is known today as "localitis." The assumption that he was at least in part "one of them" caused him to be deprived of information vital to his job. When he did well, he got little recognition; when he performed adequately, his salary and expenses were often ruinously in arrears; and when he failed, he was apt to be made to suffer. And what his own employers neglected to do to make his life miserable, his hosts often accomplished: if his own state was weak, he might be ignored, insulted, or even imprisoned. It was such bad experiences as these that drove one of the most active of Renaissance ambassadors, Niccolò Machiavelli, to write *The Prince*.

Occasionally, an ambassador acted in a manner that caused his host to determine to get rid of him. He might be simply shunned, but two Spanish ambassadors to England were early examples of the ultimate diplomatic sanction—being declared persona non grata, that is, ordered to leave. The first, Don Guerau Despés, apparently left quietly, although the hapless chargé he left behind him was packed off to the Tower of London for alleged sedition. The more famous was Don Bernardino de Mendoza, who was caught dabbling in espionage in January 1584. Knowing him to be a proud and determined diplomat, the English handled him with elaborate care. They invited Mendoza to the house of the lord chancellor, ostensibly to meet with the Privy Council. There, instead of the warm reception he had expected, he was informed that Elizabeth knew of his involvement in a plot to overthrow her, and he was ordered to leave England within fifteen days. As the English possibly expected, Mendoza refused, demanded proof, and said that he would leave only on the orders of King Philip of Spain. After what must have been a tense and bitter discussion, the ambassador agreed to leave and, remembering the fate of the last chargé, closed the Spanish embassy. The English had the goods on Mendoza but, even under the best of circumstances, an ambassador was considered, as François de Callières wrote in the eighteenth century,[84] nothing but "an honorable spy." That being the case, he would be prudent, said Callières, to "beware of doing any of the spying himself" while serving his royal master.

The royal master, especially the vigorous kings of the European Renaissance, fearing such eavesdroppers and spies, usually ran their foreign affairs almost literally out of their pockets. Ferdinand of Aragon, for example, carried the state archives with him in big leather trunks as he traveled throughout his kingdom. He may be regarded as eccentric, but his habit was followed by British foreign secretaries even in the nineteenth century. They, fortunately, kept their papers for us to read, but when Ferdinand had read his he simply discarded them as so much wastepaper.

In the next generation, while great rulers such as Francis I, Charles V, and Henry VIII still personally ran their own diplomatic and espionage establishments, their conflicts, marriage plans, and mobilization of resources placed such heavy burdens on them that they needed help just to remember what had happened. Take Francis I. He was so keen to recruit Swiss mercenary soldiers that in just the six years after 1515 he sent nearly fifty embassies to the Swiss. In acute need, in 1529 (by which time his far-flung diplomacy included an active relationship with the Ottoman sultan),[85] Francis created the ancestor of the French foreign ministry, the *Conseil des Affaires*. So complex, in fact, were Francis's affairs that by the end of his rule he maintained four "secretaries of state," each to handle relations with one or more of the French provinces and the adjoining foreign states.[86] Francis's great rival, Charles V, ruling the largest empire in the Western world, also created an imperial chancellery under the influence of a Hapsburg subject from Italy, the home of the most advanced regime of international relations—Mercurino da Gattinara, who became a sort foreign minister.[87] Under Charles's son Philip II, Spain developed his father's legacy into the most coherent department of foreign affairs in Europe of its time.

Among other pressures to create these embryo foreign departments must have been the need to have clerks to write messages to ambassadors and, particularly, to encipher them and to decipher the replies. The process was self-reinforcing: as new people were added overseas, more staff was required to service the flow of their reports and, as more people became involved in the home office, more was asked of the overseas agents. It was not, however, until the seventeenth century that any European country developed what can be considered a true department of foreign affairs. France, spearheaded by Cardinal Richelieu, took the lead, whereas England was a century and a half behind. It was not until 1782 that the Foreign Office was established in London.

We tend to think of summit meetings as peculiarly modern affairs where the shape of the table or the lineup for photo opportunities is the key issue, but they are not wholly modern. Active rulers were often unwilling to allow their underlings to decide great issues and so often took personal charge of foreign negotiations. And, like some rulers today, they sometimes tripped over their prestige. A famous (and from this distance humorous) instance occurred in 1538 when Pope Paul III, alarmed by the rising power of the Ottoman Empire, summoned Francis I and Charles V to meet to settle their differences. Where to meet? Neither ruler would go into the territory of the other. So the pope hit on the city of Nice, then in the territory of the duke of Savoy. Neutrality was satisfied, but the duke felt slighted at being asked to be little more than an innkeeper for the great kings. So, furious, Charles brought his state with him in the shape of a sumptuous galley that he had anchored in the nearby bay of Villefranche. That, in turn, annoyed Francis, who did not propose to be a guest on his rival's yacht, so he set up *his* headquarters about twenty-five miles away. That was as close as the pope could get them, but a cavalcade of courtiers led by Francis's wife set off to visit her brother Charles to bridge the gap—or, more accurately, almost to bridge the gap: the bridge that had been thrown up to join Charles's galley to the shore collapsed under the weight of the gloriously attired courtiers, dunking them into the sea.

It wasn't only prestige and protocol that counted. In earlier times, safety was a major concern. We see this vividly in the famous meeting of Edward IV of England and Louis XI of France that was designed to bring to a halt the war England and France had fought intermittently for a century over what is now northern France. Having achieved most of his objectives, Louis was anxious to end hostilities. Edward was not. To attempt to reconquer his lost territories, he arrived near Calais with an imposing army but was desperately short of supplies. The allies on whom he had counted had let him down. So both kings were ready for at least a truce. To smooth the way for their court officials and themselves, they sent ahead their heralds;[88] then out came the French privy purse. Louis not only liberally bribed the English officials but promised Edward himself a large down payment with a yearly annuity. In addition, he offered marriage between the French crown prince and one of his daughters. And finally, perhaps most important to the two sovereigns, the carpenters arrived. They built a bridge of boats across the river dividing the two armies, and in the middle of the bridge they erected a grille so that no one could pass. At the grille the two kings met and, rather clumsily I imagine, tried to embrace without exposing any vital parts to one another. Through that barrier on August 29, 1475, they concluded the Treaty of Picquigny, which marked the effective end of generations of war.

As bizarre as this meeting may appear, it was not unique. In 1807, following the battle of Friedland, Napoleon and the emperor Alexander of Russia also met—just the two of them—on a raft anchored in the middle of the Nieman River near Tilsit.

Between those two episodes, the Thirty Years' War cuts a swath across European diplomatic history. From roughly 1618 to 1648, Europe was convulsed not only by general war but also by hundreds of local conflicts between Catholics and Protestants. When everyone had been exhausted by destruction, famine, and massacres, the two main contenders, the Hapsburg Empire and France, and various of their allies settled down in 1641 to try to restore the peace. The process that ended in the Treaty of Westphalia took them seven years. There are historical records of dozens of such meetings from ancient times and even in primitive societies. The powdered and wigged ambassadors in Westphalia might not have appreciated the comparison, but one can be made to the Australian *corroborree-feasts,* in which as many as twenty tribes presented themselves to settle disputes,[89] or to the pre-Islamic Arab tribal gatherings during the yearly period forbidden (in Arabic, *haram*) to warfare. In classical times, multistate meetings are recorded at such Greek shrines as Delphi, Poros, and Delos. And, under the auspices of the church, "international" conferences dot medieval history. In later centuries, as I shall discuss, the gatherings at Westphalia in 1648, Vienna in 1814, and Paris in 1919 punctuate the history of Europe.

Today, statesmen are especially sensitive to the political cost of failure, which explains why all heads of state insist on careful preparation and agreement in advance, but rulers have long recognized this danger. Writing in 1716 François de Callières commented on the 1648 meeting that although it was "one of the most intricate negotiations I have ever known, [yet it] was not really the work of that vast concourse of ambassadors and envoys which met there and appended their signatures to the document. The essential clauses of that treaty were discussed and drawn up by a secret agent of Duke Maximilian of Bavaria sitting at a table in Paris with Cardinal Mazarin. [Indeed,] most of the great events in recent diplomatic history have been prepared by ministers sent [ahead] in secret."[90]

But a new and critical problem became immediately evident: central-ization of control over foreign affairs meant that no note could be written from one delegation to another without authorization from the home gov-ernment and that each reply would also require consultation. Not only were governments unhurried about decision-making and replies, but also travel was slow. So for weeks or even months at a time, all the diplomats could do was to wile away their boredom.

Yet the conference had proved its worth: it was cheaper than war, and so the European powers convoked another in 1713 at Utrecht (which gave Europe twenty-seven years of peace) and in 1814 at Vienna (which gave Europe nearly fifty years of peace). The very cumbersomeness of the process may, paradoxically, have been one of its virtues. It kept govern-ments talking and negotiating when otherwise they might have been fight-ing. It was also evident, however, that those who negotiated needed more authority than those at Westphalia and Utrecht were given, so at Vienna the powers were represented not by diplomats but by men of senior, even royal, rank, including the tsar of all the Russias.

Vienna became the exemplar of the "modern" conference and was closely studied by some who attended the 1919 Peace Conference in Paris. Among the "lessons" many have sought to draw from it are the conflicting aims of participants. The great unifying principal that had motivated them before the conference—defeat of a common enemy—was gone; so each party began to pursue the objectives that it saw as in its national interest. The British foreign secretary, Lord Castlereagh, strove to create a balance of powers in Europe that would prevent any single state from again achiev-ing overall military superiority; the defeated French, represented by the shrewd Prince Talleyrand, sought to regain a suitable position in the com-ity of nations; Prince Metternich was primarily concerned to defend Aus-trian territory and to prevent Prussia from dominating "Germany"; the tsar appears mainly to have wanted to assert his new position as the leader of the most powerful military force in Europe.

The inevitable question before the conference was, Who was the loser? Talleyrand wisely and rightly pointed out that if France were to be put in that position, the only option for the French would be to support the discredited and exiled Napoleon. (This lesson was not drawn by those who ran the 1919 Peace Conference, when Allied sentiment was to punish the defeated.) Talleyrand did not convince his colleagues that it was neces-sary to look ahead rather than back; indeed, he did not attack this issue head on. Rather, he organized what amounted to a "strike" by the smaller, excluded powers on the organization of the conference. Then, having alarmed the four "great powers" (the phrase was invented at the Congress), those who felt that they had earned the right to guide the discussions since they had done most of the fighting, Talleyrand used their alarm to get France admitted to the inner circle. Once inside, he was quite prepared to allow all significant matters to be handled by the inner group. Indeed, it has been said that "there never was a Congress of Vienna" since the Congress merely rubber-stamped the decisions of the major powers.[91]

Unlike France in 1814, Germany in 1919 was not invited to the peace conference for the first five months, during which time many of the key decisions were made. And no one was prepared to hear from the defeated Germans the sort of argument made by Talleyrand. This mood was set long before the conference and, because it has played such an important role in the history of our times, I will briefly ventilate it.

During the war, the Allies began to make arrangements to share the spoil. Much of this was in the Middle East and was, at the time, made subject to various secret understandings.[92] The United States was not party to these understandings and it was in part Woodrow Wilson's reaction to what he learned of Allied plans that he set out his call for the self-determination of peoples, for "open covenants of peace openly arrived at," and for a "peace without victory." Each of these issues was vigorously opposed by the other allies, who regarded Wilson as naive or worse; and each one set the other three great powers at one another's throats.

With respect to self-determination of peoples, Britain and France had already agreed on a division of the Ottoman Empire. Wilson's spokesman, Ray Stannard Baker, referred to it simply as "the old game of grab."[93] Britain finally bought France's acquiescence in its program by allowing it a share in Middle Eastern oil production. Only the Americans raised the issue of what the people in the area wanted, and their effort was too little and too late; this was in part because Colonel House turned against Wilson on this issue and in part because Wilson, as a lame-duck and sick president who faced a growing opposition in Washington, was unable to carry forward.

On "open covenants of peace openly arrived at" the American delegation quickly fell into a more traditional pattern, partly copied, in essence, from the Vienna Congress. Both groups had to answer the question, Who are the decision makers? In Vienna, the four main powers constituted the original inner group, the "great powers" that became five when France was added. In 1919, participants fit in three concentric circles. The conference as a whole, the Plenary Conference, composed of at least 1,037 delegates divided among 29 delegations, was in Wilson's theory the deciding forum, but, as at Vienna, it was from even before the opening of the conference largely ceremonial. Secretary of State Lansing wanted Wilson to put pressure on the main powers by mobilizing the small powers, who felt left out of the principal discussions, behind him as a claque. "They would have looked up to him as their champion and guide. They would have followed him." That is, he advocated exactly the tactics used by Talleyrand at the Congress of Vienna a century before.[94] The early and major decisions were made by the Council of Ten, which was composed of the heads of government and foreign ministers of the United States, Great Britain, France, and Italy plus two delegates from Japan. This group was unwieldy and routinely leaked information to the press. So, despite the first point in Wilson's Fourteen Points, a further restriction was imposed: a Council of Four (the Big Four) was established to maintain secrecy, because "secrecy was considered an essential condition for the construction of those compromises by which alone amity could be preserved."[95] Until he left for America in February 1919, President Wilson might be regarded, and was regarded by the public, as a sort of "Committee of One." As the British ambassador to Washington had said of him before the conference, "He is already a mysterious, a rather Olympian personage, and shrouded in darkness from which issue occasional thunderbolts."[96]

"Peace without victory" was a theme Wilson had set forth in a speech to the U.S. Senate in January 1917. The root causes of war, he argued, were imperialism, militarism, and the quest for a balance of power. The reaction of the European powers was furious. He had touched the point at which greed, fear, pride, and anger were focused. Anatole France spoke in public the private reactions of many of the leaders when he wrote, "Peace without victory, would this satisfy? . . . No, not even a lame peace, a peace stumbling and becrutched, but a deformed peace, squatting on its haunches, a disgusting peace, fetid, ignominious, obscene, fistulous, hemorrhoidal, in short a peace without victory."[97]

As Wilson read such comments on his program, he rejected them with scorn: he thought that ambition and greed were the only forces opposed to the crusade he had mounted and would, unless defeated, jeopardize the very civilization of Europe. That many Europeans opposed his peace-seeking therefore seemed to him so short-sighted and wrongheaded as to be irrelevant. But, further to strengthen his position, he urged the election of a Democratic majority in the U.S. Congress as a vote of confidence in his leadership.

In Great Britain, Prime Minister David Lloyd George also sought a vote of confidence by "going to the public." But the results in the two democracies were very different. I have quoted de Tocqueville as saying that a democracy was ill-fitted to conduct foreign policy. He was, of course, referring to the American system of divided governmental powers. In

Great Britain, with its parliamentary system, by winning a partisan electoral victory Lloyd George got a mandate and a supportive legislature. But Wilson's comparable electoral ploy not only made his foreign policy a partisan issue but created a split between the presidency and the Senate that doomed his program, prevented the United States from joining the League of Nations, and opened the way for the very causes of war that he had identified.

International gatherings such as the Congress of Vienna and the Paris Peace Conference are generally regarded as the high points of diplomatic activity where nations come together to end major wars. Yet ironically, among the hundreds of officials, quasi officials, nongovernmental interested groups, and hangers-on who attend, diplomats form only a small minority. The British delegation in Vienna was composed of Foreign Secretary Lord Castlereagh, three subordinate ambassadors, and a clerical staff of 12; in Paris in 1919 the British delegation numbered 420, of whom only 18 were professional diplomats—and they were little consulted by the delegation's head, Prime Minister David Lloyd George.

We naturally tend to focus on a few "historic" meetings, not only today—when international gatherings are virtually constant—but even in the last century, when, as the diplomatic historian Sir Charles Webster has written, Europe actually had an intermittent council during the whole period from the Congress of Vienna to the outbreak of World War I. He counts eight congresses and eighteen conferences.[98]

"Overt diplomacy," however, was centuries in coming. During the sixteenth, seventeenth, and eighteenth centuries, rulers set up parallel, clandestine organizations whose agents were usually unknown to the accredited ambassadors. In France, this was known as *le Secret,* and this "double diplomacy" was widely copied. Those who knew American embassies in the 1950s will not find this system unfamiliar since the local representatives of the Central Intelligence Agency often functioned as "separate but equal" partners of ambassadors and often conducted diplomatic negotiations without their knowledge.

So ambassadors faced yet another problem: trying to figure out exactly what they were supposed to do or even exactly who they were. And meanwhile, they were increasingly sent to the ends of the earth. The first French ambassador arrived in Istanbul in 1528, followed by the first British ambassador (a merchant) fifty years later; the first British ambassador did not reach Moscow until 1699. These were "hardship" posts, but it was hard enough to get ambassadors to go to European capitals. Paris was the only place where nearly everyone was willing to go; London was acceptable; Madrid was not. For centuries, there had been practically no embassies or missions in Asia except at the Ottoman and Mughal courts and none in Africa or the New World. The quest for Asian trade led, however, to the opening of consulates in various other places including the Levant, Egypt, and Morocco.[99]

The Asian experience was important in the development of diplomacy in that it tended to "promote" the role of the ambassador as the disparity in power between Europe and Asia grew. Almost generals rather than diplomats, ambassadors fought the wars of their countries on the battlefield of council chambers with money and jewels as weapons. Some of these "wars" made a larger impact on European history than battles. Perhaps the most important was the Ottoman decision to forgo an almost certain crushing victory over Peter the Great, whose army was surrounded, in Moldavia in 1711. The outnumbered, exhausted, sick, and confused Russians offered to surrender. There then ensued a much more crucial battle between the diplomats of Poland and Sweden on one side and on the other the Russians, the French, the British, and the Austrians for the favor of the Ottomans. We know almost nothing about that battle except for its result: not only was Peter allowed to extract his army (and person) intact in the treaty of Pruth but also the Russians were left in control of the Baltic provinces, which effectually neutralized Sweden, and so Peter was soon able to continue his war with the Turks. To this day, no one knows quite how to account for the Russian diplomatic success, but whatever the cause the result was fundamental to the rise of Russia, the isolation of Sweden, and the decline of the Ottoman Empire.

The Ottoman Empire was, over the centuries, host to many of the great men of European, particularly British, diplomacy. Some deserve to be described as tutors, counselors, or even supervisors to successive governments. Sir Thomas Roe, better known for his embassy to the Mughal court, was from 1621 to 1628 ambassador to the Ottoman Empire, where he was able to act as arbiter in bringing about a peace treaty with Poland in 1622. Even more intrusive was Lord Elgin, who formed a plan to split Corfu off from the empire and turn it into an independent state in 1799. Stratford Canning, who at twenty-three became chief of the British mission in 1810, was for almost half a century the key European influence in the Ottoman Empire and was, among other things, able to negotiate the independence of the new Greek state.

The reciprocal to European diplomatic activity was slow in coming. Sustained Ottoman diplomatic representation in Europe began only in 1793 with an embassy to England; other embassies set out for Paris, Berlin, and Vienna in 1797. Although the ambassadors were Turks, their assistants and advisers were Greeks.

More than most, British diplomacy had a tradition of complexity: not only were missions composed of more than one ambassador, which as we have seen was not uncommon, but, after the conquest of India, which created virtually a "second Britain," both parts of the empire sent embassies to third countries. These were always separate and sometimes in active, even vicious, competition. We see this first in the diplomacy of Britain and India in Persia (Iran); there in 1807 Napoleon's emissary got the Persians to agree to declare war on Britain and allow a French army to cross into India. In alarm, the British sent two embassies to the shah. One came from London and one from India. As Sir Denis Wright (himself later a British ambassador in Iran) wrote, "Almost inevitably there was soon an undignified clash, of major proportions, between the [two ambassadors with the representative of British India trying] to undermine Jones' [the English ambassador's] position and humiliate him in the eyes of the Persians."[100]

. . .

As diplomacy became increasingly separated from its more disreputable cousin, espionage, and then divided into that part which today we would term high-level missions by special emissaries of the ruler and that part we think of as the continuous activities carried on by resident ambassadors and their staffs, it came to be increasingly affected by prevailing social norms. In the seventeenth and eighteenth centuries, these norms were set by the monarchs and princes of the European states and their noble retainers. It was their customs, habits, dress, privileges, and concerns that dominated what was becoming the style of diplomacy and their class that furnished the personnel that make up the diplomatic establishment down to at least World War II. Even its admirers often referred to it as a caste. One of its great English practitioners, Sir Arthur Hardinge, then ambassador to Spain, pointed out how restrictive was its view of the world. Testifying before a royal commission on the eve of World War I, he said, "I think it is exceedingly difficult both for Foreign Embassies in London and for British Embassies abroad to have any real or close touch with democratic movements in the modern world."[101] This, it was generally felt, was because more than half of the officers in the British service between 1851 and 1929 belonged to the aristocracy or the gentry. During that time, candidates were required to have property yielding an income of at least £400 per annum or roughly $50,000 in today's money. From the 1850s there was an entrance exam, but only those recommended by the foreign secretary could take it. Then also it was customary for the young officer to spend two years abroad as an unpaid "attaché" to perfect a language. In short, the diplomatic service was aimed at the idle rich who wanted travel, prestige, and a life with the European aristocracy and who had the means to pay for it. The German service before World War I was even more class-conscious. It was said that in it no quality was prized so much as a noble lineage.

This social isolation has disturbed successive commissions, particularly in Great Britain and the United States, which have concerned themselves with the "reform" of the foreign service, but it was already a concern of the more enlightened practitioners of the late seventeenth century. Although his language was necessarily somewhat guarded—since he was a senior civil servant who wrote under royal patronage and since in his view the "playing-fields" of ambassadors were solely royal courts—François de Callières alluded to the same problem. "A wise prince," he wrote, "will not fall into the fault common to many princes, namely that of regarding wealth as the first and most necessary quality in an ambassador." But, he goes on to say, "It is also desirable that an ambassador should be a man of birth and breeding, especially if he is employed in any of the principal courts of Europe and it is by no means a negligible factor that he should have a noble presence and a handsome face, which undoubted are among the means which easily please mankind."[102] Given the social context and the probable use of patronage in the appointment of ambassadors—"nepotism is the damnation of diplomacy"—Callières suggested that the solution was to employ skilled men behind the scenes while leaving the "public appearance to the ignorant but high-born gentleman whose sole trouble is to maintain a fine table and a magnificent equipage." This was usually not done, he found; rather, "One may see often men who have never left their own country, who have never applied themselves to the study of public affairs, being of meager intelligence, appointed so to speak over-night to important embassies in countries of which they know neither the interests, the laws, the customs, the language, nor even the geographical situation."[103]

This sweeping and damning analysis was little heeded in the following centuries. As D. B. Horn has shown, out of nineteen British ambassadors in Paris between 1689 and the French Revolution of 1789, seven had no previous diplomatic experience, and some of the rest had very little training for the job.[104] Inevitably the result was the formation of a diplomacy very different from its more virile ancestors, a diplomacy with an excessive, at times almost exclusive, concern with ritual, protocol, and precedent. Diplomatic dispatches right up to the eve of World War I are shot through with discussions of whether an ambassador should greet the sovereign with his hat on or off, should stand or sit, and should be in front of or behind one of his colleagues.[105]

Although such concerns were tolerable before the French Revolution, they became increasingly out of place in the nineteenth century, with the result that, as Sir Arthur Hardinge noted, diplomats increasingly lived in a world cut off from the great movements of their times and, in their isolation, were increasingly regarded with suspicion and hostility not only by the general public but even by the other branches of the governments they served. Indeed, even before President Woodrow Wilson crusaded for an open diplomacy, such conservative commentators as the editor of *The Times* of London wrote of "the men who have too long played with human lives as pawns in a game of chess, who have become so enmeshed in formulas and the jargon of diplomacy that they have ceased to be conscious of the poignant realities with which they trifle."[106] It was in this spirit that diplomats were often blamed for the catastrophe of World War I and played so little part in the creation of the peace treaty that followed it.

But for two centuries, although every "expert" wrote about the need for education of "the young gentlemen," very little was done about it. An experiment was made in Oxford and Cambridge in the foundation of the chairs of modern history in 1724. Twenty young men were to be instructed in modern languages and history in each university to prepare them for government service. The results were dismal. The French effort begun under Louis XIV, more modest both in numbers (only six as compared with forty in England) and in education (being confined to work in the archives), also was judged a failure and as in England was closed down within a few years. Other efforts in Prussia (begun by Frederick II) and Russia (begun under Peter the Great) similarly died out after a few years.

Most of the diplomats who have left memoirs appear to have been profoundly anti-intellectual. Others, perhaps, were merely cynical. Lord Chesterfield spoke for many when he advised his son that "your dancing-master . . . is at this time the most useful and necessary of all the masters you have or can have." With a father's bluntness, Chesterfield went right to the bottom line: merit and knowledge alone, he wrote, "would at most raise you to . . . [the modest post of] Resident at Hamburg or Ratisbon."[107] Title, connections, and social graces were what counted.

In the United States, little attempt was made to educate anyone, would-be diplomats or others, in foreign affairs until World War I. Columbia University led the way in 1917 with courses on imperialism and international relations in nineteenth-century Europe. In 1924 Yale University offered a similar course, Harvard followed suit the next year, and the fad gradually spread. But many of the courses were rudimentary in the extreme and almost all were confined to little more than elaborate organizational charts.

The next spurt of activity came after World War II when the Foreign Service Institute was organized as a sort of finishing school for new appointees in the foreign service (which had been founded in 1924) and Columbia University set up its School of International Affairs; Harvard, Tufts University's Fletcher School of Law and Diplomacy, and the University of Virginia's Woodrow Wilson School of International Affairs soon organized programs leading to a master of arts degree in international affairs. Specialized regional programs followed at Harvard, Columbia, and other universities with, after 1951, large-scale foundation and government support. By the end of the 1950s such programs were teaching the languages, history, and culture of African, Asian, and European societies to thousands of students annually. But it was generally agreed that only a beginning had been made.

To American professional diplomats, the beginnings seemed useful but not central since the richest rewards of diplomatic service are usually not within their reach: postings to the major capitals, particularly London and Paris, are nearly always reserved for friends or supporters of an incumbent president. This is not the custom in the British, French, German, Russian, or Japanese foreign affairs establishments. Which system is better can be argued at length. Neither category is per se the best choice. Professional diplomats obviously are more likely to know how to conduct diplomatic affairs; some of them are highly intelligent and able people, but in the American system they may lack access to their titular boss, the president. Political appointees, similarly, vary from the totally incompetent to the politically highly experienced and shrewd; they usually need guidance on how to conduct an embassy, but they often are more favorably received if they are thought to be able to reach the ear of the president. About the best that can be said is that, as in all human affairs, there is no substitute for careful choice, and that is never categorical.

. . . .

26 INTERVENTION AND INTERNATIONAL LAW

"The main object of diplomacy," wrote Sir Charles Webster, "is to obtain what one wants without recourse to violence."[108] But, of course, diplomacy does not always produce the results desired by governments that believe their cause to be just, their power overwhelming, and their opportunity fleeting. In those circumstances they often seek to impose on those who have disappointed or thwarted them governments that are more likely to be amenable to their desires. Such actions have been common since relations among states were first recorded, and they remain prevalent in our times.

Consider what happened at the end of World War II, when the Allies demanded an unconditional surrender from the Axis powers so that they could extirpate the old regimes. For a short while after the initial shock of surrender, the defeated nations existed in a virtual political vacuum, being ruled by military governments. Then they were allowed to assist the occupying forces' administrations; next they were directed to form native administrations under supervision and, within a few years, governments.

Although the Western powers acted more benignly than the Soviet Union, relying on infusions of money and the techniques of public relations to accomplish their objectives, they left no doubt in the minds of the inhabitants of surrendered Axis powers that their freedom of political choice was limited. In the areas under their control, the Soviet Union was less circumspect about covering its iron fist with a velvet glove and more motivated by both strategic and ideological factors. The Soviets blatantly and often brutally imposed governments of their own persuasion not only on the former Axis powers but also on countries that had been victims of the Axis. When they (occasionally) sought to justify or explain their actions, the Soviet leaders asserted that the division of Eastern Europe agreed between British foreign secretary Anthony Eden and Soviet foreign minister Vyacheslav Molotov in May 1944 and confirmed by Prime Minister Winston Churchill and Premier Josef Stalin in October of that year gave them carte blanche in their sphere of influence just as Britain asserted similar powers in Greece.[109] Consequently, they set about imposing Communist regimes on Poland, Romania, Hungary, Bulgaria, Czechoslovakia, and what became the German Democratic Republic (East Germany) while the British imposed a monarchy on Greece. Meanwhile, in Western Europe, the United States and Britain jointly facilitated the rise to power of parties of the right or center-right, and the United States unilaterally undertook to transform the Japanese state.

Initially at least, each power believed that it had succeeded. But over time it became clear that the more blatant the action, the less it was accepted. Although sizable portions of the population of Western Europe flirted with communism, the right and center-right parties kept power long after Anglo-American influence waned; Greece was a special case in that the British, whose heavy-handed anticommunist policies were failing, were replaced by the Americans in 1947–48, and Greece underwent a turbulent series of political changes out of which emerged a military government that was both anticommunist and antidemocratic; in Eastern Europe, although all opposition was crushed either by indigenous forces or by Soviet military intervention (as in Czechoslovakia and Hungary), the regimes never acquired a firm political base and, when Soviet power eventually waned, were overturned.

These Cold War arrangements in Europe left ambiguous vast areas of what came to be called the third world, and the two sides began a half-century of competition for hegemony. Much of the competition took the relatively benign form of military and economic assistance, programs of political persuasion, formation of leagues of friendly governments, and foreign espousal of local causes, but in a number of countries such efforts were deemed insufficient and each side in the Cold War intervened more violently.

Four of these interventions have been particularly significant in our lives: the 1953 Anglo-American coup d'état in Iran, the Soviet-Chinese stimulation of an attack on South Korea in 1950, the American intervention in Vietnam (which, in various forms, took place from 1947 to 1981), and the Soviet-inspired and -supported coup d'état in Afghanistan. I will focus briefly on the Soviet intervention in Afghanistan, a venture that not only precipitated the virtual destruction of that little country but also played a major role in the collapse of the Soviet Union.

Russian intervention in Afghanistan dates from the "Great Game" of the nineteenth century and following the 1917 revolution became both more pronounced and more ideological. After initial attempts at overthrowing governments in Central Asia had failed,[110] the Soviets began a policy of indirection in Afghanistan, assigning to the Indian Communist Party the role of intermediary except in military affairs—in which, with the approval of the various Afghan governments and the tacit consent of the other powers, it always exercised a virtual monopoly. It appears that the Soviet government worked on the assumption, in accordance with Marxist theory, that Afghanistan was not "ready" for the kind of government the Soviet Union wanted it to have but that such a government would come more or less naturally in a few years. This assessment was called into question in 1977, however, following a confrontation between Soviet premier Leonid Brezhnev and the Afghan dictator Prince Muhammad Daoud. The available records do not make clear exactly what happened, but after a complex series of events, the tiny (and split) communist party managed on April 24, 1978, almost by accident, to get units of the armed forces (among whom there were more than three thousand Soviet "advisers") to seize power; the insurgents immediately executed Prince Daoud and his family, proclaimed the Democratic Republic of Afghanistan, and embarked on a program of "reform."[111]

The new regime was so thinly supported—indeed virtually unknown in most of the country—and so inexperienced, and had so few active members, that the Soviet Union immediately took control of the security forces "to protect the revolution." Under this cover, the government began to implement its policies, but these were so hastily formulated and insensitively implemented that they quickly alienated large parts of the population, particularly in the countryside. By the winter of 1979, Afghanistan was plunged into civil war. To bolster the faltering regime—in which it believed its prestige to be engaged and whose downfall, it feared, might incite unrest in fellow Muslim and culturally related Soviet Central Asia—the Soviet government began to send in troops. As in Vietnam, each new increment was judged insufficient and each local ally was deemed unreliable. So, on December 27, 1979, Soviet troops occupied the capital.

As in similar situations—those of the Egyptians in Yemen in 1961, the Americans in Vietnam and elsewhere—outside intervention triggered a nationalist reaction. In Afghanistan, this was supplemented by religious and tribal hostility toward the Soviets and their Afghan Communist allies. The overthrow of the government of the shah in Iran in January 1979 also encouraged at least the more religiously oriented Afghan movements to believe that they could win against the odds. Armed bands of guerrillas, augmented by deserters from the Afghan army, took control of the rugged mountain fastnesses of the Hindu Kush, where it was difficult for the cumbersome forces of the Russians to reach them. Each incident increased the scale and spread of hostilities so that during the autumn it began to seem likely that the communist government would collapse. As opposition increased the Soviet Union found itself in 1980 bogged down in a huge and unwinnable guerrilla war. As in the American operations in Vietnam, the Russians came to rely increasingly on technology to win against politics: the helicopter gunship became the symbol of Soviet power—and the albatross around the neck of their local allies.

At this point the war was transformed by two new but predictable influences. First, the Afghan guerrillas split into warring factions along religious, tribal, and ethnic lines. As in Yugoslavia and Greece during and after World War I, these rival armed groups battled with their neighbors (as they continue to do today) at least as strongly as with the strangers. Second, Pakistan (which then uneasily hosted more than two million Afghan refugees), encouraged and paid by the United States and, to a lesser extent, by Saudi Arabia, began to arm,[112] train, and pay thousands of Afghan and foreign volunteer guerrillas. Not only did this turn Afghanistan into a great power proxy battlefield, as it had in the days of the Great Game between Russia and Britain, but it also created armies of well-trained, seasoned, and motivated "freedom fighters." By December 1989, the Soviet Union had had enough. It began to withdraw its troops and, in a spectacular about-face, Soviet foreign minister Eduard Shevardnadze was reported to have met with the former king, Zahir Shah, in Rome to suggest that he return to head a caretaker government.

Although the Russians pulled out, Afghanistan found no peace. Virtually everyone had acquired weapons and many had learned how to use them. Rival factions fought furiously with one another for dominance, and as city after city was razed, millions were made homeless, and uncounted thousands were killed, the country found no way either toward the status quo ante or toward a stable future. And even that was not the end. The thousands of "freedom fighters," who had been recruited from other Muslim countries and who had been trained by the Central Intelligence Agency and others to fight the Russians, soon began to involve themselves in actions against others they perceived as being the enemies of their beliefs or their nations in Egypt, Saudi Arabia, Bosnia, and even in the United States.

However much events and actors in Afghanistan and other examples of outside intervention differ from one another, they evince similar patterns: each provoked reactions that usually rendered intervention not only ineffectual but also self-defeating. They caused severe dislocations to societies already split along ethnic, religious, and economic lines and in which institutions of statehood, typically newly established after long periods of foreign domination, were fragile. The results, particularly in Afghanistan but also in a number of others, have been decades of violence, sporadic civil war, and impoverishment. And they set in motion tendencies that were certainly unintended and were often costly to those who had made them possible: the spread of the drug trade, international terrorism, and severe social and political disruption as in the Soviet Union (after Afghanistan), America (after Vietnam), and France (after Algeria). Slowly and painfully, powerful states are now learning, as repeatedly their predecessors have learned in times past, that there are limits to intervention. Indeed, today, when societies are much more highly politicized than in the past, such limits are even more narrow.

. . .

At the other end of the spectrum of interstate relationships has been the attempt to find norms of conduct or laws to restrain governments and to keep their relationships within finite and peaceful limits. But "realists" have always doubted that it amounted to much. Thucydides speaks to and about us when he has Athens' envoys tell the people of Melos that "right, as the world goes, is only in question between equals in power, while the strong do what they can and the weak suffer what they must."[113] His sentiments were echoed in this century by the "father of geopolitics," H. J. Mackinder,[114] and other "realists." But still, the quest for law is very old.

In an antiquarian sense, we may trace the emphasis on law back to ancient Sumer, where the treaty evolved from domestic written contracts. Formalizing agreements between states customarily required each party to draw up its version, which was sent to the other for corrections or approval; once agreed and sealed, the document was called a "tablet of the life of the gods" because each ruler swore his oath as the servant and proxy of the city god and the treaty was seen, ultimately, as between the two gods rather than between the two rulers. Thus, to violate the terms of the treaty was a sin against the patron god of the city and risked having the god's appointment of the ruler—more or less the equivalent of the "mandate of heaven"—revoked. The conduct of foreign affairs thus arose from the practices of domestic commerce and was intimately woven into religion.

Sumer never worked out a means for its constituent cities to live in peace with one another, much less with the culturally distinct but structurally similar cities of the north and west: the cities did to one another extramurally precisely what the great law codes sought to prevent within their walls. There is no suggestion in the surviving record that anyone felt the need of an interurban code of law. And, although rudimentary arbitration might be practiced by a temporarily neutral city, there was no concept of a neutral agency or a body of precedent—law—within which treaties might be examined or acts judged.

Greece little advanced these practices or concepts although the Greeks made more use of arbitration than others. In the thirty years' peace negotiated between Athens and Sparta in 446–445 B.C.E., binding arbitration—"recourse to law and oaths"—was specified.[115] Indeed, as Sir Harold Nicholson points out, some forty-six "inter-state" matters were arbitrated between 300 and 100 B.C.E.[116] Moreover, it is possible (from a modern point of view) to interpret the role of oracles as a sort of moral arbitrator on custom and practice.

In its turn, Rome heavily emphasized domestic law but, in the vast expansion of its frontiers, incorporation of scores of ethnic and cultural groups, and subordination of other states, it effectively turned what had been "domestic" into a system that came near to encompassing the world known to the Romans. Aspects of their law passed, in imperfectly understood and only occasionally applied form, to the Europe of the Middle Ages. But that world was also without any true international institutions.

From about the ninth century, the papacy began hesitantly and often with long lapses to fill that void. It was the papacy that ultimately sanctioned treaties. The breaching of a treaty constituted perjury, which was then seen as a spiritual rather than a secular crime. The church often, as with Venice in 1177, pronounced anathemas on any who broke a truce or violated a peace. Rulers who broke their treaties could be excommunicated and their states interdicted. Despite the fact that he was also a reigning monarch of a territorial state and had far-flung interests in other states, which compromised his position, the pope (or the papacy as an institution) served as a court of arbitration to which monarchs took disputes, as Louis VI of France and Henry I of England did in 1119. The conflict between Rome, the territorial state, and the church, the *societas perfecta*, could never be resolved so long as the Vatican remained both. In Christendom, besides the papacy, there was no substitute other than the sword.

In practice, all medieval disputants, both Christian and Muslim, believed that God determined the outcome of disputes and that His court was usually the field of battle. War among Christians was regarded as wrong if "unjust" but few believed, with Erasmus, that the issue of justice was merely a pretext.

The position of Muslims both within and without Christendom was more complex. Christians generally believed that war between Christians and Muslims was right, proper, and normal whereas peace was suspect, irregular, and abnormal. Saint Francis of Assisi was a rare exception in his belief in the peaceful conversion of Muslims—he even tried to convert the sultan of Egypt in 1219—and conversion became a major thrust of the order he founded. In the following century, the great Catalan scholar Ramon Llull (Ramón Lull) gives us a more or less secular counterpart to St. Francis as he labored to bring about greater understanding between the two civilizations. But his death in 1314 may be said to have stopped missionary activity among Muslims and ushered in an age of constant hostility.

Muslims naturally took a different view of themselves and also of Muslim-Christian relations. Within the community of Islam (even when it was split into rival factions or states), war was held to be a violation of God's law. According to the Qur'an, the community of Islam was composed of "brothers" and was, as I have mentioned, treated as an evolution from a clan of kindred in which fighting was banned. Islamic society together with its "clients" was the *Daru'l-islam,* the domain of peace. Legally, no fighting was to take place within that area. And within it—provided that they lived in peace, did not make war on Muslims, and obeyed the civil authority—those who believed in "The Book" (Christians and Jews) were to be tolerated and allowed to live under their own leaders in their accustomed way. It is true that over the centuries, these principles were not always implemented, but in general they were more honored than in most other civilizations and certainly more so than in Christian Europe. Moreover, as Islam spread into areas where Christians and Jews either did not live or were small minorities, other groups, notably the Hindus of India, were accorded this status de facto.

Outside of the domain of Islam was the *Daru'l-harb,* the domain of war. The frontier between the two naturally varied over the centuries. When the Muslims were successful, as they were, for example, in Spain, the resident Christians and Jews were treated as protected clients. When the Muslims were not successful, their opponents were treated essentially as secular enemies who refused to submit to the earthly representatives of God.

On the practical implementation of these positions medieval Christian and Muslim societies reached impermanent but general internal consensuses. Christian Europeans often visited the Muslim South and East, but Muslims rarely visited Christian Europe. Large-scale conversions (Coptic Egyptians to Islam and Muslim and Jewish Spaniards to Christianity) eased some of the internal pressures. Trade increased throughout the Mediterranean and the Indian Ocean and often involved people of the three communities. And despite the trauma of the Crusades, the "reconquest" of Spain, and the Ottoman push into the Balkans, there were long periods not only of peace but even of Muslim-Christian alliances against other Muslim or Christian powers. Christians were busy fighting against other Christians and so were Muslims. Finally, the energies of both were directed away from each other, Muslims to South and Southeast Asia and Africa and Christians toward the north and northeast of Europe.

What threw at least the Christian world off balance was the discovery of the New World. The first reaction, shortly after the return of Columbus from his voyage, was that Spain and Portugal appealed to the papacy to divide the newly discovered maritime world between them. And a more profound issue was soon perceived: How was one to treat the non-Christian and non-Muslim inhabitants of that new world?

The discovery may be said to have triggered the first attempts at what we recognize as international law. At first it was not a quest for order or precedent in relations among states but rather a quest for the more general code of justice or law among peoples or nations, *jus gentium*. And, not surprisingly, it was first undertaken where the frontier of the old Europe and the New World was most keenly felt—Spain. The acquisition of a new empire posed questions that philosophers felt had to be answered.[117] A major figure among them was a "high-minded Dominican friar, Francisco de Vitoria, who in the 1530s, lectured his students at Salamanca on their right, or lack of right, as Spaniards, to dominate and exploit the Indians of the new-found world."[118] Vitoria's two volumes, *De Indis Noviter Inventis* (On the Indians recently discovered) and *De Jure Belli* (On the law of war), published about 1532, foresaw the existence of a world community and argued that international law applied to all states without limitations of geography, creed, or race.

In Europe a gap was also widening among the beliefs, laws, and mores of societies so that, quite apart from having to determine what was right conduct toward Muslims in Spain and North Africa or toward natives in the New World, at least a few scholars began to try to rethink the Christian-Roman heritage of the Middle Ages in contemporary terms. Among these, one man towers above all others.

Huig van Groot (better known by the Latin version of his name, Hugo Grotius) made the most notable contribution to international order in the terrible period of religious wars in Europe from 1618 to 1648. Born in Delft in the Netherlands in 1583, Grotius did not live to see the coming of (relative) peace from the long congress that produced the Treaty of Westphalia in 1648, but his book *De Jure Belli ac Pacis Libri Tres* (Three books on the laws of war and peace), first published in 1625,[119]

> was mainly concerned . . . with trying to save as much as possible of the old public law of medieval Christendom by providing new rationalizations for such of its rules as the governments of Europe still followed. He still spoke of the "law of nations" (*jus gentium*), not of "international law." He formulated no new rules. He seems to have invented no entirely new arguments. It is a temptation to guess that he did not, from one end to the other of his major work, *The Laws of War and Peace*, employ so much as a single fresh illustration. But he was notable for what he avoided doing. . . . He threw none of the real burden of his proofs on revealed religion. From the arguments of his predecessors he selected those which would appeal to his successors down into the nineteenth century.[120]

Early concerned with a dispute over the capture of a Portuguese ship by a ship belonging to the Dutch East India Company in the Straits of Malacca, Grotius set out to analyze both the relation of law to war and the issue of the freedom of the seas. As religious tensions in Holland broke into civil war, he attempted to find a modus vivendi for the various opinions in mutual toleration—then profoundly unpopular—and for his pains was arrested, tried, and condemned to life imprisonment in 1619. With the help of his wife, he escaped from prison in a crate supposedly containing books and smuggled himself over the frontier to France dressed as a stonemason. During the next year in exile, he wrote his great treatise. Then, unable to return to Holland, he entered the service of the king of Sweden as ambassador to France. As an ambassador he was a failure: intensely disliked by the virtual ruler of France, Cardinal Richelieu, and not popular at the royal court, he irritated everyone with whom he dealt in trivial disputes over matters of protocol. Yet failure though he was as a diplomat, he effectively set the parameters for the diplomacy that was to be practiced for the next three centuries.

Grotius wrote that "maintenance of the social order . . . is the source of law properly so called. To this sphere of law belong the abstaining from that which is another's, the restoration to another of anything of his which we may have, together with any gain which we may have received from it; the obligation to fulfill promises, the making good of a loss incurred through our fault, and the inflicting of penalties upon men according to their deserts."[121] And, as James Brown Scott wrote, "Violation of these rights or the refusal to carry out the duties resulting from them gives rise to courts where suits may be brought."[122]

The court process, thus brought into being, has produced scores of volumes of case histories; from this practical application has gradually emerged a general body of precedent that, if not "law," at least constitutes custom. This process is still evolving in our times not only on the mundane level of commercial law but into such new spheres as "crimes against humanity." The Nuremberg Tribunal,[123] convened at the end of World War II, was a major assertion of the primacy of the rule of war, of which the latest example is the Hague Tribunal, assembled to deal with alleged Serbian and Hutu genocide.

Perhaps even more important, the growing body of agreed principles gave birth to the concept that the only sure road to world peace lay in law. It was this belief that promoted treaties and conventions "outlawing" war such as the 1928 Kellogg Pact, in which the signatory powers condemned "recourse to war for the solution of international controversies, and renounce[d] it as an instrument of national policy in their relations with one another" while agreeing to settle all disputes by "peaceful means."

Beginning with the nineteenth and early twentieth centuries, there has been a growing tendency to regard international affairs as activity that takes place, or should take place, within a system of international law, yet this concept has rarely been effective in our times, when governments have more often ignored the law than abided by it and have more often abided by it when it suited their purposes than been restrained by it when it did not. It cannot be denied, however, that even among the most cynical and the most aggressive, the quest for some form of codified and agreed procedure is both ancient and real. And there can be no doubt that on a variety of important but lesser issues the corpus of international law and the institutions that have sought to apply and amplify it have played significant and positive roles in international affairs. But on the central issues of statecraft, there is far less to show. As Hannah Arendt has written, "The chief reason warfare is still with us is neither a secret death wish of the human species, nor an irrepressible instinct of aggression, nor, finally and more plausibly, the serious economic and social dangers inherent in disarmament, but the simple fact that no substitute for this final arbiter in international affairs has yet appeared on the political scene. Was not Hobbes right when he said: 'Conventions, without the sword, are but words'?"[124]

To find "the law" at fault for the continuation of war or genocide is to misread the records of our times: there will be no effective law and no effective international institutions so long as we live in a world of nation-states that refuse to diffuse their sovereignty. Despite President Dwight Eisenhower's famous 1956 admonition to Americans that there can be only one overarching code of conduct or law, most governments continue to act on the belief that there is one law for "us" and another for "them." Thus although we may hopefully inch toward the goals set forth by Vitoria and Grotius, we can expect no dramatic transformation of the international system through their chosen means. The rule of law is still on the distant horizon.

PART VII GETTING RID OF THE ALIEN

· · · · · · ·

27 PARTING COMPANY

One of the most heartrending foreign affairs issues of our century has been the expulsion or flight of millions of men, women, and children from their homes into exile. And, like most aspects of the relations among peoples, this doleful scene is not new. Moreover, it is intertwined with two other processes—the conversion of "us" into "them," which is the oldest of all changes in relations between people through resources and politics, and the conversion of "them" into "us," which, although not so ancient or so evident, came about when people began to settle, acquire larger territories, and make war. These will be the three themes of part 7. I begin with the division of groups.

As I discussed in chapter 2, throughout the long evolution of our species one of mankind's most common experiences has been emigration. The reason is clear. For millions of years, groups of humans subsisted on territories. Given the available technology, a territory could be only so large as a group could defend and exploit while keeping in contact with one another. Thus, available resources defined the group. When it got too large or when the climate worsened or prey migrated, it had to move, "downsize," or starve. We can infer from the dispersal of human beings all over the planet that the common reaction was for groups to split apart.

From accounts of tribal peoples, whose way of life at least partially echoes the common ancient experience, we know that in addition to hunger, although perhaps partially caused by it, anger sometimes burst societies apart. Jealousy, competition for mates, and the struggle for dominance have always been characteristic of animals, and our species is among the most extreme in each. As people began to acquire goods, a purely human characteristic (as I showed in chapter 3), a new divisive element was added. So, although societies usually were united against outsiders, at least while they were small, they were often bitterly divided internally; consequently, even a minor event could trigger hostilities to the point of shattering the group.

Sometimes, only a single individual was expelled—to live beyond society as an outlaw. The prehistoric oral poetry of pagan tribal Arabia is full of references to such events and people; indeed, perhaps the most famous of all that "Homeric" poetry is the bitter taunt of an expelled Bedouin who parodies his clan by pretending that it is he who has expelled them in order to live with his adopted kindred—wolves.[1] The Arabs called such people *al-sa'alik* (outcast robbers), anticipating the modern ethologists' term *lion nomad*. Since it is virtually impossible for a lone individual to survive in harsh conditions, the nomad-outcast did not live long and left few if any survivors. More common must have been the division of a clan into two or more groups, the weaker of which then moved apart to try to establish its own territory. This is so common an action that, among tribal peoples, it is possible to apply genealogies almost like maps to territory to show how groups split apart.[2]

We know very little about the early migrations except that they were a sporadic process that took millions of years. Of those that occurred over the past six thousand years or so, however, we can identify at least three great movements. One "began"—that is, may be first identified—somewhere in Central Asia or in the area near the Black Sea and sent off "shoots"—hundreds or thousands of separate groups over thousands of years—into Western Europe, the Middle East, and India. We call these people, collectively, from the family of languages they spoke, Indo-Europeans. A second wave spread across North Africa into the Nile valley and then into the Fertile Crescent and the Arabian peninsula. These people are known as Semites because their various languages are members of a single family we call Semitic or Afroasiatic, which includes Ancient Egyptian, various languages used along the Nile River, and the still-used Hebrew and Arabic.[3] A third group spoke languages and dialects of a family variously known as Asiatic or Altaic, which includes Turkish, Finnish, and Hungarian. Various other languages (and the peoples who spoke them) do not fit, at least not to the satisfaction of all scholars, in any of these three families. Sumerian, spoken in ancient Mesopotamia, is an example to which I have often referred.[4] Etruscan and Basque also continue to puzzle scholars,[5] but it is possible to construct a sort of road map of current guesses on how all these may relate to one another and to presumed earlier languages.[6]

This linguistic map can be at least approximately duplicated genetically,[7] which shows that speakers of these languages are, at least in part (since they mixed with preexisting peoples and later immigrants), descendants of tribal groups that were spewed out of three pulsating "fountains" and that fanned out into other territories. Knowing little about them, we tend to treat them as units—*the* Celts or *the* Aryans—whereas they were actually loose collections of small and separate groups. Group identity was often imposed on them by outside observers. A well-known example is the Scyths, or Scythians. They figure in the Greek historical accounts as "a people," yet it now appears that the word *scyth*, which the Greeks took to be the name of that people, simply meant "nomad."

Most of what we know about such peoples comes from settled societies that recorded, often from hearsay, some of their activities. And, naturally, those who wrote the records had a point of view: they were interested in and knew about those who were closest to them. They usually greatly exaggerated their numbers and warlike potential. Drawing on the old records, more recent historians saw the migrations of such peoples as deliberate, massive, long-range movements. The picture that is only now beginning to emerge is quite different: the migrants were more usually little groups who only inched their ways outward from their starting points, stopping years or even generations at convenient places along the way, unaware of any sense of "route" or destination. Nor were they quite the invading hordes we (or their victims) have imagined; many were themselves refugees from more powerful groups, out of sight (to the Greek and Roman observers) from "behind" in Asia or Africa.

To take the group most important to us, the Indo-Europeans: we are just beginning to piece together a vague appreciation of them. Knowing little about them in early times, we do not separate them into tribal groups or even, as we do such later Indo-European invaders, into relatively massive collections such as the Goths, the Vandals, or the Scythians. But our jumbling them all together serves to bring out a salient fact: there are shared cultural, religious, linguistic, and even genetic characteristics among people scattered from India through Persia into Greece and Rome and even to Scandinavia.

On the vast Russian plains where they lived as hunters and pastoralists the Indo-Europeans managed to domesticate the horse sometime before 4000 B.C.E.[8] That accomplishment revolutionized their society and gave them overwhelming military superiority over their neighbors. Being able to move rapidly and far and to carry with them supplies and weapons, they fanned out over Asia and eventually over Europe. Then, sometime before 1700 B.C.E., they learned to make and to use that formidable weapon most closely associated with the Indo-European invasion—the chariot. With it, their relatively small bands could achieve tactical superiority over even large concentrations of peoples. So over several hundred years, the highly mobile warriors seized control of areas from Greece to India. And for the next two thousand years, various groups of Indo-Europeans—many of whom lived as herdsmen engaging in hunting and martial activities—continued to have an impact on the settled peoples of Europe and Asia.

As they moved apart, these groups mixed with local peoples, as we can see by the mutations in their languages, their adopting of local foods and customs, and their incorporation of local gods into their pantheon. From their common but long-since-forgotten origin, they thus gradually became Indians, Persians, Greeks, Slavs, Germans, and others. In Europe, those who were becoming Greek, for example, mixed into their common Indo-European "sky" religion the earth gods they had found among the pre-Greek natives, whereas the Aryans in India incorporated into their pantheon Dravidian gods. Thus, over the centuries since their departure from Central Asia, as Indo-European brothers their progeny had become first "cousins" and then strangers.

The process did not stop there; indeed, in different forms it continues into our times. But in Greece we can see how it worked in a simpler form.[9] There, the descendants of the invading Indo-Europeans together with the native peoples they conquered created the Bronze age culture we know as Mycenaea. Around 1200 B.C.E., this civilization fell to marauding bands of "city sackers," and ultimately the survivors gave up and moved to areas where they thought they could defend themselves, including the western coast of Anatolia. We know these peoples as the Ionians (or southern Greeks) and their replacements as the northern-Greek-speaking Dorians. The diffusion that began in the Dorian invasion in Greece continued and intensified for other reasons in later centuries. One major cause was hunger. As Greece filled up, people accumulated in "pockets" created by geography, and a new pattern of civic organization was created—the city-state, or *polis*. Each city-state naturally expanded to fill its available space, just as seminomadic clansmen had filled their territories, and eventually the growing population outran its resources. Probably this promoted or at least contributed to the violent and bloody wars that occurred among the city states in archaic times.

By the eighth century B.C.E., two desperate measures had become common: female babies were "exposed" and the surplus male population was forced to migrate. Even then, with better means of transport and more knowledge of the world, migration was still so terrifying a prospect as occasionally to require the threat of execution to make those selected to go actually quit their homes.

Since the number of colonists in each venture was necessarily small, given the fact that they had to travel on oared open boats, the extant accounts suggest that they numbered only about two hundred and that these were young men who could both row and fight. Probably at least initially no women emigrated with the young men. On arrival, at least some must have kidnapped or otherwise acquired native women, who passed to their half-breed children elements of native cultures. Thus, inhabitants of distant colonies along the Black Sea, in Italy, on Sicily, and in southern France developed local dialects, acquired local habits, pursued local ambitions, feared local enemies, and so gradually grew apart from their homelands and kindred.

Expulsion of people did not stop in later times even though the reason or excuse for it changed. In the sixth century B.C.E. in the city-state of Athens, indebted farmers were expropriated and even sold into slavery. Later, Plutarch reports, Pericles sent several thousand Athenians abroad to join existing colonies and "in this way he relieved the city of a large number of idlers and agitators."[10] Greek city-states were constantly trying to get rid of "surplus" population, and many were willing to go. The lure of foreign wealth acted like a powerful magnet on this restless people. Profiting from the Persian conquest of the Ionian Greek city-states of Anatolia, Greek merchants traveled eastward, perhaps all the way to India and Central Asia. Among the Egyptians, they founded the trading city of Naucratis and ranged up and down the Nile. And they made the Mediterranean their highway. Everywhere he went, Herodotus could find local Greek informants to guide him in the lore of Egyptians, Persians, Scythians, and Indians.

These were relatively small-scale movements, but ancient empires early discovered that rearrangement of population offered a means of control. The first society that developed a thoroughgoing program of mastery through a population policy was ancient Assyria. In their many wars, the Assyrians treated defeated communities like grain in the field, using the same word, "to thresh," to describe what they did to both. The kernel was to be separated from the chaff: the defeated and broken fighting men were often slaughtered, while those with special skills and the women were put to work. But some communities were too large for this treatment, so the Assyrians hit on the idea of dividing them by moving some to new locations where they would be what might be called "internal" aliens. Syrians were moved to Iran, and Iranian colonies were planted in the south of Iraq while those from that area were moved to northern Syria. The plan had an awesome simplicity: removed from relatives and surrounded by

strangers, the defeated would find rebellion impossible. It has been estimated that the total number of people forcibly deported in the last three
centuries of Assyrian rule may have amounted to four or five million.

Quite a different form of population exchange took place in Rome.
There, it was not so much a matter of economics or hunger as of coloniza-
tion. In contrast to the exclusionary Greek city-states, Rome built its power
by incorporating its allies or those it had conquered, but as a part of the
process of consolidation, it also sent its own citizens as colonists into these
societies. In his note on Pericles' policy of sending "idlers and agitators"
abroad, Plutarch might have been describing Rome as well as Athens when
he went on to say that "by installing garrisons among the allies, [they]
implanted at the same time a healthy fear of rebellion." This was the standard policy in Italy, and the Romans extended it abroad. Thus, when they
enslaved or massacred the population of Corinth in 146 B.C.E., the Romans resettled it with Romans. Romans began to move abroad in relatively
massive numbers. This is shown by the massacres that accompanied the
war of national liberation we know as the Pontic War in Anatolia, when
about 80,000 resident Roman citizens are said to have lost their lives. Even
if that figure is an exaggeration, the resident Roman and Italian population must have been very large.[11] But each government worried about the
large, hungry, and volatile mob. In addition to diverting them with cir-
cuses and feeding them, leaders tried to get rid of them. Shortly before
he was assassinated, Caesar began to attack this issue. His plan, simply,
was the ancient Mediterranean ritual of sending the "surplus" people
abroad, and in the short time he was in power, Caesar settled an additional
80,000 Romans overseas.

◆ ◆ ◆

The barbarian invasions of the Roman and Byzantine Empires that dra-
matically altered the ethnic composition of western Asia and Europe I
discussed in previous chapters, so now I skip ahead to what is still the
greatest movement of people of all times, that of Blacks to the New World.
Spread over several centuries, it is a complex story that, after the fall of
Rome, is reshaped by European tastes in food, African politics, and Spanish disease.

At first the demand for slaves was small; it was a "luxury" trade. Demand did not become prodigious until the rise of the sugar plantations,
but that time, we now know, came much earlier than used to be thought.
Beginning in the thirteenth century, cultivation of sugar spread westward
from Egypt and Syria. The first plantation and sugar mill were set up in

Portugal in 1404 by an Italian merchant, and about 1420 the father-in-law of Columbus and his partners established Madeira as a major producer of sugar for Europe. It was partly in search of workers for this new industry that the Portuguese plunged southward along the African coast; at Elmina in 1481 they built a trading station and entered into a deal with the local ruler to supply them with slaves. To house the captives while they waited for ships, they built the first *barracoon,* or concentration camp.

Sugar was a rare luxury in the fifteenth century, but in the sixteenth century it became the major crop of New Spain and was soon followed by indigo, tobacco, cotton, and other labor-intensive "plantation" crops. At first the plantations were worked by Indians, who were both cheap and plentiful. It was not long, however, before the Indians had virtually died out—wasted away in labor, unable to withstand the diseases of the Europeans, starved, or killed in rebellions or counterguerrilla operations. The Spaniards kept plunging deeper into the jungles and deserts in search not only of gold but also of slaves to man plantations and mines. Within a generation, they could no longer find enough slaves locally, so in 1510, King Ferdinand sent to the New World the first trickle of 250 in what would become a torrent of millions of Africans.[12]

Procuring these people turned out to be relatively easy. Except for endemic diseases, conditions for slaving were nearly ideal. The west coast of Africa in the sixteenth and seventeenth centuries was divided among two main races, several kingdoms, numerous tribes, and hundreds of distinct cultures. The natives were thus engaged in constant warfare, in which the enslaving of prisoners was the common practice. And since the rulers wanted what the Europeans could offer in exchange for slaves and felt no inhibition against slavery, deals were fairly easy to strike. So eager for slaves were the Europeans that the African population declined precipitately. By 1526 the local ruler was complaining that the slave trade was ruining his country; he could not stop it, however, since the kingdom was split into various tribal domains, rather like feudal baronies, and each was anxious to profit from the trade at the expense of its neighbors.

It has been estimated that about four million slaves reached the New World just from the Loango coast (the area from the equator to the Zaire River). The area was literally "hunted out," so after 1560 the Portuguese found it necessary to move their main trading operations 400 kilometers south from the Zaire estuary to Luanda. But the whole coast from the Volta River east and south remained for three centuries a great slave emporium from which between ten and fifteen million Africans were shipped to the New World.

The Africans were usually procured in raids. The few extant descriptions show that the tactic was brutal and efficient. Small, highly mobile teams would surround an unsuspecting village. When they had overpowered the men, they often simply slaughtered those they did not want or feared and then yoked together the ones they had selected and drove them toward the coast. A large percentage, particularly of children, never reached it. Those who did were herded into barracoons to await shipment. By this time, understandably, the captives were in shock: they had lost their homes and all their possessions, seen their relatives die or be killed before their eyes, and were themselves worn by starvation, frequent beatings, and rape. Many wilted into what slavers called "fixed melancholy" and that we can now identify as a symptom of shock. Others tried to commit suicide by refusing to eat, but they were potentially too valuable to be allowed to die, so they were force-fed—the dealers and ships' crews invented a sort of reverse thumb screw they would hammer into the slave's teeth to force open his mouth.

After perhaps months of being chained together in a barracoon, the slaves would be exhibited to a ship's captain. Then they would be poked and prodded, made to skip and jump, and forced to have their mouths and anuses pried open to check for disease. (Many later said that they thought they were being inspected to be eaten.) Those who were rejected were often simply killed. After the selection had been made, the captain and the jobber would then "palaver." If they agreed on a price, the slaves would be taken, chained, out to the ship.

Slave ships were floating prisons. It is difficult even to imagine the horror they contained. Many were hardly seaworthy and, since virtually all were small, they were chronically short of water and food and had no facilities for hygiene. The slaves were chained together and packed so tightly that they often could not turn from side to side or sit upright. On a typical ship, a grown man was allotted a space that more or less equates to a coffin—72 inches by 16 by 31. During a rain or a heavy sea, the hatches were battened down, but even in good weather, there was little ventilation. Yet, many ships never let the slaves on deck during a voyage that might last half a year. The stench of the hold can scarcely be imagined; other ships' crews reported that they could smell slavers from miles away.

When an epidemic broke out, or water ran short, captains routinely threw overboard the dangerous cargo. We know this primarily because, when they did so, some tried to collect insurance. In 1781, for example, the slaver *Zong* was running low on water so the captain ordered the crew to handcuff and throw into the sea 132 slaves. When he arrived in England he claimed £30 each for them under his maritime insurance. The underwriters took the case to court and lost: the jury held that "the case of the slaves was the same as if horses had been thrown overboard." It did not help the slaves, but it is worth recording that in reply to the underwriters' appeal a higher court reversed the decision, holding that although maritime law was on the side of the captain a "higher law" required that slaves be treated as humans. That was the first such ruling. The captain was not paid, but he was not penalized. No one even thought of charging him with murder.

It wasn't just slavers who regarded exotic conquered people such as Indians and Blacks as subhuman. The most famous such character in literature is Caliban, whom Shakespeare (and his audiences) saw as a "savage and deformed slave," a "man-monster," and a "misshapen knave"— indeed, species of ape.[13]

These experiences and attitudes are not just of interest as shocking examples of inhumanity; they are formative of the "personality" of the Black community for the last two centuries. This is because what happened to the Blacks was essentially the same traumatic experience that is the essence of "breaking" a wild animal. With their natural social ties sundered, feeling isolated and exposed, frightened and humiliated, the prisoners become pliable and even ready to transfer their social instincts to their new masters. The process worked. Slaves, concentration camp inmates, and hostages of terrorists often have developed intense attachments to their tormenters.

Still, the slavers took no chances. The best way to prevent rebellion was time-honored: divide up natural groups (those who were kin, spoke the same language, came from the same village) and mix them with others with whom they had no affinity. Two additional divisions suggested themselves: about one in each seven slaves was brought to North America after an intermediate stop, or perhaps even birth, in the West Indies. These "new negroes" (as the dealers called them), unlike the "outlandish Africans," already knew the hopelessness of their situation. These differences were calculated to make conspiracy to rebel difficult and rebellion itself almost impossible. Scars of this long process of brutalization are still evident. Their history has indeed shaped the American Black community.

Until the nineteenth century, the "wastage" of slaves, who usually did not last longer than about ten years, could be made up by importation. But as the horror of enslavement became widely known, the English evangelical movement brought heavy pressure on its government to abolish slavery. Thus, after May 1, 1807, no British ship was permitted to transport slaves, and from the following year no slaves could be landed in a British possession. Slave populations declined rapidly. In the British West Indies, for example, the slave population fell from approximately 800,000 in 1808 to about 160,000 when slavery was legally ended in 1834.[14]

Plantation owners became desperate for workers at the very time that demand for sugar, tea, and coffee was rising significantly. All were labor-intensive crops. So, to take the place of Black slaves, the British turned to indentured laborers from India. Although many were seized by press gangs or sent as prisoners, hundreds of thousands went because not to go during the frequent famines (which the British administration did very little to prevent or alleviate) was to starve. Illiterate and uneducated, they could have had no idea where they were going or what awaited them; they were shipped in conditions not substantially different from those of the Black slaves whom they were replacing (with mortality rates approximating those of the slave ships); on arrival they were auctioned off to planters and forced to live under laws adapted (with changes mainly in nomenclature) from the old slave laws. Practically none of them ever returned to their native land. No one knows the total shipped to the Pacific, the Indian Ocean, and the Caribbean, but the number certainly ran into the millions.

· · ·

Yet another kind of emigre was the exile. Like the pre-Islamic Arab Bedouin, the English expelled many of their outlaws. Felons who were not executed quickly were routinely sent into enforced exile as virtual slaves. This practice dates from the 1597 "Acte for Punyshment of Rogues, Vagabonds and Sturdy Beggars." The act was ecumenical in the definition of *criminal* so that Scots and Irish prisoners of war were included, and it provided a one-way street since those who tried to return were to be hanged without further trial. In the eighteenth century at least forty thousand people—or about six in each one thousand inhabitants—were shipped out of England and many were sold off to contractors in the Caribbean or North America. Then the American Revolution closed off this escape valve in the prison system. The jails quickly clogged. Unwilling to spend the money required to build new jails and having no other out, the English "warehoused" about a thousand convicts each year in the rotting hulks of the sailing ships that were tied up along the Thames.

Few free Englishmen concerned themselves about what life was like beneath the battened-down hatches, but many worried about the prospects of plague, cholera, and typhus seeping out of the holds and onto the mainland. The answer had to be a new dumping ground. It was quickly identified as the then virtually unknown continent of Australia. To it at least 160,000 men, women, and children were exiled in the following decades. There, geographical isolation created what amounted to satisfactory supervision and the need to earn a living provided a sort of therapy so that the former offenders gradually created the nucleus of a new society.

Many of the migrations in the nineteenth and twentieth centuries have been based on decisions by individuals or small groups. Most of the vast numbers that came to America would be today classified as "economic refugees," but some were driven by the policies of governments or the attitudes and actions of majority communities. Many ethnic groups might be examined, but I will speak briefly of European Jews. Their community went through cycles of toleration and extortion, protection and massacre, invitation and expulsion that can be traced back to Roman times. The pattern becomes particularly evident in the Middle Ages. England, for example, which had no Jews before the Norman conquest, invited them in to be a sort of sponge with which to sop up the wealth of the nobles, who themselves could be squeezed when needed. Consequently, as the Magna Carta makes clear, the nobles regarded the kings and Jews as their joint enemies.

In times of fear or turmoil, the Jews were the immediate targets, as they were when each crusade began.[15] When kings and warriors were passive, cities occasionally took the initiative, as Cambridge did in 1275 when it expelled its resident Jews. There were many expulsions, but the largest occurred in the late fifteenth century when the Spanish government destroyed what was then the largest and most cultured Jewish community in the world. Most fled to Muslim countries, which were relatively open and tolerant, but some were scattered around western Europe.

Meanwhile, in eastern Europe, the Ashkenazi Jewish community underwent a different set of experiences from the Sephardic Jewish communities of the Mediterranean. Much of it was of Khazar Turkish origin and was settled on blocs of land in which Jews constituted large or even majority communities. In 1742 the Russian government, like the Spanish government of 1492, decreed that Jews were not to be allowed to live in Russia and ordered them either to convert or be deported. This order was never enforced, however, and in 1769 the province of Novorossisk was designated as an area legal for Jewish residence. Then, when Catherine the Great annexed large areas of Poland and much of what is now the Ukraine, she created the so-called Jewish pale.

After 1791, Jews were allowed to emigrate after paying double the usual rate of taxes for three years. Few then did, but over the following century, stimulated partly by the government and particularly by Tsar Aleksandr III but also encouraged by the Slavophiles and religious fundamentalists, anti-Semitism grew. Finally, in 1881, with the connivance or support of the police, anti-Jewish pogroms erupted in more than a hundred towns and cities. Alarmed by the disorder, the government set up a commission to examine Russia's more than six hundred anti-Jewish laws. Although the commission concluded that discrimination harmed the state, various new laws were enacted that, among other things, resulted in the expulsion of some twenty thousand Jews from Moscow and in further restrictions on education, professions, and residence. As a consequence, large numbers of eastern European Jews began to migrate to the West around the turn of the century.

Then, during the 1919 Peace Conference, Woodrow Wilson promoted the principle of self-determination of peoples. Although it was widely and correctly hailed as a liberating concept, it accentuated tensions in states where frontiers did not accord with ethnic concentrations. Elaborate plans were discussed to try to bring the frontiers into accord with nationality. There were many potential flash points, but one that was particularly horrible occurred in Anatolia. In May, the Peace Conference decided to support Greek claims to western, or "Ionian," Anatolia (which Italy also coveted), and to effect this decision, the Big Three (that is, minus Italy) arranged to have British, French, and American warships land Greek troops in Smyrna (Izmir). The move "resulted at once in horrible atrocities and massacres of the Turks by the Greeks."[16] The invasion and the massacres were to precipitate a revolution in the Ottoman Empire and to lead to a war that tore apart Greece and resulted in the creation of the modern Turkish state. Three campaigns were fought between the Greeks and the Turks in 1921 and 1922, in the third of which the Greeks were routed by Turkish forces under Mustafa Kemal (Ataturk). After the fall of Smyrna (Izmir), where some thirty thousand Greek and Armenian Christians were killed by rampaging Turkish soldiers, more than a million "Greeks," many of whom could speak only Turkish, fled to Greece. In 1923 the two governments agreed on a compulsory exchange of population: Turkish Orthodox Christians (primarily of the Anatolian *Karamanlis* community) were to be sent to Greece, while Greek-speaking Muslims (primarily from Crete) were to be sent to Turkey. From both sides, roughly one and a half million people were forced to emigrate.

During World War II Stalin feared that the Soviet Union's Muslims, most of whom had long shown themselves to be hostile first to Russian imperialism and then to Communism, would collaborate with the invading Germans, so he carried out a mass expulsion in which whole communities were uprooted and shipped to Siberia in conditions that ensured that many died.

Finally, even more massive population moves followed World War

II. In 1947 Muslims fled from what would become India while Hindus fled from what would become Pakistan, and in 1948 nearly a million Palestinians were forced out of or fled from the part of the Palestine Mandate that would become Israel. In the years since, other massive movements of people have occurred in Asia, Africa, and Latin America. Thus, going apart, although one of the oldest means of settling personal and communal disputes, remains a sad but persistent aspect of our times.

. . . .

28 ETHNIC CLEANSING

Every generation indulges in the conceit that it is somehow unique in the long sweep of the human experience, but even when contemporaries do not assign to themselves a distinguishing label, historians often do. So we speak of the Age of Reason or the Enlightenment. Looking back at the bloody twentieth century, some will be tempted to categorize it as the Age of Ethnic Cleansing: the destruction of the Armenians in Turkey was, in its time, almost as mesmerizing an issue as the German murder of the Gypsies and Jews, the Indian-Pakistani killings, the Hutu massacre of the Tutsis, the Serbian slaughter of the Bosnians, and a score of lesser— lesser, that is, because measured in the thousands rather than in the millions—attempts to get rid of foreigners. But as proficient as we have been in carrying out ethnic atrocities, our century cannot "claim credit" (as the media say of terrorist attacks) for inventing them. They have a long history. Indeed, we may say that they have an even longer "prehistory."

Although the prehistory does not normally command our attention, it is perhaps as significant as recent events because it informs us that below the religious, cultural, and racial criteria that figure so strongly in both condemnations and apologies are attitudes that must be embedded deep in our subconsciousness. Indeed, attempts to get rid of aliens begin in our individual bodies.

As I discussed in chapter 1, our bodies contain an immune system that is programmed to react violently when it detects what it perceives as aliens. Normally, this system, a part of which operates as an elaborate counterintelligence service, protects our bodies from pathogens, but under certain circumstances it triggers a "general war" against the intruder that also causes unacceptable damage to the self or even turns against the self. Thus, although we owe our lives to its vigilance, we have cause to fear its destructive power. In evidence of this, scores of millions of us will suffer this year from the fevers, coughing, and sneezing that are manifestations of the body's attack on flu viruses, and millions of us will die this year because of our bodies' reaction to just one such intruder: tuberculosis. It takes generations, and many deaths, for our systems to build immunities— which we might think of as "walls"—that protect us from many of the diseases suffered by our ancestors.

Long in the making also must have been the accommodations to bodily aliens on whom we depend for the quality and length of our lives. They help to digest our food, to regulate our internal environments, and to protect us from still more alien matter. Only in death do we no longer need them. Yet, although they are essential to us, we have never achieved, and probably never will achieve, a complete balance between "us" and "them." At best—in what we call health—we reach a temporary compromise.

What begins internally on a microscopic scale carries forward externally on a macroscopic scale: like our bodies, whole societies react violently to the presence of aliens. I observed in chapter 2 that what we know of animal and primitive human populations suggests not a break but a continuum, with many of the same mechanisms or propensities evident from cell to society: groups try to isolate themselves from foreigners, but they cannot; like the individual body, they need foreigners, yet they fear them. Consequently, most of the time, they chase off or try to kill intruders, and it is only slowly, over long periods of time, that they—we—have learned forms of accommodation (such as trade) while maintaining defenses (such as walls) and engaging in preparation for combat (intelligence, espionage, and armies). The protocol of our accommodations is expressed through diplomacy and politics in our civilization essentially by custom and law.

But the accommodations reached with those we regard as outsiders are not always "healthy." Frequently, they are perceived by some on one side or the other to be unfair, and from time to time that becomes the general opinion: what one party gets from the common pot may seem excessive to one or inadequate to the other; what seems appropriate to one may be viewed as outrageous to the other; what appears to the one to be defense can be perceived by the other as offense. Then the always-fragile balance breaks down and the results, as in the body, can be a violent assault on the foreigner or even the death of a whole society.

In this chapter, I discuss three examples of ethnic cleansing to bring out particular characteristics. The first is India, where Aryan invaders conquered and imposed on a preexisting civilization a religious-social order that relegated the inhabitants to a position not only of permanent segregation but even of metempsychic exclusion. The second is sixteenth- and seventeenth-century Spain, where the large population of Moriscos and the smaller Jewish community were first defeated, then subdued, and finally expelled. The third is the complex relationship, beginning with diplomacy and mutating through war to attempted extermination to segregation and finally to a form of limited incorporation, between white Americans and red (or "native") Americans during the nineteenth century. First, India.

In the Indus River valley, as I discussed above, was one of the great centers of ancient civilization, comparable in its sophisticated agriculture, industry, and urban organization with contemporary Egypt and the Sumerian city-states. Then, around the beginning of the second millennium B.C.E., groups of Indo-European–speaking Aryan nomads began to arrive from the north, and within a century the old social order was destroyed. Exactly how and when this happened is a matter of dispute, but the descendants of the Indo-European invaders boasted of their ancestors' wide-ranging works of destruction.

We know that the "Indian" Aryans shared with the Greeks, the Persians, the Scythians, and the Romans the Indo-European family of languages, myths, religious ceremonies, and forms of social organization. More pointedly, in the eyes of their victims, they also shared weapons technology—particularly the compound bow and the chariot—and the mobility given by their domestication of the horse. So crucial to them all was the horse that they venerated it as their sacred animal. So important was the horse to one of their Indo-European "cousins" that their word for themselves, *Goti* (Goths), also meant "horse," while another, the Persians, gloried in hippomorphic names. The horse gave them power, but as nomads the Aryans combined the strengths and weaknesses of that way of life: dependent not only on weather and on the health of their herds but also on settled societies both to supply what they cannot produce and to give refuge in times of famine, nomadic societies are inherently fragile. Despite a military potential awesome to settled peoples, nomads are usually relatively few in number and often near starvation.[17]

From having watched modern nomads in comparable circumstances and from what is known about other invasions—for example, the Amorites in early Mesopotamia and probably the Indo-Europeans in Greece and the Turks in Iran and Anatolia—I picture small groups of Aryans coming first as part-time workers in the agricultural areas and peddling milk products while squatting in makeshift huts on the fringes of the Indus cities.

There they would have learned of the riches (and weaknesses) of the settled peoples and gradually have become resentful of being exploited. Ultimately, perhaps after generations, they would have cooperated with later (and militarily more powerful) arrivals against the natives. At each success, they would have become further emboldened. Probably also, ambitious or fearful local individuals would have sought to enlist their strong-arm services. Finally, they would have reached a stage at which they could contend for power on their own. Probably, by that time—like the fifth millennium B.C.E. Ukrainian society and the later Etruscan society—when attacked by other Indo-European groups, the Harappan cities were too weak militarily or too divided politically to resist.

The Aryans and other Indo-European peoples took with them a distinctive military vehicle that in its time was as overwhelming as the tank in ours—the light two-wheeled, horse-drawn chariot. Apparently nothing like it had been known in the Indus civilization. It appeared there, in Syria, in Egypt, and in Greece about the same time and, although its impact was everywhere dramatic, in India it was devastating. When, much later, we can hear their voices, the descendants of the invaders boasted of their destructive power: the Indian hero Indra glories in the name *puramdara*, "city-destroyer."

Although initially clinging to their nomadic way of life, the Aryans soon began to settle and adopted much of the way of life of the conquered. Like many things in India, we see this symbolically as they substituted for the traditional Indo-European sacred animal—the horse—the Indian cow. They had brought their own horses, but the source of cows was the indigenous population: the tipoff is that the word *gavishti* in the Aryan language, Sanskrit, meant both "to search for cows" and "to go to war."

The very hazy picture we get of the invaders comes almost solely from their epics.[18] In this literature we dimly discern a warring, seminomadic tribal society engaged in heroic—indeed "Homeric"—combats with one another such as the "War of the Ten Kings." Originally seeing themselves as a band of brothers, these warriors had established themselves as aristocratic conquerors and had subdued the Dravidian-speaking natives. Those natives who remained free, driven far from the old sites of their civilization and presumably no longer able to relate to what their ancestors had accomplished, became known as "the wild tribes." Up to this point, what happened in India had happened and would happen in virtually every area where the Indo-Europeans invaded. But what happened next was more unusual.

Themselves fair-skinned, the Aryans, as reported by their descendants, came to abominate the smaller, darker native peoples, whom they envied for their riches and lands. The natives, whom they called *dasa,* were settled agriculturists, always despised by nomadic herdsmen. Another name for the natives in Sanskrit was *mleccha,* which appears to be related to the Sumerian name for India, *Me-luh-ha.* From this comes a verb, *mlech,* that means, like the Greek *barabaros* (and the Arabic *barbara*) to be unable to speak clearly, to be outlandish. The areas where people spoke in an outlandish way were alien to the gods and (civilized) man. Ultimately, as the political-religious system of the Aryans was articulated, the native people and lands into which they had retreated came to be considered "unclean," and those Aryans who ventured into the unclean land, the *mleccha-desa,* had to ritually purify themselves before returning to a normal life in the *Arya-varta,* where the Aryans lived.

Despised they were, but what they owned, including their cows and even their bodies, was booty to the conquerors. (*Dasa* came to mean "female slave.") So, being unable to defend themselves, the conquered had to try to find an accommodation. This is a common theme in conquest; both conquerors and conquered seem to need to explain their new relationship: the conquerors seek to account for their good fortune while convincing the conquered that their loss is justified, and the conquered, in turn, often seek, *in an idiom that is appropriate to the dominant society,* and so acceptable to it, to carve out for themselves a separate identity that they can maintain *and* stay alive.

Among tribal societies such as the Arab Bedouin and the Nilotic Sudanese, which emphasize kinship, resident outsiders often invent fictitious lineages. They become "cousins"—if such a position is, de facto, their current status—by alleged descent from ancestors of the dominant group. In societies where religion has replaced kinship as the defining system, the immigrant or the subjected nation may explain itself as being a member of the common religion but of a different sect or confession. The Egyptian living under the Byzantine Empire described himself as a Christian but of the Coptic church. A Persian conquered by the Arabs similarly described himself as a Muslim but a follower of the Shi'a rite. Most northern Europeans expressed their particular character within the Christian church by becoming Protestants. All of the preexisting linguistic, cultural, social differences were focused on, and partly explained by, the new idiom. Ultimately, the fine points of idiom often become so important to both adherents and opponents that they come to be regarded as the essence of belief.

So what happened in India need not seem so exotic. Under the blows of the invader, the native population sank, as the *Rig Veda* tells us, "down into obscurity" so that their name came to mean "slave." *Dasa* color meant black as contrasted with "Aryan color" or "our color," and this gave to India a lasting preoccupation that was elaborated into the remarkable social organization of *varna,* or, as we know it from the Portuguese word meaning "breed," *caste.* The defeated aborigines were ultimately assimilated into the dominant society and religion as a caste. From the four primary castes—the *brahman*s, the *kshatriya*s, the *vaishya*s, and the *shudra*s (who were the *Dasas,* or mixed races) was then elaborated a complex system of scores of *jati*s (subcastes) that were interwoven with occupational groups, races, religious sects, and geographical divisions to encompass the whole population.

What began as a matter of color was combined with the doctrine of *karma*—roughly, "fate"—to give it a transcendental justification: "I am what I am—and you are what you are—because of deeds in a former life." Therefore, what is, is right. It is right not because of any abstract moral principle but because of divine punishment or reward for actions and events in previous lives beyond the knowledge of the living. To attempt to change the status quo is thus not only sedition but also sacrilege. Seen in this light, religion became the ultimate method of control of the alien: convincing a whole society, and even its enslaved victims, of the sanctity of the existing order. No power or person, neither king nor priest nor god, could alter one's position. Acceptance of this life in the expectation that in a future life piety would be rewarded was man's only hope. Nowhere has segregation been applied in so thoroughgoing a manner.[19]

. . .

I turn now to the Spanish experience, which formed the basis for an approach to "native" peoples in Africa, Asia, and the Americas: the "Gothic" relationship with the indigenous non-Christian population of Arabs, Berbers, Jews, and people of mixed race.

When the Muslims reached Morocco in the late seventh century, the Berber population rapidly converted and under the umbrella of Islam overcame, at least temporarily, tribal fracturing; like the Arabs nearly a century before, they then thrust outward. In 711 a small Arab-led Berber army crossed into Spain. The Spain into which they arrived was ruled by descendants of Visigoths who had themselves taken over the wreckage of the Roman Empire. Initially a virile, conquering people, the later Visigoths were internally divided. The resident Jews there, as their coreligionists had in the Middle East, welcomed the Muslims as liberators.[20] As a result, the invasion met with only initial opposition, so the Muslims were able to move rapidly up the peninsula, taking all but the northernmost fringe by 715. Not to have taken it ultimately proved a fatal mistake.

For the most part, the invading Muslims, as enjoined by the Qur'an, were as tolerant of the customs and religions of the natives—who were "people of the Book"—as they had been in the Middle East: the Jews became allies, while in the treaties of surrender Christians were guaranteed freedom of religion and security of property. Indeed, it appears that even existing governors (as in other areas conquered by the Muslims) were often confirmed in their positions. The transition had been relatively (particularly for medieval invasions) peacefully achieved, and quickly hundreds of thousands of tribesmen from North Africa arrived. Many of these married native women, so the "Moorish" population was from very early days at least partly "Spanish." How to distinguish the two would only become an issue—a bitter issue—eight hundred years later.

At the time of the invasion and for centuries, the chief distinction was cultural. Unlike the Indo-European invaders of India, the Muslims brought a superior culture. Not only were they endowed with a rich civilization—their science, art, music, and philosophy being in part a legacy from the classical world—but also they were technologically far superior to any of the Europeans of the dark ages. In agriculture and crafts in particular they lifted Spain to a level no one had seen in Europe since the heyday of Rome.

Not all Christians submitted to this new order. In the far north, in the remote, poor, mountainous area of Austurias on the Bay of Biscay, the first of what would become a number of small baronies was formed, much as little states were being formed in the rest of feudal Europe, by bands of warriors and frightened peasants. To protect themselves, they implemented what we call a "scorched earth" policy, creating a wide belt of no-man's-land across which raiders from each side attacked the other. And, like the little Turkish principalities that half a millennium later similarly hung on the fringes of the Byzantine state, they were toughened by virtually constant warfare. In the rough and tumble of that dangerous epoch, the little communities were hammered into the tiny (and barbaric) states of Léon, Castile, Navarre, Aragon, and Barcelona.

Meanwhile, in 756, a descendant of the Umayyad caliphs of Damascus took control of Cordoba and set up what in the tenth century became the most civilized state of western Europe, the caliphate of Cordoba. *Al-Andalus,* or Muslim Spain, shed almost the only significant cultural light on a darkened Europe. Consequently, the Arabs exerted a powerful attraction on Christians, many of whom, like the natives of the former Sasanian Persian Empire and those parts of Byzantium conquered by the Arabs, adopted Islam. A much larger proportion adopted the Arabs' dress, customs, and language. It is a sign of this cultural transformation that the

Christian art of the period is called *mozarab,* which meant in its Arabic form "to strive to become Arab."

Then, in the late tenth century, the Muslim political consensus began to fall apart. Rivals invited the Christians to their causes: in 1009, a claimant to the caliphate of Cordoba summoned the count of Castile to his aid while his opponent secured the aid of the count of Barcelona. The end came as quickly as the beginning and, from the ruin of the great caliphate, dozens of petty rulers divided Muslim Spain among themselves. With no effective opposition, the Christians could move south, and they did: by the middle of the eleventh century, the warrior kingdoms in the north were collecting tribute from the increasingly defenseless little Muslim states.[21] This new source of revenue enabled the Christians to bring in freebooters and knights-errant from other parts of Europe so that the military balance was further shifted. Some soldiers of fortune, like the most famous of them, Rodrigo Díaz, *El Cid,* fought on both sides as their interests led them.

This confused period was brought to a ragged end by the entry of a new group from North Africa—Berbers, known in European history as the Almoravids, who, after initial successes, also lost power. The Christians used the opportunity again to advance their front line to the south. Their advance triggered a new invasion from North Africa around 1172 by the Almohads, who had little of the sophistication or tolerance of the Andalusians. It appears that during the period of the Almohads, the traditional, relatively respectful relations between Muslims and Christians began slowly and haphazardly to deteriorate. When the power of the Almohads waned, in the early thirteenth century, it happened that the Christians of Castile, Aragon, and Portugal were led by able warrior kings. In increasingly savage warfare, Castile was able in 1236 to take what had been the jewel in the Muslim crown, Cordoba, and, after a bitter siege, Seville in 1248. Within a few years, all that was left of Muslim Spain was the far south, centered on the towns of Ronda, Malaga, Granada, and Almeria. Dramatic as these conquests were, what was more significant was a change in Christian policy: in previous conquests, the Christian conquerors had been keen to keep the Muslim farmers and artisans in place. In the new conquests, the Christians began to expel the Muslims. This happened, for example, in Seville, and when Minorca was taken in 1287, the population was not only extirpated but also sold into slavery.

As a practical matter, not all Muslims could be expelled: there were just too many, and the trades they practiced were too important, particularly to the wealthy Christians who employed them. The Spaniards then were torn, as are Americans, Frenchmen, Germans, and Britons today, between their desire to get rid of the hated alien and their desire for his services. Opinions split then as they do today on the balance between these desires.

Those Muslims who stayed in Christian Spain eventually came to be called *Moriscos*.[22] Christian *Mozarabs*, who had come to be perceived by Muslims as potential subversives, flocked northward into Christian-held areas while large numbers of terrified Moriscos fled south to such cities as Granada: splits that had begun long before widened so that the "new frontier drawn on the map at about 1250 became a frontier of the mind also."[23] Caught in the crack were the Muslims who were unable to move and the Jews.

During the two and a half centuries from about 1250 to 1492, when the forces of Ferdinand and Isabella finally conquered Granada, the subject Muslim population was engaged in a long and ultimately unsuccessful process of trying to work out forms of accommodation to its new status and to its rulers. And, because Spain itself was not unified, so the treatment of the Muslims varied from place to place. In rough terms, Navarre was where they were best treated because the population was small and of long provenance; Valencia was perhaps the next best place to be if one were a farmer because Valencia needed farmers. There and elsewhere in Aragon, Muslims usually were, at least theoretically, allowed to live under royal protection. Castile, although initially lenient in its treatment of Muslims, ominously promulgated a law calling for the death by burning of any Muslim committing certain offenses against Christians. For the first time, we hear a phrase that would resonate in later times, as entering students in the University College of San Bartolomé were checked for *limpieza de sangre* (purity of blood).

In 1391, almost a century before the Inquisition was established,[24] whipped on by the inflammatory preaching of a Christian prelate, mobs of Seville Christians took to the streets against the resident Jews. From that campaign of terror can be dated the first forcibly converted Jews, known as *conversos*, some of whose descendants—including Grand Inquisitor Tomás de Torquemada—rose to key positions in the Christian elite while about one hundred thousand others who converted or said they had converted were to pay a terrible price to the Inquisition.

The fall of Granada on January 1, 1492, ended Muslim Spain. In that same month, the traditional allies of the Muslims, the Jews, despite a specific exemption in the surrender document, were offered the choice of conversion or exile.[25] The relative weakness of the North African Muslim states and the growing wealth and power of Spain in the aftermath of Columbus's discovery of the New World made the fall of Granada, although itself not a particularly dramatic event, a true turning point in history. There, despite lenient surrender terms, the trend soon became clear. Assertive Muslims and those who had distinguished themselves militarily were "encouraged" to emigrate, and among those who stayed pressure to convert began to build. In 1499, forcible conversion and burning of Muslim religious texts in Granada, despite the promise of the Castilian and Aragonese monarchs not to engage in such activities, convinced Spanish Muslims that they were on the way to losing their language, culture, and religion; so, in a disorganized, small-scale way, they revolted. The importance of the revolt lay not in its threat to Christian Spain, which was negligible, but in the license it gave the authorities to abolish the terms of surrender.

After 1502, the Muslims were given the same stark choice as the Jews: convert or leave. As a practical matter, few could leave, so many took the obvious route of pretending to convert while practicing dissimulation or what is known in Muslim theology as *taqiyah*. To find them out became one of the major tasks of the Inquisition. But the xenophobic mood went deeper than theology or law. As Roger Boase has written, purity of faith became identified with purity of blood, and all "new Christians" were regarded as *herejes en potencia*. Thus, "As a member of a vanquished minority with an alien culture, every aspect of the Morisco's way of life—including his language, dress and social customs—was despised and condemned as uncivilized and the mark of a heathen. For example, in the eyes of the Inquisition and popular opinion, to eat couscous and to dance to the sound of Berber music were un-Christian activities."[26] Angers simmered so that in 1567, when King Philip II renewed an existing but little-enforced edict making the use of Arabic language, dress, and customs illegal, he provoked another rebellion.

At that point, the Spaniards were concerned with the overseas Muslim challenge. At least one force of Ottoman infantry, allegedly sent to aid the Morisco rebels in the mountains south of Granada, landed in Spain in 1568. The mood was similar to that of England on the eve of the Armada, and although the Spaniards were to defeat the Ottoman navy at the battle of Lepanto in 1571, their worries did not cease. The Ottomans not only rapidly rebuilt their fleet but effectively eliminated the European presence in the eastern Mediterranean and urged the North Africans into a holy war against the Spaniards.[27] Justified or not, Spanish fears led to a draconian suppression of unrest. The town of Galera, to cite a particularly awful example, "was razed to the ground and sprinkled with salt, and all of its 2,500 inhabitants, including women and children, were slaughtered."[28] Local pressures continued to build, however, and in 1608, after years of debate, the government decided to get rid of the last of the descendants of the Muslims of Spain.

The Spanish navy and hired foreign merchant ships were assembled, and town criers were sent all over Spain to announce the government order. Many expellees were deported to Morocco, but some from the north went overland into the relatively tolerant France of Henry IV (and after his assassination in 1610 were forced to flee again). Many, particularly those who had gone to France, ultimately made their ways to what is now Tunisia. No accurate count was made, but perhaps six hundred thousand people were involved, and possibly two-thirds died or were killed during their emigration. Children were often detained to work as servants for the Spaniards or sold as slaves. The church proclaimed that "slavery was not only morally justifiable ('lícito en conciencia') but spiritually beneficial . . . and, as slaves rarely married, this would be another good method of ridding Spain of 'this evil race.' "[29] Finally, it was planned that the young children would not be educated so that even the memory of Muslim Spain would be expunged. As Spaniards of all sorts were to find, however, the Inquisition did not forget, and the search for those whose faith or blood was tainted was to haunt Spain for centuries.

And not only Spain: it is clear that the attitudes toward the Moriscos were quickly transferred to the indigenous population of the New World. In the hundreds of thousands Indians were enslaved, expelled, or simply hunted down and slaughtered like wild animals.[30] Those Spaniards who found such practices unsuitable were few. Fray Bartolomé de Las Casas, a missionary chaplain with the Spanish forces in Cuba and Mexico, showed his outrage at the Spanish treatment of the Indians in *La Brevísima Relación de la Destrucción de las Indias;* Francisco de Vitoria, then a professor of theology in the University of Salamanca (who, as I described in chapter 26, is now credited with being a principal founder of the field of international law), argued for a just and humane policy. Neither made any significant impact. So ethnic cleansing reached an unprecedented and, even in our century, unequaled level of barbarity and magnitude.

· · ·

As shocked as our generation is by the horror of genocide in Europe and Africa, Americans have been disinclined to weigh their own history in the same scale. That side of American history has not figured prominently or honestly in textbooks. Yet the policy toward what Chief Justice John Marshall in 1831 termed the "dependent domestic nations," the Indians, that evolved in the last century and has been carried into this is a significant aspect of the American national and foreign affairs experience.

It began, indeed, before the American independence, in the so-called French and Indian war (1755–63) when some Indian nations fought alongside the French against the English. Because of events in Europe, the French gave up most of their claims to the New World in the Treaty of Paris in 1763, and, as they evacuated their armies, they abandoned their erstwhile Indian allies. The Indian tribes north of the Ohio River, the Algonquins and the Iroquois, embittered at being deserted by the French, then formed a coalition to continue to fight. This conflict was the military school of George Washington.

To avoid future conflict, King George III issued a proclamation in 1763 forbidding further white settlement in the interior. But within five years, the British government gave in to demands for an open frontier and forced the Creeks, the Cherokees, and the Iroquois to sign treaties giving up their claims to their homelands. Land companies were quickly formed to exploit the opportunities created by the government's new "forward" policy. After the revolution, the states encouraged westward movement by awarding soldiers and others land grants in what became new states. But at the same time, the federal government negotiated treaties with several Indian nations demarcating their territories and explicitly excluding from them white immigrants. Several of the Indian nations thus came within territories claimed by states although their relationship with the United States was legally governed by treaties with the federal government. Hence the conflict over "states' rights," an issue that runs right through American history, came to challenge federal power almost before there was a federal government.

What to do with the Indians became one of the most important issues before the new government. There was immense pressure on the part of settlers to be given a free hand to take whatever they wanted. Few voices were raised against this urge, although some advocated a slow and peaceful approach. Thomas Jefferson often spoke for the moderates. As secretary of state in 1793, Jefferson was most concerned about excluding foreign powers from the acquisition of Indian lands. He put forward what he called "a kind of *Jus gentium* for America," asserting that if Indians wished to sell their lands, then only Americans could buy them. But, he said, somewhat disingenuously, "I consider our right of pre-emption of the Indian lands not as amounting to any dominion, or jurisdiction, or paramountship whatever [and] that the Indians [have] the full, undivided and independent sovereignty as long as they choose to keep it, and that this might be forever."[31]

Two issues thus were crucial to white Americans: how to keep foreign states away from the Indians and how to get their land away from them. On the first, in an act passed in 1800, diplomatic or other contacts between foreign powers and the Indian nations were prohibited,[32] while the Louisiana Purchase effectively removed France and largely removed Spain from that temptation. As to white acquisition of lands, Jefferson advocated encouraging Indian chiefs to go into debt "because we observe that when these debts get beyond what the individuals can pay, they become willing to lop them off by a cession of lands." Put another way, to end their personal problems, chiefs could be induced to compromise the communal or tribal title to the homelands of their peoples. But when debts alone did not bring about the desired result, bribes to the chiefs to commit what was tantamount to treason usually were. In 1804, for example, the chiefs of the Sac and Fox Indians agreed, for an annuity of $1,000 worth of goods and $2,234.50 worth of other presents, to make over rights to all their tribes' lands, an area now comprising most of the state of Illinois and parts of Wisconsin and Missouri.

Shortly after the 1804 treaty was ratified, President Jefferson summoned to Washington ambassadors of the eleven Indian nations party to the treaty and there promised them peace and security. However, feeling threatened by the incursion of whites, whose activities the federal government was both powerless to stop and anxious to effect, the Indians sought to protect themselves. Their best, and indeed last, opportunity to secure a foreign ally against the settlers came a few years later in the War of 1812. On the eve of the war, President James Madison was so worried about this possibility that he sought to "win the hearts and the minds" of the Indians with a new diplomacy of friendship in place of the previous "search and destroy" tactics. To this end, he assembled some thirty-three chiefs and noted warriors of the Ossage, Sac and Fox, Shawnee, Sioux, Iowa, and Winnebago in St. Louis and then brought them to Washington to dine with him in the White House.

Despite American efforts, several of the major groups of Indians made common cause with the British. Thus, all along the frontier, the war against the British merged into a war against the Indians. The governor of the Northwest Territory, William Harrison, defeated the British and the Indians in the Battle of Thames (north of Lake Erie) in 1813. Meanwhile, far to the south, Andrew Jackson broke the power of the Creek Indians and then marched to New Orleans, where, on January 8, 1815, he won a battle against the British.

The threat of British use of the Indians against the Americans had ended, but the Indian "problem" remained because the Indians remained. And their status remained unclear. One group, the so-called civilized nation—the Cherokees—had the temerity to sue the State of Georgia for the enactment of laws that, they alleged, "go directly to annihilate the Cherokees as a political society, and to seize, for the use of Georgia, the lands of the nation which have been assured to them by the United States in solemn treaties repeatedly made and still in force."[33] Speaking for the Supreme Court, Chief Justice John Marshall defined the nature of the Indian relationship to the United States as "not a foreign state in the sense of the constitution" but rather "dependent domestic nations," but a year later, in the case of *Worcester v. Georgia*, the chief justice implicitly reversed himself by reasserting the existence of Indian tribes as independent nations "having territorial boundaries, within which their authority is exclusive, and having a right to all lands within those boundaries, which is not only acknowledged, but guaranteed by the United States."[34]

That was not a popular opinion, particularly in Georgia, which had agreed with the federal government in 1802 to cede its western land claims (to what became Alabama) in return for a federal agreement to extinguish all Indian claims within Georgia. So it was not surprising that the governor of Georgia should maintain that the treaties made by the United States with the Indian nations were just "expedients by which ignorant, intractable, and savage people were induced without bloodshed to yield up what civilized peoples had a right to possess by virtue of that command of the Creator delivered to man upon his formation—be fruitful, multiply, and replenish the earth, and subdue it."[35]

During his presidency, Andrew Jackson abrogated, de facto, a score of existing federal treaties with the Indian nations by asserting that relations with the Indians were not a federal but a state prerogative since the Indians were not independent nations and had only "a possessory right to the soil, for the purposes of hunting, and not the right of domain." He then ordered the army to "persuade" the Indians to emigrate to save themselves from the states, and, in the following year, he got the Congress (retroactively) to authorize his action in the Removal Bill.

Each nation was told to move west to suitable land, but no one knew or tried to find out how the Indians were to support themselves on arrival. "Suitable" land simply meant "distant" land. Large numbers starved as they were being herded west, and when they arrived at stopping places hundreds of miles away, they were without food or shelter. Not to mince words, the removal policy was actually a death march. Those who tried to protect themselves, particularly Seminole and Sac and Fox Indians, were attacked by the American army.

A few Americans opposed this policy.[36] "Realists" among the missionaries argued that the best hope of the Indians was the creation of a refuge in the West where they would be safe from whites. Those who tried to stay in their ancestral homes would almost certainly be massacred and would cause constant hostilities with the state governments. Neither the Congress nor the administration, however, wanted to spell out a policy toward the Indians that was inherently ugly, so it was implemented piecemeal and with a combination of assurances and threats. Secretary of War Lewis Cass, in a meeting typical of a number of others, thus addressed a gathering of a thousand tribesmen from the Northwest on the Wabash River. He urged them to sell their lands and promised that a missionary well known to them would accompany them but then, ominously, ended by saying, "Look around you. You will soon be left alone. The Delawares have gone, the Shawnees are going. Be wise."[37]

Not even the whites knew what was happening, and the Indians were completely bewildered. Communications were rudimentary and the whole process was so alien to the Indian experience as to seem almost mythical. And there was no one to whom even the most immediate and practical questions could be addressed. No one knew or could predict when the march westward would begin, where the Indians would be going, how long it would take to get there, or what they would find on arrival. So when each march actually began, the Indians were completely demoralized, their tribal organization had disintegrated, and they had already exhausted what few supplies they had. But once begun, the process picked up momentum. Meanwhile, land speculators, whiskey merchants, and government agents (who sometimes combined the other two trades as well) moved among them like wolves. Militiamen evicted families from their farms and brought them, many at the point of a gun, to concentration camps. There, contractors who were supposed to supply food and equipment usually cheated on their contracts so that starvation and disease carried off unknown numbers of the very young and the old. Even an outbreak of cholera did not slow the deportations. The Indians were divided into thirteen detachments to be conveyed, on foot, the eight hundred miles to their new lands. Thus divided, families often got permanently separated. Most lost all their possessions. One detachment took six months to complete the grueling trip.

During the Civil War, the "removed" Indian nations illogically supported the Confederacy (which was based on states' rights). Apparently the Five Civilized Nations—the Chickasaw, Cherokee, Choctaw, Creek, Seminole, and other Indian nations—hoped to form themselves into a state, but before they could, the Confederacy was defeated, and on July 14, 1865, the Chickasaws became the last Confederate community to surrender. Their nation was legally extinguished only in 1906.

After the Civil War, as settlers pushed further westward, they ran into an entirely different sort of Indians. Although some of the Indians in the East were seminomads, many, including the Five Civilized Nations, were agriculturalists. In the West were true nomads who, having acquired the horse, had, like the earlier Indo-Europeans, been transformed.[38] In fact, the Comanche, the Blackfeet, the Apache, the Ute, the Crow, the Sioux (Dakota), the Kiowa, the Osage, the Wichita, the Arapaho, and the Cheyenne were warrior horsemen who resembled the Scyths, the Arabs, and the Mongols. When attacked, they fought back. As a practical matter, they had little choice because there was no new land further west into which they could "remove" and, being separate nations, they could not fall back into one another's territories. The stark fact was that there could be no retreat: they had to fight and win or fight and die. Thus, both by temperament and by lack of alternative, they resisted white encroachment. Most were to die, and the broken remnants of their tribes were to be driven into reservations.

What really destroyed them was not so much military action, most of which consisted of small battles (although "search and destroy" operations certainly killed large numbers of Indians), but the annihilation of the buffalo on which the Indians depended for their livelihood.[39] Starvation was easy to induce when the troops controlled the food supply and cut off migration, and it may be that, within the limited technology of the times, deliberate attempts were made to use what we would term biological warfare by spreading smallpox.[40] The statistics show how little the Indians were able to protect themselves. In 1866 the Comanches were thought to number nearly 5,000, but by 1884 only 1,382 were still alive. During the same period, the population of all the Plains Indians fell by at least 50 percent.

Remnants of twenty tribes were already grouped in "Indian Territory," or much of what later became Oklahoma, and some of the Sioux were already located on a reservation in about half of what is now South Dakota. Thus began, more or less without plan, what became the pattern of putting whole nations, where they still existed, on reservations and of jumbling together the scattered remains of tribes without regard to language, culture, or kinship.

Ulysses S. Grant's administration accelerated another aspect of federal relations with the Indians that dates back to the time of President Jackson—abrogating or merely ignoring existing treaties. Indian Commissioner Francis Walker set the mood and tone when he remarked in 1873 that the treaties had never been meant to be more than "a mere form to amuse and quiet savages, a half-compassionate, half-contemptuous humoring of unruly children." The Congress agreed.

By the end of the nineteenth century, no tribes were still independent. For a few more years, parts of the so-called Five Civilized Nations existed as "protectorates," but the nomadic Plains Indians were politically and militarily broken. Nor, any longer, were the overwhelming majority of the Indians able to support themselves. The buffalo were gone, and few Indians knew how to farm or had the required capital or suitable lands. What good lands remained to them lacked the necessary infrastructure, and they rapidly lost title to the economically most attractive areas. Most critical of all, the bitter frontier wars had left them psychologically shattered.

What to do with the survivors became the urgent question. No matter how little regard whites had for Indian life, it was not possible to justify further slaughter when no excuse could be offered by the disarmed, disoriented, starving rabble. Some other means of handling the Indian problem had to be found. The government was learning what not to do: some 102 Indian reservations had been created west of the Mississippi to remove some 224,000 Indians who had already lost their lands. They were supervised by some 68 agencies and 37 military posts. Managing the Indians had become a costly domestic empire. So an idea originally broached in 1869 by the Society of Friends (the Quakers), to break up tribes and give individual Indians land, finally came into focus in the Dawes Act, which was signed into law in February 1887. The act empowered the president to subdivide most Indian reservations so that individual Indians were to receive parcels of land ranging in size from 160 acres for a head of family down to 40 acres for an orphan. Then "surplus" lands could be purchased by the federal government (in funds blocked for Indian use but subject to congressional appropriation) for resale under the Homestead Act to whites. Those Indians who were born in the United States (that is, not on tribal lands or reservations) and complied (that is, who both moved apart from their tribes and adopted "White ways") were declared to be citizens.

The bill was greeted enthusiastically by reformers. The Indian Rights Association compared it to the Magna Carta and the Emancipation Proclamation and said it was "to be commemorated by the Sons of Liberty." But Dawes himself realized that the motive of his supporters was simply their desire to buy Indian lands cheaply and was stunned by the avalanche of sales. In their current situation, he noted, the Indians cannot be "left to stand alone any more than so many reeds." Yet, the act that bears his name proposed to do just that. The figures suggest he was optimistic. Of the more than 155 million acres held by Indians in 1881, half were alienated by 1900. During the same period, only about 5.4 million were divided among Indians.

But still there were Indians. The focus shifted from land to culture. In 1890, the Indians were told that a part of "becoming civilized" involved giving up their Indian names and taking white names. These should not be translations or nicknames but common American names—not White Feather or Little Fox but Tom, Dick, and Harry. Nor were Indians to continue to use their languages. In the schools to be established in the Indian areas, only English could be taught. This policy may have been influenced by, and was similar to, the French program to denationalize the Algerians and Russian efforts to wipe out the Turkic languages of the Caucasus and Central Asia.

As the unwinding of the Indian nations continued, the issue of citizenship came to the fore, as had been foreseen in the Dawes Act. In 1888, a second act granted citizenship to Indian women marrying American males; then in 1919, in the euphoria that followed the end of World War I, Indian veterans were rewarded by the grant of citizenship. And finally, in 1924, the rest of the Indians, about one-third of the Indian population, became citizens. Yet, as a practical matter, most Indians still live apart from the mainstream of American society.

· · ·

Thus, we can see that American relations with the Indians, Spanish relations with the Moriscos and Jews, and Aryan relations with the Indus valley peoples fall into a pattern. And as we attempt to understand the complex emotions and reactions of peoples who have emerged from imperialism in Central Asia, North Africa, and South Africa we find enough similarities that these episodes prove enlightening. Although some of the emotional, cultural, economic, and political problems have been partially solved, or at least ameliorated, they are apt to remain with us into the twenty-first century: *they* bear scars indicating pains and damage that we can barely appreciate while *we* are driven to deal with the fact that socially we have not risen above our bodily constraints: we find it very difficult to live with people who are different from us and in times of stress or chaos turn violently against them. It is a possibility—indeed, a probability—that in

the coming years we will see the trend that began with World War II carried much further into the fracturing of states into nations so that, as
complex as the international system has become, it is likely to become
even more Balkanized.

There are obvious contrary pressures—movements of at least partial
unification such as the European Community, supplemented by defense,
trade, and other alliances and, above all, by the worldwide "net" of the
media. And perhaps to these might be added increased emphasis on religion and culture. Some believe that future conflicts will focus on differences between the dominant cultures or civilizations. I find this less likely
than conflicts among or even within "microcultures," that "nationalism,"
as redefined away from the "nation-state" toward the community (whether
defined culturally, religiously, or racially) will be the underlying theme of
world politics in the coming decades. If I am correct, then the challenge
to be faced by the next generation will be to find a solution other than
ethnic cleansing, a means both to allow national self-determination to
come about more or less peacefully and to coalesce the resulting "ministates" into organizations that can deal with the great and growing transnational and multinational problems.

. . . .

29 COMING TOGETHER

During the centuries following Columbus's voyage to the New World
and the Portuguese venture into the Indian Ocean, Europeans were fascinated by the sorts of tales we know from Richard Hakluyt's *Voyages* and
particularly by reports of the discovery of exotic primitive peoples; for
Europeans, the Asians, Africans, and Americans appeared to be not only
outside European civilization but outside Civilization altogether. In discussing his concept of the "state of nature," Thomas Hobbes pinned it
specifically to America, where, he said, there is "no account of Time; no
Arts; no Letters; no Society; and which is worst of all, continuall feare, and
danger of violent death; And the life of man, solitary, poore, nasty, brutish,
and short. . . . For the savage people in many places of *America,* except
the government of small Families, that concord whereof dependeth on
naturall lust, have no government at all; and live at this day in that brutish manner."[41] But others puzzled over the relationship of such people to

European Christian society. We have seen that encounters with distant cultures played a significant role in Francisco de Vitoria's laying of the moral foundations of modern international law: since even distant, non-Christian peoples were obviously human, they deserved, he argued, to be treated humanely and justly. Other thinkers, notably John Locke, focused on another issue: how the experience of primitive, non-European peoples might shed light on how all societies were formed out of "the state of nature."

True, Locke (like Hobbes) used the concept of the state of nature as an intellectual device to make his contemporary political points, but he also regarded it as a real stage in human evolution and was explicit in affirming his belief "that all men are naturally in that state and remain so, till by their own consents they make themselves members of some politic society."[42] He thus put concern with "coming together" at the basis of his political thought. His emphasis, moreover, was neither wholly speculative nor antiquarian: during his lifetime individuals and groups of Locke's fellow countrymen *were* joining together to establish colonies in which aims had to be made explicit, membership defined, and laws agreed. The 101 Puritans who sailed to New England on the *Mayflower* have left us a model. John Locke, whose father was a strict Puritan, must have had that sort of model at hand as he was educated by his father at home. The Puritans' 1620 Mayflower Compact not only defined the rights and duties of members, whom they called "the Saints," but also dealt with their relationship with "strangers." Theirs was but one of a number of lesser-known or forgotten near-contemporary agreements in which groups of merchants and settlers established what were, in fact, small self-governing, isolated sodalities vested with sovereign power over property and lives of the members. Possibly Locke knew of them; it is unlikely that he knew of those of earlier times, but we now know of a few similar agreements among migrants that were forged in antiquity.

I commented in chapter 15 on communities of Assyrian merchants who about 4,000 years ago formed quasi-governmental organizations and in chapter 28 on how Greek cities around 700 B.C.E. sent abroad their surplus population to form colonies that grew into separate states. The "constitution" of one of the Greek colonies has survived. In a document rather similar to the Mayflower Compact, the new "citizens" of Cyrene in what is today Libya established the ground rules of their society. And for every written record that has survived or about which we have some information, there must have been scores that were never so explicitly set forth or have been lost.

One of the more interesting ancient experiments in forming a new society was the colony of Thurii. In 444 B.C.E., the Greek colony of Sybaris on the Gulf of Taranto in what is now southeast Italy had come close to exterminating itself in vicious civil wars. Probably fearing attack by the neighboring Italians, it appealed for immigrants from its "mother" colony in Greece and with their help managed to reconstitute itself. Then, for reasons that are not clear, it decided to establish a "daughter" colony nearby at Thurii. Not having enough people to do so by itself, Sybaris sent an appeal to both Athens and Sparta. Sparta replied that it had no people to spare, but Athens answered the appeal in an unprecedented way that would make the colony "international." It sent runners to city-states all over Greece to encourage citizens to move and settle there. Unfortunately, we do not know how these people from different city-states found their ways together in a new commonality, but they could hardly have done worse than the citizens of many relatively homogeneous Greek city-states, including those that had established Sybaris. What is noteworthy, however, is that other than the mercenary armies for which "Greece" was famous, Thurii was the only significant political manifestation of Panhellenism in Greek history. Yet it was on that weak and untested foundation that the new society was built.

So although, as the eighteenth-century philosophers stated it, the formation of societies from the "state of nature" could only have been theoretical since it would mean that individuals lived more isolated from one another than they could ever have done, there is evidence of people, often cast apart from existing societies, coalescing into new societies. There is much more evidence, of course, for such people joining existing societies. Probably, Hobbes and Locke (and Aristotle long before) got the motivation at least partly right: men feel a need to live in society. As ethologists would put it, we are social animals. Economists, at least since Adam Smith, point to an additional "practical" motivation: that living in groups enables people to specialize and so to produce more. This observation was made at least as early as the Sumerians. It was, indeed, forced on peoples from the earliest historical times to the present by the competition of their neighbors. As I mentioned in chapter 2, those groups in ancient times that did not effectively coalesce were overshadowed, incorporated, or destroyed by the communities that did. Even those who had no neighbors to fear were affected by environmental imperatives, so, for example, settlers on the American frontier went to great lengths to ensure that neighbors would be motivated to help them "raise the roof beam." In most circumstances, the loner was less likely to survive than the member of a community.

If people wanted to live in groups, they also wanted to live in successful groups in attractive environments. In the previous chapter, I alluded to the desire of large numbers of Europeans, who were already members of groups, to leave them. Their motivations were doubtless varied but high among them was the assessment that they had little opportunity where the society was unsupportive or unprogressive or where the ecology was unattractive. It was thus largely as what we today call economic refugees that millions of Europeans decided to immigrate into America. Most could not have had more than a vague sense of joining another community, but it appears that nearly all had a vision of what their lives might become. Some found fellow villagers or even relatives because someone had gone before and blazed a trail,[43] but most found, at best, neighborhoods where their language was spoken so that America spawned many "Chinatowns," "Little Italys," and "Greektowns."

Such patterns of settlement created a special form of political organization and civic government based on ethnic loyalties. Indeed, political organization fostered what became de facto foreign affairs programs, with the Irish, Italians, Jews, Poles, Lithuanians, Ukrainians, and others not only evincing a sentiment toward "the old country" but also lobbying the American government in support of programs to draw closer to or assist the places of their origin. These sentiments and forces were strongest around the beginning of this century but remain remarkably resilient despite the passage of time, the movements away from ghettos into the suburbs, and acculturation.

Much of the historically documented confluence of peoples was enforced and was achieved by conquest. But for metamorphoses to occur, more than mere force was required. We see it first in Egypt. Beset by constant threats from the upper Nile, the Egyptians began a program in the eighteenth dynasty in which "they managed to accomplish an almost perfect Egyptianization of the Nubians." So far was this policy carried with the political elite that "sons of the indigenous rulers [were taken] as hostages to Egypt, where the education at the court of Pharaoh was so successful that, allegedly, they forgot their own language."[44] For such a program to work, a dominant culture was probably the main ingredient, and for this to take effect, time was essential. China offers us an example of how it may often have worked. I described above how the Shang dynasty began to build "China" from its alien neighbors, whom the Shang kidnapped in the scores of thousands to build walls and to cultivate the fields. Most of the peasants were worked to death, but many survived and gradually a significant number adopted the language, the religion, and the customs of the elite.

The Chou were one of the *fang* peoples who, over time, adopted

Chinese culture from the Shang. They enable us to see more clearly the process of amalgamation. Like the aboriginal peoples of Greece and India, the common people of the Shang had an earth religion, whereas the Chou, like the Indo-Europeans, had a "formalistic, almost abstract heaven-religion." Indeed, as Wolfram Eberhard has written, "Chou society is the result of an *ethnic superstratification*."[45] T'ien (heaven) is their central deity and, like the Sumerians, the Chou used their paramount god's grant to them of a "mandate" to proclaim their legitimacy. As Herrlee Creel has pointed out, "This was the keynote of the propaganda by which the Chou sought, ultimately with complete success, to reconcile those they had conquered to their rule."[46] During the Chou, as I wrote in chapter 5, the classical cultural core of China was codified, and that culture—not race or religion or geographical origin—ever since has been what differentiates the Chinese from the alien.

But the process did not stop there: over centuries, China has been a great vortex, a sort of social "black hole," into which alien peoples have poured, some as refugees, some as conquerors—it mattered little because all have been transformed into Chinese. The process is by no means either complete or perfect. New groups are still in the process of transformation and many have long resisted so that, today, China still has dozens of significant ethnic, religious, and linguistic minorities; overall, however, China has been the world's greatest social synthesizer.

Apparently, a similar process on a much smaller scale was at work in ancient Greece. There the incoming Indo-European invaders were probably few in number, indeed a military elite like the Shang, who superimposed themselves on distinct and separate aboriginal populations. Not much is known about this process, but a little more is known about the subject populations. Residues of older societies continued to exist but were subjugated, although probably not so brutally as in Shang China, and usually segregated, but not so sharply as in Aryan-dominated India. The pattern of exploitation of the *Helots* and *Perioikoi* was not unique to Sparta. Thus we hear of the *Kallikyrioi* of Syracuse, the *Penestai* of Thessaly, the *Mnoitai* or *Klarotdai* of Crete, and others. The initial impact of the Indo-Europeans probably occurred sometime around 1600 or 1700 B.C.E., but for centuries the servile population continued to speak non-Greek languages as many continued to do even into the Archaic and Classical periods. Over generations, however, the bulk of the members of the native communities became joined with the Indo-Europeans and from their union was born "Greece."

The process was more or less repeated on a far larger scale in the western Roman Empire when the Goths and other peoples invaded. In part, no doubt, the invaders drove away or killed much of the existing Romanized populations of areas into which they moved, but not entirely; over time, they merged with these peoples, adopted their way of life and religion, and came to speak languages that were a mixture of Latin and their dialects. Hundreds of years later, there were no "Goths" (although the Spanish Christians of the north thought of themselves as such) but new communities from whom would eventually emerge Italians, Spaniards, and French. This conversion was one of the great results of the Middle Ages.[47]

Conversions and amalgamations were accelerated by the opening of the New World to European, African, and Asian immigration. There has been far less mixing with the indigenous population, as I pointed out in the previous chapter, but the ideal of America was summarized in the phrase "the melting pot." Americans like to believe that movement to the New World has constituted a sort of rebirth in which the old ways and old divisions were shed and a new sense of community arose. The phrase is certainly an exaggeration but it does point in the right direction. Perhaps a more accurate metaphor would suggest coagulation rather than melting because the social units that have been formed more resemble a lumpy or clotted mass than a smooth liquid. In the United States there is still a strong sense of separate ethnicity, but even in each ethnic community there is coalescence since the members of each came from disparate backgrounds. The Italian American is a special sort of American still, but if a number of Italian Americans were transported back to Italy, they would find themselves scattered in the villages of their fathers, cut off from one another, and almost as alien to one another as though they were members of other ethnic groups. America has not fully blended them with Greeks, Chinese, Ukrainians, Germans, and Scots, but it has made them, more than their ancestors, at least members of a single community.

Although the United States is an extreme example among modern societies for its multicultural, multinational, multireligious origins, it is not unique. Few modern states are truly homogeneous. Two that like to think they are are Japan and France. But despite highly exclusionary policies, they fall short of the mark. The Japanese were immigrants who conquered the indigenous population of Ainu. For centuries the Ainu were more or less confined to the island of Hokkaido and generally were segregated from the Japanese, although attempts were made in the late eighteenth century and again in the late nineteenth century to integrate them. They are forbidden to use their traditional dress, customs, and language, and intermarriage has increased. But still the Ainu stand apart from Japanese society.

Japan tried also to isolate itself culturally. In the seventeenth century, when Christian missionaries and European traders had made considerable inroads, the Tokugawa shogunate moved to suppress all foreign contacts and all native groups influenced by them. Foreign traders were expelled, Japanese Christians were hunted down and killed, and Japan closed itself off from the world. Japanese were not allowed to build ocean-going boats, and foreign traders were confined to a ghetto in Nagasaki harbor.

Perry's opening of Japan in 1853 was insignificant in scale and impact in comparison to the American occupation at the end of World War II. Today there are significant foreign communities in Japan, some of which (like the Koreans) have been there for several generations. Particularly as its own population ages, Japan is finding itself under increasing pressure to become more open, but relative to most of the world's countries, Japan is still a compact, relatively homogeneous, and culturally unified nation.

Not so extreme, but comparable, France defines itself culturally and even racially in highly conservative terms. The essence of "Frenchness" was defined by Alphonse de Lamartine, François Guizot, and their followers (and readers of Guizot's *Histoire de la civilisation en France*) in terms the Chinese would have understood and favored. But race also was brought into the definition. The problem of definition of a Frenchman is particularly acute emotionally and politically when focused on the millions of "new" inhabitants who have migrated into France from its former African, Asian, and American colonies. The French are sensitive about these immigrants' claim to nationality. That issue, indeed, is the fuel of the extreme right in French politics. But it is not, in its more subtle and less violent forms, unique to the extreme right, which, along with probably a majority of Frenchmen, would agree with Ernest Renan's statement that "a nation is a soul, a spiritual principle . . . the common possession of a rich legacy of memories from the past and consent in the present, the desire to live together and the will to continue to develop one's heritage."[48]

By this definition, newcomers cannot be French since their heritage is different; they have either no rich legacy of memories, if they come from what the French regard as a primitive people, or a different legacy. In either case, little that they express of the desire to live together with the French can matter since they have no way to assimilate the common heritage. Their Frenchness can only be skin deep; it can never grow a "soul." To the French, this issue is not theoretical because over the past two centuries immigrants have come to France (as the Indians and other colonial peoples came to England) first in a trickle, under the empire, and then in a flood as it dissolved. In the middle of the last century, there were about half a million migrants, of whom about 13,500 had acquired French citizenship. By the beginning of World War II, more than 2 million had been naturalized and about 2.5 million others who were not naturalized lived permanently in France. Today whole quarters of most French cities and even little towns are made up of Moroccans, Tunisians, and Algerians who have become quasi-French.

This issue is by no means restricted to France. Leaving aside the "quasi foreigners," those with special status and long-time residence (or their children), figures dating from 1990 indicate that foreigners make up more than 6 percent of the residents of France and Germany, more than 4 percent of Holland's residents, and more than 3 percent of England's. And, even leaving recent immigrants aside, the question of national identity is by no means resolved. The French—and outside observers—have been shocked to witness the strength of the regional "nationalisms" of the Corsicans, the Bretons, the Basques, the people of Languedoc, and others within "geographical" France. And what is true of them is even more true of the inhabitants of the long-disputed eastern frontier with Germany. If this is a problem in France, it has posed a more immediate challenge to national unity in Spain, where the Basques and the Catalans have long sought at least autonomy. Spain, unlike France, seems to have accepted, at least for the Catalans, some form of autonomy for "national" groups. Northern Italians are beginning to talk about separation from the impoverished and "Mafia-ridden" south; how far this sentiment will take them is as yet unclear. The split between eastern and western Germany has proved harder to bridge than was expected. Czechoslovakia and Yugoslavia have already come apart. In fact, the most recent statistics show that "ethnicity" is a widely shared and growing problem for which the Europeans have no answer. Certainly, not everyone wants to come together with those who fall outside their definition of "us."

Yet it cannot be denied that external forces pushing toward supraethnic affiliations are also now very strong and appear to be growing stronger, tending to pull all of us, but particularly the weaker, into larger cultural collections. We can get a measure of this from historical comparisons: whereas the process of forming "Greeks" from the mixture of Indo-Europeans and native populations was a matter of about a millennium and the conversion of "Goths" and others into Italians, French, and Spanish took about six hundred years, and even then both were imperfectly achieved, in America in the nineteenth and early twentieth centuries, most immigrants "lost" the languages of their ancestors and drastically changed their ways of life and their cultural orientations within a generation.

Today, radio, the cinema, and television are potent blenders, causing all of us, of whatever provenance, to sing the same songs, eat the same food, wear the same clothes, and dream the same dreams. To gain access to these things, we have learned that we must work the same way in similar jobs. With the partial exception of Japan and China, modernization equates everywhere to Westernization and comes through industrialization, which in turn requires urbanization. The standardization required for the process implies that access to the job markets of a modern industrial society is through command of the dominant language. In America, English is virtually a necessity, as Russian was in the Turkic republics of Central Asia under the Soviet Union. Language draws people not only across cultural frontiers but also across political boundaries, despite nationalist sentiments, in western Europe, North Africa, the Middle East, South Asia, and the Pacific basin as well as in the United States. The small, the different, the weak are all under increasing pressure to join.

In summary, we can see that although most of us, most of the time, have derived our identity through birth, our ancestors were also driven apart from those among whom they were born and slowly, hesitantly, often repeatedly, sought to assuage the pangs of insecurity and overcome the dangers of isolation by forming new associations. Such moves were not always conscious decisions, as Locke suggested, and often not a successful answer to a desperate need, as Hobbes believed, but they appear to be virtually universal. And, in general, they have positive results. Without them, our already violent world might be beyond redemption; with them, we may have a better chance for peace; but there can be no doubt that assimilation has operated through history as a double-edged sword: often, the closer the feeling of brotherhood within a community, the stronger the animosity toward the strangers without. Thus, it seems to me that the interplay of separation, migration, civil war, breakdown of nation-states, ethnic cleansing, and amalgamation of old and new nations is likely to figure strongly in our future and will pose test after painful test of international relations in the twenty-first century.

Although the future is unclear, the present experience suggests that whatever approximations of answers to these questions are brought forward, they will not be simple, will not be universally acceptable, and, above all, cannot be imposed merely by force of arms. Rather, to hope to be able to cope with them, we will have to draw on the rich heritage of the ways in which our ancestors have tried to cope with neighbors and strangers, adapt the traditional methods with great flexibility, and invent new means of action. One thing, I believe, is certain: our descendants will live in a world with many neighbors and few strangers.

NOTES

PART I: THE BOTTOM LINE

1. Laurie Garrett, "The Return of Infectious Disease," *Foreign Affairs* 75 (1996): 66; see also Garrett's *The Coming Plague: Newly Emerging Diseases in a World out of Balance* (New York: Farrar, Straus, and Giroux, 1994). I am indebted to William Clark for some of the material in this chapter.

2. See Martin A. Nowak and Andrew J. McMichael, "How HIV Defeats the Immune System," *Scientific American,* August 1995. The authors argue that it is the rapid and massive mutation of the invading viruses that finally overwhelms the immune system and that the long battle for supremacy explains why the disease appears to be dormant for so long before the final catastrophe.

3. Thucydides, *History of the Peloponnesian War,* 2:50.

4. I draw most of the following information from William Clark, *At War Within: The Double-Edged Sword of Immunity* (Oxford: Oxford University Press, 1995).

5. Thomas Hobbes, *Leviathan,* 1:13.

6. John Locke, *An Essay Concerning the True Original, Extent and End of Civil Government,* 3, "Of the State of Nature."

7. Charles Darwin, *The Descent of Man* (London: J. Murray, 1871), 162.

8. Ibid., 85, 95, 164–65.

9. See Francis Crick and Christof Koch, "The Problem of Consciousness," *Scientific American,* September 1992, in which the authors write that "the brain must use past experience (either its own or that of our distant ancestors, which is embedded in our genes) to help interpret the information coming into our eyes" (12).

10. See Sigmund Freud, *Thoughts for the Times on War and Death,* vol. 4 of *Collected Papers* (London: Hogarth, 1953), 288 ff.

11. Arthur Keith, *New Theory of Human Evolution* (New York: Philosophical Library, 1949).

12. Clark, *At War Within,* 120.

13. See Marshall Sahlins, *Tribesmen* (Englewood Cliffs, N.J.: Prentice-Hall, 1968), 10–11.

14. Hans Kruuk, *The Spotted Hyena* (Chicago: University of Chicago Press, 1972), 251 ff., 239.

15. Edward O. Wilson, *Sociobiology* (Cambridge: Harvard University Press, 1975), 274. See also James L. Gould and Peter Marler, "Learning by Instinct," *Scientific American,* January 1987, esp. 68 ff.

16. Strangers are called *zhu dole* (dangerous person) and non-Bushmen are called *zo si* (animals without hooves) because they are believed to be dangerous, like lions and hyenas. Elizabeth Marshall Thomas, *The Harmless People* (New York: Vintage, 1958), 23–24, 181.

17. Richard B. Lee, "!Kung Spatial Organization," in *Kalahari Hunter-Gatherers: Studies of the !Kung San and Their Neighbors,* ed. Richard B. Lee and Irven DeVore (Cambridge: Harvard University Press, 1976).

18. Wilson, *Sociobiology,* 249.

19. George B. Schaller and Gordon R. Lowthere, "The Relevance of Carnivore Behavior to the Study of Early Hominids," *Southwestern Journal of Anthropology* 25 (1969): 313.

20. Kruuk, *Spotted Hyena,* 260. See also Glenn King, "Society and Territory in Human Evolution," *Journal of Human Evolution* 5 (1976): 327–28.

21. A. A. Velitchko, "Dynamiques des modifications naturelles dans le Pléistocène supérieur et problème du passage des néanderthaliens à l'Homo Sapiens," in *The Origin of Homo Sapiens,* ed. F. Bordes (Paris: UNESCO, 1972).

22. James Shreeve, *The Neanderthal Enigma: Solving the Mystery of Modern Human Origins* (New York: William Morrow, 1995).

23. Patricia Phillips, *The Prehistory of Europe* (Harmondsworth: Penguin, 1981), 51–52, 75, 102, 157; Richard G. Klein, "Mousterian Cultures in European Russia," *Science* 165 (1969): 264.

24. We know a little about their diet from the structure and enamel covering of teeth. See A. Walker, "Diet and Teeth," in *The Emergence of Man: A Joint Symposium of the Royal Society and the British Academy,* ed. J. Z. Young et al. (London, 1981), 63; M. J. B. Verhaegen, "The Aquatic Ape Theory," *Medical Hypotheses* 16 (1985): 25, 28. The normally vegetarian chimpanzee may become cannibalistic during intergroup hostilities (D. Bygott, "Cannibalism among Wild Chimpanzees," *Nature* 238 [1972]: 410), while our nearest primate relatives, the bonobos, also catch and eat fish (Frans de Waal, *Peacemaking among Primates* ([Cambridge: Harvard University Press, 1989], 185).

25. Olga Soffer, *The Upper Paleolithic of the Central Russian Plain* (New York: Academic Press, 1985), 256 ff.

26. Bridget and Raymond Allchin, *The Rise of Civilization in India and Pakistan* (Cambridge: Cambridge University Press, 1982), 123.

27. James Mellaart, *The Neolithic of the Near East* (London: Thames and Hudson, 1981), 66.

28. Kent V. Flannery, "The Origins of the Village," in *Man, Settlement and Urbanism,* ed. Peter J. Ucko et al. (London: Duckworth, 1972), 28, argues that storage may have been the key factor in the origination of sedentary life. Storage

pits are identified in Iran at the Shanidar cave (Mellaart, *Neolithic of the Near East,* 72) and at various sites in Europe (Alasdair Whittle, *Neolithic Europe: A Survey* [Cambridge: Cambridge University Press, 1985], 51, 60, 63, 82).

29. For a reconstruction of the mammoth bone tent, see Patricia Phillips, *The Prehistory of Europe* (Harmondsworth, U.K.: Penguin, 1981), plate 3; Evan Hadingham, *Secrets of the Ice Age* (New York: Walker, 1979), 12 ff.; Soffer, *The Upper Paleolithic,* 72 ff.

30. Hans Helbaek, as quoted in Mellaart, *The Neolithic of the Near East,* 46.

31. See a 155–54 B.C.E. decree of the Senate quoted in Robert K. Sherk, *Rome and the Greek East to the Death of Augustus* (Cambridge: Cambridge University Press, 1984), 33; Mario Liverani, "The Ideology of the Assyrian Empire," in *Power and Propaganda: A Symposium on Ancient Empires,* ed. Mogen Trolle Larsen (Copenhagen: Akademisk Forlag, 1979), 311.

32. Some words for "slave" are derived from names for conquered native populations. We see this in the Indo-European *dasa,* the Etruscan *Etera,* and many others. Commonly, the Indo-European languages' terms for "slave" embody the concepts of alienness and seizure: Middle Iranian, *dast-grab;* Latin, *captus;* Greek, *doulos.*

33. Among a vast literature, I have found most useful J. P. V. D. Balsdon, *Romans and Aliens* (London: Duckworth, 1979), 79 ff.; Orlando Patterson, *Slavery and Social Death* (Cambridge: Harvard University Press, 1982), 345 ff.; Kenneth Hughes, *Slavery* (London: Allen & Unwin, 1975), 59; Keith Hopkins, *Conquerors and Slaves* (Cambridge: Cambridge University Press, 1978), esp. 76–77; Joseph Vogt, *Ancient Slavery and the Ideal of Man* (Oxford: Blackwell, 1974), 39 ff.

34. As M. I. Finley writes, the "ethical position was summed up by the elder Seneca, with reference to the passive partner in buggery: 'Unchastity (impudicitia) is a crime in the freeborn, a necessity for the slave, a duty (officium) for the freedman.'" *Ancient Slavery and Modern Ideology* (Harmondsworth, U.K.: Penguin, 1983), 96. See also K. R. Bradley, *Slaves and Masters in the Roman Empire* (Oxford: Oxford University Press, 1987), 113 ff.

35. Plutarch, *Roman Questions,* 278E; Suetonius, *On Grammarians,* 2; and Horace, *Epistles,* 2.1.156, all quoted in Hopkins, *Conquerors and Slaves,* 76–77. Also see Vogt, *Ancient Slavery and the Ideal of Man,* 123.

PART II: DEFENSE

1. Marilyn Roper, "A Survey of the Evidence for Intrahuman Killing in the Pleistocene," *Current Anthropology* 10 (1969): 429.

2. See Giovanni Pettinato, *Ebla: Un Impero incisa nell' Argilla* (Milan: Arnoldo Mondardori, 1979), 106, 165 ff., 226.

3. Robert McCormick Adams and Hans Nissen, *The Uruk Countryside* (Chicago: University of Chicago Press, 1972). See also Adams's study of the area to the north and east of Baghdad, *Land Behind Baghdad* (Chicago: University of Chicago Press, 1965); and his *Heartland of Cities* (Chicago: University of Chicago Press, 1981).

4. Hans Jörg Nissen, "The City Wall of Uruk," in *Man, Settlement and Urbanism*, ed. Peter J. Ucko et al. (London: Duckworth, 1972), 793 ff.; C. C. Lamberg-Karlovsky and Jeremy A. Sabloff, *Ancient Civilizations* (Menlo Park, Calif.: Cummings, 1979), 172.

5. Wilhelm Solheim, "An Earlier Agricultural Revolution," *Scientific American*, April 1972, 107.

6. J. P. Mallory, "The Chronology of the Early Kurgan Tradition," *Journal of Indo-European Studies* 4 (1976): 258.

7. Bridget and Raymond Allchin, *The Rise of Civilization in India and Pakistan* (Cambridge: Cambridge University Press, 1982), 123.

8. A. Berriedale Keith, "The Age of the Rigveda," in *The Cambridge History of India* (Cambridge: Cambridge University Press, 1921), 77.

9. C. C. Lamberg-Karlovsky, "Sumer, Elam and the Indus: Three Urban Processes Equal One Structure?" in *Harappan Civilization*, ed. Gregory L. Possehl (Warminster: Aris and Phillips, 1982), 61–67.

10. Romila Thapar, *A History of India* (Harmondsworth, U.K.: Penguin, 1966), 1:43; Mortimer Wheeler, *Civilizations of the Indus Valley and Beyond* (London: Thames and Hudson, 1966), 78; Wendy D. O'Flaherty, trans. and annot., *The Rig Veda* (Harmondsworth, U.K.: Penguin, 1981), 148.

11. Kwang-Chih Chang, *Shang Civilization* (New Haven: Yale University Press, 1980), 273 ff.

12. Herbert Franke, "Siege and Defense of Towns in Medieval China," in *Chinese Ways in Warfare*, ed. Frank A. Kierman Jr. and John K. Fairbank (Cambridge: Harvard University Press, 1974), 151.

13. F. Wendorf et al., "Egyptian Prehistory: Some New Concepts," *Science* 169 (1970): 1161 ff. The newcomers, who apparently came down the Nile, brought not only new animals and plants but "well made pottery, permanent adobe-walled houses, storage structures, and a lithic tradition radically different from that of the immediately preceding Terminal Paleolithic people in this area" (1170).

14. B. G. Trigger, "The Rise of Egyptian Civilization," in *Ancient Egypt: A Social History*, ed. B. G. Trigger et al. (Cambridge: Cambridge University Press, 1983), 48.

15. John Maynard Keynes, *The General Theory of Employment, Interest and Money* (London: Macmillan and Cambridge University Press, 1936), 131.

16. Carlo Cipolla, *Before the Industrial Revolution* (New York: Norton, 1993), 33 ff.

17. Quoted in H. Frankfort et al., *The Intellectual Adventure of Ancient Man* (Chicago: University of Chicago Press, 1946), 95.

18. I. E. S. Edwards, *The Pyramids of Egypt* (Harmondsworth, U.K.: Penguin, 1947), 85.

19. See John A. Wilson, *The Burden of Egypt* (Chicago: University of Chicago Press, 1951), 156 ff.

20. Not himself sympathetic to religion, Edward Gibbon laconically com-

mented that during the barbarian invasions of Europe, "the hostile myriads were poured with resistless violence into the Belgic provinces. The consternation of Gaul was universal, and the various fortunes of its cities have been adorned by tradition with martyrdoms and miracles. Troyes was saved by the merits of St. Lupus; St. Servatius was removed from the world that he might not behold the ruin of Tongres; and the prayers of St. Genevieve diverted the march of Attila from the neighborhood of Paris. But as the greatest part of the Gallic cities were alike destitute of saints and soldiers, they were besieged and stormed by the Huns." *The Decline and Fall of the Roman Empire* (New York: Modern Library, n.d.), 4:279–80.

21. Eugen Weber, *The Hollow Years: France in the 1930s* (London: Sinclair-Stevenson, 1995), 274.

22. Wolfram Eberhard, *Conquerors and Rulers* (Leiden: Brill, 1970), 33.

23. See Herrlee Creel, *The Origins of Statecraft in China* (Chicago: University of Chicago Press, 1970), 312; Joseph Needham, *Science and Civilization in China* (Cambridge: Cambridge University Press, 1971), 4:71.

24. E. T. Salmon, *The Making of Roman Italy* (London: Thames and Hudson, 1982), 28. The city-state was then less than 1,000 square kilometers (386 square miles), or roughly five times the size of Washington, D.C., according to K. J. Beloch, quoted in William Harris, *War and Imperialism in Republican Rome* (Oxford: Oxford University Press, 1985), 60.

25. Livy, *The Early History of Rome*, 5:38.

26. According to Frederick W. Mote in *The Cambridge History of China* (Cambridge: Cambridge University Press, 1988), 7:401.

27. Arthur Waldron, *The Great Wall of China: From History to Myth* (Cambridge: Cambridge University Press, 1990).

28. Thucydides, *History of the Peloponnesian War*, 2:12.

29. Henri Pirenne, *Economic and Social History of Medieval Europe* (New York: Harcourt Brace, 1956), 54.

30. Daniel Waley, *The Italian City-Republics* (New York: McGraw-Hill, 1969), 35.

31. This was admitted by a senior Russian official, the former first deputy head of the International Department of the Soviet Communist Party, at a 1994 gathering of the Nobel Institute in Oslo when he remarked that "any price which is necessary to pay for security will be paid and finally it was that price which destroyed the country." Quoted in Melvyn P. Leffer, "Inside Enemy Archives," *Foreign Affairs*, July–August 1996, 127–28.

32. Quentin Hughes, *Military Architecture* (Hants, U.K.: Liphook, 1974), 222 ff.

33. Quoted in Donald Kagan, *On the Origins of War and the Preservation of Peace* (London: Hutchinson, 1995), 355–56.

34. Supreme Headquarters, Allied Expeditionary Force, Counter-Intelligence Sub-Division, *Handbook of the Organisation Todt*, MIRS/MR-OT/5/45 (1945; reprint, Osnabrück: Biblio Verlag, 1992), 6.

35. Chester Wilmot, *The Struggle for Europe* (London: Collins, 1952), 192.

36. Allied Expeditionary Force, *Handbook of the Organisation Todt*, 16.

37. Ibid., 173.

38. He was speaking to the deputy director of the National Security Council staff, Walt W. Rostow, as quoted in Kagan, *On the Origins of War*, 480.

39. Omitted, among others, are the Antonine wall; Hadrian's wall; the innumerable medieval city walls; and the twentieth-century "walls" (mainly composed of wire and minefields) that the Italians built to separate Libya from Egypt, the French built to separate Tunisia from Algeria, and the Israelis built to separate Israel from Jordan and Syria. I have also not discussed the American DEW line, NORAD, or the abortive Strategic Defense Initiative (the "Star Wars" program).

PART III: ARMIES AND WARFARE

1. Edward Gibbon, *The Decline and Fall of the Roman Empire* (New York: Modern Library, n.d.), 1:69.

2. *Discourses on Livy* (Chicago: University of Chicago Press, 1996), 189.

3. *Vom Kriege*, bk. 1, "What Is War?" chap. 1, sec. 24. I have used the edition by Anatol Rapoport: *Clausewitz on War* (Harmondsworth, U.K.: Penguin, 1971) and Peter Paret: *Clausewitz and the State* (Princeton: Princeton University Press, 1985).

4. Roy Rappaport, *Pigs for the Ancestors: Ritual in the Ecology of a New Guinea People* (New Haven: Yale University Press, 1968), 143.

5. See chapter 28 on ethnic cleansing.

6. E. E. Evans-Pritchard, *The Nuer* (Oxford: Clarendon, 1940), 121–23.

7. Günter Wagner, "The Political Organization of the Bantu of Kavirondo," in *African Political Systems*, ed. M. Fortes and E. E. Evans-Pritchard (London: Oxford University Press, 1940), 228 ff.

8. Described in the Chinese chronicle *Tso-chuan*, quoted and analyzed by Frank A. Kierman Jr. in *Chinese Ways in Warfare*, ed. Frank A. Kierman Jr. and John King Fairbank (Cambridge: Harvard University Press, 1974), 27 ff.

9. Quoted in Kierman, *Chinese Ways in Warfare*, 60.

10. Sima Qian, *Shi ji (Records of the Grand Historian)*, rev. ed., trans. Burton Watson (New York: Columbia University Press, 1993), 43.

11. Wagner, "Political Organization of the Bantu," 226–27; Ruth Landes, "Dakota Warfare," *Southwestern Journal of Anthropology* 15 (1959): 46.

12. Thorkild Jacobsen, *Toward the Image of Tammuz and Other Essays on Mesopotamian History and Culture* (Cambridge: Harvard University Press, 1970), 137 ff.; Rappaport, *Pigs for the Ancestors*, 28–29.

13. Mogens Trolle Larsen, *The Old Assyrian City-State and Its Colonies* (Copenhagen: Akademisk Forlag, 1976), 85.

14. Mario Liverani, "The Ideology of the Assyrian Empire," in *Power and Propaganda*, ed. Mogens Trolle Larsen (Copenhagen: Akademisk Forlag, 1979), 307.

15. D. D. Luckenbill, ed., *Ancient Records of Assyria and Babylonia* (Chicago: University of Chicago Press, 1926–27), 1:144–45.

16. J. N. Postgate, "The Economic Structure of the Assyrian Empire," in *Power and Propaganda,* ed. Mogens Trolle Larsen (Copenhagen: Akademisk Forlag, 1979), 210, 216.

17. Claude Nicolet, *The World of the Citizen in Republican Rome* (London: Batsford Academic and Educational [Press], 1980), 89.

18. William Harris, *War and Imperialism in Republican Rome* (Oxford: Oxford University Press, 1979), 9–10, 53.

19. Livy, *The War with Hannibal,* 23:40; Polybius, *On Roman Imperialism,* 1: 79.

20. Keith Hopkins, *Conquerors and Slaves* (Cambridge: Cambridge University Press, 1978), 66–67, table 1.2.

21. N. Sherwin White, *The Roman Citizenship* (Oxford: Oxford University Press, 1980), 439, 454.

22. Chester Starr, *The Roman Empire* (New York: Oxford University Press, 1982), 75–90. Louis XIV apparently spent about 75 percent of his revenues on war; Peter the Great is said to have spent at least 10 percent more; Cromwell probably spent 90 percent during the 1650s, as did Frederick the Great a century later. I draw these figures from Geoffrey Parker, *The Military Revolution and the Rise of the West, 1500–1800* (Cambridge: Cambridge University Press, 1988), 62, 148.

23. A. H. M. Jones, *The Latter Roman Empire* (Oxford: Oxford University Press, 1973), 619 ff.

24. Wagner, "Political Organization of the Bantu," 226–27.

25. Johan Huizinga, *The Autumn of the Middle Ages* (Chicago: University of Chicago Press, 1996), 89.

26. Barbara Tuchman, *A Distant Mirror: The Calamitous 14th Century* (New York: Knopf, 1978), 85.

27. Quoted in Bertold Spuler, *History of the Mongols* (London: Routledge and Kegan Paul, 1972), 40–41.

28. Richard Lee and Irven DeVore, *Man the Hunter* (Chicago: University of Chicago Press, 1968), 299.

29. W. W. Tarn, *Hellenistic Navy and Military Developments* (Cambridge: Cambridge University Press, 1930), 2.

30. Plutarch, *The Age of Alexander,* "Timoleon," 28.

31. M. E. Mallett, J. R. Mallett, and J. R. Hale, *The Military Organization of a Renaissance State, Venice c. 1400–1617* (Cambridge: Cambridge University Press, 1984), 24–25, 144–46.

32. Parker, *The Military Revolution,* 60.

33. George Stein, *The Waffen SS* (Ithaca, N.Y.: Cornell University Press, 1966), 137–38, 167, 296 ff.

34. Herodotus, *The Histories,* 7:60. See also A. R. Burn, "Persia and the Greeks," in *The Cambridge History of Iran,* ed. Ilya Gershevitch (Cambridge: Cambridge University Press, 1985), 2:320 ff.

35. Herodotus, *The Histories,* 6:31.

36. In September 1996, the U.S. Department of Defense released docu-

ments showing that U.S. Army manuals used to train Latin American military officers between 1982 and 1991 at Fort Benning, Georgia, advocated false arrest, blackmail, torture, and execution of insurgents, according to *The Washington Post* (as reprinted in *The Guardian Weekly* [London], 29 September 1996).

37. This was Bernardo de Vargas Machuca's *Milicia y descripción de las Indias* (Madrid, 1599), noted in Parker, *The Military Revolution*, 120.

38. As head of the U.S. government task force, which was attempting to broker a peace in Algeria, I had a unique opportunity to observe events there.

39. *Sepoy* is an Anglicized version of the Persian-Turkish *sipahi* (soldier).

40. C. A. Bayly, *The New Cambridge History of India: Indian Society and the Making of the British Empire* (Cambridge: Cambridge University Press, 1988), chap. 1.

41. John Maynard Keynes, *A Treatise on Money*, 2:156–57, quoted in Karl de Schweinitz, *The Rise and Fall of British India* (London: Routledge, 1983), 43.

42. K. M. Panikkar, *Asia and Western Dominance* (London: Allen and Unwin, 1953), 100.

43. Adam Smith, *The Wealth of Nations* (New York: Modern Library, 1937), 602–6.

44. P. J. Marshall, *The New Cambridge History of India: Bengal, the British Bridgehead* (Cambridge: Cambridge University Press, 1987), 2:168.

45. The vision of English women being raped by dark Indian men was spread by some eighty English novels published in the years between the revolt and World War I. See Nancy L. Paxton, "Mobilizing Chivalry: Rape in British Novels about the Indian Uprising of 1857," *Victorian Studies* (Fall 1992): 5 ff.

46. "Minute on Education" of 2 February 1835, quoted in Philip Lawson, *The East India Company* (London: Longman, 1993), 153.

47. Eric Stokes, *The Peasant Armed: The Indian Revolt of 1857*, ed. C. A. Bayly (Oxford: Clarendon, 1986), 82.

48. Quoted in R. C. Majumdar, "Atrocities," in *The History and Culture of the Indian People* (Bombay: Bharatiya Vidya Bhavan, 1965), 9:591 ff.

49. Bernard Cohn, "Representing Authority in Victorian India," in *The Invention of Tradition*, ed. Eric Hobsbawm and Terence Ranger (Cambridge: Cambridge University Press, 1983).

50. Otto Kurz, "Cultural Relations Between Parthia and Rome," in Ehsan Yarshater, *The Cambridge History of Iran* (Cambridge: Cambridge University Press, 1983), 3:562.

51. He was given due credit by Winston Churchill in a letter to Lord Justice of Inventions Sir Charles Sargant (Churchill Papers: 2/107) reprinted in *Winston S. Churchill*, ed. Martin Gilbert (London: Heinemann, 1977), vol. 4, pt. 2, "Documents, June 1919–March 1921," 886 ff.

52. Gilbert, *Churchill*, 886.

53. J. F. C. Fuller, *The Decisive Battles of the Western World, 1792–1944* (London: Granada, 1970), 2:365.

54. Carlo Cipolla, *Guns and Sails in the Early Phase of European Expansion, 1400–1700* (London: Collins, 1965), 21.

55. Noel Perrin, *Giving Up the Gun* (Boulder, Colo.: Shambhala, 1979), 58 ff.

56. Joseph Needham, *Science and Civilisation in China* (Cambridge: Cambridge University Press, 1971), vol. 4, pt. 3, p. 476 ff.

57. Ibid., pt. 2, p. 413, and pt. 3, p. 667.

58. I am indebted for this and the following information to Parker, *The Military Revolution,* chap. 3, and Cipolla, *Guns and Sails.*

59. J. R. Hale, *War and Society in Renaissance Europe, 1450–1620* (Leicester: Leicester University Press, 1985), 222–29.

60. John Nef, *War and Human Progress* (London: Routledge and Kegan Paul, 1950), 239 ff., chap. 14.

61. Cipolla, *Guns and Sails,* 43, 82–83.

62. Gunther Rothenberg, *Napoleon's Great Adversaries* (Bloomington: Indiana University Press, 1982), 97.

63. Correspondence in the possession of my family and reproduced in William M. Polk, *Leonidas Polk, Bishop and General* (New York: Longman Green, 1894), vol. 2, chap. 2.

64. Michael Howard, *War in European History* (Oxford: Oxford University Press, 1976), 108.

65. John W. Wheeler-Bennett, *The Nemesis of Power* (London: Macmillan, 1954), 5.

66. The peace treaty was signed on June 28, 1919, and the Volkskommission für das Friedensheer was created on July 5.

67. Quoted by Wheeler-Bennett, *Nemesis of Power,* 118, n. 1.

68. In the first, he forced the two senior generals and sixteen "unreliable" generals into retirement and reassigned forty-four other generals and many other senior officers. In the second, following the failure of the Russian campaign in December 1941, Hitler purged a further thirty-five generals and assumed the role of Oberbefehlshaber des Heeres (commander-in-chief). Meanwhile, he had reneged on his promise not to create a Nazi Party army and had allowed the Waffen-SS to rise to equivalence with the regular army. Hitler's final purge of the army generals took place after the abortive coup of July 20, 1944.

69. Carlo Cipolla, *Before the Industrial Revolution,* 3d ed. (New York: Norton, 1993), 38, 199.

70. Taiwan was first, followed (in order) by North Korea, Israel, South Korea, and France, with the USSR in twelfth place. See Bruce M. Russett et al., *World Handbook of Political and Social Indicators* (New Haven: Yale University Press, 1964), 74 ff.

PART IV: NONGOVERNMENTAL RELATIONS

1. Edward O. Wilson, *Sociobiology: The New Synthesis* (Cambridge: Harvard University Press, 1975), 551.

2. Adam Smith, *The Wealth of Nations,* bk. 1, chap. 2.

3. Marcel Mauss, *Essai sur le don,* trans. Ian Cunnison (London: Cohen & West, 1954), esp. chap. 2, secs. 1, 4, 5.

4. Marshall Sahlins, *"The Spirit of the Gift" in Stone Age Economics* (London: Tavistock, 1974), 169.

5. Elizabeth Thomas, *The Harmless People* (New York: Knopf, 1958), 215; Mauss, *Essai sur le don,* 105. See also Lorna Marshall, "Sharing, Talking, and Giving, Relief of Social Tensions among the !Kung," in *Man the Hunter,* ed. Richard B. Lee and Irven DeVore (Chicago: Aldine, 1968), 361 ff.

6. Quoted in Stephanie Dalley, *Mari and Karana: Two Old Babylonian Cities* (London: Longman, 1984), 153.

7. Ruth Benedict, *The Chrysanthemum and the Sword* (Boston: Houghton Mifflin, 1947), 133 ff.

8. That is, they inscribed the name of the person they wished to humiliate or even exile on an *ostrakizein* (potsherd) and, when enough of these "ballots" mentioned the same person, he was banished.

9. E. Adamson Hoebel, *The Law of Primitive Man* (Cambridge: Harvard University Press, 1954), 169.

10. Herodotus, *The Histories,* 4:33.

11. Taqwin al-Buldan, *The Geography* (in Arabic), ed. Joseph Toussaint Reinaud (Paris, 1840), 250 ff. His work is based mainly on earlier sources.

12. Herodotus, *The Histories,* 4:196.

13. Bronislaw Malinowski, *Argonauts of the Western Pacific* (1922; reprint, New York: Dutton, 1961), 81, 85.

14. Napoleon Chagnon, *The Fierce People* (New York: Holt, 1968), 7, 100 ff.

15. Roy Rappaport, *Pigs for the Ancestors* (New Haven: Yale University Press, 1968), 99 ff. This was not true of sea trade and piracy, where the actors were not in fixed or constant contact with one another and so could afford to be more opportunistic.

16. His *Arthasastra,* written for the the first emperor of the Mauryan dynasty, has been published in various editions. The one I have used is translated by R. Shamasastry (Mysore, India: Mysore Printing and Publishing, 1961), 7th ed.

17. See Elizabeth Carter and Matthew Stolper, *Elam* (Berkeley: University of California Press, 1984), 10.

18. Ying-shih Yü, *Trade and Expansion in Han China* (Berkeley: University of California Press, 1967), 37.

19. On the Ottoman, British, and French policies in the nineteenth century in the Middle East see William R. Polk, *The Opening of South Lebanon* (Cambridge: Harvard University Press, 1963), 167, 225, and *The Arab World Today* (Cambridge: Harvard University Press, 1991), 67 ff., 115 ff.

20. Michael A. Hoffman, *Egypt Before the Pharaohs* (London: Ark, 1980), 201.

21. Hoffman, *Egypt Before the Pharaohs,* 247. See also 164, 207 ff., 213–14.

22. J. E. Dixon, J. R. Cann, and Colin Renfrew, "Obsidian and the Origins of Trade," *Scientific American,* March 1968, 38 ff.

23. That such a sequence is plausible is shown to us by its replication in

trading patterns in other areas at later dates. For examples, see Patricia Phillips, *The Prehistory of Europe* (Harmondsworth, U.K.: Penguin, 1981), 154, 157, 163, 171, 179, 192, 207.

24. Philip L. Kohl, "The Balance of Trade in Southeastern Asia in the Mid-Third Millennium B.C.E.," *Current Anthropology* 19 (1978): 463 ff. In this article Kohl shows that a trading area centered on Uruk and the other Sumerian cities encompassed the Indus valley, Syria, and lands as far north and east as present-day Uzbekistan by approximately 2600 B.C.E.

25. Even today, in the same areas, it is difficult for a traveler to "live off the land," particularly in the spring before the crops come in, as I learned when I lived for a year in a remote village in the Lebanese mountains.

26. Nilakanta Sastri, *A History of South India* (Madras: Oxford University Press, 1975), 79–81. A Persian mission in the late sixth century B.C.E. found that Indian sailors were so accustomed to the deep sea route that they were ignorant of the Persian coastal waters. Certainly by T'ang times, for which we have records, and probably long before, Indian merchants (by then joined by Arabs and Persians) had established a large-scale trade with what is today Vietnam. See Edward Schafer, *The Vermilion Bird* (Berkeley: University of California Press, 1967), 28.

27. Yvon Garlan, *War in the Ancient World* (London: Chatto and Windus, 1975), 40.

28. William R. Polk, trans., *The Golden Ode of Labid ibn Rabia* (Chicago: University of Chicago Press, 1974; Cairo: American University at Cairo Press, 1977), 159.

29. Mauss, *Essai sur le don*, 51.

30. Mogens Trolle Larsen, *The Old Assyrian City-State and Its Colonies* (Copenhagen: Akademisk Forlag, 1976), 86 ff.

31. Quoted in C. J. Gadd, "Assyria and Babylon c. 1370–1300," in *The Cambridge Ancient History* (Cambridge: Cambridge University Press, 1926), 2:25.

32. We catch a revealing glimpse of him in a charming eighteenth-dynasty Egyptian wall painting. The artist grandly displays the unloading of a Phoenician merchant vessel with the bulk of the cargo lovingly depicted, front and center. It was obviously intended for the official market, but on the fringes of the picture, under the noses of the officials, a merchant-sailor can be seen hawking his private stock of oil or wine to the common people. Norman Davies and R. O. Faulkner, "A Syrian Trading Venture to Egypt," *Journal of Egyptian Archaeology* 33 (1947): 40 ff. One of their ships has been reconstructed and is a museum in southern Turkey.

33. Peter Garnsey, "Grain for Rome," in *Trade in the Ancient Economy*, ed. Peter Garnsey et al. (London: Chatto and Windus, 1983), 118 ff.

34. The great Jewish medieval traveler Benjamin of Tudela has left us an account of his journey in *The Itinerary of Benjamin of Tudela* (New York: Joseph Simon, 1983), and the chance finding of documents and scraps of paper on which the Jewish community of medieval Egypt recorded its transactions has been marvelously exploited by S. D. Goitein in *A Mediterranean Society* (Berkeley:

University of California Press, 1967). More detail for the Indian area is given by K. N. Chaudhuri, *Asia Before Europe* (Cambridge: Cambridge University Press, 1990).

35. Goitein, *Mediterranean Society*, 1:217, 242.

36. Translating and editing Ibn Battuta's account was one of the major contributions of my late teacher, Sir Hamilton Gibb. He began his affair with Ibn Battuta with a summary published in London in 1929 and ultimately produced a three-volume scholarly edition that he finished shortly before his death more than thirty years later.

37. For observations on the Western and Muslim travelers, see Bertold Spuler, *History of the Mongols* (London: Routledge and Kegan Paul, 1972); for notes on the missions before the Polos, see Leonardo Olschki, *Marco Polo's Precursors* (Baltimore: Johns Hopkins University Press, 1943), and Ch'en Yuan, *Western and Central Asians in China Under the Mongols* (Los Angeles: University of California, Monumenta Series, 1966).

38. Joseph Needham thinks it possible or even probable that other Chinese sailed to the west coast of North and South America; see his *Science and Civilisation in China* (Cambridge: Cambridge University Press, 1971), 4:487 ff.

39. See Kenneth R. Andrews, *Trade, Plunder and Settlement* (Cambridge: Cambridge University Press, 1984), 22 ff.

40. Kwan-wai So, *Japanese Piracy in Ming China During the Sixteenth Century* (Ann Arbor: University of Michigan Press, 1975), 1, 162. The Chinese ran together the characters *wo* (Japanese) and *k'ou* (bandits, robbers), but in fact many of the pirates were Chinese.

41. Edward William Bovill, *The Golden Trade of the Moors* (1958; reprint, Princeton: Marcus Wiener, 1995).

42. Needham, *Science and Civilisation in China*, vol. 4, pt. 3, p. 528. See also J. H. Parry, *The Discovery of the Sea* (Berkeley: University of California Press, 1981), 134.

43. Fernand Braudel and F. C. Spooner, "Prices in Europe from 1450-1750," in *The Cambridge Economic History of Europe*, ed. E. E. Rich (Cambridge: Cambridge University Press, 1967), 4:445.

44. Estimated at between 0.1 and 1 percent annually. Carlo Cipolla, *Before the Industrial Revolution*, 3d ed. (New York: Norton, 1993), 171.

45. See Walter Minchinton, "Patterns and Structure of Demand 1500-1750," in Carlo M. Cipolla, *The Fontana Economic History of Europe* (London: Collins-Fontana, 1974), 2:144.

46. Geoffrey Parker, "The Emergence of Modern Finance in Europe 1500-1750," in Cipolla, *Fontana Economic History*, 2:530.

47. Quoted in Carlo Cipolla, *Guns and Sails in the Early Phase of European Expansion, 1400-1700* (London: Collins, 1965), 36.

48. Jaime Vincens Vives, "The Decline of Spain in the Seventeenth Century," in *The Economic Decline of Empires*, ed. Carlo Cipolla (London: Methuen, 1970), 121 ff.

49. Quoted in Eric Roll, *A History of Economic Thought* (New York: Prentice-Hall, 1942), 61.

50. See William L. Schurz, *The Manila Galleon* (1939; reprint, Manila: Historical Conservation Society, 1985), 30 ff.

51. M. Huc, *A Journey Through the Chinese Empire* (New York, 1855), quoted in Ping-ti Ho, "Economic and Institutional Factors in the Decline of the Chinese Empire," in *The Economic Decline of Empires*, ed. Carlo M. Cipolla (London: Methuen, 1970), 274.

52. As reported by the contemporary Italian traveler Gemelli Careri, quoted in Schurz, *Manila Galleon*, 59.

53. D'Avenant, quoted in Roll, *History of Economic Thought*, 63.

54. As J. H. Parry has pointed out (*Trade and Dominion* [New York: Praeger, 1971], 278), it was not until British "dominion in India was virtually complete, that the proportional share of Asia [open to British commerce] significantly increased." Until 1812, Jamaica alone consumed the same amount of British produce as all of India.

55. By R. Delcher, in Cipolla, *Before the Industrial Revolution*, 223.

56. Hoh-Cheung Mui and Lora H. Mui, *Shops and Shopkeeping in Eighteenth-Century England* (Montreal: McGill–Queen's University Press, 1989), 13–14.

57. Jonathan D. Spence, *The Search for Modern China* (New York: Norton, 1990), 120 ff.

58. Quoted in Chang Hsin-pao, *Commissioner Lin and the Opium War* (Cambridge: Harvard University Press, 1964). See also John King Fairbank, *Trade and Diplomacy on the China Coast* (Cambridge: Harvard University Press, 1953); Maurice Collis, *Foreign Mud* (London: Faber, 1969). A contrary view is put forward by Desmond Platt, who argues that the Anglo-Chinese wars of 1839–42 and 1856–60 were fought simply "to open up the markets of China to world trade." *Finance, Trade and Politics in British Foreign Policy, 1815–1914* (Oxford: Oxford University Press, 1968), 262 ff. It seems to me that this is to take what the diplomats said solely at face value and not to understand either the economic issues at stake or what was happening on the ground.

59. G. Botero, *Relationi Universali* (Venice, 1659), quoted in Cipolla, *Guns and Sails*, 86–87.

60. Moustafa Fahmy, *La Révolution de l'industrie en Égypte et ses conséquences sociales au 19ᵉ siècle, 1800–1850* (Leiden: Brill, 1954).

61. Omar Celal Sarçaa, quoted in Charles Issawi, *The Economic History of the Middle East* (Chicago: University of Chicago Press, 1966), 54–55. Almost identical words were used by an eighteenth-century Portuguese writer. "The English," he said, "produce, sell, and resell everything which is needed in our country. The ancient manufactures of Portugal have been destroyed." Quoted in Cipolla, *Before the Industrial Revolution*, 52.

62. William R. Polk, *The Opening of South Lebanon*, 224.

63. Its use is discussed by Machiavelli in *The Prince* (esp. chap. 18) and *The Discourses* (bk. 2, chaps. 11, 30).

64. The British paid subsidies to the Dutch continuously even earlier, during the reign of Elizabeth, and later when they were fighting Louis XIV—and Louis himself was perhaps the greatest donor of policy-linked subsidies.

65. Allen Guttmann, "Old Sports," *Natural History,* July 1992, 50 ff.

66. Richard J. Barnet and Ronald E. Müller, *Global Reach* (New York: Simon & Schuster, 1974), 60 ff., 81 ff.

67. Richard J. Barnet and John Cavanaugh, *Global Dreams* (New York: Simon & Schuster, 1995), 14.

68. Their remarkable documentary record of work among the American Indian nations and communities in various parts of Asia is housed at Houghton Library of Harvard University; I have discussed aspects of their work in the Middle East in *The Opening of South Lebanon.*

PART V: INTELLIGENCE AND ESPIONAGE

1. Michael J. Barrett in *The Journal of Defense and Diplomacy,* 1984, quoted in Phillip Knightley, *The Second Oldest Profession* (London: Andre Deutsch, 1986), xii.

2. As D. B. Horn, *The British Diplomatic Service* (Oxford: Clarendon, 1961), 259, and the great French student of diplomacy François de Callières, *De la manière de négocier avec les souverains,* trans. A. F. Whyte (1716; reprint, London: Constable, 1919), 26, have written.

3. The figure was put at "at least 80 percent" for French intelligence before World War II by Henri Navarre, quoted in Robert J. Young, "French Military Intelligence and Nazi Germany, 1938–1939," in *Knowing One's Enemies,* ed. Ernest R. May (Princeton: Princeton University Press, 1984), 276. Young says that this figure was independently confirmed for him by British officers.

4. Classical accounts including Thucydides, *History of the Peloponnesian War,* and Plutarch, *The Rise and Fall of Athens,* are full of accounts of betrayals.

5. A. R. Burn, "Persia and the Greeks," in *The Cambridge History of Iran,* ed. Ilya Gershevitch (Cambridge: Cambridge University Press, 1985), 2:300.

6. Sima Qian, *Shi Ji,* trans. Burton Watson as *Records of the Grand Historian,* rev. ed. (New York: Columbia University Press, 1993), 2:231 ff.

7. Peter Wright's book *Spy Catcher* (Richmond, Vict., Australia: William Heinemann, 1987) horrified the British public, which had naively thought that its government, unlike other, more tyrannical governments, did not engage in such activities. I will discuss the counterintelligence aspects of these activities below; here I am talking about their use for foreign intelligence.

8. Christopher Andrew, "Codebreakers and Foreign Offices," in *The Missing Dimension: Governments and Intelligence Communities in the Twentieth Century,* ed. Christopher Andrew and David Dilks (London: Macmillan, 1984), 46.

9. J. A. Brinkman, "Babylonia Under the Assyrian Rule," in *Power and Propaganda,* ed. Mogens Trolle Larsen (Copenhagen: Akademisk Forlag, 1979), 235.

10. Procopius, *Secret History*, trans. G. A. Williamson (Harmondsworth, U.K.: Penguin, 1981), 189–90.

11. There is even a tradition, recounted by Gabriel Ronay in *The Tartar Khan's Englishman* (London: Cassell, 1978), that an unidentified Englishman defected to the Mongols and served them as an intelligence agent to the West in the 1220s. This is apparently based on the confession of an Englishman recorded in 1243 by Mathew Paris and printed in C. Raymond Beazley, *The Texts and Versions of John de Plano Carpini and William de Rubruquis* (London: Hakluyt, 1903).

12. J. R. Hale, "International Relations in the West," in *The New Cambridge Modern History* (Cambridge: Cambridge University Press, 1971), 269.

13. Conyers Read, *Mr. Secretary Walsingham and the Policy of Queen Elizabeth* (Oxford: Clarendon, 1925), 3:293. See also Garrett Mattingly, *Renaissance Diplomacy* (London: Jonathan Cape, 1962), 260.

14. Callières, *Manière de négocier*, 26.

15. Horn, *British Diplomatic Service*, 276.

16. The surviving document has been translated and explained by V. L. Ménage in "The Mission of an Ottoman Secret Agent in France in 1486," *Journal of the Royal Asiatic Society*, 1965.

17. Florence alone had more than sixty firms with agents in the Ottoman capital. Hale, "International Relations in the West," 265.

18. As that shrewd observer King Henry VIII remarked to the Venetian ambassador to London, quoted in Hale, "International Relations in the West," 264.

19. Robert Baden-Powell, *My Adventures as a Spy* (London: Arthur Pearson, 1915), 70.

20. Peter Hopkirk, *The Great Game* (Oxford: Oxford University Press, 1990).

21. Gertrude Schroeder, "Soviet Realities Sans Potemkin," classified "Confidential and No Foreign Dissem[ination]," reprinted in H. Bradford Westerfield, *Inside CIA's Private World* (New Haven: Yale University Press, 1995), 43.

22. Quoted in B. J. Kemp, "Old Kingdom, Middle Kingdom and Second Intermediate Period," in B. G. Trigger et al., *Ancient Egypt : A Social History* (Cambridge: Cambridge University Press, 1983), 162.

23. Livy, *The War with Hannibal*, 23:33. The text of the agreement is given by Polybius, On Roman Imperialism, 7:9. For comments, see J. F. Lazenby, *Hannibal's War* (Warminster: Aris & Phillips, 1978), 169.

24. David Kahn, *The Codebreakers* (New York: Macmillan, 1969), 108–9.

25. Kahn, *The Codebreakers*, 116–17.

26. In the Eisenhower and Kennedy administrations senior officials were often denied access to information that was essential to the performance of their duties, as I learned when a member of the Policy Planning Council. For example, no one—including the administrator, who ranked as an undersecretary of state— in the whole Administration for International Development was officially informed of the military intelligence programs that actually set the levels of aid programs in Turkey, Iran, and Pakistan.

27. Andrew, "Codebreakers and Foreign Offices," 37–38.

28. Bradford Perkins, *The Cambridge History of American Foreign Relations* (Cambridge: Cambridge University Press, 1993), 1:108.

29. Conyers Read (*Mr. Secretary Walsingham,* 3:285) says that there is no contemporary evidence for this feat.

30. British intelligence in France at this time was exceptionally highly developed. See the excellent article by Alfred Cobban, "British Secret Service in France, 1784–1792," *English Historical Review* 69 (1954): 226 ff.

31. Geoffrey Parker, *The Military Revolution* (Cambridge: Cambridge University Press, 1988), 150–51.

32. Gunther Rothenberg, *The Art of Warfare in the Age of Napoleon* (London: Batsford, 1977), 211.

33. For a trip by camel I made from Riyadh, Saudi Arabia, across the Great Nafud Desert to Amman, Jordan, in 1972, I used the best maps then available and found them often inaccurate. They have since been totally remade using satellite imaging along with ground surveys.

34. Possibly first made by Giambattista della Porta in Italy sometime around 1558.

35. They were found to be unstable platforms for observation and were vulnerable to the powerful rifles issued in that war, so they were given up in 1863. See Donald E. Markle, *Spies and Spymasters of the Civil War* (New York: Hippocrene, 1994), 37–38.

36. David Kahn, *Hitler's Spies* (New York: Macmillan, 1978), 115 ff. The U-2 episode was the exception to the norm. On the pilot's story, see Francis Gary Powers, *Operation Overflight* (New York: Tower, 1970).

37. Daniel Dupont, "Up, Up and Away: The U.S. Military Brings Back the Balloon," *Scientific American,* June 1996, 28–29.

38. Plutarch, *The Rise and Fall of Athens,* "Lysander."

39. Rommel himself had previously profited by the German breaking of the code used by the American military attaché in Cairo, but the code had been changed just before El Alamain. See David Kahn, "Codebreaking in World Wars I and II," in Andrew and Dilks, *The Missing Dimension,* 144.

40. See Ralph Bennett, *Ultra in the West* (London: Hutchinson, 1979). When I questioned my cousin, Colonel (later General) James H. Polk, who commanded the advance unit of General Patton's Third Army, on what Ultra had meant to him, he said that he did not then know the source of the intelligence he was given but that when he received it, he was told that it was absolutely accurate, and he found it to be so.

41. The story of the breaking of the German codes is one of the greatest intelligence stories of all time. General Gustave Bertrand, *Enigma, ou la plus énigme de la guerre 1393–1945* (Paris: Plon, 1973) explains how the Polish studies reached the British.

42. Kahn, *The Codebreakers,* 468.

43. It was a long ordeal for Hull, who was so desperately ill with tuberculosis

and diabetes that he could hardly get out of bed. He met with the Japanese ambassador about fifty times in the buildup to Pearl Harbor.

44. Quoted by David Kahn in Andrew and Dilks, *The Missing Dimension*, 147.

45. While a member of the Policy Planning Council, I was deeply involved in the events of that week, later took part in a major U.S. government war game that went over much of the buildup of the crisis, and still later discussed it in detail with Russian officials and academics while lecturing at the Soviet Academy of Sciences' Institute of World Economy and International Affairs.

46. James Rusbridger and Eric Nave, *Betrayal at Pearl Harbor: How Churchill Lured Roosevelt into War* (London: Michael O'Mara, 1991), esp. 261–62. David Kahn casts doubt on this interpretation in "The Intelligence Failure of Pearl Harbor," *Foreign Affairs*, Winter 1991, 149.

47. Livy, *The War with Hannibal*, 24:22.

48. Herodotus, *The Persian Wars*, 5:91, 6:68. Paul Cartledge, in *Sparta and Lakonia: A Regional History 1300–362 B.C.E.* (London: Routledge and Kegan Paul, 1979, 201), comments that the oracle's responses were "plainly intended to discourage resistance."

49. Herodotus, *The Persian Wars*, 7:145–47.

50. Eugen Weber, *The Hollow Years: France in the 1930s* (London: Sinclair-Stevenson, 1995), 178.

51. In the rise to imperial majesty of the Persian Empire, as J. M. Cook has written (*The Persian Empire* [London: Dent, 1983], 106–7), only one significant conquest took place without the help of treachery from within.

52. Mattingly, *Renaissance Diplomacy*, 257 ff.

53. H. R. Roemer, "Timur in Iran," in *The Cambridge History of Iran*, ed. Peter Jackson (Cambridge: Cambridge University Press, 1986), 6:51–52.

54. Dmitri Volkogonov, *Lenin* (New York: Free Press, 1994), 332–33, 145, 146.

55. Curt Gentry, *J. Edgar Hoover: The Man and the Secrets* (New York: Norton, 1991), 314.

56. David Fromkin, "Daring Amateurism," *Foreign Affairs*, January–February 1996, 165.

57. Henri Navarre, quoted in May, ed., *Knowing One's Enemies*, 277.

58. Roger Hilsman, "Does the CIA Still Have a Role?" *Foreign Affairs*, September–October 1995, 107–8.

59. *The Secret History of the Mongols* (San Francisco: North Point, 1984), 165.

60. *Kautilya's Arthasastra*, 7th ed., trans. Rudrapina Shamasastry (Mysore, India: Mysore Printing and Publishing, 1961), 32–33.

61. From the Siasset Nameh as quoted in W. Barthold, *Turkestan Down to the Mongol Invasion* (London: Oxford University Press, 1928), 306.

62. Fromkin, "Daring Amateurism," 171.

63. Gerald Barrier, "The Punjab Disturbances," in *Peasant Resistance in India, 1858–1914*, ed. David Hardiman (New Delhi: Oxford University Press, 1993), 227.

64. Thomas Hughes, *The Fate of Facts in a World of Men* (New York: Foreign Policy Association, 1976), 8.

65. Donald Cameron Watt, "British Intelligence and the Coming of the Second World War in Europe," in May, ed., *Knowing One's Enemies*, 263.

PART VI: DIPLOMACY

1. Sir Nevile Bland, *Satow's Guide to Diplomatic Practice* (London: Longman, 1968), 1.

2. In the original Latin, "Legatus est vir bonus peregre missus ad mentiendum Reipublicae causa," there was no pun: it translates as "to tell lies," but in the better-known English version there is a play on the word *lie*, meaning both to "tell lies" and to "reside" or "sleep." Almost the same words (as the English) were later used by the eminent Victorian historian William Stubbs. Apologists have tried to explain away the less attractive part of the Wotton/Stubbs pun. But there was no pun in the way it was put by King Louis XI of France; Louis, who made more use of ambassadors than any European monarch before him, bluntly instructed them on dealing with foreign princes: "If they lie to you," he ordered, "lie still more to them." Quoted in David J. Hill, *A History of Diplomacy in the International Development of Europe* (London: Longmans Green, 1906), 2:153. As Hill comments, "It was the example of Louis XI, even more than the precepts formulated a quarter of a century afterward by Machiavelli, that made the 'raison d'etat' the foundation of European politics for centuries."

3. I deal with this splitting apart of groups more fully in chapter 27.

4. The "Comanche" called themselves the *Nemene*. Like most tribal names, *Nemene* meant "the People." *Comanche* comes into English through Spanish from the Ute Indian language. In Ute, *comanche* means "enemy." Similarly, the "Apache" called themselves *Dine*, which also means "the People," whereas *apache* is the Zuni Indian word for "enemy."

5. Abdur-Rahman Ibn Khaldun, *Al-Muqaddimah*, 2:7. My translation.

6. Giovanni Pettinato, *Ebla: Un impero incisa nell'Argilla* (Milan: Mondardori, 1979), 96 ff.

7. It is known to us in two versions since it was preserved both on clay tablets found in the ruins of the Hittite capital in Anatolia, in cuneiform, and, in hieroglyphs, on two Egyptian temples. International relations had already developed a highly articulated diplomatic tradition, and this treaty, apparently for the first time, set up means for authentication and so may be said to be the earliest document allowing for the study of what would come to be called diplomatics.

8. Quoted from *Keilschrifturkunden aus Boghazköi* (Leipzig and Berlin, 1921–63) in A. Goetz, "The Hittites and Syria (1300–1200 B.C.)," in *The Cambridge Ancient History*, ed. I. E. S. Edwards et al. (Cambridge: Cambridge University Press, 1975), vol. 2, pt. 2, p. 258.

9. Hans G. Gütterbock, "The Hittites and the Aegean World: Part I. The Ahhiyawa Problem Reconsidered," *American Journal of Archaeology* 87 (1983): 136.

10. Cho-yun Hsu, *Ancient China in Transition* (Stanford: Stanford University Press, 1965), 3, 26, 53.

11. See Ying-shih Yü, *Trade and Expansion in Han China* (Stanford: Stanford University Press, 1967), 10 ff. In his "Han Foreign Relations" in *The Cambridge History of China*, ed. Denis Twitchett (Cambridge: Cambridge University Press, 1987), Ying-shih Yü points out that dynastic marriages that were aimed to create "harmonious kinship" (in Chinese, *ho-ch'in*) were undertaken from 198 B.C.E. (386 ff).

12. The *Shi ji* of Sima Qian, bk. 10, translated by Burton Watson as *Records of the Grand Historian*, rev. ed. (New York: Columbia University Press, 1993), 1: 304.

13. Wolfram Eberhard, *Conquerors and Rulers* (Leiden: Brill, 1970), 119.

14. See, for example, R. B. Mowat, *A History of European Diplomacy, 1451– 1789* (London: Oxford University Press, 1928), 38 ff., on marriage ties among the ruling families of Spain, Scotland, England, and France.

15. It appears that the U-2 exception came about in part because Soviet premier Nikita Khrushev was under great pressure from his own military to overcome their shame at being unable to stop the high-flying American planes. They had developed a missile of which they were proud and, for using it successfully, wanted credit.

16. Polybius, *The Rise of the Roman Empire*, trans. Ian Scott-Kilvert (Harmondsworth: Penguin, 1979), 5:103–4.

17. Bradford Perkins, *The Creation of a Republican Empire*, vol. 1 of *The Cambridge History of American Foreign Relations* (Cambridge: Cambridge University Press, 1993), 56 ff.

18. "Five or six commercial agreements with major powers, some thought, should be about the limit." Ibid., 77.

19. Lien-sheng Yang, "Historical Notes on the Chinese World Order," in *The Chinese World Order*, ed. John King Fairbank (Cambridge: Harvard University Press, 1968), 27.

20. The idea of Islam being imposed on conquered peoples dies hard but is mainly a myth. In fact, because non-Muslims paid an extra tax, Muslims were loath to have them convert. Africa and Southeast Asia were converted mainly by merchants. And in India, lower-Caste Hindus and Untouchables have found the egalitarianism of Islam alluring, as have many American Blacks.

21. Itamar Singer, "Western Anatolia in the Thirteenth Century B.C. According to the Hittite Sources," *Anatolian Studies* 33 (1983): 212.

22. J. W. McCrindel, trans. and ed., *Ancient India as Described by Magasthnes and Arrian* (Calcutta: Chuckervertty, Chatterjee), 1926.

23. The *Arthasastra* was not rediscovered until the early years of this century. Since then, it has been published in various editions. I have used the edition translated by Rudrapina Shamasastry (Mysore, India: Mysore Printing and Publishing, 1961), 7th ed. Among recent studies of it are M. V. Krishna Rao, *The Techniques of Statecraft* (Delhi: Munshiram Manoharlal, 1987).

24. In *The Techniques of Statecraft: A Study of Kautilya's Arthasastra* (Delhi: Atma Ram, 1987), 41, reflecting modern Indian ideas, Aradhana Parmar (rather foolishly) turns him into a sort of Fabian social philosopher whose "state resembles the modern 'welfare state.'"

25. The work has been handed down on the basis of a Chinese version prepared during the Ming dynasty. Either that version or the original Mongol text influenced works by later historians in Persian and Arabic. I have used the edition prepared by Paul Kahn, which is based on the translation of Francis Woodman Cleaves (San Francisco: North Point, 1984).

26. Inside the U.S. government, for example, are the Bureau of Intelligence and Research, the Office of Politico-Military Affairs, the Policy Planning Council, the Office of International Security Affairs, the U.S. National Intelligence Board, the staff of the National Security Council, and, supported by the government, the RAND Corporation and various other research bodies; in the former Soviet Union, there are various institutes of the Academy of Sciences, notably the Institute of World Economy and International Affairs.

27. Of which the most famous are the American Foreign Policy Association, the Council on Foreign Relations, and the British Royal Institute of International Affairs.

28. I will discuss this development below but here I will merely mention that the 1959 National Defense Educational Act of 1959 together with support from various foundations brought about the creation of scores of university programs that supported hundreds of specialists and serviced tens of thousands of students each year.

29. Such as *Foreign Affairs, Foreign Policy, World Politics,* and *The Journal of Conflict Resolution,* to name just a few.

30. For example, Thucydides, *History of the Peloponnesian War,* 1:1:31.

31. Herodotus, *The Persian Wars,* 8:140–44.

32. Thucydides, *History of the Peloponnesian War,* 1:3:73.

33. Ibid., 13:21.

34. Perkins, *Creation of a Republican Empire,* 78.

35. Henry Kittredge Norton, "Foreign Office Organization," *Annals of the American Academy of Political and Social Science,* 1929:20.

36. Dozens of studies of needed reforms have been undertaken, of which the more publicized are the 1947 Hoover Commission, the 1953 Herter Committee, and the 1970 Peterson Task Force, which referred to "two decades of atrophy" and commented that "conditions of the profession [the fact that it is 'a closed hierarchical professional corps'] engender a clan mentality, a sense of detachment from the physical environment of the moment and from the community of ordinary Americans as a whole."

37. Zara Steiner, *The Foreign Office and Foreign Policy, 1898–1914* (Cambridge: Cambridge University Press, 1969), ix.

38. S. F. Nadel, *The Nuba* (London: Oxford University Press, 1947), 159, 259, 302, 453. The term that Nadel translates as "blood brothership" comes from

the Arabic *tawassal,* which means to have a connection or to gain access to someone. The ambassadors were those who had "access."

39. Raganar Numelin, *The Beginnings of Diplomacy: A Sociological Study of Intertribal and International Relations* (Copenhagen: Ejnar Munksgaard, 1950), chap. 4, describes use of a *churinga,* or "sacred staff," among the Australian aboriginals and similar symbolic equipment among Ghanaian tribes and even in Ireland.

40. Thucydides, *History of the Peloponnesian War,* 2:7:67; Frank Adcock and D. J. Mosley, *Diplomacy in Ancient Greece* (London: Thames and Hudson, 1975), 152–53; Plutarch, "Timoleon," 39; Yvon Garlan, *War in the Ancient World* (London: Chatto & Windus, 1975), 44.

41. Xenophon, *Hellenica,* 3:4:19; Thucydides, *History of the Peloponnesian War,* 1:2:29, 1:5:130, 2:6:2. See also W. Kendrick Pritchett, *The Greek State at War, Part 1* (Berkeley: University of California Press, 1971), of which chapter 3 of volume 1 deals with booty.

42. Thucydides, *History of the Peloponnesian War,* 5:16:1, 79.

43. Ibid., 1:5.125.

44. Xenophon, *Hellenica;* 2:2:19, 7:1:1. Thucydides notes instances when embassies were accorded full powers.

45. Herodotus, *The Persian Wars,* 7:148 ff.; Xenophon, *Hellenica,* 2:2:19, 7:1:1. See also Plutarch, "Nicias," 10, and "Alcibiades," 14.

46. As in the truce between Athens and Sparta in 423 B.C.E., which specified free passage to both heralds and embassies. Thucydides, *History of the Peloponnesian War,* 4:14:118.

47. Herodotus, *The Persian Wars,* 7:133 ff.; Thucydides, *History of the Peloponnesian War,* 3:10:72–73.

48. Thucydides, *History of the Peloponnesian War,* 2:7:67. See also Adcock and Mosley, *Diplomacy in Ancient Greece,*176.

49. Herodotus, *The Persian Wars,* 6:107. If this is bizarre, it is not unique. Many of the "messengers" or ambassadors of primitive African societies were also runners.

50. Harold Nicolson, *The Evolution of Diplomatic Method* (London: Constable, 1954), 34.

51. Ta-tuan Ch'en, "Investiture of Liu-Ch'iu Kings in the Ch'ing Period," in Fairbank, ed., *The Chinese World Order,* 156–57.

52. Thucydides, *History of the Peloponnesian War,* 5:16:59–60; Russell Meiggs, *The Athenian Empire* (Oxford: Oxford University Press, 1979), 145–46.

53. Meiggs, *Athenian Empire,* 165, 211-219.

54. Livy, *The Early History of Rome,* 1:32; Maurice R. Davie, *The Evolution of War* (New Haven: Yale University Press, 1929), app. L.

55. Polybius, *On Roman Imperialism,* 3:15. Although Polybius is our best source, we must evaluate his reportage with respect to his viewpoint: he saw Rome as the ultimate power of his time, a nation against which no one could prevail and with whom only the irresponsible would contend. Rome had a right deriving from power, even if cruelly used, whereas opponents, even when acting with jus-

tice, could create only chaos and therefore were to be opposed. Hannibal was seen as acting in "all the heat of youth," whereas the dour Romans were pillars of authority.

56. Louis Bréhier, *Le monde Byzantin: Les institutions de l'empire byzantin* (Paris: Albin Michel, 1949), 229, my translation.

57. Edward Gibbon, *The Decline and Fall of the Roman Empire*, chap. 52.

58. I will discuss the "reconquest" from another angle in chapter 28.

59. Reported in Ruy Gonzáles de Clavijo, *Historia del Gran Tamorlan e itinerario y enarración del viaje y relacién de la Embaxada que Rue Goncalez de Clavijo le hizo, por mandado del Rey D. Henrique Tercero de Castilla* (Seville, 1582).

60. These events are dealt with in Speros Vryonis's brilliant *Decline of Medieval Hellenism in Asia Minor and the Process of Islamization from the Eleventh through the Fifteenth Centuries* (Berkeley: University of California Press, 1971), and in Claude Cahen, *Pre-Ottoman Turkey* (London: Sidgwick and Jackson, 1968).

61. V. Minorsky, "The Middle East in Western Politics in the 13th, 14th and 15th Centuries," *Asian Affairs* 10 (1979): 427 ff.

62. Donald E. Queller, *The Office of the Ambassador in the Middle Ages* (Princeton: Princeton University Press, 1967), 90–91.

63. Paul Pelliot, "Les Mongols et la Papaute," quoted in Bertold Spuler, *History of the Mongols* (London: Routledge and Kegan Paul, 1972), 68–69.

64. Spuler, *History of the Mongols*, 141–44.

65. On which see John Wansbrough, "A Mamluk Ambassador to Venice in 913/1507," *Bulletin of the School of Oriental and African Studies of the University of London* 26 (1963): 503.

66. S. A. Skilliter, "The Organization of the First English Embassy in 1583," *American Historical Review* 74 (1968): 159.

67. See Melvyn P. Leffer, "Inside Enemy Archives," *Foreign Affairs*, July–August 1996, 131.

68. I speak from personal experience.

69. J. R. Hale, "International Relations in the West," in *The New Cambridge Modern History* (Cambride: Cambridge University Press, 1971), 266 ff.

70. See Conyers Read, *Mr. Secretary Walsingham and the Policy of Queen Elizabeth* (Oxford: Clarendon, 1925), 2:194, speaking of King James of Scotland.

71. Donald E. Queller, *The Office of Ambassador in the Middle Ages* (Princeton: Princeton University Press, 1967), 90.

72. As portrayed in the famous "manual" by Baldesar Castiglione, *The Book of the Courtier* (New York: Doubleday, 1959).

73. See D. B. Horn, *The British Diplomatic Service, 1689–1789* (Oxford: Oxford University Press, 1961), 56.

74. Ibid., 63. British ambassadors in Constantinople before 1809 made nearly 50 percent of their income in this way.

75. C. G. Picavet, *La diplomatie française au temps de Louis XIV (1661–1715)* (Paris: Librairie Félix Alcan, 1930), 83; Horn, *British Diplomatic Service*, 64, 88.

76. Numelin, *Beginnings of Diplomacy*, 125–26. C. T. Onions, in *The Oxford Dictionary of English Etymology*, gives the Old English form *ambeht*, meaning "servant" or "messenger."

77. Laurence Lockhart, "European Contacts with Persia, 1350–1736," in *The Cambridge History of Iran*, ed. Peter Jackson (Cambridge: Cambridge University Press, 1986), 6:392.

78. Mark Mancall, "The Ch'ing Tribute System," in Fairbank, ed., *The Chinese World Order*, 65.

79. David Jayne Hill, *A History of Diplomacy in the International Development of Europe* (London: Longmans, Green, 1911), 456–57.

80. Quoted in Horn, *British Diplomatic Service*, 28.

81. Ogier Ghiselin de Busbecq, *Life and Letters*, trans. C. T. Forster and F. H. B. Daniell (London: C. K. Paul, 1881).

82. Quoted in Stanford J. Shaw, *History of the Ottoman Empire and Modern Turkey* (Cambridge: Cambridge University Press, 1976), 1:163.

83. J. R. Hale, "International Relations in the West," 269–70.

84. François de Callières, *The Practice of Diplomacy*, trans. A. F. Whyte (London: Constable, 1919), 27, 68, 50; originally published as *De la manière de négocier avec les souverains* (Paris, 1716).

85. When Francis was captured by Charles V at the battle of Pavia and imprisoned in Spain in 1525, he smuggled a letter to Sultan Suleiman asking for Ottoman action against Charles. Suleiman replied with just a flowery letter, but when Francis's ambassador shrewdly warned Suleiman that the war between Charles and Francis was not just a European affair since what Charles really aimed at was world domination, the Ottomans launched an army into the Balkans, overwhelmed the Hungarians at the battle of Mohács, and threatened Vienna.

86. This arrangement, although probably unknown to the members of the first United States Congress, was similar to the duties entrusted to the newly founded Department of State, which handled correspondence with the states as well as foreign countries.

87. On his diplomacy with England and the spread of the Italian regime see Hill, *History of Diplomacy*, 153 ff., 363 ff.

88. Heralds were still widely used in Europe in the late Renaissance. Among their duties then were officiating at tournaments, arranging truces in battles, and ransoming captives after the fighting had ended. The latter was particularly the function of the Spanish *alfaqueque* (in Arabic, *fakkak*) in the numerous wars between the Muslims and the Christians in medieval Spain. And violation of their "sacred character" was regarded as tantamount to an act of war. For example, when the pro-French inhabitants of Lugano in 1511 seized and killed a herald, the neighboring Swiss were so shocked that they declared war on the French. See Mowat, *History of European Diplomacy*, 35.

89. See Numelin, *Beginnings of Diplomacy*, 140–41 (based on J. Dawson, *The Australian Aborigines* [Melbourne, 1887], 72).

90. Callières, *Practice of Diplomacy*, 68.

91. Harold Nicholson, *The Congress of Vienna* (London: Constable, 1946), 143, quoting Friedrich von Gentz.

92. Since I have discussed them in detail in *The Arab World Today* (Cambridge: Harvard University Press, 1991, chaps. 8–13), I will not duplicate the story here.

93. Ray Stannard Baker, *Woodrow Wilson and World Settlement, Written from His Unpublished and Personal Material* (New York: Doubleday, Page, 1922), 2:190.

94. Baker, *Woodrow Wilson*, 1:180.

95. H. W. V. Temperley, ed., *A History of the Peace Conference of Paris* (London: Oxford University Press, 1920), 1:263.

96. Quoted in Arthur S. Link, *Wilson: Campaigns for Progressivism and Peace* (Princeton: Princeton University Press, 1965), 275.

97. Quoted in ibid., 274.

98. Charles Webster, *The Study of Nineteenth Century Diplomacy* (London: G. Bell, 1915), 379.

99. William Foster, *England's Quest of Eastern Trade* (London: A. & C. Black, 1933), 68 ff.

100. Denis Wright, *The English among the Persians* (London: Heinemann, 1977), 5–7. Ambassador Harford Brydges-Jones tells his own story in *An Account of the Transactions of His Majesty's Mission to the Court of Persia in the Years 1807–11* (1834; reprint, Tehran: Imperial Organization for Social Services, 1976).

101. Quoted by A. F. Whyte in his introduction to Callières, *Practice of Diplomacy*, xix.

102. Callières, *Practice of Diplomacy*, 39–40.

103. Ibid., 9.

104. Horn, *British Diplomatic Service*, 96.

105. See, for example, a report by the British ambassador to Spain to King James I of England on this matter, quoted by Charles H. Carter in *The Western European Powers, 1500–1700*, ed. Charles H. Carter (Ithaca, N.Y.: Cornell University Press, 1971), 275–76. Even as late as 1962, when the author, then a government official, called on the shah of Iran in the company of the American ambassador, the ambassador was primarily concerned with whether we should bow or shake hands.

106. 23 November 1912, as quoted by A. F. Whyte in his introduction to Callières, *Practice of Diplomacy*, x.

107. Quoted in Horn, *British Diplomatic Service*, 127 ff.

108. Charles Webster, *The Art and Practice of Diplomacy* (London: Chatto & Windus, 1961), 2.

109. Churchill had proposed to Stalin in the summer of 1944 (without informing President Roosevelt) that the Soviet Union should have a "controlling interest" in Romania and Bulgaria while Britain be agreed to have a similar position in Greece and Yugoslavia. See Chester Wilmot, *The Struggle for Europe* (London: Collins, 1952), 636–37.

110. See Peter Hopkirk, *Setting the East Ablaze: Lenin's Dream of an Empire in Asia* (Oxford: Oxford University Press, 1986).

111. Perhaps the best available book is still Henry S. Bradsher, *Afghanistan and the Soviet Union* (Durham, N.C.: Duke Press Policy Studies, 1983).

112. Especially with the Stinger surface-to-air missile, which more or less overcame the great advantage given to Soviet troops by their helicopter gunships.

113. Thucydides, *History of the Peloponnesian War,* 5:91.

114. See H. J. Mackinder, *Democratic Ideals and Reality* (1919; reprint, Harmondsworth, U.K.: Penguin, 1942). Mackinder believed that "the rule of the world still rests on force . . . let us be rid of cant: Democracy must reckon with Reality" (150–51).

115. Thucydides, *History of the Peloponnesian War,* 5:8.

116. Harold Nicholson, *The Evolution of Diplomatic Method* (London: Constable, 1954), 8.

117. See James Brown Scott, *The Spanish Origin of International Law* (Oxford: Oxford University Press, 1934).

118. Garrett Mattingly, *Renaissance Diplomacy* (London: Jonathan Cape, 1962), 283.

119. Hugo Grotius, *Three Books on the Laws of War and Peace,* trans. Francis W. Kelsey (Oxford: Oxford University Press, 1925).

120. Mattingly, *Renaissance Diplomacy,* 293–94.

121. Quoted by James Brown Scott in his introduction to Grotius, *Three Books on the Laws of War and Peace,* xxxv.

122. Scott, *Spanish Origin,* xxxv.

123. On which see Telford Taylor, *The Anatomy of the Nuremberg Trials* (New York: Knopf, 1992).

124. Hannah Arendt, *On Violence* (New York: Harcourt Brace, 1969), 5.

PART VII: GETTING RID OF THE ALIEN

1. The "L" poem of Shanfara has been reprinted in numerous editions in Arabic (e.g., in *Al-Mujani al-Hadith* [Beirut: Munashif al-Arab ash-Sharqiyah, 1946], 1:3) and has been translated into English by J. W. Redhouse in *The L-Poem of the Arabs* (London: Trübner, 1881).

2. As I did in *The Arab World Today* (Cambridge: Harvard University Press, 1991), 16.

3. Joseph H. Greenberg, *Language, Culture and Communication* (Stanford: Stanford University Press, 1971).

4. Some believe it is related to Altaic and Dravidian. See K. H. Menges, "Dravidian and Altaic," *Anthropos* 72 (1977): 129 ff.; David W. McAlpin, "Toward Proto-Elamo-Dravidian," *Language* 50 (1974): 89 ff.

5. On Etruscan see Francisco Adrados, "Etruscan as an IE Anatolian (but not Hittite) language," *Journal of Indo-European Studies* 17 (1989): 363 ff.

6. The latest is provided by Philip E. Ross in "Hard Words," *Scientific American,* April 1991, 69.

7. Luigi Luca Cavalli-Sforza has been a pioneer in this field; the clearest

presentation of his work is "Genes, Peoples and Language," *Scientific American*, November 1991, 104 ff. Also see his *The Great Human Diasporas* (Reading, Mass.: Addison-Wesley, 1995).

8. Discussion of the date of domestication of the horse may seem a recondite issue, the kind scholars love to discuss, but it set off a social and military revolution. Until recently, most scholars believed that it did not come about until the chariot was invented in about 1800 B.C.E. and that the bit (which was thought essential to cavalry) came much later. Now, because of studies of the teeth of horses dating from 4000 B.C.E. and found in the Ukraine, we know that riders then used antler cheekpieces to control their mounts. See David Anthony, Dimitri Telegin, and Dorcas Brown, "The Origin of Horseback Riding," *Scientific American*, December 1991, 44 ff. Even without this discovery, the use of horses for war with little or no equipment comes as no surprise. The Great Plains Indians, probably like the Scythians, rode bareback and without bridles or stirrups. In my own cavalry training, I was made to ride over a difficult obstacle course without bridle or stirrups. Of course, having these pieces of equipment was an advantage that made possible, thousands of years later, armored "heavy" cavalry, where the rider used the weight of the horse to thrust a lance. On these inventions see Lynn White Jr., "The Crusades and the Technological Trust of the West," in *War, Technology, and Society in the Middle East*, ed. Vernon J. Parry and Malcolm E. Yapp (London: Oxford University Press, 1975), 97 ff.

9. For a stimulating discussion of these events, see Robert Drews, *The Coming of the Greeks: Indo-European Conquests in the Aegean and the Near East* (Princeton: Princeton University Press, 1988).

10. Plutarch, "Pericles," in *The Rise and Fall of Athens*, trans. Ian Scott-Kilvert (Harmondsworth, U.K.: Penguin, 1960), 177.

11. See Plutarch, *Fall of the Roman Republic*, "Gaius Marius," 31; and A. N. Sherwin-White, *Roman Foreign Policy in the East* (London: Duckworth, 1984), 240 ff.

12. I draw much of the following information from James Duffy, *Portuguese Africa* (Cambridge: Harvard University Press, 1959); Duffy, *Portugal in Africa* (Cambridge: Harvard University Press, 1962); Robert Harms, *River of Wealth, River of Sorrow* (New Haven: Yale University Press, 1981); Basil Davidson, *The African Slave Trade* (Boston: Little, Brown, 1961); James Rawley, *The Trans-Atlantic Slave Trade* (New York: Norton, 1981); Daniel Mannix and Malcolm Cowley, *Black Cargoes* (New York: Viking, 1962); Richard S. Dunn, *Sugar and Slaves* (New York: Norton, 1972); Herbert Aptheker, *American Negro Slave Revolts* (New York: International, 1941[?]); Melville J. Herskovits, *The Myth of the Negro Past* (Boston: Beacon, 1942); Howard Jones, *Mutiny on the 'Amistad': The Saga of a Slave Revolt and Its Impact on American Abolition, Law and Diplomacy* (Oxford: Oxford University Press, 1987).

13. Dale Peterson and Jane Goodall, *Visions of Caliban: On Chimpanzees and People* (Boston: Houghton Mifflin, 1993), 14–15.

14. I am indebted to Hugh Tinker's *A New System of Slavery: The Export of Indian Labour Overseas, 1830–1920* (London: Oxford University Press, 1974) for this and the following information.

15. For contemporary chronicles giving the Jewish version of these events, particularly in Germany, see Shlomo Eidelberg, ed., *The Jews and the Crusaders* (Madison: University of Wisconsin Press, 1977).

16. H. W. V. Temperley, *A History of the Peace Conference of Paris* (London: Oxford University Press, 1924), 6:26.

17. Pre-Islamic Arabic poetry is full of descriptions of starvation, as are later travelers' accounts. See also A. M. Khazanov, *Nomads and the Outside World* (Cambridge: Cambridge University Press, 1984), 69 ff. Despite the propensity of settled peoples to think of them as vast "hordes," their ecosystem would not have allowed the congregation of large numbers of people.

18. The *Puranas*, like the Persian *Shahnameh*, are books of kings. They set the scene for the national epics, the *Mahabharata* and the *Ramayana*. They are far from reliable historical documents. They are thought not to have been composed even orally until centuries after the Aryan invasions.

19. The segregating aspects of the caste system are discussed in Mary Douglas, *Purity and Danger* (London: Routledge and Kegan Paul, 1985), esp. chap. 7. See also M. N. Srinivas, *Religion and Society among the Coorgs of South India* (Oxford: Oxford University Press, 1952), 24 ff.

20. As Herwig Wolfram writes in *History of the Goths* (Berkeley: University of California Press, 1988), "the anti-Jewish legislation of Visigothic Spain codified frightful excesses of hate" (234).

21. In a treaty of 1069 (quoted in Richard Fletcher, *Moorish Spain* [Berkeley: University of California Press, 1992], 99), the Muslim ruler of Zaragoza promised to deliver to the ruler of the little Basque state of Navarre a thousand gold pieces a month so that the two rulers would "both be bound together in one brotherhood."

22. The term is of uncertain origin. See the excellent work by L. P. Harvey, *Islamic Spain, 1250 to 1500* (Chicago: University of Chicago Press, 1990).

23. Given their superior skills, the Muslim refugees created what L. P. Harvey calls "a medieval economic miracle" in Granada.

24. I am indebted to Professor L. P. Harvey for this and subsequent supplementary information in a personal communication.

25. Those who chose exile went primarily to such Muslim areas as North Africa or the Ottoman Empire. Those who converted put themselves under the authority of the Inquisition, on which the classic study is Henry Charles Lea, *The Inquisition of the Middle Ages* (London: Macmillan, 1887–80); Edward Peters, *Inquisition* (Berkeley: University of Calfornia Press, 1989) is both more modern and wider in scope. Benzion Netanyahu, *The Origins of the Inquisition in Fifteenth Century Spain* (New York: Random House, 1995) focuses on the legal background.

26. Roger Boase, "The Morisco Expulsion and Diaspora: An Example of Racial and Religious Intolerance," in *Cultures in Contact in Medieval Spain*, ed. David Hook and Barry Taylor (London: King's College, 1990), 10.

27. Based on information from his Marrano or Ottoman Jewish adviser, Sultan Selim II began an active diplomacy with France, the Spanish Netherlands, and probably (covertly) with the Spanish Muslims against Hapsburg Spain. On this see

Andew C. Hess, "The Moriscos: An Ottoman Fifth Column in Sixteenth Century Spain," *American Historical Review* 74 (1968), and *The Forgotten Frontier: A History of the Sixteenth-Century Ibero-African Frontier* (Chicago: University of Chicago Press, 1978), esp. 87 ff.

28. Boase, "The Morisco Expulsion," 11.

29. Ibid., 12–13.

30. Estimates for the native population of the New World have been revised upward by modern research methods so that a reasonable guess today is about 100 million before the Spanish invasion. See the summary of studies in David E. Stannard, *American Holocaust* (Oxford: Oxford University Press, 1992), 266 ff., 341–42.

31. Quoted from *Writings of Thomas Jefferson* (1:340–41) in Francis Paul Prucha, *American Indian Policy* (Cambridge: Harvard University Press, 1962), 140–41. Jefferson's doctrine was essentially confirmed by a series of decisions by the Supreme Court including *Fletcher v. Peck* in 1810 and *Johnson v. McIntosh* in 1823.

32. Prucha, *American Indian Policy*, 264–65.

33. *Cherokee Nation v. Georgia*, United States Supreme Court, 1931, 5 Peters 1.

34. Quoted in Francis Paul Prucha, ed., *Documents of United States Indian Policy* (Lincoln: University of Nebraska Press, 1975), 60.

35. Quoted in ibid., 242.

36. The best known was a newspaper editor from Georgia by the name of Samuel Worcester, but he, along with a number of missionaries, was arrested and sentenced by a Georgia court to four years of hard labor. When his case came before the Supreme Court, Chief Justice John Marshall, speaking for the Court, overturned the conviction, but Georgia at first refused to obey, so Worcester stayed in prison for months. These were early days for the new republic, and the power of the Supreme Court had not yet been fully accepted. President Jackson is said to have remarked, "Justice Marshall has decided. Now let him enforce his decision."

37. Quoted in George Schultz, *An American Canaan* (Norman: University of Oklahoma Press, 1972), 86.

38. E. Adamson Hoebel, *The Law of Primitive Man* (1954; reprint, New York: Atheneum, 1979), 129–31; Frank Gilbert Roe, *The Indian and the Horse* (Norman: University of Oklahoma Press, 1955), chap. 12.

39. For the incoming whites, the buffalo was a convenient fertilizer that the farmers needed to turn pasture into farm. In Kansas alone the bones of an estimated 31 million buffalo were sold as fertilizer in the 13 years after 1868. Buffalo skins were even more sought after. In Texas, in just December 1877 and January 1878, hunters killed and skinned more than 100,000 buffalo. A skin fetched more than a week's wages for a skilled craftsman, so the hunt became a sort of gold rush.

40. Stannard, *American Holocaust*, 242, 335.

41. Thomas Hobbes, *Leviathan*, 1:13.

42. John Locke, *An Essay Concerning the True Original, Extent and End of Civil Government*, 3, "Of the State of Nature."

43. From a Lebanese Druze village whose history I portrayed in *The Opening of South Lebanon* (Cambridge: Harvard University Press, 1963), the first migrants had established a pied-à-terre in Cincinnati, so those who went later invariably went first to that city.

44. Paul John Frandsen, "Egyptian Imperialism," in *Power and Propaganda*, ed. Mogens Trolle Larsen (Copenhagen: Akademisk Forlag, 1979), 169.

45. Wolfram Eberhard, *Conquerors and Rulers: Social Forces in Medieval China* (Leiden: Brill, 1970), 28–31.

46. Herrlee Creel, *The Origins of Statecraft in China* (Chicago: University of Chicago Press, 1970), 44–45.

47. Dante is the best known of the "spokesmen" for the new cultures, his *Divina Commedia* establishing a high status for Italian and his *De vulgari eloquentia* (in Latin) analyzing it, but there were many others, including the troubadours who wrote in the "national" language of Provence, Langue d'Oc.

48. Quoted in Theodore Zeldin, *France 1848–1945: Intellect and Pride* (Oxford: Oxford University Press), 13–14.

INDEX

Abbas, Shah (Safavid Persian ruler), 254

Abbasid caliphate. *See* Islamic states, caliphates

Abu'l-Fida' (Arab geographer), 132

Achaemenian Persian Empire, 109

Adams, John (in Continental Congress), on trade, 193

Afghanistan
refugees in Pakistan, 271
resistance encouraged, 271–72
Soviet intervention, 270–72

Africa. *See* Money; Slaves, slavery; Tribes, African

Agriculture, first practiced at Mureybet, 39–40

Ahhiyawa (Mycenaea), 221

Aid to less-developed countries, 164

Ainu (original Japanese people), 316

Al-Andalus (Muslim Spain), 149, 299–300

Alexander I (tsar of Russia), 259

Alexander the Great (king of Macedon), 109

Almohads (African dynasty), 300

Almoravids (Berber dynasty), 300

American Indians
biological warfare against, 308
citizenship, 310
clash with settlers, 308, 348n. 39
coups among, 77–78
Indian Rights Association, 309
Indian Territory (Oklahoma), 308
land, 309–10
migration routes, cut off by army, 308
names to be changed, 310
nation, attempt to form a new, 308

policy of French, British, and U.S. government toward, 304
population, 308, 348n. 30
removal, 306–7
reservations, 308–10
See also Tribes, American Indian

Amorites (Syrian nomads), 97, 295

Amritsar massacre (by British in India), 107

Anatolia, 137–38, 247, 292

Angeloi. See Diplomats

Angleton, James Jesus (CIA counterintelligence chief), 211

Anschluss, 122

Anthropology, origins of, 26–27

Apartheid, in India, 104

Aragon, 299, 301

Arbitration, 141, 273

Arendt, Hannah (American scholar), 278

Arghun Khan (Mongol ruler of Ilkhans of Persia), 249

Aristotle, 313

Armed forces, 76
conscription: Assyrian, 85; Chinese, 81; Mesopotamian, 84
cost of, 120, 123–24, 327n. 22
divisions: cavalry, 82, 85, 108–10; infantry, basis of Chinese armies, 81; sappers, early Assyrian development, 85
mercenaries, 93–96; *condottiere* (medieval Italy), 123
militias: possible origin in Mesopotamia, 83–84; use by Assyria, 96; Xerxes' force against Greece, 96
rearmament, German, 121

Armed forces (*continued*)
  size of, 81, 93, 116, 123–24
  units: *Landwehr* (Prussian national
    guard), 118, 226; Luftwaffe, 121; na-
    vies, creation and growth of, 113–14;
    Prussian/German army, 118–22; Red
    Army, rebuilt by Germans, 121; Royal
    Air Force (RAF), 121; Schutz Staffeln
    (SS), 95–96, 122; Wehrmacht, 95,
    122
  "volunteers," 96
Arms
  gun control, attempts at, 113
  gunpowder, 113, 117
  industry, expansion of, 112–15, 124
  trade, 112, 124–25, 164
  See also Weapons
Aryans (Indo-Europeans), 295–98
  Arya-varta (Aryan homeland), 297
  suppression of Dravidian speakers,
    296–97
'Asabiyah concept of social unity, 218
Assassination attempts, 207
Associations, quasi-governmental
  Mayflower Compact, 312
  merchants in ancient world, 142, 312
Assyria
  displacement of citizens by mercenaries,
    86
  early relations with Hittites, 229–30
  empire, 84–85
  fall of, 87
  homeland, small area in north Iraq, 84
  military organization, 85
  terror and propaganda, 85, 86–87
  veterans, social policy toward, 86
Ataturk/Mustafa Kemal, 292
Aztec rulers of Mexico, 83

Bailey, Col. F. M. (British agent), 185
Baker, Ray Stannard (spokesman for
  Woodrow Wilson), 261
Balance of payments
  English with China, 158
  European early modern, 153
Barcelona, 299
Barnet, Richard J. (American writer),
  168
Bartolomé de Las Casas, Fray, 303
Battles
  Amiens (1918 Allied-German, first tank
    success), 111

Ankara (1402 Mongol-Ottoman), 110
Armada (1588 Anglo-Spanish naval),
  115
D-Day, intelligence on, 199–200,
  204–5
El Alamain (1942 Anglo-German), 199
Jena (1806 Franco-Prussian), 118
Jutland (1916 Anglo-German naval),
  191
Kadesh (c. 1470 B.C.E. Egyptian-
  Hittite), 94
Lepanto (1571 Ottoman-Spanish na-
  val), 114, 251, 302
Manzikert (1071 Byzantine-Seljuk), 247
Marne (1914 Franco-British-German),
  110
Midway (World War II, Japanese-
  American naval), 202
New Orleans (1815 American-British),
  306
Plassey, (1757 British-Mughal), 103
Pydna (168 B.C.E. Roman-Macedonian),
  42
Somme (1916, first use of tanks), 111,
  120
Thames (1813 American–American In-
  dian), 305
Tours (732 Muslim-Frank), 109
Ulm (1805 Franco-Austrian), 117
Verdun (1916, beginning of trench war-
  fare), 120
Waterloo (1814, defeat of Napoleon),
  118
Beaumarchais, Pierre de (French agent in
  England), 193–94
Benjamin of Tudela, 331n. 34
Berbers, 298
Biological weapons, 20–21, 308
Bismarck, Prince Otto von, 119, 222
Black Death ("the pestilence"), 19
Boase, Roger (English Hispanicist), 302
Body, human
  bacteria, role of, 14, 21–22
  foreigners, coping with, 22
  immune system, 2–3; circumvented dur-
    ing pregnancy, 23–24; functioning of,
    22–23; overreaction, 23; triggering of,
    18, 22
  labor, value for, 41
  medical interventions, 2, 17
  as model for foreign affairs, 8
  parasites, 15, 16

pathogens, 14, 16–17, 19–20; mutation of, 19
Brezhnev, Leonid, 270
Brotherhood, 29–30
  of ambassadors, 238, 340n. 38
  of Muslims, 228–29
  of rulers, 220–23; and Cold War, 223, 255
Burn, A. R. (historian), 177
Burton, Capt. Sir Richard (English explorer), 185
Byzantium, 243–44

Callières, François de (eighteenth-century diplomat and author), 181, 257, 259, 266
Camel, in warfare, 109
Camus, Albert, 99
Cannibalism, 37
Canning, Stratford (later Viscount Stratford de Redcliffe), 264
Capitulations, 160
Caravans, 149, 161
Carthage, 88–89, 94–95, 132–33, 144, 242–43
Cass, Lewis (American secretary of war), 307
Caste system in India, 298
Castile, 299, 300, 301
Castlereagh, Viscount (British foreign secretary), 260–61
Cavanaugh, John (American writer), 168
Chagnon, Napoleon (anthropologist), 134
Chandragupta (founder of the Mauryan Empire), 231–32
Charles V (Hapsburg emperor)
  foreign affairs, personal control of, 257
  murder of French ambassador, probable, 255
  priests as spies, use of, 180
  "summit" with Francis I, abortive, 258
Charles VIII (king of France), 184
Chinese dynasties or eras
  Chou (c. 1122–ninth century B.C.E.), 56; "barbarian" origin, 56, 314–15; cultural barrier to aliens, 55–57
  Han (206 B.C.E.–220 C.E.), 58–59
  Manchu (1644–1912), 112
  Ming (1368–1644), 60–61, 112; Great Wall, 61; Treasure Fleet, 151; wars with Mongols, 61

Qin (221–206 B.C.E.), 58, 82
Shang (first Chinese dynasty, before 1200 B.C.E.), 53, 314–15; amid "barbarian" neighbors, 43
Song (907–1279), 112–13
"Spring and Autumn" and "Warring States" (c. 722–221 B.C.E.), 58, 80–82, 108
T'ang (618–907), 113
Three Kingdoms (221–265), 113
Yuan (1279–1368), 61, 114
Chingis Khan, 92–93
Christie, Walter (tank pioneer), 111
Churchill, Winston
  deal with Soviet Union on eastern Europe, 269, 344n. 109
  on tanks in World War I, 110–11
Cipher. See Code; Code breaking
Cipolla, Carlo (economic historian), 54, 112, 117, 123
Clausewitz, Carl von (military philosopher), 6, 76, 118, 119
Code
  encoding machines; Enigma (Axis powers), 199; scrambler, 201; scytale (Greek), 198–99; Thomas Jefferson's device, 199
  use of: Caesar, 187–88; Woodrow Wilson, 188; promoted early growth of foreign offices, 257–58
Code breaking
  American (Magic), 200–1, 209
  British, 191; in World War II, 200, 209
  French: Cardinal Richelieu's cabinet noir, 188
  German: in World War I, 191–92; in World War II (Ultra), 200, 209
  Japanese: JN-25, 203, 337n. 46; Purple, 201
  revealed: French to Germans, 189; Henry IV to Venetians, 189
  use of: against Germans, 199–200; against Japanese, 202; against Russians, 189–90
Cold War, 115, 124
Commerce, unifying influence in early United States, 226
Conferences, congresses
  "cheaper than war," 260
  Congress of Vienna (1814), 4, 182, 260–61
  diplomats' limited role in, 262

Conferences, congresses (*continued*)
 intermittent, 262
 Paris Peace Conference (1919), 4,
  261–62, 292
 Utrecht (1713), 260
Conolly, Lt. Arthur (British agent),
 185
Constitution, U.S., and foreign affairs,
 123, 226
Conversos (converted Jews), 301
Cook, Captain James, 133
Corroborreefeasts, Australian aboriginal
 peace conferences, 259
Counterinsurgency
 American in Vietnam, 99, 327n. 36
 French in Indo-China, 98–99
 Spanish sixteenth-century manual on,
  99, 328n. 37
Counterintelligence
 dangers of, 211
 effectiveness in World War II, 210
 Indian, 210–12
 Mongol, 210
 secure storage, use of, 192
Coups d'etat promoted by United States
 Chile, 206
 Guatemala, 206
 Iran, against Prime Minister Mossadegh,
  206–7, 270
Cow, replaces horse as symbol of Aryans,
 296
Creel, Herrlee (sinologist), 315
Crusades, 247–48
Cryptology. *See* Code; Code breaking
Cuban Missile Crisis, 198, 202, 337n. 45
Culture
 assimilation into different, 318
 as tool of statecraft, 314–15
Curzon, Lord, 179

Da Gama, Vasco, 156
Daoud, Prince Muhammad (Afghan
 ruler), 270
Daru'l-harb (domain of war, the non-
 Muslim world), 229
Daru'l-islam (domain of peace, Islamic
 heartland), 229
Darwin, Charles, 25–26, 34
Dasa (Dravidian speakers of India), 297
Dawes, Sen. Henry, 309–10
Dawes Act (1887), 309
"Dear enemy mechanism," 31–32
De Gaulle, Gen. Charles, 99

Dei, Benedetto (Florentine merchant),
 154
Democracy and foreign affairs, 236
 contrast of parliamentary and American
  systems, 262–63
Department of State. *See* Foreign affairs institutions
Descartes, René (French philosopher),
 13–14
Despés, Don Guerau (Spanish ambassador
 to Elizabethan England), 256
Díaz, Rodrigo (*El Cid*), 300
Diplomacy
 aim, 268
 definition of, 4
 institutions (*see* Foreign affairs institutions)
 kinship, basis in, 218 (*see also* Kinship)
 open, 261
 origin of the term, 217, 338n. 2
 signaling as negotiation, 237
Diplomats
 citizenship, 253, 264
 disloyalty of, 254
 distrust and ill treatment of, 237, 240,
  245, 253
 duties: reports, 251–52, 256; serving visitors, 252; Venetian *relazione,* 251
 education of, attempts at, 267–68
 expulsion (declared persona non
  grata), 256–57
 hardship of, 254
 immunity of, 240; violation of as pretext for war, 255
 isolation of, 255
 merchants as, 237
 moonlighting, 253
 multiple ambassadors in missions, 239
 murder of, 255
 pay, 253–54
 posts, 262–64
 powers of, 239, 264
 resident, 252–53
 social background, 240, 254, 265–66
 specialization, 237, 240, 253
 symbol of office, 238, 341n. 39
 types of: *angeloi* (Greek, foreigner),
  239; Chief of the Path (Sudanese
  Nuba tribal), 238, 340n. 38; *fetial* (Roman, priest), 241–42; governor general (Athenian *episkopoi,* Spartan *harmost,* T'ang *Chuan yün shih,* Mongol
  posoly), 241; herald, 238, 343n. 88;

nuncios (messengers), 252; *prebeis* (Greek, native), 239; *proxenos* (honorary consul), 234, 240–41; *wakilu'l-tujjar* (merchants' representative), 148–49
Diseases, 16–21
   AIDS, cost of, 20
   attack on, strategy of, 17
   Black Death ("the pestilence"), 19
   cerebro-spinal meningitis, 20
   deaths from "traditional," 20
   Ebola virus, 19–20
   human granulocytic ehrlichiosis, 16
   Lyme disease, 16
   pandemics, causes of, 20
   Rocky Mountain spotted fever, 16
   smallpox, 18
Divine intervention
   execration texts, Egyptian, 55
   relics: medieval Europe, 55–56, 324–25n. 20; modern France, 56
Donne, John, 15, 16–17
Donovan, William (head of the Office of Strategic Service), 209
Dravidian, language of pre-Aryan Indians, 296
Dulles, John Foster (American secretary of state), 164, 252

Eberhard, Wolfram (sinologist), 315
Eden, Sir Anthony (British statesman), 269
Edward IV (king of England), 258–59
Egypt, 53–55, 136
   cultural "virtual" wall, 56
   High Dam refused, 164
   Hittites, relations with, 220–21
   invaders, Hyksos, 186–87
   Maadi (trading town), 136
   pharaohs: Amenophis IV, 143; Hatshepsut (queen), 142; Kamose, 186–87; Khufu (Cheops), 55; Narmer/Menes, 54, 55; Necho II, 144; Sesostris III, 55
   predynastic, 54
   pyramid building, impact of, 54
   trade, 138
Eisenhower, Dwight, 278
Elgin, Lord (British ambassador to Ottoman Empire), 264
Elizabeth I (queen of England), 251
Embargo, ineffective against Muslims, 147, 250
Espionage. *See* Intelligence

Ethnic cleansing
   American policy toward American Indians, 306–7
   Aryan policy toward Dravidian Indians, 295
   German: of Gypsies, 293; of Jews, 293
   Hutu, of Tutsis, 293
   instinct for, 293–94
   Serbian, of Bosnian Muslims, 293
   Spanish Christian: of American Indians, 303; of Moriscos, 303
   Turkish, of Armenians, 293
   See also Expulsion
Ethology, l, 7–8
   relevance, 28
   students of: Keith, Arthur, 27–28; Kruuk, Hans, 322n. 14; Schaller, George B., 322n. 19; Wilson, Edward O., 129
Etruscans (Rasenna), 52, 59–60, 295
European Union, 311
Exile. *See* Expulsion
Exploration
   of Central Asian route, 151
   by Indians, 140
   by Phoenicians, 144–45
   by Polos, 151
   by Portuguese, 154–56
Expulsion, 33–34, 281
   American government, of American Indians, 306–7
   Arab, 282
   British, 290–91
   Greek, 35, 284–85
   Indians and Pakistanis, 293
   Palestinians, 293
   Soviet, of Turkic peoples, 292
   Spanish Christians, of Muslims and Jews, 300–1, 347n. 25
Extraterritoriality
   Assyrian *karum*, 142
   Sumerian *kâru*, 140

Ferdinand (king of Spain)
   fights Muslims, 301
   starts the slave trade, 287
Feudalism, 109
Fichte, Johann Gottlieb, 118, 226
Finance, 162–64
   access to capital markets, 163
   European loans to Asian countries, 163
Foreign affairs
   academies: Council on Foreign

Foreign affairs (*continued*)
Relations, 340n. 27; Institute of World Economy and International Affairs (Russian), 6
scholars: Fromkin, David, 209; Horn, D. B., 266; Mattingly, Garrett, 7; Nicholson, Harold, 7, 273; Queller, Donald, 252; Steiner, Zara, 237; Webster, Sir Charles, 4, 262, 268
study of, 3–7; at American universities, 233, 267–68, 340n. 28; little attention paid to non-European, 7
study of other cultures by Americans, 178
war as natural condition, 231
Foreign affairs institutions
American, creation of, 226; Continental Congress, 235; Department of State, 235–36, 340n. 36; Policy Planning Council, 5, 252
British Foreign Office, creation of, 258
Byzantine: office of barbarians, 244; post office, 245
French foreign ministry, 257–58
Greek city-state assemblies, 234
parallel operations, 262
Vatican, 239
Foreign Office. *See* Foreign affairs institutions
Foreign Service Institute, 268
Foundations, 169
France
domestic nations: Basques, Bretons, Corsicans, and Languedoc, 318
foreigners, attitude toward, 317
immigrants, 317
self-image, 317
Francis, Saint, 274
Francis I (king of France)
Conseil des Affaires, creation of, 257
Ottoman attack on Hapsburg Empire, encouragement of, 251, 343n. 85
foreign affairs, personal supervision of, 257
mercenaries, recruitment of, 257
spies, extensive use of, 180
"summit" with Charles V, abortive, 258
Francisco de Vitoria (Spanish philosopher), 276, 303, 312
Franke, Herbert (sinologist), 53
Franklin, Benjamin, 194–95
Freud, Sigmund

on residual memory of primitive times, 26
on stress of civilization, 8

Galera (Spanish Arab town massacred), 302
Gapon (Russian priest and police agent), 206
Garrett, Laurie, on public health strategy, 17
Gattinara, Mercurino da (Spanish foreign minister under Charles V), 257
Gauls (seminomadic Celtic peoples), 59
Generals. *See* Military leaders
Geniza (Jewish documents in Egypt), 149, 331n. 34
Genoa, maintains relations with Ottoman Empire, 183–84
Genocide, 303–4. *See also* Ethnic cleansing
Geographical knowledge
decline of, after fall of Rome, 146–47
Ebla gazetteer, 49
Imagio Mundi (Cardinal Pierre d'Ailly), 147
Indian Ocean sailing instructions, 155
Pratica della Mercatura (Francesco Balducci Pegolotti), 151
George III (king of England), 304
Georgia, State of, sued by Cherokees, 306
German Democratic Republic, 70, 96
German Federal Republic, 70
Ghent, Treaty of. *See* Treaties
Ghiselin de Busbecq, Ogier (ambassador to and writer on Ottoman Empire), 255
Gibbon, Edward, 75, 245–46, 324–25n. 20
Golden bridle, 180, 186
Golden Horde (Mongol army/state), 110, 248
Goldschmidt, Walter (anthropologist), 133
Gorbachev, Mikhail, 207–8
Goths, 246, 295, 315–16
Governments, imposed by outside powers
Allies in Western Europe, 269
Britain in Greece, 269–70
Soviet Union in Eastern Europe, 269
U.S. in Japan, 269
Granada (last Muslim city in Spain), 301, 302

Great Game, 185–86. *See also* Intelligence

Great powers, phrase invented, 260–61

Great Wall of China, 61–62

Greece, origin of, 315

Greeks
Dorian and Ionian, 284
Mycenaean, 229, 284

Grotius, Hugo (Huig van Groot), 276–77

Guerrillas, 96–101

Guizot, François (French nationalist historian), 317

Hakluyt, Richard (publisher of travelers' tales), 26, 311

Hale, J. R. (English historian), 115, 180, 329

Hardinge, Sir Arthur (British ambassador), 265

Hebrews conquer Palestine, 143

Henry, Prince ("the Navigator"), 155

Henry III (king of Castile), 246–47

Henry IV (king of France), 303

Henry VIII (king of England), 257

Herald. *See* Diplomats

Hernu, Charles (French minister), 205

Herodotus, 96, 98, 132–33, 144, 205, 234, 285

Hinduism, 104

Hitler, Adolf
approved by senior German general, 103
purges the German general staff, 122, 329n. 68

Hittites
Ahhiyawa (Mycenaea), relations with, 221
Egypt, relations with, 220
peace, concept of, 221, 230, 338n. 7
trade, importance of, 230

Hobbes, Thomas, 24–25, 130, 278, 311, 313, 319

Holland, alien population, 318

Holy Alliance, 222

Homestead Act (on American Indian lands), 309

Horses
domesticated, 283, 346n. 8
venerated by Indo-Europeans, 295
in warfare, 108–10, 283–84

Hughes, Thomas (American diplomat), 212

Hull, Cordell (American secretary of state), 201, 336–37n. 43

Human beings, *Homo sapiens* and Neanderthals, 35

Human Rights Watch, 170

Ibn Battuta, Mohammed (medieval traveler), 150–51, 332n. 36

Ibn Khaldun, Abdur-Rahman (North African historian), 218–19, 246

Impressment, British, of American sailors, 227

Indenturing Indian workers, 290

Indus/Harappan civilization
cities: existence of doubted, 51–52; Ganweriwala, 52; Harappa, 52; Mohenjo-daro, 52
impact of Indo-European invasion, 51, 231, 295; described in *Rig Veda*, 52

Innocent IV, Pope, 248

Inquisition, 301

Intelligence, 175–213 passim
Achamenid Persian (under Xerxes), 176–77, 205
aircraft, use in, 196–98
American organizations: FBI (Federal Bureau of Investigations), 208, 210; OSS (Office of Strategic Services), 208, 209; CIA (Central Intelligence Agency), 206, 209, 262; DIA (Defense Intelligence Agency), 208; NSA (National Security Agency), 208, 223
Assyrian, 179–80
British: Elizabethan, 180–81, 189, 193, 208; mail, 181; merchants, use of, 181; MI5 (British security service), 208, 210; MI6 (British intelligence service), 206, 208
Byzantine, 180
collection, 178
cost, 202
couriers, 181, 182
criticism of, 209
disguise, 185–86
German Intelligence Service (*Sicherheitsdienst*), 204, 206
Great Game, 185–86
Han Chinese, 177–78
intercepted, 179; Carthaginians, 187; German in World War I, 191–92; Hyksos invaders in Egypt, 186–87
Israeli organization (*Mossad*), 209–10; attack on U.S. facilities in Egypt, 206
Italian (Renaissance states), 180
mails, tampering with, 181

Intelligence (*continued*)
  Mongol: English agent, 335n. 11;
    "golden bridle" merchants, 180, 186
  Ottoman, 192
  overflights, 197–98
  personnel, 180
  Russian organizations, 207–8
  satellites, use in, 198
  size, 210
  varieties, 175–76, 178–79
International Bank for Reconstruction
  and Development (World Bank), 170
International Monetary Fund, 170
International Postal Union, 170
International Telephone and Telegraph
  Co. (ITT), 168
Intervention
  American, in Vietnam, 270
  Chinese-Soviet, in Korea, 270
  Egyptian, in Yemen, 271
  Imperial Russian and Soviet Union, in
    Afghanistan, 270–72
Iran, agrees to declare war on Britain,
  265
Isabella (Queen of Castile), 301
Islam, 228–29, 339n. 20
Islamic invasion of Europe, 245–46
Islamic states, caliphates
  Abbasid, reliance on foreign troops, 91
  Cordoba, 246
  Ilkhanate of Persia, 249
  mamluks in Egypt, 107; relations with
    Venice, 250
  Mughal, 102, 106
  muluk al-tawa'if (petty kingdoms of Mus-
    lim Spain), 246
  Ottoman, 110; aid to Moriscos, 302
  Seljuk: Alp-Arslan on counterintelli-
    gence, 211; Manzikert, Battle of, 247;
    rise of, 247
  Umayyad (of Cordoba), 299
Italy, sentiment for split into two parts,
  318

Jackson, Andrew, 306, 309
Japan, attempts to "open," 162, 317
Jefferson, Thomas, 236, 304–5
Jem (pretender to Ottoman throne),
  182–84
Jerusalem, captured by Seljuks, 247
Jews
  Ashkenazi and Khazar Turks, 291

  Russian policy toward, 291–92
  Spanish, allied with Arabs, 298–99
John of Cârpine, Friar (ambassador to
  Mongols in 1271), 248
Jung, C. G., 8
Justice. *See* Law, concept of
Justinian (Byzantine emperor), 69, 179–
  80

Kadesh, Battle of, 94
Kahn, David (American author), 188
Kamose. *See* Egypt
Karakorum, Mongol royal camp, 248
Karma, 298
Kautilya. *See* Strategists
Keith, Berriedale (English Indianist), 51–
  52
Keith, Sir Arthur, 27–28
Kennan, George (American diplomat and
  historian), 251
Kennedy, John F., 70–71
Keynes, John Maynard, 7, 54, 102
Khazars (Turkish people), 244
Khrushchev, Nikita, 70–71
Khufu (Cheops; Egyptian pharaoh), 55
Khusrau I (Sasanian Persian shah), 69
Kinahu (Canaanites/Phoenicians), 143–
  45
Kinship
  applied to government and foreign rela-
    tions, 221–22
  basis of all peaceful relationships, 29
  defined at birth, 29
  deme, 29–30, 219
  fictitious, 219–20
  words denoting, 29, 219
  See also Diplomacy
Knatchbull-Hugessen, Sir Hughe (British
  ambassador), 192–93
Küyük Khan (successor to Chingis Khan),
  248, 249

Lamartine, Alphonse de (French writer),
  317
Language
  policy of Americans, French, and Rus-
    sians, 310
  role in nation building, 319
Lansing, Robert (American secretary of
  state), 261–62
Lavon Affair (Israeli attack on U.S. facilities in Egypt), 206

Law, concepts of
  effect of discovery of New World, 275
  Greek, 235
  Grotius, Hugo (*De Jure Belli ac Pacis Libri Tres*), 276–77
  Hague Tribunal, 277
  jus gentium, 276
  medieval Europe, 274
  Muslims: "People of the Book" to be protected, 275; war as violation of Divine law, 274; on war with Christians, 274
  Nuremberg Tribunal, 277
  origin in Sumerian commercial law, 273
  Roman, 273–74
  slaves, regarding, 289
Lawrence, T. E. (British guerrilla leader), 97–98
Laws. *See* Treaties
Leachman, Col. Gerald (British agent), 185
League of Nations, 170
Lee, Arthur (American secret agent), 193–94
Lee, Richard (American anthropologist), 93
Leeuwenhoek, Antonie van (Dutch microscopist), 15
Lenin, Vladimir, 121
León, 299
Le Secret, 262
Levant Company, 102–3, 160
Library of Congress, 176
Limpieza de sangre (purity of blood), Spanish Christian concept, 301
Lion nomads, 33
Livy (Titus Livius), 60, 88, 241, 325, 327
Lloyd George, David (British prime minister), 262–63
Llull, Ramon, 274
Locke, John (English philosopher), 24–25, 312, 313, 319
Louis XI (king of France), 258–59
Louis XV (king of France), 117
Louisiana Purchase, 305
Lugal (big man), Sumerian war leader/king, 83

Macaulay, Thomas (later Lord), 105
Machiavelli, Niccolò. *See* Strategists
Machine gun, in trench warfare, 115
Mackinder, H. J. *See* Strategists

Madison, James, 305
Magic. *See* Code breaking
Magyars, 63
Malinovsky, Roman (Russian labor leader and police agent), 206
Malinowski, Bronislaw (anthropologist), 133, 134
Mandate governments, 136
Mao Tse-tung, as strategist of guerrilla warfare, 98
Maps
  carta Pisana, 195
  espionage, a principal task of, 195
  Indian Ocean charts, 195–96
  Japanese street maps, 176
  quality poor until recently, 196, 336n. 33
  U.S. Air Force, 176
Maratha (Indian state), 103
Marshall, John (Chief Justice, U.S. Supreme Court), 304, 306
Martel, Charles (Frank leader), 109
Mary, Queen of Scots, 188–89
Massilia (ancestor of Marseilles), 242
Maurice, Prince (Dutch military reformer), 112–13
Mauryan Empire (India), 231–32
Mauss, Marcel (French sociologist), 130
Maximilian of Bavaria, Duke, 259
Mazarin, Cardinal, 259
McCarthy, Sen. Joseph, 252
McCone, John (CIA director, ITT director), 168
Mecca, 228
Medina (Arabian holy city), 228
Mehmet Ali Pasha (Albanian ruler of Egypt), 82
Mehmet II, "the Conqueror," 182
Mendoza, Don Bernardino de (Spanish ambassador), 256–57
Mercantilism, 158–59
Merchants
  as diplomats, 237
  expatriate citizenship, 141
  Jews, 148–49, 331–32n. 34
  Hansa, 150
  living arrangements in foreign countries, 148–49
  as spies, 142–43, 175
  trade fairs, 149
Metternich, Fürst Clemens von (Hapsburg statesman), 260

Migration, 34
 of foreigners into France, 317–18
 of *Homo sapiens* into Europe, 35–36
 Indo-Europeans, 282–84
 of Jews from east Europe, 291–92
 mixed with local peoples, 284
 of Semites across Africa, 282
 of Turks into western Asia, 248, 282
Military leaders
 Alaric (Gothic), 91
 Alexander the Great, 109
 Bonaparte, Napoleon, 55; on importance of cavalry, 110, 117, 118; meets Tsar Alexander, 259; takes Vienna, 65, 110, 117, 118
 Clive, Robert (English), 103, 157
 Gaius Crassus (Roman), 109
 Gamelin, Gen. Maurice (French), 68, 69
 Grant, Gen. Ulysses S. (American), 118, 309
 Guderian, Gen. Heinz (German), 111
 Hannibal, 88, 187, 203–4, 242
 Hindenburg, Paul von (German), 192
 Ludendorff, German Gen. Erich (German), 192
 Marshall, Gen. George C. (American), 201
 Maurice, Prince (Dutch military reformer), 112–13
 Moltke, Gen. Helmuth von (German), 212
 Montgomery, Gen. Bernard (British), 199
 Nimitz, Admiral Chester (American), 202
 Polk, Gen. James H. (American), 336n. 40
 Polk, Gen. Leonidas (American Confederate), 118
 Pyrrhus, Macedonian king, 242
 Rommell, Marshal Erwin (German), 69, 111, 199
 Scharnhorst, Gen. Gerhard von, 95, 118
 Schlieffen, Gen. Alfred von (German), 119
 Seeckt, Gen. Hans von (German), 67, 120–21
 Sherman, Gen. William T. (American), 118
 Sulla, Cornelius (Roman general), 88

Yamamoto, Adm. Isoroku (Japanese), 202
Minorities
 accommodation, of defeated to victors, 297
 China, 315
 Islam, 275
 Japan, 316
 United States, in neighborhoods, 314, 316
Missionaries, 169
 among American Indians, 307
 in India, 104
Mitterrand, François (French president), 99
Molotov, Vyacheslav (Soviet foreign minister), 269
Money
 British exports reverse flow of precious metals, 161
 circulation of, through cathedral building in medieval Europe, 54
 coins, worn away, 332n. 44
 copper, tin, and silver, as media of exchange, 139
 gold: Columbus on value of, 157; sought in Africa, 154
 gold and silver: British export, to buy Chinese goods, 158; British loot, in Bengal, 157; European need for, 154, 156–57; French loot, in Algiers, 157; imports from New World, 157, 158–59
 suftaja, medieval Islamic "traveler's check," 149
Mongols
 European perception of, 248–50
 hegemony, 150
 Russia, rule of, 110
Montesquieu, Charles-Louis, 24
Moriscos (Andalusian Muslims), 299
Mozarab art in al-Andalus, 300
Muluk al-tawa'if (petty kingdoms of Muslim Spain), 246
Mun, Thomas (English mercantilist), 158–59
Mycenaea. *See* Ahhiyawa (Mycenaea); Greeks

Nam-lugal (Sumerian term for kingship), 83
Nationalism, 43, 118, 226

Navarre, 299, 301
Neolithic Revolution, 134
Neumann, John von (American mathematician), 5
Neutrality
  Indian view of, 231–32
  possible origin of concept, 230–31
  Woodrow Wilson on, 190
Nobel Peace Prize, 170
Nomad sedenterization, 295–96
Nongovernmental organizations (NGOs), 6–7, 169–70
  clash with governments, 166
Norton, Henry Kittredge (American historian), 236
Novikov, Nikolai (Russian ambassador), 252
Numelin, Ragnar (Danish historian), 254

Odysseus, 141
Oil, in 1919 Paris Peace Conference, 261
Olympic Games, 167
Open diplomacy, 261
Opium, 159–60
Oracle, Delphic, 204, 337n. 48
Organisation Todt, 59, 69–70
Organization of Petroleum Exporting Countries (OPEC), 170
Ottoman Empire
  besieges Vienna, 65
  bought off from destroying Peter the Great's army, 264
  military reform in, 82
  sultans: Bayezid I, 110; Bayezid II, 183; Mehmet II, "the Conqueror," 182; Suleiman the Magnificent, 143
  tribal policy, 136
  vaccination, pioneers in, 18
Ownership. See Possessions
Özgüç, Tahsin (Turkish commentator), 142

Palmerston, Lord (British statesman), 107
Papacy, as medieval court of arbitration, 274. See also Popes
Parker, Geoffrey (historian), 196
Parthian Persian Empire, 109
Party kings (muluk al-tawa'if), 246. See also Islamic states, caliphates
Paul III, Pope, 258
"Peace without victory," 261, 262

Pedro I ("the Cruel," king of Castile), 246
Pedro IV (king of Aragon), 246
Peloponnesian Confederacy, 234–35
Peloponnesian War, 62
Pericles, 62
Periplus of Africa, 145
Perkins, Bradford (American historian), 235
Persian Gulf War, 115–16
Peter the Great (tsar of Russia), 264
Philip II (Spanish Hapsburg emperor), 64, 188
Philip IV ("the Fair," king of France), 249
Philip V (king of Macedonia), 187
Phoenicians (Canaanites), 135, 143–44
Phoenix program in Vietnam, 99, 327n. 36
Piracy and privateers
  African gold trade, stimulated by, 155
  British, 102, 160
  Chinese view of, 332n. 40
  See also Seafaring
Pirenne, Henri (historian), 63, 325
Pisa, 63–64
Pliny the Elder, 89
Plutarch, 94, 198–99
Poincaré, Raymond (French statesman), 179
Polis, poleis, 225, 234
Polk, Gen. James H. (American), 336n. 40
Polk, Gen. Leonidas (American Confederate), 118
Polybius, 88, 89, 195, 341n. 55
Popes
  Innocent IV, 248
  Paul III, 258
  Sixtus IV, 239
  Urban II, 247–48
Population
  Assyrian, 285
  balance with resources, 218, 284
  exchange, 292
  Greek: expulsion to reduce, 284, 285; infanticide to reduce, 284
  medieval European cities, 153
  Roman policy, 88, 90, 286
Portugal, 300
Possessions, types of
  bodies, as, 37

Possessions, types of (*continued*)
  crops, 39
  facilities, 38–40, 51
  houses, 39
  territories (*see* Territory, territoriality)
Post Office Act of 1711, British, 181
Potlatch, 130
Prebeis. See Diplomats
Prester John (mythical Asian Christian),
  248
Procopius (Byzantine historian), 180
Propaganda, 85, 244
Protocol, 244–45
  Chinese, disliked by ambassadors, 254–
    55
  excessive concern with, 258, 266–67,
    344n. 105
  Muscovite tsars, 255
  Xiongnu, 255
Public Record Office, British, 181, 192
Pugwash, 169–70
Purple. *See* Code breaking

Quakers (Society of Friends), on American Indian policy, 309

Religion, role in legitimizing government,
  315
Renan, Ernest (French writer), 317
Rhodes, as headquarters of the Knights of
  St. John, 183
Richelieu, Cardinal
  creates *cabinet noir,* 188
  creates French foreign office, 258
Rig Veda (Aryan epics in India), 297
Roe, Sir Thomas (British ambassador to
  Mughals and Ottomans), 264
Romanus IV Diogenes (Byzantine emperor), 247
Rome
  early organization of, 87
  failure of strategy, 17–18
  fall of, in the West, 91–92
  foreign troops, 90–91
  militarism, 87–88
  origin, 59–60
  population policy, 88–90
  sacked by Gauls, 60
  Syracuse occupation, 204
  terror amounting to genocide, 89–90
  trade policy, 146–47
Rulers, role of the military in creating, 83

Rusk, Dean (American secretary of state),
  176

Sahlins, Marshall (American sociologist),
  130
Sanctuaries, 132
Sanskrit, Indo-European language of
  Aryans, 296
Santayana, George (American philoso-
  pher), 3
Sargon (Semite conqueror of Sumer),
  136–37
Satellites, 198
Savoy, duke of
  helps Ottoman spy, 184
  as intermediary, 258
Schlieffen Plan (for invasion of France),
  119
Scott, James Brown (American legal
  scholar), 277
Scrambler (telephone device), 201. *See
  also* Code; Code breaking
Seafaring
  Chinese, 150; Ming Treasure Fleet,
    151, 332n. 38
  Indian, 140, 331n. 26
  Mediterranean routes, 149–50
  monsoon winds and navigation, 140
  Phoenician, 144–45
  Pirates: Barbary, 250; Chinese view of,
    152, 332n. 37; English, 250; Vene-
    tian, 147 (*see also* Piracy and priva-
    teers)
  Portuguese, 154–55
Security clearance, 189, 335n. 26
Self-determination of peoples, 292
Seligman, M. E. P., 8
Seljuk. *See* Islamic states, caliphates
Shakespeare, image of primitive man, 289
Shevardnadze, Eduard (Soviet foreign
  minister), 272
Ships
  Atlantic caravel (*Niña*), 153
  Chinese, 114, 150, 332n. 38
  galleons, 156
  Mediterranean, 114, 152–53
  sails, 153
  Spanish Armada, 114, 180–81
  Venetian, 152
Signaling, as negotiation, 237
Sima Qian (Chinese historian), 82, 326
Sindabad the Sailor, 148

Sixtus IV, Pope, 239
Slaves, slavery, 37, 41–43, 323n. 32
  African coast, ideal for slave trade, 287
  barracoon (slave prison), 155, 287
  British law of 1807, 289
  broken to obedience, 289
  European trade, 154
  Greek, in Rome, 42, 323n. 34
  impact on Rome, 42
  method of capture, 287–88
  New World, 42–43
  numbers of, 287
  plantation crops, 154–55, 286–87
  shipment, 288
Smith, Adam (English philosopher/economist), 103, 129, 134, 328, 329
Smith, Captain John (mercenary in Ottoman service), 250
Soane, Major E. B. (British agent), 185
Sogdiana (Central Asian area), 109
Soldiers
  janissaries (Ottoman), 107, 110
  mamluks (Egyptian), 107
  native/auxiliary, 109; numbers and recruitment, 116
  Samurai (Japanese), 113
  sepoys (Indian), 101–7; used in China, 160
Spies, 205–6
  Ames, Aldrich (American spy for the Soviet Union), 198, 205
  Baden-Powell, Lt.-Gen. Sir Robert, 185
  Bancroft, Edward (American spy for the British), 194
  Barak (Ottoman in Europe), 182–85
  Blunt, Anthony (English spy for the Soviet Union), 205
  Burgess, Guy (English spy for the Soviet Union), 205
  Cicero (Albanian spy for the Germans), 192–93
  Deane, Silas (American spy for the British), 194
  Kim (novel), 185–86
  McLean, Donald (English spy for the Soviet Union), 205
  Nicholson, Harold (American charged as spy for Soviet Union), 205
  Philby, Kim (English spy for the Soviet Union), 198
  Walker Ring (American spies for Soviet Union), 211

Stalin, Joseph, 121, 204, 255, 269
Standard of living, European, 153
Starr, Chester (American historian), 90, 327n. 22
State, formations of, 313–14
  Cyrene, 312
  Thurii, 313
States' rights (conflict between federal and state government), 304, 308
Storage pits, 38–40, 51
Strategists
  Chia I (Chinese), 135–36
  Fuller, J. F. C., 111
  Kautilya/Vishnugupta, 18, 134, 210–11, 231–32
  Machiavelli, Niccolò, 18, 75, 231, 233, 256
  Mackinder, H. J. (English geographer, "geopolitics"), 272
  Mao Tse-tung, on guerrilla warfare, 98
  "mirrors for princes," 232–33; modern industry of, 233, 340nn. 26–29; Mongol Secret History, 233, 340n. 25
  rise of, in recent times, 5–6
  Sun Tzu, 18, 231, 232
Strategy
  Anglo-French, in World War I, 190
  Byzantine, 244
  German, in World War I, 190–91
  Indian, 231–32
Sugar, role in slave trade, 287
Sumer (Mesopotamia), 83–84
Sun Tzu. See Strategists

Talleyrand-Périgord, Prince Charles Maurice de, 260, 262
Taqiyah (dissimulation), 302
Tarn, W. W. (classical historian), 93
Taxes
  catasto (Florentine), 122–24
  on land, first known (China), 81
  medieval urban, to build walls, 63
T cells. See Body, human
Tea trade, China, 159
Territory, territoriality, 30–31, 38
  defined, 31
  large size reduces intergroup contact, 32–33
  limits size of groups, 32
  as possession, 38
Terror, use of, 85, 89–90
Terrorists, in Algeria and France, 99–100

Theodosius (Roman emperor), 91
Thomas, Elizabeth (anthropologist), 130
Thucydides, 19, 234, 239
Timbuktu, entrepot of the African gold trade, 154
Timur (Tammerlane), 110, 143, 250
Tlatoque, Aztec Mexican term for city-state ruler, 83
Tocqueville, Alexis de, 236
Torquemada, Tomás de (Grand Inquisitor), 301
Torture, 99
Tournaments, 92
Towns and cities
  Carthage, 88–89, 94–95, 132–33, 144
  Çatal Hüyük (early Anatolian), 41
  Clusium (Etruscan), 60
  Ebla (north Syrian city-state), 49, 220, 237
  Jericho, 41, 47, 49, 75, 134, 137–38
  Mari (north Syrian city-state), 42
  Massilia (Greek, ancestor of Marseilles), 242
  medieval European, 63; growth of, 63–64; walls required, 63
  Ugarit (Phoenician entrepot), 230
  Ur (Mesopotamian port), 139
  Uruk (early Mesopotamian), 42, 49–50, 135
Trade
  cocoa, 159
  Egypt, ancient, 142
  Europe, fairs in, 149
  European demand for free, 162
  giri (Japanese gifts), 131
  Hebrew, and war, 134, 135
  impact of European on Middle East, 161
  items of ancient: cedar, 143; copper, 136, 138; jade, 138; lapis lazuli, 138; relics, 147; obsidian, 137, 139; turquoise, 138
  kula (Trobriand Islands), 133
  Mauryan Indian favoring foreign merchants, 232
  origin of, 130, 132
  Phoenician, 143–44, 331n. 32
  reciprocal gifting, 130–32
  Red Sea–Indian Ocean, 136
  Roman, 141; grain imports, 146; trade policy, 146
  silent, 132–33
  slave (*see* Slaves, slavery)

Treaties, 94, 273
  Biological Weapons Convention (1972), 21
  Ghent (1814), 239
  Hague War Regulations of 1899, 97
  Kellogg Pact, 277
  Paris (1763), 304
  Pruth (1711), 264
  Versailles (1919), 261–63
  Westphalia (1648), 259
Tribes
  based on kinship and neighborhood, 219–20
  Hittite view of, 229
Tribes, African
  Bantu (South African people), 79
  Bushmen, !Kung (South African people), 130
  Dinka (Sudan Nilotic tribe), 79
  Nuba (Sudan tribe), 238
  Nubians, 314
  Nuer (Sudan Nilotic tribe), 29, 79
Tribes, American Indian
  Algonquin, 304
  Apache (Dine), 218, 308, 338n. 4
  Blackfoot, 308
  Cherokee, 304, 306
  Cheyenne, 131, 308
  Chickasaw, 308
  Choctaw, 308
  Comanche (Nemene), 78, 218, 308, 338n. 4
  Creek, 304, 305–6, 308
  Crow, 308
  Delaware, 307
  Iowa, 304
  Iroquois, 304
  Kiowa, 308
  Nomlaki, 133
  Osage, 305, 308
  Sac and Fox, 305
  Seminole, 308
  Shawnee, 305
  Sioux (Dakota), 305, 308
  Ute, 308
  Wichita, 308
  Winnebago, 305
Tribes, Asian
  Bedouin, control from the air, 197
  Hsuing-nu/Xiongnu (northeast Asian people), 135
  Jürchen (nomad invaders of China), 113

Yuezhi (Central Asian people), 177–78
Tribes, New Guinea
  Kurelu, 77–78
  Maring, 79, 134
  Wittaria, 77–78
Tribes, South American
  Yanomamö (South American Indians), 134

U-2, 197–98
Ultra. *See* Code breaking
Umayyad caliphate. *See* Islamic states, caliphates
United Nations, 170
Universities
  schools of foreign affairs, 267–68
Ur. *See* Towns and cities
Urban II, Pope, preaches the crusade, 247–48
Uruk. *See* Towns and cities
Utrecht, 260

Valencia, 301
Varna, 298
Vauban, Marshal Sébastien de (French military architect), 67
Venice, active diplomacy with Mamluks and Ottomans, 250
Venlo Incident, 206
Vienna, growth of civic sense, 65–66
Vietnam, overthrow of Diem regime, 207
Vikings, ravage Europe, 63
Viruses. *See* Diseases
Vishnugupta. *See* Strategists
Voyages of exploration
  Indian, 140
  Phoenician, 144–45
  Portuguese, 154–56

Wagner, Günter (anthropologist), 92, 327
Waldron, Andrew (sinologist), 61, 325
Walker, Francis (American Indian commissioner), 309
Wall building
  Chinese, 57–58, 60–61
  cost forces growth of towns, 49
  failure to build walls, result of, 50
  impact on community, 48–49, 59
  organizational skills, need for, 50–51
Walls
  Athenian, 62
  Atlantic, 59, 69–70, 199–200

Berlin (Ulbricht), 70–71
Byzantine-Persian, sixth century, 69
Great Wall of China, 61–62
Han, 58
Italian, 64
Jericho, 47–48
Maginot Line, 67–68
Qin, 58
Siegfried Line, 69
Uruk, 49–50
Vienna, dismantling medieval, 64–65
Walsingham, Sir Francis (Elizabethan intelligence chief), 180–81, 189, 193, 208
Warfare
  attitudes toward, 92
  Chinese, "Spring and Autumn" and "Warring States," 80–82
  classical warfare, pomp and circumstance, 78
  Cold War, 115, 124, 164, 197
  extrawar hostilities, 78–79
  impact on society, 82–83
  leadership in as basis of rule, 83–84
  primitive: counting coups among American Indians, 77–78; total war, 79; violent theater in New Guinea, 77
  substitutes for, tournament and hunt, 92
  trench, 110
Wars
  Algerian, 99–100
  American Civil, 97–115, 117–18
  Crimean, 115
  Franco-Prussian (1870), 119
  French and Indian (1755–63), 304
  among Greek city-states, 93
  Greek-Turkish (1921–22), 292
  Revolt of 1857/Sepoy Rebellion, 105
  Seven Years' War (1756–63), 304
  Spanish Civil, 121
  Thirty Years' War (1618–48), 259
  World War I: beginning of, 119; casualties, 66–67, 119–20; fortifications, 66; outbreak welcomed, 93
  World War II, 124
Washington, George, 182, 190, 304
Watt, Donald Cameron (English writer), 213
Weapons
  aircraft, 196
  ballistae, 111
  balloon, 196, 198
  bayonet, 117

Weapons (*continued*)
cannon, 112
catapults, 111
chariots, 108–9, 283–84, 296
crossbow, 82, 110, 111
cruise missiles, 115
Enfield rifle, in Sepoy Rebellion, 106
gunpowder, 112, 117
handguns, 111–13
machine gun in trench warfare, 115
matchlock, used in Europe and China
c. 1530, 112
rockets, 115
submarine, 190–91
tank, origin of, 110
trébuchets, 111
Webster, Sir Charles. *See* Foreign affairs
Weimar Republic, 120
Wellington, Duke of, 96–97
Wells, H. G., and origin of the tank, 110
Wen (Han Chinese emperor), 135
Westphalia, Treaty of. *See* Treaties
West Point (U.S. military academy), 117–18
William of Rubruck (French-Flemish
priest and ambassador to Mongols), 249
Wilson, Woodrow, 188, 190–91, 261–62
Winterbotham, F. W. (British intelligence
official), 199

Women, 222
Worldview
as bipolar, 229; Egyptian-Hittite, 229–30; "Third World," 229–30
as collections of states, 224; American
colonies and early states, 226–27; Germany, 226; Greek cities, 225–26; Sumerian cities, 224–25
as peerless, 224, 227; Byzantium, 244;
China, 227–28; Islam, 228–29
Wotton, Sir Henry (British ambassador),
338n. 2
Wright, Sir Denis (British ambassador),
265

Xenophobia, 33
Xenophon, 94
Xerxes (Achamenid Persian shah), 96,
101, 205, 225

Yeltsin, Boris, 207
Yemen, 271

Zahir Shah (exiled Afghan king), 272
Zenanas (Indian harems), 104
Zhang Qian (Han Chinese ambassador in
Central Asia), 177
Zimmermann Telegram, 190–91
Zong (slave ship), 288–89